Geographic Information
How to Find It, How to Use It

Geographic Information
How to Find It, How to Use It

Jenny Marie Johnson

GREENWOOD PRESS
Westport, Connecticut • London

Library of Congress Cataloging-in-Publication Data

Johnson, Jenny Marie.
   Geographic Information / Jenny Marie Johnson.
      p. cm. — (How to find it, how to use it)
   Includes bibliographical references and index.
   ISBN 1–57356–392–7 (alk. paper)
   1. Geography—Bibliography. 2. Cartography—Bibilography. I. Title. II. Series.
   Z6001.A1J65   2003
[G116]
0016.91—dc21   2003048545

British Library Cataloguing in Publication Data is available.

Library of Congress Catalog Card Number: 2003048545
ISBN: 1–57356–392–7

First published in 2003

Greenwood Press, 88 Post Road West, Westport, CT 06881
An imprint of Greenwood Publishing Group, Inc.
www.greenwood.com

Printed in the United States of America

The paper used in this book complies with the
Permanent Paper Standard issued by the National
Information Standards Organization (Z39.48–1984).

10 9 8 7 6 5 4 3 2 1

The following figures are courtesy of the Map and Geography Library, University of
Illinois at Urbana-Champaign: 3.1, 3.2, 3.3, 3.4, 3.5, 3.6, 3.7, 3.8, 3.9, 3.10, 3.11, 5.1,
5.2, 5.3, 5.4, 5.5, 6.1, 6.2, 6.3, 6.4, 6.5, 6.6, 6.7, 6.9, 10.2, 10.3

Contents

Preface

The world is shrinking before our eyes. Through television, and the greatly extended selections of cable television, we can see events occurring thousands of miles away as they are happening. The Internet has shortened the time to receive a letter from days or weeks to mere hours; at times, e-mail can have the feeling of conversation as queries and replies are rapid-fired back and forth. Instant messaging and chat rooms create temporary communities out of individuals separated by tens or hundreds of miles, communities that dissolve after discussions are over. Web sites (along with cable news networks) bring news media resources from London, Moscow, Cairo, Kabul, and Beijing into North American homes any time of the day or night.

But with increased connectivity comes increased unfamiliarity as well as increased information. News is coming from places never heard of before or from places that are vaguely familiar from other contexts. Individuals, and their families, are discovering an increased need or desire to find out about other places and also to discover how similar familiar places might be to those far away and how far away places are having local impacts.

Geographic data and information about the world, about specific places, and about connections between places can be found in many different locations. Geographic information is contained in materials that go beyond maps and atlases. When investigating a place, tabular, textual, and graphic resources should all be considered, as should the vast assortment of information sources including libraries, government agencies, professional associations, map dealers and data vendors, and no-cost or low-cost Web sites. A map is not always the best answer. Many geographical questions need only a single number or perhaps a descriptive paragraph or two.

SCOPE AND PURPOSE

Geographic Information: How to Find It, How to Use It is a first step in discovering a wide variety of commonly available geographic information resources. It includes descriptions of many core or foundation titles and titles that illustrate particular attributes or have become somewhat universal because of long-standing publication patterns (multiple editions) or geographic ubiquitousness. *Geographic Information: How to Find It, How to Use It* should not be considered a comprehensive guide—it is a sampler or idea guide. Information resources are described within the context of other information resources and technological developments.

The titles and items chosen for inclusion are *the best* or are highly regarded by users and librarians, are fundamental to understanding specific kinds of information resources, or illustrate specific points or outputs from publishers of interest. Of course, the author's personal bias played a large role in the choice of titles described, so some of the titles are simply the author's favorites.

A work like this could never be comprehensive. There are too many possible resources, although most will fall into broad genres of publications. New publications and new editions are being released constantly, and Web sites change even faster than printed publications. Most of the titles included should be available for use in large- or medium-sized libraries or available for purchase from standard book-purchasing venues; nearly all of the on-line resources described are available for use without charge.

INTENDED AUDIENCE

Geographic Information: How to Find It, How to Use It is intended for those interested in adding geographic information resources to their repertoire of research options including non specialist librarians, students, or anyone else working on a project that could benefit from using geographically related resources. The broad range of information sources included may mean that not all chapters or items described are of interest—but they might be of interest at some other time. No prior knowledge of map reading or geographic investigation methods is assumed.

ORGANIZATION

Geographic Information: How to Find It, How to Use It includes 12 chapters—each describing a different genre of information resources. The first chapter, "Geography," and the last, "Connecting Geographic Information to the Curricula," form a contextual envelope for the other 10 chapters that focus on very specific and different kinds of geographical information sources. Although there are some references between chapters and a few assumptions in later chapters that material in earlier chapters has been read, the chapters stand alone for the most part.

Because the format of geographic information resources impacts their possible uses, *Geographic Information: How to Find It, How to Use It* is organized primarily by format type. Some chapters, "Topo-

graphic Maps" and "Gazetteers" as examples, explain only one or two kinds of resources along with publications that might be helpful in their use. Other chapters, such as "Thematic Atlases" and "Special Format Maps," are illustrative of the broad variety of information available. Still other chapters, such as "Map Basics" and "Geographic Information Systems," will help guide readers in establishing a basic foundation for working with geographic information.

An outline and a list of major sources discussed appear at the start of each chapter. Bibliographies at the end of each chapter give full publication information for all of the major sources and any additional sources discussed.

A Web site (http://door.library.uiuc.edu/max/Geo Info/GeoInfo.html) has been developed to assist in accessing and maintaining current URLs for on-line information resources.

Acknowledgments

Books, and other information resources, always are prepared in a broader context of community, friends, and family. The University of Illinois at Urbana-Champaign Library Research and Publication Committee assisted by funding a research assistant, Alicia Anderson, to format bibliographies and create the accompanying Web site. Scott McEathron and all of the Map and Geography Library student assistants were enthusiastic about everything they heard; Kate Swan was the lioness at the gate. Edythe and David always knew the right time to ask about progress, and Tom verified that the project was worthwhile.

My two smallest helpers, Kelda and Krista at age three-and-a-half, had this conversation on a Wednesday afternoon: "Mommy's upstairs. She's writing on her book." "She needs privacy!" "Mom, do you need privacy? I'm coming to tell you something!" My Ladies, many thanks for telling me "something." There are no more pages to write! The book is done!

Jmj

CHAPTER 1
Everything Happens Somewhere

TOPICS COVERED

Descriptions of Geography
Web Sites on Geography
Organizations
About Geographers
Finding Geographers and Geographical Collections
Geography Journals
History of Geography
Quotations

MAJOR SOURCES DISCUSSED

Don't Know Much about Geography
Harm de Blij's Geography Book
10 Geographic Ideas that Changed the World
Geography: A Global Synthesis
Geography in America
Geography's Inner Worlds
The Student's Companion to Geography, 2nd ed.
Rediscovering Geography
Geography: Guide to Geographical Resources
Geography About.com

Yahoo! Geography
Association of American Geographers
American Geographical Society
Geographers: Biobibliographical Studies
A Biographical Dictionary of American Geography in the Twentieth Century
Biographical Dictionary of Geography
Guide to Programs in Geography in the United States and Canada; AAG Handbook and Directory of Geographers
Schwendeman's Directory of College Geography of the United States
Annals of the Association of American Geographers
Professional Geographer
AAG Newsletter
Geographical Review
Focus on Geography
History of Modern Geography: An Annotated Bibliography of Selected Works
All Possible Worlds: A History of Geographical Ideas
Geography and Geographers
Dictionary of Quotations in Geography
Carto-Quotes

Geography is more than knowing that the state capital of California is Sacramento, that apples are grown in Washington State, and that the Danube both flows through Vienna and is part of the border between Hungary and the Czech Republic. Geography is about understanding how locating a state capital directly influences the pattern of the area's economic and social development. Geography is about connecting the area just east of the Cascade Mountains in Washington where apples are grown to the regions in Mexico from where the migrant workers who pick and process the apples might have come. Geography is about discovering how landscape and specific landscape features have influenced cultural ties between people and historical developments through many centuries.

Geography is important because everything happens somewhere, and all of the *where*s are connected. Geographers study the why of where and how places are interdependent at many different levels: local, regional, national, and global. Geographers think about places and events, searching for connections and spatial patterns, and then finding ways to explain those patterns through charts and tables, articles, books, atlases, and maps. In fact, the word *geography* is derived from these Earth-describing activities, *geo* (Earth) and *graphe* (to write).

Geography has both earth science components (physical geography) and social science components (human geography). Physical geographers focus on things like animal species distribution and migration, modeling climate change and analyzing the effects of climate change on human activities, and determining pollution sources and forecasting potentially affected areas. Human geographers look at problems such as the relationship of workplace location to choosing a place to live, finding the best sites for car dealerships or discount department stores, and how the transmittal of infectious diseases has been impacted by modern transportation. Sometimes geographers study a situation locally to develop global hypotheses. Geography could be considered an *interdisciplinary discipline.* Individuals with diverse interests are tied together through their interest in understanding how places or locations affect activities (human and otherwise), how places are connected, and how those connections facilitate movement between places or cause an event at one location to impact another location. "The core of geography is an abiding concern for the human and physical attributes of places and regions and with the spatial interactions that alter them" (*Geography's Inner Worlds,* 392).

Geography has not always been about connections between places or the connection between humans and their environment. During the classical period, geography was central to a scholar's understanding of the world. Almost by default, many scholars were geographers because they either wrote descriptions of places they had been or collected descriptions from others. During the same period, foundation techniques for measuring the Earth were being developed using trigonometry and astronomy. Unfortunately, many of these descriptions and methods were lost to the Western world during Europe's Middle Ages, but some bits and pieces were preserved and enhanced by Arab scholars.

After the Middle Ages, geography was reincarnated as the backbone for the discovery and systematic exploration of the world. With discovery came the need to describe new places, with particular emphasis on natural resources that could potentially be extracted, cultivated, or in some way exploited by the discoverers. In Europe, geography reached a highpoint during the nineteenth century and the age of far-flung colonial empires. Geography's identity and primary function was closely tied to creating qualitative inventories of resources and descriptions of land use and defining regions through identifying similar characteristics.

Geography remained very much a qualitative discipline until the 1950s and 1960s when quantitative methods were adopted. The discipline began shifting away from descriptive methods for describing regions to statistical methods and modeling. Instead of describing the world as a patchwork of different kinds of regions, it could be described as many different kinds of interacting or linked systems. Until the quantitative revolution, many geographers were experts in a particular place or kind of place. After the quantitative revolution, geographers began developing expertise in systems or themes such as transportation, hydrology, population migration, locational analysis, and climatology. Many of these specializations overlap with or are informed by other fields: biogeography with biology, medical geography with medicine, locational and regional analysis with economics (Figure 1.1).

Geography is changing again. Qualitative techniques are making a comeback but sophisticated quantitative techniques are still heavily emphasized because vast amounts of statistical data can be processed so efficiently using computers and statistical analysis packages, digital imaging packages, and geographic information systems. Geographers focusing on regions use quantitative techniques and investigations into specific systems and system interactions to build new understandings of regions and their connections to the world.

DESCRIPTIONS OF GEOGRAPHY

Don't Know Much about Geography
Harm de Blij's Geography Book
10 Geographic Ideas that Changed the World

There are a number of books that either examine the world from a geographic viewpoint or put geographic ways of thinking into a global context. *Don't Know Much about Geography* is full of interesting geographical factoids and antidotes. It is intended not as a description of the discipline but as a reinterpretation and re-explanation of bare-bones geographical facts memorized in school but perhaps never placed into a physical, historical, or cultural context. The first chapter is somewhat historical, covering a little of the history of geography and the history of discovery and exploration. The second and third chapters focus on physical geography, the fourth on human history viewed through geography's lens, and the fifth on climatology and meteorology. The last chapter, titled "Lost in Space?," is not geographical in the strictest sense because it answers extraterrestrial, not earthbound, questions. All of the chapters are outlined at the beginning by a list of questions covered by the chapter. The first four chapters also include "Milestones in Geography" sections, chronological listings

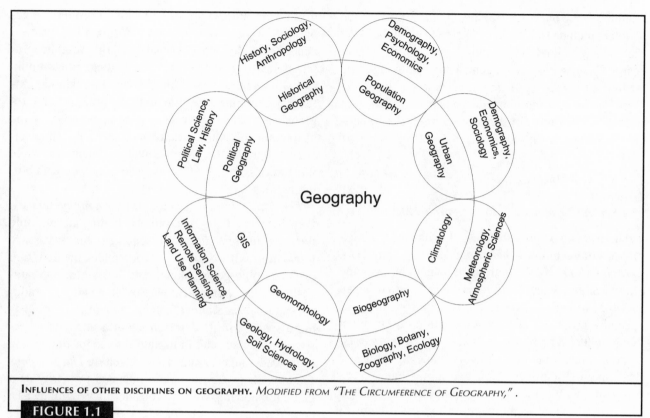

INFLUENCES OF OTHER DISCIPLINES ON GEOGRAPHY. *MODIFIED FROM "THE CIRCUMFERENCE OF GEOGRAPHY,".*

FIGURE 1.1

of explorations, technical advances, publications, and political events. The appendices include a list of states with information about the derivation of their names and nicknames and a list of nations. The volume concludes with a bibliography and index.

For viewers of ABC's *Good Morning America* program during the early and mid-1990s, Harm de Blij might be the personification of geography; he was the geography editor for the program from 1990 to 1996. *Harm de Blij's Geography Book* is based on subjects covered by de Blij during broadcasts, in particular topics about which de Blij received written correspondence from viewers. Fourteen chapters show how geography and geographical thinking can be applied to a wide variety of topics and concerns. After broadly describing geography and the history of geography in the United States, de Blij surveys map basics; landscape creation and interpretation; weather, climate, and the greenhouse effect; cities and the geography of national government; boundaries; population geography and the effects of population growth; the oceans; and changes in nations and states and how those changes are felt globally. A number of appendix lists follow, full of basic geographic trivia: highest, lowest, coldest, wettest, largest. *Harm de Blij's Geography*

Book is written in an easy-to-read approachable style. It will provide foundation information, answer basic questions, put information into context, and perhaps whet the reader's appetite for more geography.

10 Geographic Ideas that Changed the World is a book of 10 chapters written by geographers about how geography and geographic thinking have impacted the world. "These ten are not the only geographic ideas that have changed the world; they might not even be the ten most important geographic ideas ever to have emerged. Each does, however, have its origins in one or more core geographic concept, and each has been around long enough to have had an impact to the world beyond our discipline and on the world outside the walls of universities" (*10 Geographic Ideas,* x). The "ideas" include maps, weather maps and forecasting, geographic information systems, "human adjustment" to environmental changes, climatic water budgets, human transformation of the Earth, connections and interdependencies between locations, central place theory, megalopolis, and sense of place. The essays/chapters are scholarly in nature but primarily are intended to be accessible for upper-level high school students and college undergraduates or for anyone who was not introduced to geography in an academic setting but is developing an interest. All of the chapters include references, and at the end of the book there is a paragraph introducing the education and research interests of each contributor. Although the writing in *10 Geographic Ideas that Changed the World* is for the most part jargon-free, readers will probably glean more if they have some prior experience reading scholarly or research articles.

Geograpy: A Global Synthesis
Geography in America
Geography's Inner Worlds
The Student's Companion to Geography. 2nd ed.

There are also books that describe the many subdisciplines of geography. *Geography in America* and *Geography's Inner Worlds* both focus on geography in the United States. Work on *Geography in America* began in 1985, in part to expand the role and visibility of specialty groups within the Association of American Geographers. The structure of *Geography in America* clearly shows that geography is made up of many thriving subdisciplines. After two introductory chapters that survey modern geography and geography's place in twentieth-century education, there are 33 chapters that explore the human and physical, the systemic and regional facets of the discipline. The chapters are grouped into seven sections: Environmental Processes and Resources; Historical and Cultural Contributions to Geographic Understanding; Analysis and Management of Societal Growth and Change; Assessment and Management of Hazards and Infirmity; International Understanding through Regional Synthesis; Emerging Perspectives on Geographic Inquiry; and Analysis and Display of Geographic Phenomena. The volume concludes with a name and a subject index. All of the chapters include extensive bibliographies. *Geography in America* focuses on specific areas of inquiry in geography; it does not intend or attempt to show geography as a unified discipline.

Geography's Inner Worlds, like *Geography in America,* is a set of contributed chapters. But unlike *Geography in America, Geography's Inner Worlds* looks for commonalties among geography's subdisciplines, going beyond descriptions of the subdisciplines to create a more unified view of the discipline as a whole. Work began on *Geography's Inner Worlds* in the mid-1980s at approximately the same time that *Geography in America* was in preparation. *Geography's Inner Worlds* was primarily intended for geographers, "to reintroduce geographers to each other, and to introduce overseas geographers—especially from outside the English-speaking realm—to American geography." (*Geography's Inner Worlds,* xviii) Seventeen chapters divided into four parts describe what geography is, what geographers do, how geographers think, and why geographers think the way that they do. Although examples are drawn from systemic and regional, human, and physical geography, none of the chapters revolve around any one geography subdiscipline. Many of the chapters include black-and-white illustrations, and all of the chapters conclude with bibliographies.

The Student's Companion to Geography takes a British view of the discipline including its multiple foci, its history and subdisciplines, the necessary foundation skills needed by geographers, the literature of geography, geographical data resources, and suggestions for geographical employment and postgraduate studies. *The Student's Companion to Geography* is more specific in its descriptions of academic and research processes and in its suggestions for finding the right academic program. This is because *The Student's Companion to Geography* is intended primarily as a guide for students who are considering geography as a potential academic pursuit and those who are already studying geography, although it also serves as a general introduction to the discipline.

Rediscovering Geography

Rediscovering Geography takes yet a different view of the discipline. Prepared by a committee of the Board on Earth Sciences and Resources of the National Research Council, this publication broadly describes geography and how geographical methods are used in education and research, and at different levels of government. The first two chapters are introductory in nature: the first summarizes recent changes in the discipline and the reasons for the report, and the second gives an overview of six critical areas where geography can play an instrumental role. Chapters 3 and 4 present a digest of geographic viewpoints and techniques. After two chapters about geography's contributions to scientific research and decision making, the final two chapters suggest ways to increase the use of geographical techniques, increase the number of geography degrees granted by universities and colleges along with increasing general geographical competencies, and strengthen the discipline as a whole. The last chapter includes 11 recommendations for improving geographic understanding and literacy, strengthening geographic institutions, and encouraging implementation of the recommendations.

All of the chapters include black-and-white illustrations, mainly maps and graphs, along with sidebars that explain concepts in greater depth or that illuminate a case study. The volume follows the standard National Research Council format with an extensive preface and executive summary at the beginning. *Rediscovering Geography* concludes with a lengthy list of references and three appendices: "Enrollment and Employment Trends in Geography," reprinted from the August 1995 issue of *Professional Geographer*; contact information for professional geographical organizations; and biographical sketches of the committee members who authored the volume.

Searching for "geography" as a subject in library catalogs will result in an overabundance of matches. Many of the matches may be introductory physical or human geography texts or texts for survey courses with titles like *Introduction to Geography* and *Geography: Realms, Regions, and Concepts*. Searching "geography" could also yield books on specific places and maps. Any results list from searching "geography" will need to be examined carefully to identify appropriate titles. Given geography's diverse nature, it should come as no surprise to find many books describing specific geography subdisciplines. Fortunately, searching for books on subdisciplines can be focused through terms such as "economic geography," "historical geography," "physical geography," and "urban geography." Works on the field of geography in specific places can be found by searching "Geography—[place name]," while works about the geography of specific places can be found by searching "[Place name]—Geography."

WEB SITES ON GEOGRAPHY

As with other disciplines, geography has a large number of information resources available through the World Wide Web. Many geography departments have Web sites, as do professional organizations, publications, and—occasionally—individual researchers. Fortunately, links to many of these sites are provided by Web link aggregators.

Geography: Guide to Geographical Resources
 (http://www.library.wisc.edu/libraries/Geography/
 guide/geoglist.htm)
The Geography Library at the University of Wisconsin–Madison has compiled a Web site subject guide to geography that includes links or references to a number of helpful geographic resources; not all of the references are available on-line. The first part of the Web site, "Geography: Geographers Define and

Describe Geography," compiles citations to works that define or describe geography. The Web site also includes citations to geography bibliographies and links to other selected sites with geographic content. There are also descriptions of journal indexing/abstracting services, lists of geography dissertations, geography dictionaries and encyclopedias, and gazetteers, as well as links to geography department indexes and association and agency Web sites.

Geography About.com (http://geography.about.com)
Yahoo! Geography (http://dir.yahoo.com/Science/
 geography/)
Geography About.com is geared more toward non-geographers than toward people already involved in the discipline. The site includes a number of definitions of geography from A.D. 150 (Ptolemy) through 1995 (Wassmansdorf), an explanation of how geography differs from geology, and very brief descriptions of geography's history and why geography is important. This site also includes links to information about careers in geography, geographic education at all educational levels, human and physical geography, and cartography and map resources. There are also blank (or outline) maps, clip art, and a number of resources for "homework help." Geography About.com has something for everyone.

Yahoo! Geography is also directed primarily toward the needs of non-geographers. Like other Yahoo! directories, Geography is an extensive collection of annotated links to Web sites. Some of the linked sites are very specific, such as "Medical Geography in Ukraine," while others are links to yet other resource directories on the Web, including Geography About.com. Yahoo! Geography does not give quite as much guidance as Geography About.com nor does it contain any real content beyond the links.

ORGANIZATIONS

Organizations that center on the discipline of geography, in contrast to organizations that are geographical in nature (the National Geographic Society is a prime example), will have available information about studying geography, making contact with geographers, and recent developments in the field.

Association of American Geographers
 (http://www.aag.org)
The Association of American Geographers (AAG), founded in 1904, "advances professional studies in

geography and encourages the application of geographic research in education, government, and business. It promotes discussion among its members and with scholars in related fields, supports the publication of scholarly studies, and performs services to aid the advancement of its members and the field of geography." (AAG Web site) The AAG has over 6,700 members, mostly from the United States, but more than 60 other countries are also represented. The association includes geographers with regional and systemic specialties, as well as physical and human focuses. Accordingly, there are 52 specialty groups within AAG that give the members an opportunity to interact with others who have similar interests. Many of the specialty groups produce a newsletter or have a Web site. AAG holds a spring annual meeting with paper sessions sponsored by different specialty groups. The AAG Web site includes information about careers in geography and an "Ask a Geographer" section with contacts to people with discipline specialties. The Web site also includes links to a number of other geography organization sites.

American Geographical Society (http://www.amergeog. org)

The American Geographical Society (AGS) was founded in 1851 in New York City; it is the oldest professional geographical association in the United States. "The mission of the American Geographical Society is to link business, professional, and scholarly worlds in the creation and application of geographical knowledge and techniques to address economic, social, and environmental problems." (AGS Web site) Besides information about the Society, *Ubique,* the Society's thrice-yearly newsletter, is available on-line through the AGS Web site; print copies of *Ubique* are sent to AGS members (fellows).

There are also a number of smaller regional or state organizations that might be helpful for making connections. Many publish a regular journal or newsletter, and most have an annual meeting. Web sites for this kind of organization can generally be found by searching for the state or region of interest along with "geographical" or "geographers." Typical organizations include:

• North East Map Organization (http://ublib. buffalo.edu/libraries/units/sel/collections/maps/ nemo.html)
• Association of Pacific Coast Geographers—serves as the Pacific Coast Regional Division of the Associa-

tion of American Geographers and publishes an annual *Yearbook* (http://www.csus.edu/apcg/)
• California Geographical Society—publishes *The California Geographer* annually (http://www. calgeog.org/)
• Illinois Geographical Society—publishes the refereed *Bulletin of the Illinois Geographical Society* twice each year (http://lilt.ilstu.edu/igs/default.htm)
• Pennsylvania Geographical Society—publishes *The Pennsylvania Geographer,* a refereed journal, twice each year (http://www.thepgs.org)

ABOUT GEOGRAPHERS

Geographers: Biobibliographical Studies

Geographers: Biobibliographical Studies, published somewhat annually, contains bibliographical/ biographical essays about more than 300 individuals who have made significant contributions to geography. Entries go beyond geographers and cartographers; some of the essays describe zoologists, crowned heads of state, alchemists, economists, philosophers, and nineteenth-century travelers. The only commonality among the subjects, beyond a connection to geography, is that they are all dead. The contributions of the entry subjects to geography vary widely—some have obvious geographical connections such as map or atlas publishing, leading important surveys or voyages of discovery, recording or organizing descriptions of places, or developing new techniques or moving forward important research agendas. But some of the geographical connections may seem tentative or somewhat nebulous. Fortunately, each essay follows a standard outline that always includes a section on "geographical thought." All of the essays have three major text sections: Education, Life, and Work; Scientific Ideas and Geographical Thought; and Influence and Spread of Ideas. These are followed by a bibliography section with three or four subsections: "Obituaries and Other Accounts," a select bibliography of works, other references and a description of archival sources, and a chronology. At the start of most entries is a black-and-white portrait of the subject: sometimes a photograph, sometimes a painting, sometimes a photograph of a sculpture. Each volume concludes with two indexes. The first is an index to names, organizations, and geographical concepts appearing in that specific volume. The second index is a cumulative index of all of the biobibliographies that appeared in the previous volumes. *Geographers: Biobibliographical Studies* goes beyond Anglo-American and European geography to include individuals from Asia and Africa, many of whom may not have otherwise come to a reader's attention. Because of the extensive bibliographies and the straightforward synthesis of individual's lives and works, *Geographers: Biobibliographical Studies* might be an ideal place to begin reading about specific geographers or about geographers who flourished during specfic time periods of interest.

A Biographical Dictionary of American Geography in the Twentieth Century. 2nd ed.

A Biographical Dictionary of American Geography in the Twentieth Century contains over 680 brief biographical entries for geographers and non-geographers who were intimately connected to the discipline. Entries include the subject's name, lifespan dates, place of birth, names of parents and spouses, dates and degree-granting institutions, title of dissertation, places and dates of employment and special connections to the Association of American Geographers, such as being a charter member or president. All of the geographers included are deceased. Many, but not all, of the entries were involved in higher education. The entries are in alphabetical order by last name. There is no index nor is there any kind of cross-referenced list to degree-granting institutions, research interests, or places of employment. While entries also do not include references to living geographer offspring, connections can be made from deceased offspring to their deceased parents. *A Biographical Dictionary of American Geography in the Twentieth Century* is best as a quick reference, a starting point to confirm or determine the most appropriate institution to contact when needing to find details about an individual's career.

Biographical Dictionary of Geography

Biographical Dictionary of Geography is narrower in scope than *Geographers: Biobibliographical Studies* and broader (although containing fewer entries) than *A Biographical Dictionary of American Geography in the Twentieth Century.* Seventy-seven European or North American geographers, a mix of alive and dead individuals at the time of publication, are explored in short essays, most two-and-a-half pages or less, with an accompanying selected bibliography and chronology and occasionally a short list of references. The essays briefly survey the highlights of each individual's life as well as contributions to the discipline of geography. There are three appendices, an alphabetical list of the geographers included in

the volume, a chronological list, and lists by country of birth. The chronological and country of birth appendices are especially interesting because the reader will be able to quickly see that more than 80 percent of the geographers included in *Biographical Dictionary of Geography* either flourished during the nineteenth century or were born during the nineteenth or twentieth centuries. Also, nearly 75 percent of the geographers included were born in Germany, the United Kingdom, or the United States. Both of these are indicative of geography's development into an academic discipline during the nineteenth century in those three nations.

FINDING GEOGRAPHERS AND GEOGRAPHICAL COLLECTIONS

Guide to Programs in Geography in the United States and Canada; AAG Handbook and Directory of Geographers

Guide to Programs in Geography in the United States and Canada; AAG Handbook and Directory of Geographers, published annually by the Association of American Geographers, describes undergraduate and graduate degree programs in the United States and Canada. Each entry includes a description of the program and department; admissions and financial aid information, or contact information for obtaining this information; and a list of faculty including degrees and research or teaching interests, along with basic contact information. The entries are alphabetical by state name and then by university or college name; Canadian provinces follow the United States. Included with the program entries are entries describing some of the federal agencies that often employ geographers as well as major geographical associations. Following the descriptive entries is a multiple-page table that summarizes program specialties; there also is a listing, arranged by state and degree-granting institution of Ph.D. dissertations and master's theses completed during the previous year. The portion of the volume devoted to geography degree programs concludes with a list of programs not described, primarily those at two-year colleges, and some aggregated statistical data about geography programs and degrees granted.

The second portion of *Guide to Programs in Geography in the United States and Canada; AAG Handbook and Directory of Geographers,* slightly less than half of the volume, describes the Association of American Geographers and its membership. Included are the association's constitution; names and contact information for the association's executive committee and councilors; descriptions of committees and appointments; lists of past AAG presidents, publication editors, membership totals, and locations of annual meetings. The section also includes brief descriptions of AAG specialty groups and lists of awards and honors recipients. More than three-quarters of the *AAG Handbook and Directory of Geographers* is alphabetical directory information for AAG members; entries include name, address, telephone and fax numbers, e-mail address, birth date and place, degrees with year and granting institution, and current title and place of employment. After the directory, the members' names are resorted geographically by zip code or country.

Guide to Programs in Geography in the United States and Canada; AAG Handbook and Directory of Geographers will help track down geographers if they are members of AAG or if their academic departmental affiliation is known. This publication also highlights the diversity of study pursued in geography through the descriptions of departmental specialties and the AAG specialty groups.

Schwendeman's Directory of College Geography of the United States

Like the AAG *Guide to Programs, Schwendeman's Directory* describes geography programs at U.S. colleges and universities, but the description is done through tables and charts, not text. The tables and charts are divided into eight chapters that focus mainly on enrollment levels in regional, systemic, and techniques courses. The introductory chapter includes a table with contact information for all of the programs included in the *Directory,* a table showing the number of bachelor's, master's, and Ph.D. students, and a listing of faculty in the departments. The final two chapters serve as summaries for the first six chapters. Because the information for individual geography programs is divided among the many tables, it is difficult to used *Schwendeman's Directory* to build a description of any one program. *Schwendeman's* will be more useful when comparing specific parts or emphases of different programs, and older editions of *Schwendeman's* could be used to track the growth or decline of geographic subdisciplines.

There are four library/information organizations that might be helpful in making connections with geographers and geographic information. The American Library Association's Map and Geography Round Table (MAGERT; http://magert.whoi.edu:8000/) and the Special Libraries Association's Geography and Map Division (SLA G&M; http://www.sla.org/division/dgm/index.htm) are two of the biggest professional organizations for librarians in the United States who specialize in maps, geography, and geographic information. Both organizations have meetings in conjunction with their parent organizations' annual general meetings and winter business meetings. MAGERT publishes a newsletter, *baseline,* six times a year. Like MAGERT and SLA G&M, the Western Association of Map Libraries (WAML; http://www.waml.org/) is an organization primarily of map librarians. Unlike MAGERT and SLA G&M, WAML has a specific primarily membership region, generally the western United States and western Canadian provinces. WAML meets twice a year, and for people in the principal membership region who are interested in geographic information sources, WAML is an especially invaluable resources for making connections with specialists and collections. WAML's journal, *Information Bulletin,* appears three times a year.

The North American Cartographic Information Society (NACIS; http://www.nacis.org/) has a slightly different focus from the previous three organizations. Its membership is made up of a mixture of U.S., Canadian, and Mexican geographers who have an interest in cartography or geographic information resources; professional commercial cartographers; and map librarians. NACIS meets once a year, usually in October. *Cartographic Perspectives,* NACIS's refereed journal, is published three times a year.

Additionally there are directories to map collections. The most recently printed directory to map collections is the *Guide to U.S. Map Resources,* 2nd ed. Although published in 1990, *Guide* is still useful for finding basic contact information for most large- and medium-sized or important map collections in the United States. On the Web, lists maintained at the University of Minnesota John R. Borchert Map Library(http://map.lib.umn.edu/map_libraries.phtml), the University of Virginia Geospatial & Statistical Data Center (http://fisher.lib.virginia.edu/collections/maps/othermaplibs.html), WAML (http://www.waml.org/maplibs.html), and the Association of Canadian Map Libraries and Archives (http://www.ssc.uwo.ca/assoc/acml/acmla.html) may also prove to be useful in finding the right person to talk with or the right set of materials to look at.

GEOGRAPHY JOURNALS

Annals of the Association of American Geographers
Professional Geographer
AAG Newsletter

The Association of American Geographers (AAG) publishes three general titles on a regular schedule. *Annals* and *Professional Geographer* are both quarterly and are both refereed and indexed in the major journal indexes such as *GeoBase, Social Science Abstracts,* and *Social Science and Science Citation Index.* There are subtle differences in the articles presented by *Annals* and *Professional Geographer. Annals* is the AAG's flagship professional publication with high-quality research articles and book reviews covering all of geography's subdisciplines. Generally, the articles fall into four broad categories: Environmental Sciences; Methods, Models, and GIS; Nature and Society; and People, Place, and Region. The articles are always well-grounded in geographical literature and include extensive references or bibliographies. The book reviews are thoughtful and also often include references to related works that have been used as context or comparisons.

Professional Geographer also publishes research articles drawing from the entire discipline, but the articles tend to be shorter than those in *Annals* and more often emphasize focused empirical studies and methodologies rather than the more synoptic articles in *Annals.* Methodologies and viewpoints slightly out of the mainstream are also more apt to be found in *Professional Geographer.* The style of book review is also slightly different. While the reviews in *Annals* often place the focus book into a broader context, the *Professional Geographer* reviews focus tightly on only the book being reviewed.

The *AAG Newsletter,* issued monthly, has a completely different mission. It keeps members up-to-date on association activities, lists books that have been received by the *Annals* and *Professional Geographer* book review editor, and alerts geographers to potential grant funding opportunities, as well as announcing who has received grant money for research projects. Each month, a substantial portion of the *Newsletter* is devoted to "Jobs in Geography"—announcements of open positions at colleges and universities primarily in the United States but also including some from Canada and elsewhere.

Geographical Review (http://www.amergeog.org/gr/ grhome.html)
Focus on Geography (http://www.amergeog.org/ focus_magazine.htm)

The American Geographical Society publishes *Geographical Review* and *Focus on Geography;* both

are issued quarterly. *Geographical Review* is more scholarly with refereed articles that often reflect the regional geography aspects of the discipline. Sections titled "Geographical Record," "Geographical Field Note," and "Geographical Review Essay" appear regularly. Each issue also includes a number of book reviews.

Focus on Geography is a glossy, popular treatment of geographically based inquiry. Articles are short, often written in a lively and entertaining style, and are amply illustrated with color photographs and maps. Articles usually conclude with a brief "References and Further Readings" bibliography.

Most geographers would agree that titles like *Annals of the Association of American Geographers, Professional Geographer,* and *Geographical Review* are "core" to the discipline. But these three titles are general in nature. Geographers' mental lists of important journals will include many additional titles. A number of geography's subdisciplines have journals devoted to their interests that are considered core by much smaller and more focused groups. The specialist journals are published either by specialty groups or by commercial publishers. Especially important, or long-running, titles include: *Progress in Human Geography, Progress in Physical Geography, Economic Geography, Antipode, Cartographica, Monthly Weather Review, Political Geography, Papers in Regional Science,* and *Urban Geography.* For geographers specializing in regional studies, there are titles such as *Eurasian Geography and Economics, Asia Pacific Viewpoint, Polar Geography and Geology,* and *Revue de Geographie Alpine.* Journals for geographic subdisciplines can be found in the same way as searching for books.

HISTORY OF GEOGRAPHY

Books on the history of geography, as distinguished from historical geography, which is a subdiscipline of the field, can be found in library catalogs by searching "Geography—History."

History of Modern Geography: An Annotated Bibliography of Selected Works
History of Modern Geography focuses on sources about academic geography during the eighteenth, nineteenth, and twentieth centuries. The citations are organized in three large sections (the first of which is the largest): General and Topical, Geography in Various Countries, and Biographical Works. "General and Topical" is divided into 12 chapters that list sources on geographic subdisciplines; geographic societies

and organizations; discovery and exploration; cartography, survey, and navigation; and teaching geography in higher education and at other levels. The history of cartography and exploration is not fully covered because that portion of the literature is so extensive. "Geography in Various Countries" includes seven chapters with specific chapters on the United States, Great Britain, France, Germany, Italy, and other European countries and the former USSR. The final section, "Biographical Works," includes three chapters: United States, Europe, and other countries. The publications listed in *History of Modern Geography* include books and journal articles and are in a variety of Western European languages, with English and German predominant. All of the entries include a brief annotation. *History of Modern Geography* concludes with an index to authors and one to subjects.

Other geographical bibliographies that include titles on the history of geography are described in Chapter 2.

All Possible Worlds: A History of Geographical Ideas. 3rd ed.

All Possible Worlds is a broad survey of the development and evolution of geography from the classical era through the later portion of the twentieth century. After an introductory chapter, the remaining text is divided into two parts, Classical and Modern. The chapters in the Classical part describe how geography evolved in the Greek and Roman worlds; the effects of the dissolution of the Roman world and the rise of Christianity, as well as geography in other parts of the world during the European Middle Ages; the Age of Exploration with its corresponding explosion of cartographic and navigational techniques; the impacts of discoveries on government, science, and philosophy; and the influence of Alexander von Humboldt and Carl Ritter. The second part, Modern, examines *new* geography—geography in which no one could be a universal expert, but instead the experts are all specialists. Ten of the chapters in this part describe developments in individual nations (Germany, France, Great Britain, Russia/Soviet Union/Commonwealth of Independent States, Canada, Sweden, Japan, and three chapters on the United States). The last three chapters show some applications of geography, briefly discuss the development of observation and analysis techniques, and summarize foundations of geographic inquiry at the end of the twentieth century. There is a list of references for each chapter and an index of personal names with life extents and very brief biographical information. *All Possible Worlds* will provide

good grounding for those interested in the differences between national schools of geography.

Geography and Geographers. 5th ed.

Geography and Geographers is a description and history of geography, specifically human geography, as an academic discipline. "The book is basically a reconstruction, from published material, of philosophical and methodological debates within human geography; it is more concerned with writing about human geography than with writings that are human geography.... [not] to summarize what human geographers have done, but rather to concentrate on how they have done it, and why" (*Geography and Geographers,* xiii). The book is organized into 10 chapters; the first and last provide a contextual envelope while the center eight chapters focus on the development of theory and specialties within human geography. Chapters on geographical foundations, the rise of systematic studies and the use of the scientific method, and spatial analysis are followed by chapters on behavioral, humanistic, radical, cultural, and applied geography. *Geography and Geographers* is not the most appropriate choice for a *first* book about geography; other works will create easier entries into the foundations and developments of geographical thought and subdisciplines. The bibliography at the end of *Geography and Geographers* may prove to be a useful starting point in developing a bibliography for directed readings or for surveying a wide variety of writings about human geography.

There are many other possible choices available for reading about the development of the geographical discipline, each with a different emphasis or viewpoint. *The Geographical Tradition* highlights key events in the history of cartography. Chapters discuss geography during the "Age of Reconnaissance" (not the Renaissance), the impact of the Scientific Revolution on geography, the Age of Enlightenment, pre-Darwinian geography, the impacts of Darwinism, the age of (European) empires, the early to mid-twentieth century, and the quantification of geography. All of the chapters are footnoted. There also is a bibliography that focuses on English-language materials.

On Geography and Its History explores the history of geography's developments primarily in Great Britain within a European and global context. There are chapters specifically focusing on the Royal Geographical Society, geography at the University of Cambridge, Darwin, and geography during the Victorian era. All of the chapters are extensively footnoted.

The "Index to Persons" will be especially helpful in finding references to individuals that appear in multiple chapters.

The Association of American Geographers (AAG) Centennial Coordinating Committee has been working on a "Geography in America Timeline" as part of its preparations for the 2004 centennial association meeting. Previews of the timeline appeared in the *AAG Newsletter* between November 2001 and March 2002. A beta version of the timeline can be viewed through the Web (http://home.gwiu.edu/~icheung/gat/gat.html) Events described in the timeline generally range from 1749 to 2000. Each entry describes an event or publication, and all entries include substantial references to materials, most in print but some on-line.

QUOTATIONS

Books of quotations can serve as inspiration for writing or can assist in quickly setting the thoughts of a particular author into the context of the thoughts of others.

Dictionary of Quotations in Geography

The compilers of *Dictionary of Quotations in Geography* gleaned their selections from more than 80 years of writing in the United States about geography and geographical matters. Most of the quotations came from standard American geographical journals including *Annals of the Association of American Geographers, Bulletin of the American Geographical Society, Geographical Review, Journal of Geography,* and *Professional Geographer.* The compilers intended with their selections to "review and identify some of the salient features of American geography. . . . to characterize a variety of themes as the discipline has evolved" (*Dictionary of Quotations in Geography,* x).

The quotations are arranged chronologically within five themes, four of which are derived from William Pattison's 1964 article, "The Four Traditions of Geography." Pattison's traditions or themes are: spatial, area studies, man-land, and earth science. In *Dictionary of Quotations in Geography,* the earth science section contains quotations about physiography, geomorphology, "Earth-Sun Relations," climatology, biogeography, and physical geography—all writings about the Earth and its systems. "Man-Land Tradition," part two, focuses on humans and their activities, including how the physical environment seems to affect or is affected by human activities. Specific topics are: "Racial Geography and the Tropics," "Environment and Civilization,"

"Environment and Behavior," "Climate and Man," and "Man-Land Geography." The quotations in the third part, "Area Studies Tradition," have a point of view that attempts to explain how complex regions operate and interact with other regions. "The Spatial Tradition," part four, contains quotations about methodology, theory, process, and geographic organizations. The final section, titled "Other," focuses on a variety of general topics: Applied Geography, Political Geography, Mapping Science, Field Techniques, Geographic Education, and History of Geographic Thought.

Each quotation begins with the author's full name, the date of the publication, and a page number. These tie to the alphabetical-by-author list of sources cited near the end of the volume. The volume also includes a single index to authors, places, and topics.

Dictionary of Quotations in Geography could be used in a number of different ways. A broad topic of interest could be selected, for example "Geographic Education," and the selected quotations could be read chronologically for a quick overview of how thoughts and attitudes about geographic education have evolved between the time of the first quotation, 1813, and the last, 1984. The index makes possible the targeting of specific topics or authors. Materials written by Wilber Zelinsky, a well-known cultural geographer, appear on three different pages; thoughts about Illinois appear twice. The "Sources Cited" section could serve as a foundation for reading some of the core American geographic literature produced during the early to mid-twentieth century.

The compilers of *Dictionary of Quotations in Geography* did not attempt to be all inclusive. Their selections are intended to be samples that illustrate or illuminate particular patterns of thought within the discipline of geography at specific times. Nor did the compilers "judge" the correctness or ethicalness of the ideas. Some of the thoughts expressed by geographers of the past, in particular those quoted in the "Man-Land Tradition" section that reflect ideas of environmental determinism, may be seen today as biased, prejudiced, or racist, but they need to be acknowledged because they were widespread and accepted at the time of original publication. The context of composition needs to be kept at the forefront when using *Dictionary of Quotations in Geography.*

Carto-Quotes

Carto-Quotes has a diffuse scope and set of literature from which the quotations are drawn and a less-focused theme than found in *Dictionary of Quotations in Geog-*

raphy. Each of the quotations in *Carto-Quotes* "has as its central theme some connection—albeit at times quite oblique—with the world of maps and/or mapmaking, or else it simply conveys a particular sense of place or time that will hopefully strike a chord with the surveyor, the urban planner, the architect or the traveller" (*Carto-Quotes,* 7). The chronological time period spanned by the quotations is from the fifth century B.C. to 1996. The quotations come from literature (both prose and poetry), official reports, letters, speeches, newspapers, and textbooks. The topics are diverse including, but not limited to, political events, boundary changes, surveying, discovery and exploration, attitudes about places, and descriptions of peoples' appearances through maplike metaphors. The quotations are arranged alphabetically by author and are followed by an author index, a bibliography, and an acknowledgment list for the use of copyrighted materials.

While most authors are quoted only once or twice, Shakespeare is included 19 times. Some of the quotations are well-known—Jonathan Swift, 1733, "So Geographiers, in Afric-maps, With savage-pictures fill their gaps." Others may lead to laughter—Israel Tourist Bureau, 1979, "If you liked the book [Old Testament], you'll love the country." Others are less statements on geography than they are statements about society—Muhammad Ali, 1975, "Wars on nations are fought to change maps, but wars on poverty are fought to map change." Few of the quotations are from geographers or are about the discipline of geography. The emphasis of *Carto-Quotes* is describing the world and how it is perceived. The selected quotations are not presented in either an intellectual or a chronological context. *Carto-Quotes* is fun reading but it will not serve as a barometer of geographic thought. Instead it might spark ideas for paper topics or help locate just the right quotation to spice up a presentation.

Geography is a diverse field with many subdisciplines. The underlying questions for geographers are: What there is there? Why is it there? What are the impacts of this being here? How does here connect with over there? After centuries of being a fundamental descriptive tool for explorers and exploiters, geography evolved into ways of thinking about connections and impacts between places. Geography in the late twentieth and early twenty-first centuries goes well beyond describing landscapes, people, and natural resources. Now geography is the science of why the wheres and the whats of locations are important and how the wheres are tightly woven together. Geographers use a wide variety of tools, data, and methods to answer the question, "Why should we care that this is here?"

BIBLIOGRAPHY

10 Geographic Ideas that Changed the World. Susan Hanson, ed. New Brunswick, N.J.: Rutgers University Press, 1997. ISBN 0-8135-2356-7.

AAG Newsletter. Washington, D.C: Association of American Geographers, 1967– . 12 per year. ISSN: 0275-3995.

All Possible Worlds: A History of Geographical Ideas. 3rd ed. Geoffrey J. Martin and Preston E. James. New York: J. Wiley & Sons, 1993. ISBN: 0-471-63414-X.

Annals of the Association of American Geographers. Washington, D.C.: Association of American Geographers, 1911– . Quarterly. ISSN: 0004-5608.

Antipode: A Radical Journal of Geography. Oxford: Basil Blackwell, 1969–. 3 per year. ISSN: 0066-4812.

Asia Pacific Viewpoint. Oxford: Basil Blackwell, 1996– . 3 per year. Former title *Pacific Viewpoint.* ISSN: 1360-7456.

Association of Pacific Coast Geographers Yearbook. Corvallis, Ore.: Oregon State University Press, 1935– . Annual. ISSN: 0066-9628.

A Biographical Dictionary of American Geography in the Twentieth Century. 2nd ed., rev. Gary S. Dunbar, comp. Baton Rouge, La.: Geoscience Publications, Dept. of Geography and Anthropology, Louisiana State University, 1996. ISBN: 0-938909-00-2.

Biographical Dictionary of Geography. Robert P. Larkin and Gary L. Peters. Westport, Conn.: Greenwood Press, 1993. ISBN: 0-313-27622-6.

Bulletin of the American Geographical Society. New York: American Geographical Society, 1859–1915. Frequency varied. Continued by: *Geographical Review.*

Bulletin of the Illinois Geographical Society. Normal, Ill.: Illinois Geographical Society, 1955– . Biannual. ISSN: 0019-2031.

California Geographer. Los Angeles, Calif.: California Geographical Society, 1960– . Annual. ISSN: 0575-5700.

Cartographic Perspectives: Bulletin of the North American Cartographic Information Society. University Park, Penn.: The Society, 1989–. Triannual. ISSN: 1048-9053.

Cartographica. Toronto: University of Toronto Press, 1980– . Quarterly. Former title *Canadian Cartographer.* ISSN: 0317-7173.

Carto-Quotes: An Inspirational Companion for the Map-Maker and the Map-User. Gary Brannon and Les Harding, eds. Kitchener, Ontario: Upney Editions, 1996. ISBN: 0-9681403-1-9.

"The Circumference of Geography." Nevis M. Fenneman. *Annals of the Association of American Geographers* vol. 9 (1919): 3–11.

Dictionary of Quotations in Geography. James O. Wheeler and Francis M. Sibley, comps. New York: Greenwood Press, 1986. ISBN: 0-313-24196-1.

Don't Know Much about Geography: Everything You Need to Know about the World but Never Learned. Kenneth C. Davis. New York: William Morrow, 1992. ISBN: 0-380-71379-9.

Economic Geography. Worcester, Mass.: Clark University, 1925– . Quarterly. ISSN: 0013-0095.

Elementary Statistics for Geographers. rev. ed. James E. Burt and Gerald M. Barber. New York: Guilford Press, 1996. ISBN: 0-89862-282-4.

Eurasian Geography and Economics. Palm Beach, Fla.: V.H. Winston and Son, 1960– . 8 per yr. Former titles: *Soviet Geography, Post-Soviet Geography* and. *Post-Soviet Geography and Economics.* ISSN: 1538-7216.

Focus on Geography. New York: American Geographical Society, 1950– . Quarterly. Also titled *Focus.* ISSN: 0015-5004.

"The Four Traditions of Geography." William D. Pattison. *The Journal of Geography* Vol. 63, no. 5 (May 1964): 211–216.

Geographers: Biobibliographical Studies. International Geographical Union, Commission on the History of Geographical Thought. London: Mansell, 1977– . Annual. ISSN: 0308-6992.

Geographical Review. New York: American Geographical Society, 1916– . Quarterly. Formerly: *Bulletin of the American Geographical Society.* ISSN: 0016-7428.

The Geographical Tradition. David N. Livingstone. Oxford: Blackwell, 1993. ISBN: 0-631-18586-0.

Geography: A Global Synthesis. Peter Haggett. New York: Pearson, 2001. ISBN: 0-582-32030-5.

Geography: Realms, Regions, and Concepts. 10th ed. Harm J. de Blij and Peter O. Muller. New York: J. Wiley & Sons, 2002. ISBN: 0-471-40775-5.

Geography and Geographers: Anglo-American Human Geography since 1945. 5th ed. R.J. Johnston. New York: Arnold, 1997. ISBN: 0-340-65263-2.

Geography in America. Gary L. Gaile and Cort J. Willmott. Columbus, Ohio: Merrill, 1989. ISBN: 0-675-20648-0.

Geography's Inner Worlds. Pervasive Themes in Contemporary American Geography. Ronald F. Abler, Melvin G. Marcus, and Judy M. Olson, eds. New Brunswick, N.J.: Rutgers University Press, 1992. ISBN: 0-8135-1830-X.

Guide to Programs in Geography in the United States and Canada; AAG Handbook and Directory of Geographers. Washington, D.C.: Association of American Geographers, 1993– . Annual. Previous titles include: *Association of American Geographers Directory of Geographers; AAG Handbook and Directory of Geographers; AAG Directory of Geographers; Guide to Programs of Geography in the United States and Canada; Guide to Programs of Geography.* ISSN: 0882-1542.

Guide to U.S. Map Resources. 2nd ed. David A. Cobb, comp. Chicago: American Library Association, 1990. ISBN: 0-8389-0547-1.

Harm de Blij's Geography Book: A Leading Geographer's Fresh Look at Our Changing World. Harm J. de Blij. New York: J. Wiley & Sons, 1995. ISBN: 0-471-11687-4.

History of Modern Geography: An Annotated Bibliography of Selected Works. Gary S. Dunbar. *Bibliographies of the History of Science and Technology,* vol. 9. New York: Garland Publishing, 1985. ISBN 0-8240-9066-7.

Information Bulletin. Sacramento, Calif.: Western Association of Map Libraries. 1969– . Triannual. ISSN: 049-7282.

Introduction to Geography. 8th ed. Arthur Getis, Judith Getis, and Jerome Donald Fellmann. Boston: McGraw-Hill, 2002. ISBN: 0-07-248504-3.

The Journal of Geography. Indiana, Penn.: National Council for Geographic Education, 1902– . Bimonthly. ISSN: 0022-1341.

Monthly Weather Review. Boston: American Meteorological Society, 1872– . Monthly. ISSN: 0027-0644.

On Geography and Its History. D.R. Stoddart. New York: B. Blackwell, 1986. ISBN 0631134883.

Papers in Regional Science: The Journal of the Regional Science Association International. Urbana, Ill.: Regional Science Association International in cooperation with the Regional Science Program, University of Illinois at Urbana-Champaign, 1921– . Quarterly. ISSN: 1056-8190.

The Pennsylvania Geographer. Johnstown, Penn.: Pennsylvania Geographical Society, 1963– . Semiannual. ISSN: 0553-5980.

Polar Geography. Silver Spring, Md.: V.H. Winston, 1980– . Quarterly. Former title: *Polar Geography and Geology.* ISSN: 1088-937X.

Political Geography. England: Pergamon, 1982– . 8 per year. Former title: *Political Geography Quarterly.* ISSN: 0962-6298.

Professional Geographer. Washington, D.C.: Association of American Geographers, 1946– . Quarterly. ISSN 0033-0124.

Progress in Human Geography: An International Review of Geographical Work in the Social Sciences and Humanities. London: Edward Arnold, 1977– . Bimonthly. ISSN: 0309-1325.

Progress in Physical Geography: An International Review of Geographical Work in the National and Environmental Sciences. London: Edward Arnold, 1977– . Quarterly. ISSN: 0309-1333.

Rediscovering Geography: New Relevance for Science and Society. National Research Council. Washington, D.C.: National Academy Press, 1997. ISBN: 0-309-05199-1.

Revue de Geographie Alpine. Grenoble, France: Imprimerie Allier Frères, 1913– . Quarterly. ISSN: 0035-1121.

Schwendeman's Directory of College Geography of the United States. Richmond, Ky.: The Geographical Studies and Research Center at Eastern Kentucky University, 1949– . Annual. ISSN: 0734-8185.

The Student's Companion to Geography. 2nd ed. ISBN: 0-631-22132-8.

Urban Geography. Silver Spring, Md.: V.H. Winston, 1980– . 8 per year. ISSN: 0272-3638.

On-line References

The American Geographical Society. Home page. American Geographical Society. <http://www.amergeog.org> (14 October 2003).

Association of American Geographers. Home page. Association of American Geographers, <http://www.aag.org> (14 October 2003).

Association of Canadian Map Libraries and Archives Home page. ACMLA, 1 September 2003. <http://www.ssc.uwo.ca/assoc/acml/acmla.html> (14 October 2003).

Association of Pacific Coast Geographers Home page. APCG, 20 August 2003. <http://www.csus.edu/apcg/> (14 October 2003).

California Geographical Society. Home page. CGS, 2003. <http://cgs.csusb.edu> (14 October 2003).

Focus on Geography: The Magazine of the American Geographical Society. American Geographical Society, 5 September 2003. http://www.amergeog.org/focus_magazine.htm> (14 October 2003).

"The Four Traditions of Geography." William D. Pattison, 1964. National Council for Geographic Education, 2003. <http://www.ncge.org/publications/journal/classic/fourtraditions.doc> (14 October 2003).

Geographical Review. American Geographical Society, 27 May 2003. <http://www.amergeog.org/gr/grhome.html> (14 October 2003).

Geography About.com. About, Inc., 2003. <http://geography.about.com> (14 October 2003).

Geography: Guide to Geographical Resources. Miriam Kerndt. University of Wisconsin-Madison, Geography Library, 1 November 2000. <http://www.library.wisc.edu/libraries/Geography/guide/geoglist.htm> (14 October 2003).

Geography and Map Division. Home page. Special Libraries Association, Geography and Map Division, 25 August 2003. <http://www.sla.org/division/dgm/index.htm> (14 October 2003).

Geography in America Timeline. Association of American Geographers, AAG Centennial Coordinating Committee. Donald C. Dahmanna and Ivan Cheung, 6 June 2002. Site part of George Washington University, Columbian College of Arts and Sciences. <http://home.gwu.edu/~icheung/gat/gat.html> (14 October 2003)

Illinois Geographical Society. Home page. Illinois State University, 5 June 2003. <http://lilt.ilstu.edu/igs/default.htm> (14 October 2003).

Map and Geography Round Table (MAGERT). Home page. American Library Association, 30 June 2003. <http://magert.whoi.edu:8000/> (14 October 2003).

Map Collections at Other Major Research Libraries. University of Virginia Geospatial & Statistical Data Center, 2 September 2003. <http://fisher.lib.virginia.edu/collections/maps/othermaplibs.html> (14 October 2003).

Map Libraries on the World Wide Web. John R. Borchert Map Library, University of Minnesota, 8 May 2001. <http://map.lib.umn.edu/map_libraries.phtml> (14 October 2003).

North American Cartographic Information Society. Home page. NACIS, 2003. <http://www.nacis.org> (14 October 2003).

North East Map Organization. Home page. David J. Bertuca. North East Map Organization, 4 October 2003. <http://ublib.buffalo.edu/libraries/ast/maps/nemo.html> (14 October 2003).

Pennsylvania Geographical Society. Home page. Bloomsburg University of Pennsylvania, 24 April 2003. <http://www.thepgs.org> (14 October 2003).

WAML Principal Region Map Collections. Western Association of Map Libraries, 7 March 2002. <http://www.waml.org/maplibs.html> (14 October 2003).

Western Association of Map Libraries. Home page. WAML, 28 March 2002. <http://www.waml.org> (14 October 2003).

Yahoo! Geography. Yahoo! Inc., 2003. <http://dir.yahoo.com/Science/geography> (14 October 2003).

CHAPTER 2
General Works

TOPICS COVERED

Bibliographies and Literature Guides
Indexes and Abstracts
Dictionaries and Glossaries
Country Guides

MAJOR SOURCES DISCUSSED

Bibliography of Geography
A Geographical Bibliography for American Libraries
A Bibliography of Geographic Thought
The Literature of Geography
A Guide to Information Sources in the Geographical Sciences
Current Geographical Publications/Online Geographical Bibliography
Geographical Abstracts/Geobase
GeoRef

Social Sciences Abstracts
Social Sciences Citation Index/Science Citation Index Expanded
The Dictionary of Human Geography
The Dictionary of Physical Geography
A Dictionary of Geography
The Penguin Dictionary of Geography
Dictionary of Geography
A Modern Dictionary of Geography
Longman Illustrated Dictionary of Geography
Geographic Dictionary
Geographical Dictionary
Geography Glossary
Fundamentals of Physical Geography—Glossary
CIA World Factbook
Background Notes
Country Studies
Worldmark Encyclopedia of the Nations

Administrative Subdivisions of Countries

Although geography is a diverse discipline, and geographers have widely varied interests, there are commonalties in where geographers begin the search for the ideas and information that help to shape their view of the world. Many of the guides to the literature, including bibliographies and indexes to journal articles, contain citations to works about human and physical geography. Both sides of geography are covered by foundational dictionaries, and country guides usually describe many different geographical aspects including physiography, economics, politics, and society

BIBLIOGRAPHIES AND LITERATURE GUIDES

The 1970s and 1980s were prolific years for bibliography publication; there are very few recent bibliographies or literature guides that have been compiled

and published on paper. Some specialized bibliographies are available through the Web.

Bibliography of Geography

Two of the University of Chicago Department of Geography's Research Paper series are volumes in Chancy Harris's projected multi-volume *Bibliography of Geography;* Research Paper number 179 is "Part I. Introduction to General Aids," and Research Paper number 206 is "Part II: Volume 1. The United States of America." Harris had planned additional bibliographies for human and physical geography systematic fields and for regional geography. From the introductory material of the United States volume, it appears that the *Bibliography of Geography's* second part, regional geography, was intended to be published in five segments: United States; Soviet Union; the Americas excluding the United States; Europe excluding the Soviet Union; and Africa, Asia, Australia, and the Pacific. Only the volume on the United States and the volume on general works have been published. Based on Harris's work with graduate students in the University of Chicago Department of Geography, both of the published volumes emphasize titles in English, French, German, and Russian with the majority of entries being for English-language titles. The titles listed in *Introduction to General Aids* tend to have been published between 1946 and 1975 and the titles in the United States volume were generally published between 1970 and 1985.

Introduction to General Aids does not substantively cover publications prior to 1946 because Harris felt that they had been "admirably summarized" by Wright and Platt in *Aids to Geographical Research*, published in 1947. *Introduction to General Aids* contains 585 main entries, many of which include a substantial description or analysis of the contents. Some of the entries, especially in the cases of serial publications, are for multiple titles. The entries are divided into 16 chapters: 4 on bibliographies; 11 on specific material types such as books, serials, government documents, photographs, maps, gazetteers, and dictionaries; and 1 on geographic methodology. The chapters all begin with a bibliographic essay that is followed by full entries to specific titles. The volume also includes two appendices, one on United States Board on Geographic Names gazetteers and the other describing Harris's personal office reference collection, and concludes with an index to authors, titles, and subjects.

The volume on the United States has a cutoff date of approximately 1970 because Harris's intention was to provide a guide to literature that would be valuable for research on "contemporary geography," not historical. He again refers the reader to Wright and Platt for older titles. Although there are only 974 entries, as with *Introduction to General Aids,* some include multiple references leading to more than 1,250 total references. Most of the entries include annotations, primarily indications of the extent of included bibliographies. The first 52 entries are for "World-Wide Bibliographies and Guides." The remaining entries, specific to the United States, are divided into four sections: General Aids; Physical Geography, Related Earth Sciences, The Environment, and Resources; Human Geography and Related Social Sciences; and Regions of the United States. The sources in "General Aids" mirror the types of items included in *Introduction to General Aids*. The physical and human geography sections are divided into subspecialties, such as climate, land use, ethnic geography, political geography, and geographic education. The regions section is divided into four

large, subnational geographical regions. The chapters or sections include only bibliographic entries; there are no bibliographic essays to place the entries into a context. The volume concludes with an index to authors, titles, and subjects.

Although dated, *Bibliography of Geography* is a key entry point into the geographic literature published between 1945 and 1985, identifying core resources and creating links to past scholarship.

A Geographical Bibliography for American Libraries
A Geographical Bibliography for American Libraries was a joint project of the Association of American Geographers and the National Geographic Society and focuses on publications produced between 1970 and 1984. Titles published before 1970 were covered by an earlier title, *A Geographical Bibliography for American College Libraries,* which was published in 1970. The volume was compiled to assist American libraries in building collections of geographic materials, and the titles included, primarily in English and generally available for acquisition at the time that the bibliography was compiled, would be of interest to public, school, and academic libraries as well as geographers, scholars in related fields, and the general public. The bibliography does not include maps, journal articles, or government agency reports except in exceptional cases where these kinds of items were considered core to the topic covered by the chapter.

Seventy-one area specialists contributed 2,903 numbered bibliographic entries; nearly all have short annotations. The 78 chapters, which are attributed to their contributors, are arranged in 8 parts: General Aids and Sources; History, Philosophy, and Methodology; Systematic Fields of Physical Geography; Systematic Fields of Human Geography; Applied Geography; Regional Geography; and Publications Suitable for School Libraries. Most chapters have multiple sections dividing the coverage of the chapter by type or format of publication; bibliographies, serials, atlases, general works, and special topics are the most common sections. The volume concludes with a combined index to authors, editors, compilers, short titles, and major subjects.

A Geographical Bibliography for American Libraries presents a bibliographic view of the core literature of geography, and its many subdisciplines, that was published in the 1970s and the first half of the 1980s. Fifteen years after its publication, *A Geographical Bibliography for American Libraries* continues to be an aid for entering the literature of geography because many of the titles described were widely distributed and continue to be central to the discipline, either in the edition listed or in a subsequent edition.

A Bibliography of Geographic Thought

A Bibliography of Geographic Thought is the outgrowth of four previous, and much smaller, bibliographies compiled by James O. Wheeler. The volume "is intended as a comprehensive listing of books and articles in English on the history, philosophy, and methodology of geography—a definitive bibliography on the history of what geographers have thought about geography and other geographers" (A Bibliography of Geographic Thought, ix). Nearly 6,000 citations to journal articles and books, primarily published during the twentieth century, up to 1988, with a scattering of nineteenth-century titles and an occasional eighteenth-century title, are included. The entries are citations only; there are no descriptions or annotations.

The first chapter is devoted to books solely, listed alphabetically by author. The other nine chapters are all journal articles, also arranged alphabetically by author, focusing on specific topics: Biographical, Geography and Other Disciplines, Geography in Various Countries, Geographic Techniques and Models, Philosophy in Geography, The Profession of Geography, Subdisciplines in Geography, Applied Geography, and Educational Geography. The three indexes, author, subject, and biographical, are the keys to decreasing undirected browsing through A Bibliography of Geographic Thought. The author index includes primary and secondary authors and editors. The subject index uses very broad terms, such as "Applied geography," "Physical geography," and "Social geography (see also Human geography)," and is essentially an index to the "Subdisciplines in Geography" chapter. The subjects are overly broad and are not as helpful as could be desired. Both the author and the biographical indexes list people with their last name and only initials for the first and second names.

A Bibliography of Geographic Thought will be of interest to readers interested in citations to a broad cross-section of geographic literature, especially that part of the literature rooted in the historical and philosophical development of the discipline. It may be too diverse for a novice scholar or an undirected reader.

The Literature of Geography

The Literature of Geography is a series of chapter-length bibliographic essays and was intended by the author to serve "as an introductory guide, identifying the most useful, the most significant, and the most authoritative sources within each branch of the subject" (The Literature of Geography, 9). The emphasis is on English-language reference works published prior to 1977, recent titles in the context of The Literature of Geography's 1978 publication date. The first two chapters are general introductions to geographical literature and how it can be found or how it is organized in libraries. There are also chapters on specific types of information sources, statistical sources, and governmental agencies. The final five chapters cover the history of geography, geographic techniques, and systemic and regional geography. An index to authors, titles, and broad subjects is also included.

The Literature of Geography has a strong British emphasis, and it could serve as a lodestone for an initial determination of core literature. The chapters are easy to read; they do not devolve into lists of book titles without descriptions. The Literature of Geography is a good general guide to the kinds of literature produced by geographers.

A Guide to Information Sources in the Geographical Sciences

A Guide to Information Sources in the Geographical Sciences is a collection of 13 bibliographic essay chapters written by, and attributed to, subject specialists. The initial overview chapter is followed by four chapters focusing on systematic approaches (geomorphology, historical geography, agricultural geography, and industrial geography), four on regions (Africa, South Asia, the United States, and the Soviet Union), and four on "Tools for the Geographer" (maps, atlases, gazetteers, and cartographic serials; aerial photographs and satellite information; statistical methods and computing; and archival materials). Unfortunately, Guide to Information Sources does not include an index; the only way to access the titles listed is by scanning the chapters appropriate to the reader's interests. This is not easy because many of the chapters, and in particular the chapter on the United States, become paragraphs of citation after citation. The value of Guide to Information Sources in the Geographical Sciences is that information resources are grouped with similar titles with text that provides a small amount of evaluation or context.

The previously mentioned University of Chicago Department of Geography's Research Paper series also includes International List of Geographical Serials, in three editions, and Annotated World List of Selected Current Geographical Serials, in four editions. Unfortunately, the serials publication world is very volatile, and neither of these publications reflects the full spectrum of current geography journal publication, but they will be useful for identifying older and ceased titles.

INDEXES AND ABSTRACTS

There are two indexes that specifically cover geographic literature appearing in journals and others that include journal geographic literature within a much larger universe of writing.

Current Geographical Publications

Current Geographical Publications contains bibliographical references to books, journal articles, other textual documents, maps, and atlases received by the American Geographical Society Collection at the University of Wisconsin-Milwaukee Golda Meir Library. Issued 10 times a year, *Current Geographical Publications* is arranged in four sections: Topical, Regional, Maps, and Selected Books and Monographs. A list of "Periodicals Analyzed in this Issue" appears in each issue.

The items indexed in the "Topical" and "Regional" sections, the true heart of *Current Geographical Publications,* are arranged according to the American Geographical Society Collection's classification scheme. The topical section includes references to books and articles on all aspects of geography: general geography, travel and exploration, mathematical geography, physical geography, hydrology, oceanography, climatology, biogeography, human geography, economic geography, political geography, geographical methodology, history of geography, geographical and related institutions, and aids to geographical research. The regional section arranges bibliographic citations according to the state, country, or region that the book or article describes. Items often have more than one access point. An article titled "Development of flood hazard maps of Bangladesh using NOAA-AVHRR images with GIS" is indexed in the regional section under Bangladesh, in the topical section under Geographic Information Systems in the Mathematical Cartography subsection, and under Natural Disasters in the Physical Geography subsection.

Current Geographical Publications is straightforward in the choice of terms used as section and subsection headings. Most of the items indexed are English-language and tend to be from mainstream geography literature. *Current Geographical Publications'* structure and use are more transparent to a first-time user than other indexes because the organizational scheme is clearly illustrated in the table of contents, the primary access mechanism.

Generally, to find articles in *Current Geographical Publications* by topic, the user only needs to find an appropriately titled subsection and turn to the indicated page. A cumulative annual index that includes access by author name usually is issued four to six months after the end of the calendar year. The text of the monthly issues is available through the American Geographical Society Collection's Web site (http://leardo.lib.uwm.edu/cgp/index.html); it is used in much the same way as the paper with access through a table of contents. Beginning in 2004, *Current Geographical Publications* will be published online only.

The American Geographical Society Collection had made all issues of *Current Geographical Publications* available through a searchable Web interface, Online Geographical Bibliography (http://geobib.lib.uwm.edu). Currently, data published since 1985 can be searched using either a simple one-field search for subject, author, or title, a more complex multiple-field advanced search, or a single-field keyword search. A thesaurus to subject terms used by the society is provided through the Web site. The entries include full bibliographic information for the specific article with links to other article citations possible through the author's name, journal title, and subjects. Searching "Aids to geographical research" results in 63 citations. Picking one as an example, "'The Dead Don't Answer Questionnaires': Researching and Writing Historical Geography" by Alan R. Baker, leads to the full citation with links through Baker's name to nine other articles, links through the journal title (*Journal of Geography in Higher Education*) to 152 entries, and links through the two subject headings ("Aids to geographical research" and "Historical geography") to 63 and 1,291 entries, respectively.

Current Geographical Publications is the most straightforward index solely devoted to geography. Lower-division geography students and non-geographers will find *Current Geographical Publications,* in either format, readily accessible.

Geographical Abstracts/Geobase

Geographical Abstracts is the most extensive geographically-oriented indexing and abstracting service in the English language. Most of the items indexed are journal articles, but a number of monograph publications are also included. Prior to 1989, *Geographical Abstracts* was published in seven sections, each with a closely defined topic: A, Landforms and the Quaternary; B, Climatology and Hydrology; C, Economic Geography; D, Social and Historical Geography; E, Sedimentology; F, Regional and Community Planning; and G, Remote Sensing, Photogrammetry, and Cartography. In its current paper form, *Geographical Abstracts* is published in two parts, "Human Geography" and "Physical Geography," merging the contents of the original seven sections and issued monthly with a cumulative index after the close of the year. The electronic version, *Geobase,* merges the two paper publications with additional data from *Geomechanics Abstracts, Ecological Abstracts, International Development Abstracts, Oceanographic Literature Review,* and *Geological Abstracts.*

Geographical Abstracts, in paper format, can be cumbersome to use. The monthly installments have tables of contents that make general browsing of abstracts possible. But different aspects of the same topic can appear in both parts so topics that are interdisciplinary in nature may necessitate searching both parts of the paper *Geographical Abstracts.* The annual cumulative indexes, and each of the monthly installments, has three index sections: subject, regional, and author. The indexing terms are followed by entry numbers keyed to specific citations and abstracts. Some terms might have only one entry while others have hundreds. Because the indexes in the monthly listing are for that installment only, using the individual monthly issues is not too difficult. Using the cumulative index is more complex because it does not indicate in which monthly installment the numbered citation and abstract appears, leading to a need to scan the cover of each installment for the number range of the entries it includes. The regional index is arranged alphabetically and hierarchically; Seattle is listed under Washington, which is part of the United States entry in the *U*s. All authors and coauthors are indexed; the *Geographical Abstracts* editors have not necessarily attempted or been able to standardize how authors' names are listed, although most are last name with initials. There is the possibility that the same person may be listed in the index under multiple forms of his name. There also is the possibility that a single name may represent more than one person.

The entries in *Geographical Abstracts* include article title, authors, journal title, year, volume and issue number, and pagination. The abstracts usually have been prepared by the author. Non-English publications are listed with an English translation of the title followed by the original title. All of the abstracts are in English. The abstracts do not include other subject indexing terms.

Geobase, "The Bibliographic Database for the Earth, Geographical and Ecological Sciences," indexes approximately 2,000 journals. Coverage is available via the Web or on CD-ROM for more than 1,000,000 records from 1980 to the present; 74,000 new records are added to the database each year through monthly updates. Fortunately, when searching *Geobase,* the entire database is being searched; there is no need to consider whether the search topic is more closely aligned with physical geography or human geography.

The indexing for major journals in *Geobase* is upto-date; indexing for the February 2001 issue of *Professional Geographer* was available through *Geobase* before the first week of May. For other journals, in particular those with a smaller subscription base or those that are less mainstream, indexing may lag or may be incomplete.

Because the universe of literature that they index is so large and diverse, *Geographical Abstracts* and *Geobase* can be difficult and even frustrating to use initially. Nevertheless, *Geographical Abstracts* and *Geobase* should be among the indexing and abstracting tools of choice for geography majors and for anyone with an advanced interest in geographic topics.

GeoRef

Some geographers, especially those interested in how natural earth-shaping and earth-moving processes effect or are effected by human activities, work and publish in both geography and geology. *GeoRef* is the geoscience bibliographic database developed by the American Geological Institute based on records that the institute has kept describing publications about the geology of North America since 1785 and the rest of the world since 1933. Like *Geobase, GeoRef* is the equivalent of multiple print publications: *Bibliography of North American Geology, Bibliography and Index of Geology Exclusive of North America, Geophysical Abstracts,* and *Bibliography and Index of Geology.* The items indexed include journal articles, books, and conference proceedings. Some entries include abstracts and all include descriptors or subject terms that are live links to other items on the same or a similar topic.

Social Sciences Abstracts

Readers interested in the interdisciplinary social science aspects of geography might do well by searching *Social Sciences Abstracts.* Just as with *GeoRef, Social Sciences Abstracts* will assist in identifying articles by geographers which have appeared either in a publication that is broader than just geography or in a publication that is not traditionally affiliated with geography. *Social Sciences Abstracts* indexes articles and book reviews in more than 550 English-language social science, including geography, journals. There will be cases of interdisciplinary titles where *Social Sciences Abstracts* has indexed more issues of a journal than *Geobase*. The journals included in *Social Sciences Abstracts* that are strongly affiliated with geography tend to be central to the discipline. Entries include active links through authors' names to other articles and reviews. Abstracts do not appear in all of the entries; subject headings do, although they are not active links.

Social Sciences Citation Index
Science Citation Index Expanded

Social Sciences Citation Index and *Science Citation Index Expanded* are both part of the ISI Web of Science. The lists of geographic journals indexed in the separate databases differ substantially. *Social Sciences Citation Index* indexes many of the core journals with broader content, such as the *Annals of the Association of American Geographers, Canadian Geographer, Geographical Review,* and *Professional Geographer.* Focused titles, including *Economic Geography, Area, Political Geography,* and *Progress in Human Geography,* are also indexed. The geographically-related journals indexed in *Science Citation Index Expanded* tend to be physical geography and remote sensing titles; *Arctic, Antarctica, and Alpine Research; Geomorphology; Progress in Physical Geography;* and *Photogrammetric Engineering and Remote Sensing* are typical titles. The appropriate database needs to be selected depending on the specific subdiscipline interests. In many cases, it might be most advantageous to search both *Social Sciences Citation Index* and *Science Citation Index Expanded* simultaneously. In some cases, *Arts and Humanities Citation Index* could also be an appropriate choice, especially if searching for articles that discuss architecture, archaeology, or religion from a geographical viewpoint.

Using multiple databases when working with Web of Science is also necessary when searching for specific authors. Colin E. Thorn is a periglacial geomorphologist and also has interests in the methodology and philosophy of geomorphology. Searching "thorn ce" in *Social Sciences Citation Index* yields only five articles attributed to Thorn, though searching *Science Citation Index Expanded* leads to eight articles; none of the results from the first search duplicates the results of the second. As a word of caution, like *Geographical Abstracts* and *Geobase,* the indexing does not differentiate between different authors who share

the same last name and initials. It may help to also include an author's institutional affiliation, if known, to narrow a search that appears to have results written by multiple authors with the same name.

Social Sciences Citation Index and *Science Citation Index Expanded* do not appear to index some journals fully or consistently. Some journals that might be considered to be somewhat core are not indexed at all, perhaps because they do not appear as regularly as they should. The advantage to using the ISI Web of Science databases is the instant connectivity to abstracts and indexing for the articles that a core or targeted article cites. *Social Sciences Citation Index* and *Science Citation Index Expanded* will help build bibliographies of related works, but they should not be relied upon for a comprehensive view of literature from the geographic discipline. A view of the current journal literature must be cobbled together using a number of citation sources.

DICTIONARIES AND GLOSSARIES

Printed dictionaries will give the most complete, comprehensive, and in-depth coverage of terms and concepts. On-line glossaries might be preferred for quick information needs but their coverage of the language of geography may be spotty and the quality of the definitions uneven.

The Dictionary of Human Geography. 4th ed.
The Dictionary of Physical Geography. 3rd ed.

These "sister" dictionaries are the premier dictionaries for the discipline of geography. Encyclopedic in nature with extended articles, they describe terms, theories, and concepts in context. Both are edited by internationally acknowledged experts and include attributed articles and definitions by an Anglo-American group of scholars.

The Dictionary of Human Geography includes more than 900 entries; this may not seem extensive, but the volume has only 907 pages. Most of the entries are essay in nature, extensively footnoted with cross-references to other entries, a list of references, and a bibliography of suggested readings. Cross-references are indicated by capitalization. The entries generally begin with a foundation definition that is a sentence or two long, then expand with contextual information, examples, and connections to other concepts. For instance, the essay "Locational analysis" begins:

An approach to HUMAN GEOGRAPHY focusing on the spatial arrangement of phenomena and on related flow patterns: its usual methodology is that of SPATIAL SCIENCE. The philosophy of POSITIVISM underpins the approach, which is closely linked to the discipline's QUANTITATIVE REVOLUTION. (*The Dictionary of Human Geography*, 464)

The following three-and-a-half pages of text traces the development of locational analysis from its beginning in the United States during the 1950s and its spread to the United Kingdom during the 1960s. The work of scholars in the area is described, as are the connections between scholars and how they influenced the development of the method. The method is also discussed in the context of its influence on other areas of geography. Reading the entry will lead a student to foundation works on locational analysis. The entry also includes ample cross-references to other entries in the dictionary. The entry concludes with an extensive list of references, many of which are core works in the discipline.

The Dictionary of Physical Geography is similar in nature. It has more entries that are short, closer to traditional dictionary structure than *The Dictionary of Human Geography,* but nearly all of the entries are signed and many include references or suggested reading. Even very short entries, such as "**oceanography** The study or description of the oceans encompassing the sea floor, the physics and chemistry of the seas and all aspects of marine biology" (*The Dictionary of Physical Geography,* 346), often include a suggested reading. Again, the more than 90 contributors tend to be Anglo-American but all are recognized experts in their fields. Featuring more than 2,000 entries, *The Dictionary of Physical Geography* covers all areas of physical geography including geomorphology, climatology, pedology, geographic information systems and remote sensing, and human impacts on physical geography. Because of the nature of the concepts covered in *The Dictionary of Physical Geography,* there are more illustrations included than in *The Dictionary of Human Geography.* Some were created especially for the dictionary while others were selected from previous publications. The captions for illustrations from other sources include full citations for easier follow-up.

Both of these dictionaries include extensive alphabetical indexes. The indexes will assist in making connections between concepts and terms that appear in different contexts or influence the content of other en-

tries. *The Dictionary of Human Geography* and *The Dictionary of Physical Geography* should be considered essential dictionaries for the geographic discipline. The short definitions in combination with longer interpretative essays provide concepts in context. Both will be ideal companions for reading the literature of geography. *The Dictionary of Human Geography,* in particular, could easily serve as a primer on geographic thought and trends.

A Dictionary of Geography. 2nd ed. (Mayhew)
The Penguin Dictionary of Geography. 3rd ed. (Clark)
Dictionary of Geography (Skinner/Redfern/Farmer)
A Modern Dictionary of Geography. 4th ed. (Witherick/Ross/Small)

There are a number of smaller, general dictionaries that are less encyclopedic in nature than *The Dictionary of Human Geography* and *The Dictionary of Physical Geography.* Closer to the traditional idea of a dictionary with shorter articles or definitions, they have similar titles but each has its own unique aspects. Interestingly, most geography dictionaries are British publications or have their roots in British publications.

A Dictionary of Geography (Mayhew) contains definitions for more than 6,000 terms connected to geographic subdisciplines, including, but not limited to, cartography, statistics, climatology, biogeography, population, geomorphology, and transportation. The terms and concepts defined are central to the discipline. Most of the definitions are succinct and easy to understand. Cross-references to other definitions are indicated by asterisks. There are some black-and-white illustrations, primarily diagrams, and a few tables, but Mayhew is not as fully illustrated as *Dictionary of Geography* (Skinner/Redfern/Farmer) or *A Modern Dictionary of Geography* (Witherick/Ross/Small). Unlike *The Dictionary of Human Geography* and *The Dictionary of Physical Geography,* Mayhew does not include full references to source material or suggestions for further reading. Instead, some of the definitions, in particular those for specific theories, include the author's name and date of publication assuming that the reader will be able to consult a library catalog or on-line database to locate the source material. Meyhew's *A Dictionary of Geography* is a portable and well-rounded dictionary. It would assist readers who are beginning their study of geography because the definitions are mainstream and to-the-point.

The Penguin Dictionary of Geography (Clark) is similar in scope and size to Mayhew with a balanced coverage of human and physical geography and including vocabulary that has been appropriated by geography from other disciplines. The third edition has expanded on the coverage provided by previous editions of terms related to studying the environment and globalization. Although some of the definitions are lengthy, perhaps as long as half a page, most are fewer than 10 lines. Most of the entries include cross-references (indicated by small capitals), and the volume includes 43 black-and-white illustrations. There are no references to other resources or to source materials. Like Mayhew, this third edition of a classic dictionary is easily portable and will be a good choice for finding up-to-date and succinct definitions of standard terms applied to geography.

Dictionary of Geography (Skinner/Redfern/Farmer) contains nearly 1,450 terms. Approximately half of the definitions begin with a sentence that uses the term being defined as the first word or words. The definition for *literacy* begins "**literacy** is the ability of a person to read and write." The definition then puts literacy into economic and social contexts:

The literacy rate of a country is used as a means of measuring its level of economic development. It is an indication of the quality of education in a country, which in turn is an indicator of the wealth and social development of that country. Literacy may vary between different social groups, and between different sexes in a population. (*Dictionary of Geography,* 161)

References to other entries are indicated in italics. Some entries are little more than references elsewhere:

load: the material transported by a river. It may be transported by:

- suspended load
- saltation
- solution. (*Dictionary of Geography*, 161)

There are a number of black-and-white illustrations throughout the dictionary. The definitions are readable and are not overly technical. The scope of the dictionary is not well defined; it includes terms from the entire breadth of geography, from all aspects of both physical and human geography. Some of the terms included are organizations or individuals while other terms are colloquial name for regions. Surprisingly there are a number of included terms that border on slang, and although they may be finding acceptance in the literature, this does not seem to be the first place that someone would look to find a definition for:

swiss cheese effect: a distribution across an area that is patchy, the patchiness being described as the "swiss cheese effect," i.e. there are holes in it. (*Dictionary of Geography*, 269)

A Modern Dictionary of Geography (Witherick/Ross/Small) falls between Mayhew and Clark and Skinner/Redfern/Farmer in size with definitions for 2,400 terms and 200 illustrations. The authors balance their coverage between human and physical geography with a slight emphasis on human. The dictionary is intended for advanced high school and college level students. The authors based their section of terms on syllabi and examinations used in Great Britain. Cross-references are indicated by terms in small capitals; terms printed in italics do not have a separate entry but are only defined in the context of the host entry. In preparing the fourth edition, the editors emphasized current use of terminology and rewrote a number of entries to reflect changes in the political world that had occurred since the publication of the previous edition.

Longman Illustrated Dictionary of Geography

This dictionary is much smaller than the other dictionaries, containing only 1,800 words, but its organization is interesting. Instead of terms being listed alphabetically they are grouped with related terms into 25 different themes. The themes are arranged in four sections: Physical Geography, Human and Economic Geography, Applied Geography, and General Terms. The four sections are followed by three appendixes and an index.

The index is the key to finding meanings of words. Looking up *quickflow* in the index leads to this definition on page 96:

quickflow (*n*) the rapid runoff ($\uparrow$) which is made up of direct channel (p. 23) precipitation (p. 55), surface runoff, and rapid interflow ($\downarrow$), including pipeflow ($\downarrow$). It makes up the largest part of stream discharge (p. 98) during a flood (p. 99).

The upward pointing arrow indicates that the term in front of it is included above the defined term on the same page or on the preceding facing page. A downward pointing indicates that the term in front of it is included after the defined term on the same page or on the following facing page. Bracketed numbers are references to nonfacing pages where other terms are defined. The arrows and page references can be followed to create a definitional context for the first term that was looked up in the alphabetical index.

Related terms are grouped together in themes, but even within themes they are not alphabetical. Hierarchies and relationships determine the order in which terms are displayed. As an example, the section on settlement theories and models begins with a definition of *settlement*. It is followed by a short entry for Walter Christaller, the German economist who formulated the central place theory—a theory that describes the relationships and the resulting hierarchies of the sizes of places, the goods and services available at differently sized places, and the distances between places of different sizes and with different functions assuming that transportation between all places requires equal effort. Christaller's entry is followed by definitions, in order, for *central place, central place theory, hierarchy, isotropic surface, market center,* and *range of good.* Reading the definitions and examining the illustrations on the first four pages of the settlement theories and models section will give a short-hand overview of Christaller's theory and its components. This structure of flow and connections between sequential definitions is repeated throughout the dictionary.

The *Longman Illustrated Dictionary of Geography* can also be used as a thesaurus and will help recall specific vocabulary. Because of the dictionary's organization, words can be located without knowing what they are beforehand. Perhaps someone is trying to describe the hot, dry winds that blow in northern Africa during the spring and fall. Knowing that a word for a particular kind of air movement is being sought, the dictionary user could go to the "Atmosphere/Winds" section and quickly read through the definitions until *sirocco* was found.

The *Longman Illustrated Dictionary of Geography* includes many color illustrations helping to explain processes and making more clear verbal descriptions. Some appear more decorative than useful, but for the most part, the illustrations are an essential part of the definitions. The interesting structure of the *Longman Illustrated Dictionary of Geography* may make its use initially difficult. Intuitively, dictionaries are alphabetical, not thematic. But after a short period of use, the structure will become apparent as will the benefits of being able to read definitions in their disciplinary context.

"Geographical Dictionary" (http://www.kesgrave. suffolk.sch.uk/Curric/geog/diction.html)

"Geographical Dictionary" is part of The Geography Portal at Kesgrave High School, Ipswich, Suffolk, England. The terms included come from human and physical geography with a bias toward concepts related to geomorphology. All of the definitions are short and clearly written. Nearly 170 of the terms or their definitions are linked to "on-line tutorials" that set the terms into a broader context, explain processes and consequences, and often provide photographs, diagrams, and graphs as illustrations. The on-line tutorials fall into eight basic categories and can be read separately from the dictionary.

"Geography Glossary" (http://geography.about.com/ library/misc/blgg.htm)

The "Geography Glossary" at About.com includes 167 basic definitions for human and physical geography terms, 80 of which have links to other About.com pages for additional information sources or articles and expanded definitions with illustrations. Some of the expanded definitions and About.com-generated articles include references and suggestions for further reading. About.com also has a page of links to other geographically or geologically related on-line glossaries and dictionaries (http://geography.about.com/ science/geography/msub39.htm).

Fundamentals of Physical Geography (http://geog. ouc.bc.ca/physgeog/physgeoglos/glossary.html)

Fundamentals of Physical Geography is an on-line textbook that was developed over three years to support an introductory course on physical geography offered at Okanagan University College in Kelowna, British Columbia, by supplementing traditional print textbooks. The glossary of terms can be used on its own. Many of the definitions include active cross-reference links to other definitions. The 11-chapter text relies heavily on the glossary with many active links directly from the text to definitions. Each of the chapters also has a study guide with a list of key terms linked to definitions. The definitions are generally short and to the point. Because of the text it accompanies and the course that the Web site is intended to support, there will be few terms in the glossary not related to physical geography.

COUNTRY GUIDES

Information about countries such as demographic statistics, history, and economic development is available through a number of different sources with a wide variety of depth of information. Dictionary and encyclopedic gazetteers, discussed in the chapter on gazetteers, also include basic statistical and descriptive information as part of their entries.

The World Factbook (http://www.odci.gov/cia/ publications/factbook/index.html)

The statistics found in *The World Factbook,* prepared by the CIA, are standard statistics, "basic intelligence," which are often repackaged by other agencies and commercial publishers. Information about 267 regions, countries, and dependencies worldwide is presented in a standard profile format. The profiles begin with a simple map and color illustration of the areas' flags, if appropriate. The descriptive and statistical information is divided into nine sections. The first, "Introduction," usually contains a paragraph of background information which forms the contextual setting for the detailed descriptive and statistical information in the remaining sections: Geography, People, Government, Economy, Communications, Transportation, Military, and Transnational Issues. Each time that *The World Factbook* is released, new information categories are included.

The "Geography" section focuses on location, climate, terrain, and natural resources. Some of the information presented is statistical, percentages or numerical values, while other information categories are filled by descriptive text and lists. Measurements of heights, distances, and areas are all in metric units. *The World Factbook* is intended for a U.S. readership, specifically for U.S. government officials; nowhere is this more obvious than in the "Area—comparative" section, which compares the country or region being described with the United States or part of the United States. The "People" section is statistics-intensive and contains standard demographic information, such as population growth rate, infant mortality rate, HIV/AIDS, ethnic groups, and literacy. "Government" is largely descriptive with information on government form, national holidays, legal system, suffrage, and the branches of government along with "political pressure groups and leaders" and international participation. The "Government" section is also where information about diplomatic representation to and from the United States is listed. The "Economy" section begins with an overview paragraph, which is followed by standard economic statistics including gross domestic product, inflation rate, unemployment rate, a list of core industries, and information about electricity production and consumption and imports and exports. "Communications" and "Transportation" both demonstrate the country's connectivity, listing numbers of telephone lines, radio and television stations, and numbers of radios and televisions. Descriptions of connectivity continue in "Transportation" with lengths of railways, highways, and pipelines, number of airports with the

lengths of the paved runways, and names of port cities. "Military" lists the military branches and indicates the size of the available fighting force along with the amount of military expenditures. There are only two broad categories of information in "Transnational Issues": Disputes—international and Illicit drugs. "Disputes—international" might include information about other claims on the nation's territory or claims that the country may have on other nations' territory, border disputes, and occasionally, information about internal ethnic disputes that have ramifications for relationships with other nations. "Illicit drugs" is a general description of the country's place in the illegal drug production and trade world. Many countries are identified as being transshipment points, gateways for movement, and production points for raw materials, refining chemicals, or final products.

Background Notes

Produced by the United States Department of State, Bureau of Public Affairs, *Background Notes* are good basic sources of information about individual nations. Each follows approximately the same template: statistical data about geography, people, government, and economy, followed by text describing the history, current government and political conditions, economy, foreign relations, U.S.-[nation] relations, and travel and business information.

The content of each *Note* begins with the country's official name. The statistical data is based largely on data from *The World Factbook.* The geography section includes area, identifies the capital city, and gives a brief description of the terrain and climate. Beyond the square kilometers and miles occupied by the country, the area data includes a comparison with areas in the United States. The people statistics list the nationality of the country's inhabitants, basic population size and growth rate data, proportions of ethnic groups and religions, languages spoken, educational attainment, mortality rate and life expectancy, and percentages of employment sectors. Government quickly describes the type of government and governmental bodies, constitution, and political parties. Economy lists basic production statistics.

Publications in the *Background Notes* set tend to be 20 pages or fewer; all are pre-punched for storing in ring binders. Updated Notes are not issued on a set schedule; a few are as old as 1986 or 1987. *Background Notes* has undergone some substantial format and content changes in the last 10 to 15 years. Through the late 1980s, a black-and-white map, suitable for photocopying, was included on the inside, or second, page with a small regional map on the front page. There also usually was a bibliography of other information resources in a boxed section, primarily books, near the end of each Note. In the early to mid-1990s, both the "Further Information" section and the photocopy-appropriate map were dropped from the publications. The small region map was changed into a hemispherical view with a large arrow pointing to the appropriate country. Most recently, in 1999, the format was changed again to completely delete all geographic graphics. This may correspond to a push by the Department of State to make the content of the *Background Notes* series available through their Web site (http://www.state.gov).

The same types of information are presented as in the paper version of the *Background Notes* regardless of publication date: History, Government, Political Conditions, Economy, Foreign Relations, and U.S. Relations. The on-line *Background Notes* include links to other Web sites embedded in the text, primarily to other Department of State information such as travel warnings, daily press briefings, and *Country Commercial Guides.*

There are a number of other sources of information about countries available through the Web. About.com has repackaged *The World Factbook* and is making the data available through its Web site, along with links to a number of other data sources including the Department of State *Background Notes.*

Country Studies

Country Studies are a core resource for discovering a wide variety of basic information about many different nations. Sponsored by the United States Department of the Army, the *Country Studies* set is prepared by the Library of Congress Federal Research Division. Typical titles are *Poland: A Country Study* or *Turkey: A Country Study. Country Studies* are revised and reissued on an irregular basis. Older editions may be titled *Area Handbooks,* for example, *Area Handbook for Malaysia,* and the entire group is officially titled the *Area Handbook Series.*

The set includes individual book-length publications, written to an established standard for content and writing style, for slightly more than 100 countries. The set does not cover a number of Western nations; Canada, France, the United Kingdom, and Scandinavian nations (excluding Finland) are among those without a volume because the Department of the Army was more interested in developing descriptions of lesser-known areas where troops might be deployed.

Country Studies are textual descriptions and analyses of a country's historical and cultural settings and current social, economic, political, and security systems along with the institutions responsible for these systems. *Country Studies* examine how the systems are interrelated within a country and how the country relates to other nations. The foreword of each *Country Study* states that, although produced in the United States by an agency of the U.S. government, the book "represents the analysis of the authors and should not be construed as an expression of an official United States government position, policy, or decision."

A typical *Country Study* will have a lengthy introductory section that sets the volume into the context of the political and economic situations at the time of compilation and publication. A "Chronology of Important Events" might be included, and a "Country Profile" will precede the introduction; these will be useful for quick facts. The body of the volume will be divided into five chapters: Historical Setting; The Society and Its Environment; The Economy; Government and Politics; and National Security. Each chapter concludes with a short section about other materials to read. The appendices are substantial and include tables of demographic and economic data, a bibliography divided by chapter, and often a glossary. The volume concludes with an index. Illustrations in *Country Studies* are black-and-white and will include sketches, maps, and photographs. The maps will all be small enough to photocopy on a standard self-service machine.

Country Studies are available through the Library of Congress Web site (http://memory.loc.gov/frd/cs/cshome.html). The complete text of the print volumes has been converted for display. Instead of long chapters, each section displays separately with forward and back buttons to move to adjoining sections. Each section will have a currentness date at the end. Occasionally there will be a link from the displayed section to the glossary, bibliography, or tables. Most, but not all, of the illustration graphics (maps, photographs, sketches, and tables) have been included as PDF files. The Web site takes advantage of digital information to allow searching for terms across *Country Studies.* Terms can be searched for across all of the on-line *Country Studies* or the search can be restricted to specific countries. Entering "Greek Catholic Church" as a search results in seven sections from six different *Country Studies* that include that precise phrase and nine sections that include the three words in close proximity to each other. This kind of indexing and search capability will allow for quick comparisons between countries. The on-line *Country Studies* can also be used in a more linear fashion by selecting the country of interest from an alphabetical list to access a table of contents that is linked to textual sections. The headings in the on-line table of contents are more detailed than the headings in the print volumes; they show chapter sections and subsections, not just sections.

Although not every *Country Study* includes a chronology and a glossary, all of the publications in the set follow the same pattern of five substantial chapters, an appendix of statistical tables, and a bibliography. The same information is found on-line as is available in the print volumes. The on-line version allows for the flexibility of searching for the same term in a number of *Country Studies* at the same time. On-line *Country Studies* will be useful for a quick dive into information while the print volumes will be more appropriate for long reading and studying sessions. A fiscal point in the on-line versions' favor: on-line access is free!

Worldmark Encyclopedia of the Nations. 10th ed.

The information available through *Worldmark Encyclopedia of the Nations* is more extensive than *The World Factbook* or the Department of State *Background Notes,* but not as full as the *Country Study* approach of an individual volume devoted to each nation. Two of the volumes in this six-volume set are not strictly devoted to national descriptions. Volume one describes the nature, structure, and functions of the United Nations. Volume six contains biographical profiles of national heads of government, organized alphabetically by country name. The set revolves around the contents of the central four volumes: 2. Africa; 3. Americas; 4. Asia and Oceania; and 5. Europe. The uniformly organized descriptions for the countries of each continent are arranged alphabetically. Each description begins with an introductory section that includes the country's name, illustrations of the coat of arms and flag, name of the capital, description of the flag, title of the national anthem, information about the national monetary unit and official system of weights and measures, a list of national holidays, and time zone. Each entry is divided into 50 numbered sections of varying length that describe physical, demographic and ethnographic, political, economic, educational, and cultural aspects of the nation. The 50th section is a bibliography of book titles that may be of additional interest. Each of the entries is accompanied by a simple black-and-white map of the country with an inset map showing the country's location. The endpapers in each

of the volumes ties to the contents; in the Africa volume, for example, the front endpapers are a political map of Africa and the back are color illustrations of African national flags.

Worldmark Encyclopedia of the Nations is straightforward to use. The consistent entry structure makes information on specific aspects easy to locate. Users will find that the entries are more extensive than found in the *Background Notes* and that they require less effort to navigate than the *Background Notes* because sections are more specifically defined. Of particular interest are the bibliographies that could function as foundation bibliographies for entry-point research.

Administrative Subdivisions of Countries: A Comprehensive World Reference, 1900 through 1998

Administrative subdivisions, such as counties, provinces, or parishes, are important because they may be good indicators of how a country is governed or how it is divided to provide infrastructure services such as road maintenance. Law enforcement is usually undertaken at a less-than-national level. Physical descriptions of countries are often arranged by regions.

Administrative Subdivisions of Countries is a compilation of information about nations and how they are divided into smaller units. Important background information for understanding entries is included in "The Elements of the Entries." Entries are arranged alphabetically by country name following a standard format. Prior to the entries is a "Registry of Countries," an alphabetical list of current, obsolete, and foreign names with page references to the appropriate national entry. The entries begin with brief information about the country's ISO code, languages, time zone, and capital followed by a short summary history. A list of non-English names for the country and a short history of the country's name precede an alphabetical table of first-level administrative units. The information most commonly included about the administrative units includes ISO and FIPS codes, population, area in both kilometers and miles, and capital. Sometimes names of subdistricts, other statistical area codes, and postal codes are listed. Notes about information sources follow the table. The notes sometimes are quite extensive and may include information about the origins of subdivision names, how the subdivisions are further divided, and specifics about subdivision territorial extent. Some, but not all, of the country entries include a chronological listing of changes to subdivisions, such as splits, consolidations, name changes, status changes, and capital moves. There also may be a listing of alternate subdivision names or information about population changes at the subdivision level. The volume concludes with a short bibliography and an index to all administrative subdivisions listed in the book.

The author of the book is maintaining a Web site of useful links about countries at the Statoids Web Page (http://www.mindspring.com/~gwil/statoids.html). This is also the mechanism for keeping *Administrative Subdivisions of Countries* up-to-date. The site includes alphabetical tables of countries showing primary and secondary divisions, links to statistical and postal code tables and scanned maps, and the international dialing prefix and time zone. A monthly newsletter, also posted through the Web site, keeps users apprised of recent changes in the world and at the site.

Bibliographies, indexes and indexes with abstracts, dictionaries, and country guides provide entry points into geography literature and understanding. They serve as information organizers and often can provide alternative ideas for the next step in a research path.

BIBLIOGRAPHY

Administrative Subdivisions of Countries: A Comprehensive World Reference, 1900 through 1998. Gwillim Law. Jefferson, N.C.: McFarland, 1999. ISBN: 0-7864-0729-8.

Aids to Geographical Research: Bibliographies, Periodicals, Atlases, Gazetteers and Other Reference Books. 2nd ed. John Kirtland Wright and Elizabeth T. Platt. New York: Published for the American Geographical Society by Columbia University Press, 1947. Reprint, Westport, Conn.: Greenwood Press, 1971. ISBN: 0-8371-3384-X.

Annals of the Association of American Geographers. Washington, D.C.: Association of American Geographers, 1911– . Quarterly. ISSN: 0004-5608.

Annotated World List of Selected Current Geographical Serials. 4th ed., rev. Chauncy D. Harris. University of Chicago, Department of Geography Research Paper, no. 194. Chicago: University of Chicago Press, 1980. ISBN: 0-89065-101-9.

Arctic, Antarctic, and Alpine Research. Boulder, Colo.: Institute of Arctic and Alpine Research, University of Colorado at Boulder, 1999– . Quarterly. Former title *Arctic and Alpine Research.* ISSN 1523-0430.

Area. London: Published on behalf of the Royal Geographical Society with the Institute of British Geographers by Blackwell, 1969– . Quarterly. ISSN: 0004-0894.

Arts and Humanities Citation Index. Computer file. On-line database. Philadelphia, Pa.: Institute for Scientific Information, 1987– . Data from 1975 forward.

Background Notes on the Countries of the World. Washington, D.C.: U.S. Department of State, Bureau of Public Affairs, 1980– . Irregular updates.

A Bibliography of Geographic Thought. Catherine L. Brown and James O. Wheeler, comps. Bibliographies and Indexes in Geography, no. 1. Westport: Greenwood Press, 1989. ISBN: 0-31326-899-1.

Bibliography of Geography, Part I. Introduction to General Aids. Chauncy D. Harris. University of Chicago, Department of Geography Research Paper, no. 179. Chicago: University of Chicago, Committee on Geographical Studies, 1976. ISBN: 0-89065-086-1.

Bibliography of Geography, Part II. Regional, Vol. 1. The United States of America. Chauncy D. Harris. University of Chicago, Department of Geography Research Paper, no. 206. Chicago: University of Chicago Press, 1984. ISBN: 0-89065-112-4.

Canadian Geographer. Toronto: Published for the Canadian Association of Geographers by the University of Toronto Press, 1950– . Quarterly. ISSN: 0008-3658.

Country Studies. Various eds. Area Handbook Series. Main titles after subject countries, e.g.: *Poland: A Country Study.* Washington, D.C.: Federal Research Division, Library of Congress, 1990– .

Current Geographical Publications. American Geographical Society. Milwaukee, Wis.: University of Wisconsin, Milwaukee Library, 1938–2003. Monthly except July and August. ISSN: 0011-3514.

A Dictionary of Geography. 2nd ed. Susan Mayhew. New York: Oxford University Press, 1997. ISBN: 0-19-280034-5.

Dictionary of Geography. Malcolm Skinner, David Redfern, and Geoff Farmer. London: Fitzroy Dearborn, 1999. ISBN: 1-57958-154-4.

The Dictionary of Human Geography. 4th ed., rev. R.J. Johnston, et al., eds. Malden, Mass.: Blackwell, 2000. ISBN: 0-631-20561-6.

The Dictionary of Physical Geography. 3rd ed. David S.G. Thomas and Andrew Goudie, eds. Malden, Mass.: Blackwell, 2000. ISBN: 0-631-20472-5.

Economic Geography. Worcester, Mass.: Clark University, 1925– . Quarterly. ISSN: 0013-0095.

Geobase. Computer file. Norwich, England: Elsevier/Geo Abstracts, 1990– ; distributed by Silver Platter and OCLC. On-line database. New York: Elsevier Science. Includes citations for 1980–present. Updated monthly.

Geographical Abstracts: Human Geography. Norwich, England: Elsevier/Geo Abstracts, 1989– . Monthly. ISSN: 0953-9611.

Geographical Abstracts: Physical Geography. Norwich, England: Elsevier/Geo Abstracts, 1989– . Monthly. ISSN: 0954-0504.

A Geographical Bibliography for American College Libraries. Rev. ed. Gordon R. Lewthwaite, Edward T. Price, Jr., and Harold A. Winters, comps. Washington, D.C.: Association of American Geographers, Commission on College Geography, 1970.

A Geographical Bibliography for American Libraries. Chauncy D. Harris, ed. Washington, D.C.: Association of American Geographers, 1985. ISBN: 0-89291-193-X.

Geographical Review. New York: American Geographical Society, 1916– . Quarterly. ISSN: 0016-7428.

Geomorphology. Amsterdam: Elsevier, 1987– . Quarterly. ISSN: 0169-555X.

GeoRef. Computer file. Boston: SilverPlatter Information System, 1990– . WebSPIRS on-line search interface. Includes citations for 1785–present.

A Guide to Information Sources in the Geographical Sciences. Stephen Goddard, ed. London: Croom Helm; Lanham, Md.: Rowman & Littlefield, 1983. ISBN: 0-389-20403-X.

International List of Geographical Serials. 3rd ed. Chauncy D. Harris and Jerome D. Fellman, comps. University of Chicago, Department of Geography Research paper, no. 193. Chicago: University of Chicago, Department of Geography, 1980. ISBN: 0-89065-100-0.

Journal of Geography in Higher Education. Abingdon, England: Carfax, 1977– . 3 per year. ISSN: 0309-8265.

The Literature of Geography: A Guide to its Organisation and Use. Rev. ed. Gordon J. Brewer. London: Clive Bingley, 1978. ISBN: 0-208-01683-X.

Longman Illustrated Dictionary of Geography: The Study of the Earth, Its Landforms and Peoples. John Kingston. Harlow, Essex: Longman, 1988. ISBN: 0-582-02163-4.

A Modern Dictionary of Geography. 4th ed. M. E. Witherick, Simon Ross, and John Small. London: Arnold, 2001. ISBN: 0-340-80713-X.

The Penguin Dictionary of Geography. 3rd. ed. Audrey N. Clark. New York: Penguin, 2003. ISBN: 0140515054.

Photogrammetric Engineering and Remote Sensing. Falls Church, Va.: American Society of Photogrammetry, 1975– . Monthly. ISSN: 0099-1112.

Political Geography. Oxford, England: Pergamon, 1992– . Bimonthly. Former title Political Geography Quarterly.

Professional Geographer. Washington, D.C.: Association of American Geographers, 1946– . Quarterly. ISSN: 0962-6298.

Progress in Human Geography: An International Review of Geographical Work in the Social Sciences and Humanities.. London: Edward Arnold, 1977–. Bimonthly. ISSN: 0309-1325.

Progress in Physical Geography: An International Review of Geographical Work in the Natural and Environmental Sciences. London: Edward Arnold, 1977– . Quarterly. ISSN: 0309-1333.

Science Citation Index Expanded. Computer file. On-line database. Philadelphia, Pa.: Institute for Scientific Information, 1987– . Data from 1945 forward.

Social Sciences Abstracts. Computer file. On-line database. New York: H. W. Wilson, 1997– . Data from 1983 forward.

Social Sciences Citation Index. Computer file. On-line database. Philadelphia, Pa.: Institute for Scientific Information, 1987– . Data from 1956 forward.

Worldmark Encyclopedia of the Nations. 10th ed. Detroit, Mich.: Gale Group, 2001. ISBN: 0-7876-0511-5.

On-line References

Administrative Divisions of Countries ("Statoids"). GwillimLaw, 13 October 2003. <http://www.mindspring.com/~gwil/statoids.html> (14 October 2003).

Background Notes. Current issues. United States Department of State, 2003 <http://www.state.gov/r/pa/ei/bgn>(14 October 2003).

Country Studies. Library of Congress, 24 March 2003. <http://memory.loc.gov/frd/cs/cshome.html> (14 October 2003).

Current Geographical Publications. Additions to the American Geographical Society Collection. University of Wisconsin-Milwaukee, Golda Meir Library, 8 July 2003. <http://leardo.lib.uwm.edu/cgp/index.html> (14 October 2003).

Fundamentals of Physical Geography <http://geog.ouc.bc.ca/physgeog/physgeoglos/glossary.html>

"Geographical Dictionary." The Geography Portal. Kesgrave High School Geography Department, 4 October 2002. <http://www.kesgrave.suffolk.sch.uk/Curric/geog/diction.html> (14 October 2003).

"Geography Glossary." About.com, 2003. <http://geography.about.com/library/misc/blgg.htm> (14 October 2003).

"Glossary." Fundamentals of Physical Geography. Michael J. Pidwirny. Okanagon University College, Dept. of Geography, 20 May 2003. <http://geog.ouc.bc.ca/physgeog/physgeoglos/glossary.html> (14 October 2003).

Online Geographical Bibliography. American Geographical Society Collection. University of Wisconsin-Milwaukee, Golda Meir Library, 29 July 2003. <http://geobib.lib.uwm.edu/> (14 October 2003).

The World Factbook. Central Intelligence Agency, 1 January 2003. <http://www.odci.gov/cia/publications/factbook/index.html> (14 October 2003).

CHAPTER 3
Map Basics

One of the most simple, on the surface, definitions of *map* was coined by Arthur Robinson and Barbara Petchneik in *The Nature of Maps:* A map is a graphic representation of the milieu. But this definition, while elegant, does not illuminate the many decisions that need to be made in generalizing a complex, multi-dimensional world to fit into a comparatively simple two-dimensional "sketch" or the interpretive skills and graphical and cultural literacy necessary to glean meaningful information from a cartographic item.

Maps can be real or virtual. Real maps are physical products that can be held and include most of the items typically thought of as maps, along with some related materials: for example, road maps, topographic maps, nautical charts, maps of bird migratory routes, aerial photographs. Virtual maps fall into three broad cate-gories: mental maps, images viewed on computer screens, and digital geospatial data. Real maps flow into the virtual when users read, interpret, and apply the information that the maps contain. Virtual maps flow into the real through the process of interpreting a geographical situation and applying symbolic lan-guage onto paper to transform the mental map that rep-resents the situation into a physical object.

THINKING ABOUT MAPS

The single most important thing to remember about maps is that they lie. Shapes are distorted, information is generalized and selectively displayed, features are classified and replaced by symbols, and the symbols are not always placed exactly where the features they represent are located in the real world. These "lies" are necessary for maps to convey the intended infor-mation successfully. "What was this map intended to do?" should always be considered when looking at a map. The author's purpose for the map, along with the author's point of view on a situation, will have a strong impact on how a map is compiled, its final appearance, and its ultimate usefulness for other purposes.

Broadly grouped, there are two basic types of tangible maps: general (or reference) and thematic (or special-purpose). Fundamentally, both types perform the same task of symbolically displaying extracted and generalized geographic data. The difference is that general maps often are multipurpose, show many different data themes all with the same level of importance, and often are used as base information for producing thematic maps. Thematic maps usually have a much narrower focus, show a limited number of themes (often only one), and sometimes have a very specific intended audience.

Reference maps emphasize location, direction, and area. Natural and man-made features are shown. Reference maps are good for finding specific places or determining what is located in a designated area and usually are stand-alone products. Topographic maps and maps in general atlases are typical examples, as are nautical charts and road maps.

Thematic maps often sacrifice details of location, direction, and area, leaving only enough as background information for placing the theme data into an appropriate geographic context. The themes come from both the natural and the man-made world. Many different techniques have been used to produce thematic maps. Thematic maps most often will be found in atlases, in particular world and national atlases. Because the focus and audience for most thematic maps will be very narrow, too small to support producing the map as a stand-alone product, map publishers tend to bundle thematic maps together in atlases.

A number of books that can assist in building a foundation of map-reading, interpretation, and use skills have been published. Cartography textbooks, intended for use in university and college courses, will be useful for understanding map compilation, creation, and production, leading towards a better understanding of mapping constraints and appropriate usage.

Cartographic Citations: A Style Guide

Part of using maps appropriately is being able to cite them correctly in bibliographies. Suggestions for cartographic citation forms are not included in standard writing style guides such as the *Chicago Manual of Style* or the *MLA Handbook*. To fill this gap, the Map and Geography Round Table of the American Library Association has published *Cartographic Citations*. Citation forms and examples using real cartographic publications are divided into six main sections: manuscript maps, printed cartographic materials, atlases, models, remote-sensing imagery, and computer spatial-data files. Each of the sections has multiple parts reflecting different kinds of cartographic materials and publication formats. Each part begins with a basic form that generically illustrates the entry type and then follows with examples. The citation elements are defined, and a glossary is included. As more instructors ask students to include maps in class projects and as interest in cartographic materials grows, *Cartographic Citations* will assist in including cartographic items in bibliographies with all other source material types.

The Language of Maps. 16th ed.

The Language of Maps was originally compiled for use as a textbook at the University of Minnesota. Concepts about map reading and interpretation are communicated in a straightforward, non-jargony manner. After covering basics such as determining distance and direction along with location methods in the first part, the following four parts discuss topographic map reading and interpretation and thematic map use and interpretation. Interspersed through the parts are practice quizzes; the answers are at the back of the volume along with a combined glossary and index. *The Language of Maps* is heavily illustrated with black-and-white line drawings and reproductions of maps, all examples of commonly seen U.S. maps. Prior knowledge is not needed to understand the information presented by *The Language of Maps*. New concepts are defined as part of the text so that there is no need to flip back and forth between text and glossary to successfully follow the discussion. *The Language of Maps* is a good crash course in map reading and will be an excellent well-rounded foundation for further exploration.

Map Use & Analysis. 4th ed.
Map Use: Reading, Analysis, and Interpretation. 4th ed., rev.

Map Use & Analysis is an introduction to maps and their many uses. Attention is not paid specifically to thematic maps but is devoted to the many pieces that go into making and interpreting maps. The work is made up of 21 information-packed chapters accompanied by 5 appendices and a glossary. The author does not presuppose any prior knowledge on the part of the reader and begins with a general description of maps, followed by basic information about the Earth, map projections, location systems, map scales, measuring distances and areas on maps, and route finding and navigation. There are three chapters devoted to representing terrain and interpreting terrain representations and four chapters focusing on concepts related to thematic maps. Chapter 16 emphasizes how easy it is to misuse maps, and the final five chapters discuss aspects of the digital era: remote sensing, computer-assisted cartography, applications of digital maps, and geographic information systems. Chapters are illustrated, in both black-and-white and color. Some footnotes are included and all chapters conclude with a suggested readings list. The text is easy to scan because many central terms are printed in bold for their first occurrence or at the time of definition. *Map Use & Analysis* would be appropriate to use both as a survey of mapping and map use as well as a quick reference when looking for specific information.

The authors of *Map Use: Reading, Analysis, and Interpretation* "stress that a good map user must understand what goes into the making of a map" (*Map Use: Reading, Analysis, and Interpretation,* vii). Twenty-five richly illustrated chapters are divided into three sections that emphasize "Map Reading," "Map Analysis," and "Map Interpretation." "Map Reading" breaks map creation into small steps so that readers can focus attention on separate, but intertwined, topics such as the environment being mapped, data availability, reducing real-world complexity into symbols, four basic kinds of maps, the problem of time, computer software, and Web-based resources. The "Map Analysis" section describes methods for analyzing "spatial structures and relations of the mapped environment" (*Map Use: Reading, Analysis, and Interpretation,* ix) including location, direction, and distance on maps, using global positioning systems (GPS), making measurements on or from maps, identifying and comparing patterns and structures, and using geographic information systems (GIS) to analyze mapped data. The chapters included in "Map Interpretation" bring the reader back to the content of the first chapter with its focus on the environment being mapped as "environmental comprehension and understanding, for it is our surroundings, not the map, which is the real subject of map use" (*Map Use: Reading, Analysis, and Interpretation,* ix). Here readers will be introduced to fundamentals of physical environment systems and how they interact, human impacts on the environment, interpreting aerial photographs and satellite imagery, and the all-important and complementary differences between maps and reality. All of the chapters begin with an outline, and some include boxed illustrative

text drawn from literature and the news media. Key terms appear in a bold font. Chapters conclude with lists of selected readings that are drawn from the academic, professional, and research literature. The appendices include lengthy discussions, all of which could nearly be chapters in their own right, of map scale, remote sensing, map projections, and navigation instruments, along with a more traditional appendix of standard numeric tables. As with *Map Use & Analysis, Map Use: Reading, Analysis, and Interpretation* can be sampled or read cover-to-cover.

Cartography: Thematic Map Design. 5th ed.—(Dent)
Elements of Cartography. 6th ed.—(Robinson)

Cartography: Thematic Map Design (Dent) and *Elements of Cartography* (Robinson) are long-standing classic cartography textbooks. Dent is made up of 18 chapters divided into 5 sections: Thematic Mapping Essentials, Techniques of Quantitative Thematic Mapping, Designing Thematic Maps, Electronic Map Production, and Effective Graphing for Cartographers. Each chapter has extensive illustrations, an endnotes section, a glossary, and a bibliography of suggested expanded readings. There are also five appendices and an index. A Mercator poster published by the United States Geological Survey that explains projections is bundled with the volume. The entire focus of Dent is specifically on techniques for creating thematic maps, maps with special purposes. But Dent will be helpful to non-cartographers because reading for background on how thematic maps are designed can create a better understanding of how to use and interpret the end results. Readers easily can bypass information about the actual map creation process. Dent is not technical in the sense of needing to have prior knowledge of how computers and software packages function; the book is global in its approach and not tied to specific mapping packages. Basic mathematical understanding is required.

Robinson's focus is more diffused than Dent's although its intended emphasis is also thematic maps. The text is made up of 31 chapters divided into 7 sections followed by 6 appendices and an index. The sections are titled: Introduction (discussions of cartography in general, map types, and the history of cartography), Earth-Map Relations, Sources of Data, Data Processing, Perception and Design, Cartographic Abstraction, and Map Execution and Dissemination. Chapters are heavily illustrated and conclude with a "Selected References" list. There are no footnotes or endnotes to tie the references to specific points or parts of the chapters. While not tied to specific software packages, Robinson emphasizes the process of map production much more than Dent. Readers interested in increasing their map interpretation skills will be able to bypass some of the more technical chapters, but some chapters important to understanding maps are located in the middle of technical sections. For example, the "Data Processing" section's six chapters, chapters 12 through 17, focus primarily on working with data in digital form, including information on image processing, digital databases and working with digital databases, and geographic information. Chapter 16, "Data Measurement and Basic Statistical Processing," is an essential chapter for understanding measurement types and fundamental statistical functions, but because it is embedded in the middle of a highly technical section, a casual browser may miss it. As with Dent, some understanding of mathematics is necessary. Robinson's basic chapter covering the history of cartography is information not included in Dent.

As these two titles have evolved through numerous editions, the technological focus has shifted away from manual map production toward computer-assisted production. This change is especially obvious in Robinson. The fourth edition (1978) devoted a chapter to manual map construction; in the sixth edition this information has been reduced and compressed into the final appendix. In 20 years, completely new chapters on digital data have been added to Robinson, but they have been added in such a way that the text, taken in its entirety, seems disjointed. At this point in their evolution, Dent may prove to be the easier title for an interested non-cartographer to browse or read selectively.

How to Lie with Maps. 2nd ed.

How to Lie with Maps is a thinking person's guide to the tricks and traps of using maps, in particular thematic maps. The author hopes to create map skeptics by making the reader more aware of how "real world truth" is distorted in order to produce legible, and sometimes not-so-legible, maps. *How to Lie with Maps* is not about reading maps but rather about being *map aware.* A chapter on scale, projection, and symbols; a chapter on generalization; and a chapter on map production errors precede chapters on specific map types and uses. The final chapters are on data-intensive maps, in particular census maps, the use of color, and the impact of computer-generated dynamic cartography. Although not as heavily illustrated as a standard cartography textbook would be, the illustrations are appropriate and often essential for better understand-

ing of the text. There are no footnotes; a selected bibliography divided by applicable chapter and an index complete the book. Potential readers of *How to Lie with Maps* will find Monmonier's text enjoyable reading and may be more apt to read this work cover-to-cover instead of hopscotching through looking for specific information bits. While the concepts presented are sophisticated and rich in context, *How to Lie with Maps* will not require extensive technical or mathematical background to make good use of its content.

The Map Catalog: Every Kind of Map and Chart on Earth and Even Some above It. 2nd ed.

The Map Catalog is a compilation of descriptions of many different kinds of maps and possible map themes, complete with lavish illustrations in both black-and-white and color, and sources from which to acquire maps. This volume has four central sections: Land Maps, Sky Maps, Water Maps, and Map Products; each section is divided into chapters on specific kinds of thematic maps. After a brief description and history of the focus map type, both domestic and foreign commercial sources, as well as government sources, are described with information about products produced and how to contact the sources from which to purchase publications. Some sections include information about how specific kinds of maps can be used or tips about making map use easier. If appropriate, there are references to other chapters at the end of each chapter; references in the business maps chapter point to atlases, census maps, land ownership maps, and utilities maps. This book will be ideal to browse in order to find ideas for appropriate maps and map sources. But it needs to be used with caution, because the specifics about contacting map-producing companies and agencies are badly out of date. Nor is there any information included about contacting map producers through the Internet.

LOCATION SYSTEMS

A number of different systems have been developed to describe where places are on Earth. The system used depends on the kind of information needed. Some systems are used worldwide; others are used for only particular countries or parts of countries.

Geographic Coordinates

Geographic coordinates are expressed as an (x, y) pair. X stands for the degrees of latitude north or south of the equator; Y stands for the degrees of longitude east or west of a prime meridian. Together the lines of latitude and longitude intersecting at right angles form the Earth's graticule. Latitude and longitude are commonly designated using degrees, minutes, and seconds. Just like telling time, there are 60 minutes in a degree and 60 seconds in a minute. Latitude and longitude can also be indicated using decimal degrees, where the minutes and seconds have been converted to hundredths of degrees. The location of the Miami International Airport in Florida can be written as 25°47′35″ N/80°17′25″ W or 25.793° N/80.29° W. Web sites are available that will do the math automatically after the coordinate that needs transformation has been input (http://www.fcc.gov/mb/audio/bickel/DDDMMSS-decimal.html; http://web.library.uiuc.edu/asp/max/DD2DMS.asp). There may be some slight difference between answers because of rounding.

Lines of latitude can alternatively be called parallels. Parallels do not converge; they run around the globe east to west, making concentric circles with ever smaller circumferences as they move away from the equator, 24,901.55 miles, and get closer to the poles, 0 miles. Latitude's highest value is 90° north or south, the value at the poles. Its lowest value is 0° at the equator, located halfway between the two poles. In some places, instead of referring to latitude north or south of the equator, people describe using plus (+) for north and minus (–) for south. The distance from one degree of latitude to another varies between 68.7 miles (0°–1°) and 69.4 miles (89°–90°). The slight variation occurs because of the Earth's bulge at the equator and mild flattening at the poles. Lines of latitude are somewhat "natural" because their origin is at the widest part of the earth. Latitude was calculated in the ancient world using the Sun, Polaris (the current North Star), and other stars as reference points. Latitude, because of the tilt of the Earth relative to the Sun, has a direct tie to the seasons. The Tropic of Cancer and Tropic of Capricorn, approximately 23.5° north and south, are the farthest north and south of the equator that the sun is ever directly overhead. The sun is directly overhead at the tropic of Cancer at the northern hemisphere's summer solstice and directly overhead the tropic of Capricorn for the winter solstice.

Lines of longitude, or meridians, are a much more recent "invention" because there was no natural starting place or easy system of celestial references. Lines of longitude converge, intersecting at both the North and South Poles, and all have the same length, 24,859.82 miles. As with latitude, plus (+) and minus (–) can be used to describe the relationship to the east (+) or west (–) of Greenwich, England, the currently most widely recognized prime meridian. The distance between degrees of longitude varies from 0 miles at the poles to 62.2 miles at the equator.

The Illustrated Longitude

The Illustrated Longitude covers the history of the search for a method to measure time accurately enough to be able to calculate longitudinal position. For centuries, European nations, especially those with a high interest in navigating on the high seas, pursued one scheme after another that purported to determine longitude. They included observing the moons of Jupiter along with other heavenly bodies and listening for cannon fire of signal ships. The tie between time and determining longitude at sea was acknowledged as early as 1530 but an accurate-enough clock, or chronometer, was not invented until 200 years later. *The Illustrated Longitude* includes lavish illustrations and a bibliography of materials that might be of interest to those excited about exploration, the history of cartography, and the history of mensuration.

Greenwich's identification as the prime meridian is a fairly recent occurrence. Depending on the origin of the mapmaker or publisher and the area covered by the map, it was not uncommon to find prime meridians ranging from Jerusalem in the east to Washington, D.C., in the west on maps created by Western cartographers. Greenwich, England, became the official world prime meridian in 1884 as an action of the International Meridian Conference held in Washington, D.C. The International Date Line was defined at the same time.

Some older maps exist that number meridians from 0 to 360 degrees to completely circumnavigate the globe instead of the current practice of 0 to 180, then 180 back to 0. On these kinds of maps, if Greenwich is the prime meridian, longitudinal values in England to the west of Greenwich will be in the 300s while those to the east will be in single digits. Typically the maps that number from 0 to 360 circumnavigate the Earth—eastward from the prime meridian. This is an especially important detail to note for maps of the Western Hemisphere.

Because older maps cannot be relied upon to use Greenwich as their prime meridian, creative mathematical thinking may be necessary to convert coordinates found in gazetteers that use Greenwich as the prime to coordinates on older maps that use other locations.

Depending on where the meridian is, amounts will need to be added or subtracted to convert mapped coordinates to Greenwich prime coordinates. After

Greenwich-based coordinates are determined using a modern gazetteer, the maps to be used need to be checked for non-Greenwich prime usage.

The connection between time and longitude has been formalized in the system of international time zones. Exactly opposite the Greenwich Meridian, the other half of its great circle, is the 180th meridian. This meridian is the primary portion of the International Date Line. When it is noon at Greenwich, England, it is midnight at the International Date Line. This is the only time that the entire world has exactly the same date. The International Date Line is where the new day begins and from which each day advances from east to west. The day advances at the rate of 1 hour for every 15 degrees of Earth's rotation around its axis, translated into 15 degrees of longitude. Noon occurs when the sun passes over the central meridian in the zone. Although their foundations are straight meridians, both the International Date Line and many divisions between time zones have zigs and zags to keep areas that are connected economically or politically, like urban areas, states or countries, in the same time zone.

Time zones 15° wide had been adopted in the United States in 1883, a year before Greenwich as the prime meridian and a host of other resolutions regarding universal time had been passed by the International Meridian Conference. Prior to this, towns kept "sun time" which was proving to be unworkable as places far apart became more closely tied together by the expansion of the transcontinental railroad system. *Greenwich Time and the Longitude* discusses ties between time and longitude. This book includes numerous illustrations and a bibliography leading to more in-depth reading. *The Illustrated Longitude* and *Greenwich Time and the Longitude* are similar to each other with the first emphasizing the development of the chronometer and the second placing greater emphasis on finding a system of timekeeping that could be applied worldwide.

Universal Transverse Mercator System

The Universal Transverse Mercator (UTM) grid is based on maps in the transverse Mercator projection. Sixty zones, each a column 6° of latitude wide and numbered from 1 to 60, circle the Earth beginning at the 180th meridian. The columns extend between 84°N and 80°S. A false origin is established 500,000 meters west of the zone's central meridian and on the equator for locations north of the equator. The false origin for areas south of the equator is 500,000 meters west of a zone's central meridian and 10,000,000 me-

ters south of the equator. Places are located as being a number of meters east and meters north of the zone's false origin plus an indication of the zone number (1–60) and hemisphere (N or S). Although the numbers needed to describe where a point is will be very long, features can be located within 1 meter of their real-world locations. The UTM grid is supplemented by the Universal Polar Stereographic (UPS) grid to cover the areas north of 84° N and south of 80° S. There is also a military version of both the UTM and UPS grids which uses lettered-grid zones within the UTM and UPS zones to decrease the length of the numerical location designations. The UTM grid appears on United States Geological Survey topographic quadrangles.

State Plane Coordinates

The State Plane Coordinate (SPC) system divides each state into two or more zones that follow state and county boundaries and are oriented in the same direction as the predominant length of the state. Illinois is long north to south and its two zones are also oriented to run north to south. Montana has three zones that run east to west. There are a total of 125 zones nationwide. A false origin is developed for each zone west and south of the zone and measurements are made, in feet, from the false origin to the desired location. The location is notated as feet east then feet north of the false origin, state name, and state zone. Because the areas of the zones are relatively small, SPC coordinates are accurate to 1 foot in 10,000 feet. SPC 10,000-foot grids are indicated on United States Geological Survey topographic maps by black tick marks along the maps' edges. SPC is no longer widely used but should be kept in mind when interpreting the many options given by topographic quadrangles for determining locations.

Public Land Survey System

The Public Land Survey System (PLSS) is a "rectangular" system that was put into place in the late 1780s to facilitate land description and property ownership identification. The PLSS is used only in the United States and is plotted directly on the land by surveying. PLSS is not a regular grid that can be applied by laying it over a map. It does not take into account the curvature of the Earth's surface with meridians that converge. All meridians and parallels remain approximately parallel for their entire lengths. Because of this rigidity, the portion of the United

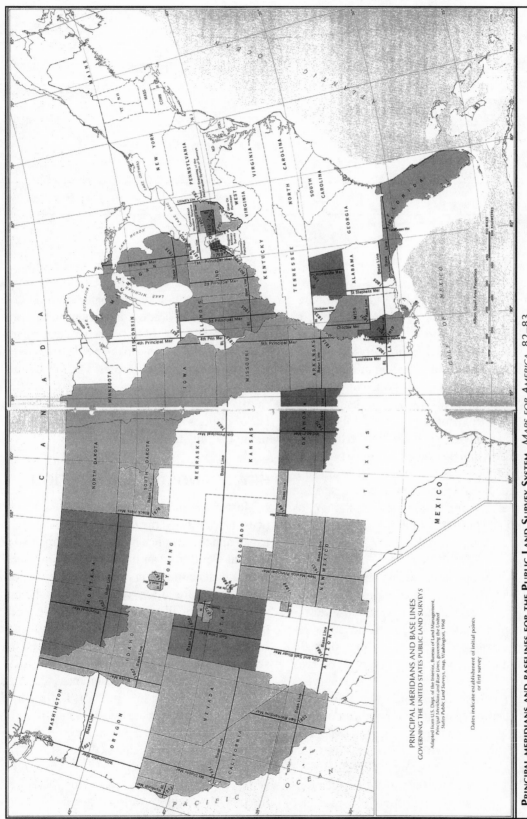

PRINCIPAL MERIDIANS AND BASE LINES
GOVERNING THE UNITED STATES PUBLIC LAND SURVEYS

Adapted from U.S. Dept. of the Interior, Bureau of Land Management,
*Principal Meridians and Base Lines, governing the United
States Public Land Surveys*, map. Washington, 1968

Dates indicate establishment of initial points
or first survey

PRINCIPAL MERIDIANS AND BASELINES FOR THE PUBLIC LAND SURVEY SYSTEM. *MAPS FOR AMERICA*, 82–83.

FIGURE 3.1

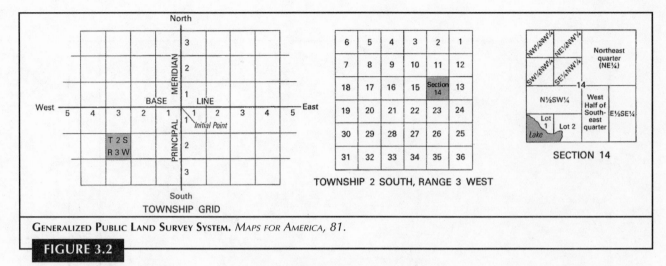

GENERALIZED PUBLIC LAND SURVEY SYSTEM. *MAPS FOR AMERICA, 81.*

FIGURE 3.2

States covered by PLSS, roughly west from the 13 original states, has been divided into a number of areas, each with its own principal meridian and baseline (Figure 3.1). The basic unit of measure is the acre, combined with other acres to form townships, typically a 6-by-6 mile square divided into 36 square mile sections. A township is defined as being in a particular range west or east of a particular principal meridian and in a specific tier, or township, north or south of the principal baseline. Rural roads typically follow section and base lines and occasionally "jog" where corrections were made in the surveying. Property within townships is described "inside out" first defining subfractions and fractions of a section, then the specific section, then the township and range with the appropriate meridian. A typical description for a location in Washington State would look like: SW 1/4, NE 1/4, Sec. 15, T 5N, R 2 W, Willamette Meridian. The smallest area that can be described using this method is half of a quarter-quarter section, or 20 acres. Smaller areas, and irregular plats, are usually designated by lot numbers (Figure 3.2). There are some regions where sections are numbered higher than 36 because the land had been surveyed before PLSS was put into place. In these areas, the PLSS surveys around the previously surveyed land leaving the original descriptions in place with new number designations. PLSS is shown on United States Geological Survey topographic maps with red section lines and numbers. The Wisconsin Department of Natural Resources has developed a sequence of Web pages that uses a series of simple maps to illustrate how to read a PLSS designation (http://www.dnr.state.wi.us/org/land/forestry/Private/PLSSTut/legaldesc.htm).

Part of The Geographer's Craft Web project located at the University of Colorado at Boulder Department of Geography is a "Coordinate Systems Overview" (http://www.colorado.edu/geography/gcraft/notes/coordsys/coordsys_f.html). It includes many definitions, examples, and links to illustrations, all in a quick-to-read bulleted format. The Geodetic Tool Kit Web site, hosted by the National Geodetic Survey (http://www.ngs.noaa.gov/TOOLS/), includes a number of utilities that facilitate conversions between different coordinate and grid systems.

SCALE AND GENERALIZATION

Most maps include some kind of scale statement. Scale is the ratio of the distance between two points on a map and the distance between the same two points in the real world. It is an indication of how much reduction and generalization were necessary to create the map. Maps are often referred to as being large-, medium-, or small-scale. The world is reduced less to produce a large-scale map than a small-scale map. Large-scale maps generally show less area than small-scale maps but with more detail. Small-scale maps show fewer details but more landmass than large-scale maps (Table 3.1, Figures 3.3a–d). The scale of a map needs to be appropriate to the kind of information shown and the intended uses for the map.

The scale of a map can be communicated in a number of different ways: representative fraction or ratio; verbal expression; bar or area scale. A representative fraction is a unitless ratio; it always takes the form 1:xxx or 1/xxx. Units can be assigned by the map reader as long as the same unit is applied to both sides of the ratio. Representative fractions work with any

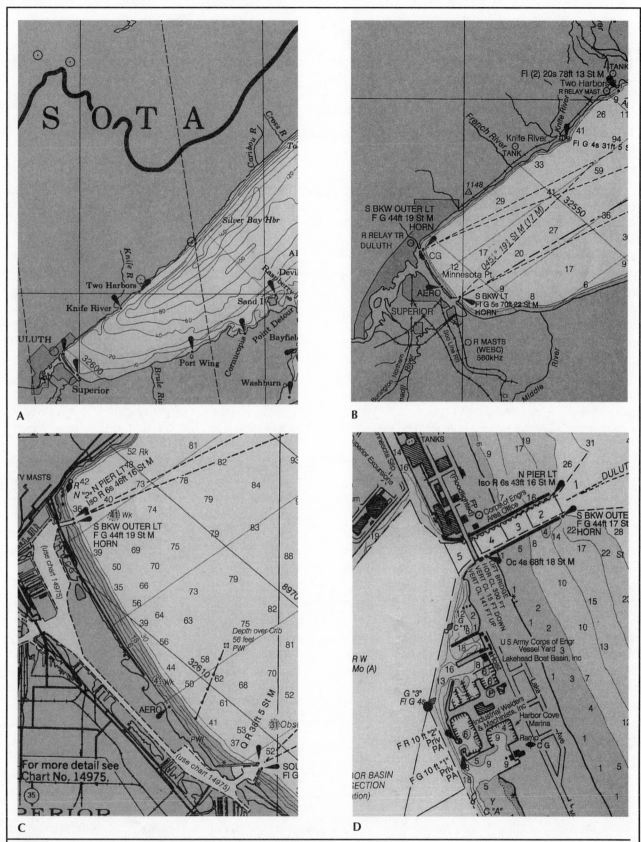

As the scale becomes larger, the amount of generalization decreases and more details about the Duluth ship canal and harbor area appear. (a) Scale 1:1,500,000. *Great Lakes, Lake Champlain to Lake of the Woods.* 1:1,500,000. 26th ed. NOAA Chart 14500. 1997. **(b) Scale 1:600,000.** *Lake Superior.* 1:600,000. 11th ed. NOAA Chart 14961. 1999. **(c) Scale 1:120,000.** *Little Girls Point to Silver Bay, including Duluth and Apostle Islands.* 1:120,000. 24th ed. NOAA Chart 14966. 1999. **(d) Scale 1:15,000.** *Duluth-Superior Harbor.* 1:15,000. 32nd ed. NOAA Chart 14975. 2000.

FIGURE 3.3

TABLE 3.1

RELATIONSHIP BETWEEN SCALE, REPRESENTATION OF LAND AREA, AND LEVEL OF DETAIL.

Scale	Denominator	Land Area Shown	Details Shown
Large-Scale	⇓	⇓	⇑
Small-Scale	⇑	⇑	⇓

unit: inches, centimeters, even lengths of pencils and hands. In the United States, a commonly-found scale expressed as a representative fraction is 1:24,000. This could be interpreted to mean one inch on the map represents or equals 24,000 inches in the real world, or one hand width on the map represents 24,000 of exactly the same hand width in the real world. As the number to the right of the ratio sign (the denominator of the fraction) becomes larger, the scale becomes smaller. Small-scale maps tend to have denominators larger than 250,000. Large-scale maps have denominators of 50,000 or less. If two sets of maps for the same area are being examined, the set with the larger scale will have more sheets than the smaller scale. For example, 1,084 topographic map sheets are needed to cover the State of Illinois at 1:24,000, while only 19 are needed at 1:250,000 and fewer still, only one, at 1:1,000,000.

A second common way of representing scale is a verbal expression. Many are found on highway maps: one inch equals 26.5 miles; one inch equals approximately 12 miles; 1 cm = 16 km. Strangely, it often seems that the amounts measured are never convenient for calculating how far away a place is. That is because the amount of reduction, and thus the scale, is driven by the size of paper that the map is printed on. The calculation should be straightforward; measure the number of inches, if that is the appropriate unit of measure on the map, and multiply by the real-world factor. Verbal expressions can be transformed into representative fractions by multiplying or dividing by appropriate conversion factors. In the United States, there is one important conversion to remember: a mile contains 63,360 inches or 5,280 feet. It doesn't hurt to remember that there are 12 inches in a foot, too. To convert the verbal scale, "1 inch equals 26.5 miles," just multiply 26.5 miles by 63,360 inches per mile to get 1,679,040. This converts both units of measurement into inches, which can be dropped to create the ratio 1:1,679,040. Converting to representative fractions is not necessary for using a map, but it may

make comparisons between different maps easier if all scales are represented in the same way.

Scale can also be shown graphically using a bar scale. A bar scale functions just like a ruler; a line is divided and subdivided to represent appropriate distances on the map. Looking at a bar scale will give the map user a quick and rough estimation of distances. Unfortunately, unless the scale is detached or cut off of the map sheet it cannot be laid over the map to measure with. A ruler or a strip of paper that the bar scale can be transferred to using tick marks along the edge will need to be used. Bar scales can be transformed to representative fractions or verbal expressions by measuring a distance, one mile or one kilometer, as carefully as possible on the bar scale using appropriate units of measurement (inches for mile, centimeters for kilometer). Then divide the distance (mile or kilometer) that has been converted into the units of measurement (inches or centimeters) by the amount measured on the bar scale. The quotient will be the right side, or denominator, of the representative fraction.

Because maps are never at the scale 1:1, there is always a certain amount of generalization or simplification needed. More or less generalization is needed depending on how small or large the scale of the map is (Figures 3.3a–d). There are five basic generalization techniques: selection, simplification, combination, shift, and exaggeration. Selection occurs because not every detail of the landscape can be shown on the map; some must be omitted. Usually, larger features are selected to be displayed while smaller features do not appear. Simplification reduces the complexity of shapes by removing less essential bends; often shorelines, streambeds, and roads are simplified. A feature should never be simplified so much that it loses all identity. Combination occurs when a number of small features are merged to create a single larger feature on the map. This technique is used if the features are important as a group but not necessarily important enough to be shown individually. Sometimes features have to be shifted on the map because they are nearly

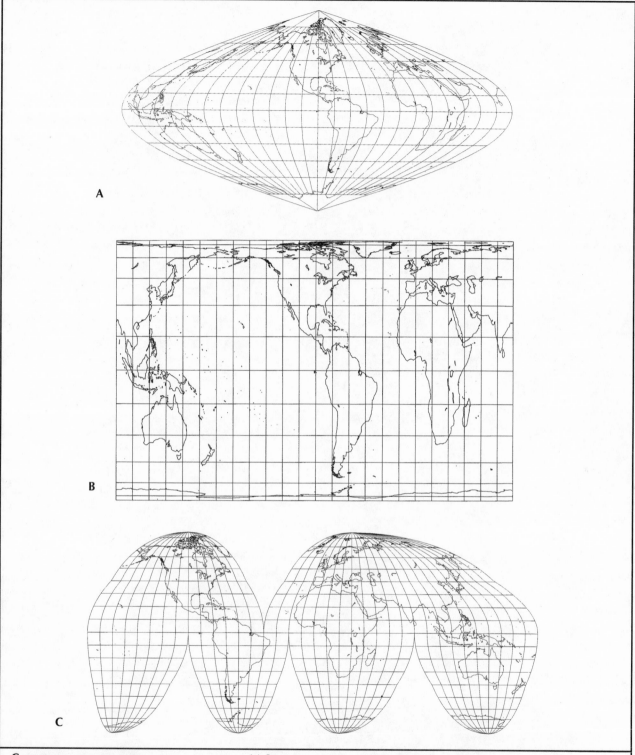

A

B

C

COMMON MAP PROJECTIONS AND THEIR PROPERTIES. (A) SINUSOIDAL—EQUAL-AREA, PSEUDOCYLINDRICAL. *AN ALBUM OF MAP PROJECTIONS*, 38. (B) GALL (PETERS) ORTHOGRAPHIC—EQUAL AREA, CYLINDRICAL. *AN ALBUM OF MAP PROJECTIONS*, 21. (C) GOODES HOMOLOSINE (INTERRUPTED)—EQUAL AREA, PSEUDOCYLINDRICAL. *AN ALBUM OF MAP PROJECTIONS*, 67.

FIGURE 3.4

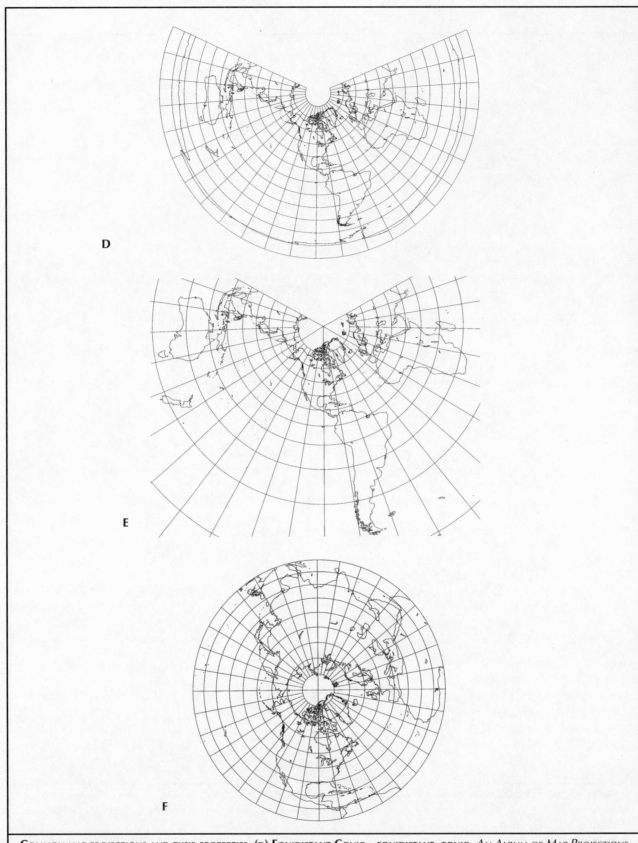

COMMON MAP PROJECTIONS AND THEIR PROPERTIES. (D) EQUIDISTANT CONIC—EQUIDISTANT, CONIC. *AN ALBUM OF MAP PROJECTIONS,* 93. **(E) LAMBERT CONFORMAL CONIC—CONFORMAL, CONIC.** *AN ALBUM OF MAP PROJECTIONS,* 96. **(F) LAMBERT AZIMUTHAL EQUAL-AREA—EQUAL AREA, AZIMUTHAL.** *AN ALBUM OF MAP PROJECTIONS,* 137.

FIGURE 3.4 (continued)

co-located in the world. This happens often for transportation systems that run side-by-side along the same access corridors, such as roads, railroads, and power lines. Features also may need to be exaggerated in size if they are to be "seen" at the scale selected for the map. Generalization does not necessarily impact a map's accuracy even though details may be lost or locations may be slightly shifted. Generalization is required for map production to occur.

Scale, and the necessary generalization, will determine how particular maps can be used. Maps of utility lines will be very large-scale because relatively small areas are shown with large amounts of detailed features precisely located. Outline maps included in textbooks will usually be very small-scale; they often show large areas, such as continents, on a relatively small piece of paper with very few details.

Chapter 5, "Scale and Generalization Concepts," in *Map Use & Analysis* does a good job of explaining scale with samples of converting scales and instructions on how to determine a map's scale if none is given. Appendix A of *Map Use: Reading, Analysis, and Interpretation* reviews scale extensively. *The Language of Maps* includes a page of scale conversion exercises and an answer key.

PROJECTIONS

Earth is an ellipsoid; it is slightly flattened at the poles and bulges around the equator. Maps transform this complex three-dimensional shape into two-dimensional planes through projections. The term *projection* applies to both the mathematical equations and the resulting graphical form.

No projection is perfect; all projections have particular inherent distortions of distance, size, shape, or direction. All projections distort at least one of these characteristics. No projection can maintain correct distance, size, shape, and direction all at the same time. Projections can be classified by the kind of attribute that is least distorted. Equidistant projections can be used to accurately measure distances, but only along specific lines or from specific points. Equal-area, or equivalent, projections maintain the relationships between sizes of shapes; these projections can be used to compare the sizes of countries or states. Conformal projections maintain angular relationships so that shapes are transformed from the ellipsoid correctly. Azimuthal projections allow for direction finding, but only from one or two specific points or for a very small area (Figures 3.4a–f).

Projections are also classified by the kind of surface or construction technique from which the projection is derived. Maps can be projected onto cylinders and cones, which are "unrolled" to create sheetlike surfaces, or flat planes. Each kind of projection technique results in maps with particular characteristics, mainly in how the meridians and parallels are represented, either by straight or curved lines, and at what kinds of angles the meridians and parallels meet. There are seven types of projection: cylindrical, pseudocylindric, conic, pseudoconic, polyconic, azimuthal, pseudoazimuthal, and retroazimuthal. The resulting projection can also be altered by changing the lines or points at which the globe is tangental to the projection surface (Figures 3.5a and b; Figures 3.6a and b).

Flattening the Earth
An Album of Map Projections

Flattening the Earth is a history of map projections written by the United States' "dean" of map projections, John Snyder. The work is organized chronologically beginning with Claudius Ptolemy (A.D. 150) and working through to the last part of the twentieth century. Each projection is discussed in the context in which it was developed; many discussions include mathematical equations and black-and-white line drawings. All chapters conclude with a table of map projections used or developed during the period covered by the chapter. The tables are keyed to figures within the text and often include the inventor's name, date of invention, and either design or appropriate applications. The chapters that cover pre-nineteenth-century projection development also include a timeline that places projection invention and use into the contexts of world exploration and mathematical advances. An extensive bibliography is included. This work may be difficult for a novice cartographer or cartographic historian to access. From the very first page, a firm understanding of cartographic and projection basics is necessary. Nevertheless, *Flattening the Earth* should be considered a core resource and is required reading for anyone with a deep interest in projections.

An Album of Map Projections, also a work by Snyder, will not require as much advance knowledge for comfortable reading as *Flattening the Earth. Album* is a United States Geological Survey publication that presents information about 90 different projections organized by construction technique, many in different variations, using a consistent format. Two basic pages are devoted to each projection; the first describes the projection and includes information about the projec-

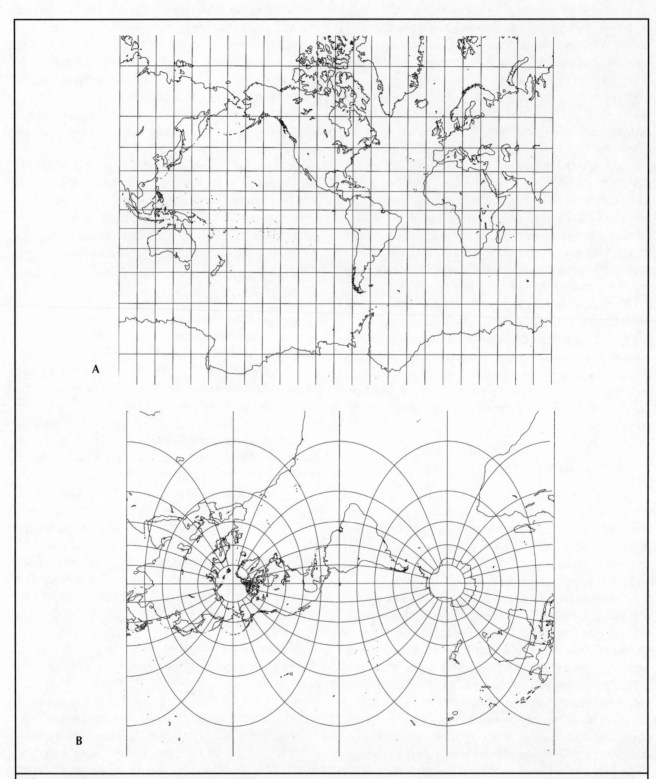

A

B

CHANGING THE PROJECTION TANGENT LINE. (A) MERCATOR PROJECTION WITH LINE OF TANGENCY AT THE EQUATOR. *AN ALBUM OF MAP PROJECTIONS*, 11. (B) TRANSVERSE MERCATOR PROJECTION WITH LINE OF TANGENCY ON A CENTRAL MERIDIAN. *AN ALBUM OF MAP PROJECTIONS*, 13.

FIGURE 3.5

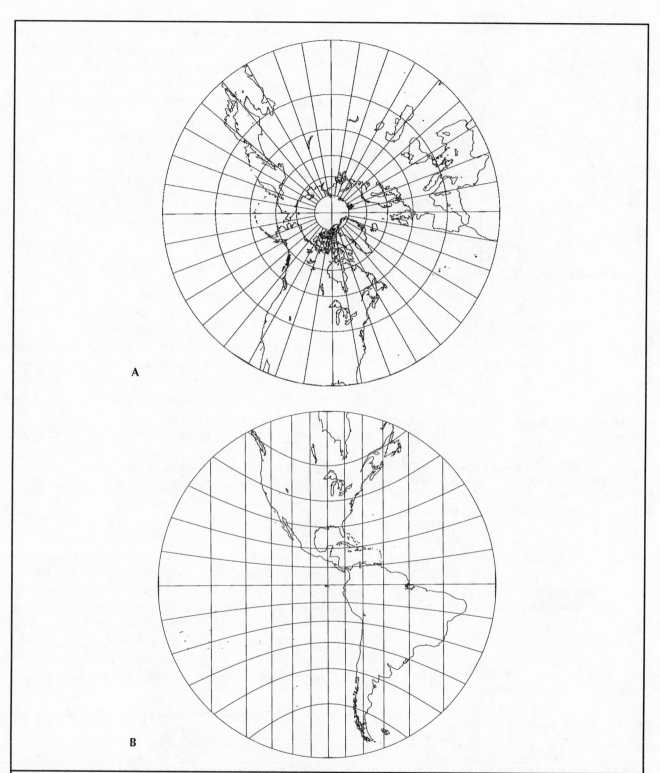

A

B

CHANGING THE PROJECTION POINT OF TANGENCY. (A) POLAR GNOMONIC PROJECTION WITH POINT OF TANGENCY AT THE NORTH POLE. *AN ALBUM OF MAP PROJECTIONS*, 117. **(B) EQUATORIAL GNOMONIC PROJECTION WITH POINT OF TANGENCY ON THE EQUATOR.** *AN ALBUM OF MAP PROJECTIONS*, 118.

FIGURE 3.6

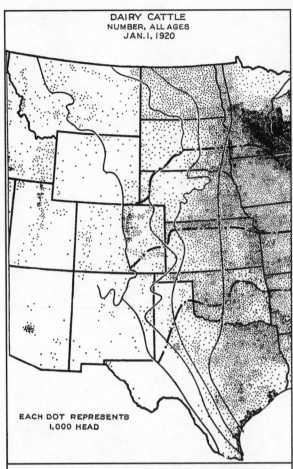

DAIRY CATTLE
NUMBER, ALL AGES
JAN. I, 1920

EACH DOT REPRESENTS
1,000 HEAD

DOT MAP. FROM THE DISTRIBUTION OF DOTS, IT APPEARS THAT THIS DATA MAY HAVE BEEN AGGREGATED TO THE COUNTY LEVEL. COUNTY-LIKE SHAPES POSSIBLY CAN BE DISCERNED IN NORTHEAST TEXAS, EASTERN KANSAS, AND MINNESOTA. "THE AGRICULTURE OF THE GREAT PLAINS REGION." O.E. BAKER. *ANNALS OF THE ASSOCIATION OF AMERICAN GEOGRAPHERS.* VOL. 14, NO. 3 (1923): 151.

FIGURE 3.7

pendix; readers of this work do not need to understand complex computations to make use of the information. A short bibliography also is included. Because of its formulaic outline and consistent graphic approach, *Album* makes it easy to compare the qualities and appearance of different map projections.

SYMBOLIZATION FOR THEMATIC MAPS

Symbolization method depends primarily on the type of data. Raw counts cannot be correctly shown using some techniques while percentages cannot be shown using others.

Dot or Nonproportional Symbol

Dot maps are used to depict nominal and raw count data. These maps show generalized locations of phenomena and are ideal for illustrating variation in spatial density (Figure 3.7). More dots in an area indicates a greater number of occurrences. Any small symbol can be used; dots are the most common. A dot can represent one occurrence or many occurrences, so legends need to be read carefully. Dots on the map can be counted and multiplied by the number of occurrences each dot represents to calculate an approximate total number. The result is only approximate because having the symbols stand for multiple occurrences can underrepresent actual numbers. For instance, if there were 350 dairy cows in a specific area, and the dot symbol stands for 100 cows, then 300 cows can be represented with three dots, but 50 cows will remain unaccounted for. Different classes of objects, for example, different breeds of cattle, can be shown on the same map by using differently colored dots or different shapes all with the same size. Dot maps are often used to show locations of natural point phenomena such as earthquake epicenters and hot springs. They are also used quite often to illustrate agricultural activities.

Proportional or Graduated Symbol

Proportional symbol maps use the size of the symbol to convey the value or amount of the attribute being mapped (Figure 3.8). Proportional symbols are not used to differentiate between different classes or categories; a small circle and a larger circle would not be used to represent trout and salmon spawning sites, respectively. Circles traditionally have been most used along with other geometric shapes such as squares and triangles. Sometimes a symbol that appears to have

tion's classification, graticule, scale, distortions, usage, origin, aspect, other names, and similar projections. A Tissot indicatrix, or distortion diagram, showing areas and kinds of distortions using circles is included for many projections. The second page for each projection is a black-and-white line drawing showing the projection. The line drawings throughout the book are centered at 90°W (slightly east of the Mississippi River), if appropriate for the projection being shown. A glossary, "Guide to Selecting Map Projections," and a short introduction to distortion diagrams precede the specific projection descriptions. Some projection formulas are included but as an ap-

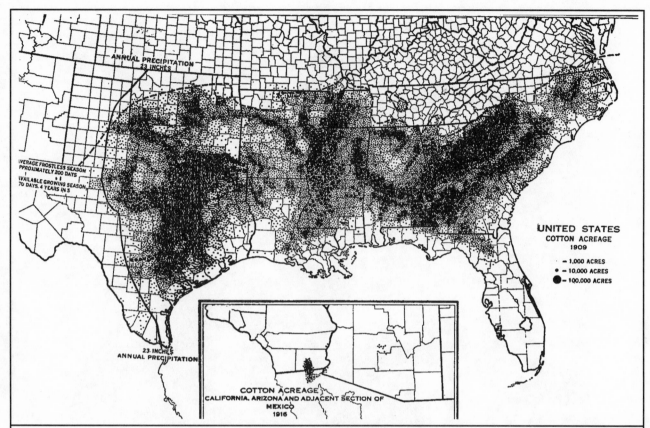

PROPORTIONAL SYMBOL MAP. THE PLACEMENT OF THE LARGER, AND SEEMINGLY DARKER, DOTS MAKES IT EASY TO SEE WHERE INTENSE COTTON FARMING WAS TAKING PLACE IN 1909. "THE INCREASING IMPORTANCE OF THE PHYSICAL CONDITIONS IN DETERMINING THE UTILIZATION OF LAND FOR AGRICULTURAL AND FOREST PRODUCTION IN THE UNITED STATES." O.E. BAKER. *ANNALS OF THE ASSOCIATION OF AMERICAN GEOGRAPHERS.* VOL. 11 (1921): 41.

FIGURE 3.8

volume, such as a sphere, is used. Pictographic symbols, shapes that resemble the attribute being mapped, are also used. Proportional symbol maps can be tricky to interpret correctly because it can be difficult to differentiate between different-sized symbols and because symbols often overlap each other.

Choropleth

Choropleth maps show data that is geographically bounded by administrative areas such as states, counties, and townships. The administrative areas serve as aggregation areas, and the same kind of administrative area will be used throughout the map (Figure 3.9). The boundaries of the areas are not formed because of how the data is classified. A traditional soils map is not a choropleth map because the boundaries between soil types are dependent on the data. It is not strictly correct to map raw totals, things like number of births, number

of cows, or number of acres of corn, using choropleth maps because the enumeration areas most likely will not be equal in size, and the map will be difficult to interpret correctly. Raw totals need to be transformed into derived data, customarily ratios, densities, or proportions. Choropleth maps can be used correctly to show the number of births per number of women over the age of 18, the number of cows per acre of farm land, or the average value received for a bushel of corn.

Enumeration areas with the same or similar values will be classified together and shown using the same areal pattern or color. A fairly recent development, with the application of computing power to mapping, is the creation of unclassified choropleth maps; each enumeration area will be in its own class, except areas that have exactly the same value. Unclassified choropleth maps, while preserving the data, will be difficult for the reader to use to identify patterns and relationships.

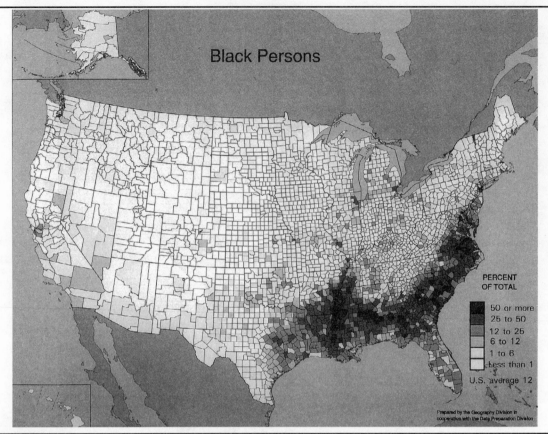

CHOROPLETH MAP. TYPICALLY DARKER OR BOLDER COLORS REPRESENT HIGHER CONCENTRATIONS. *RACE AND HISPANIC ORIGIN POPULATION DENSITY OF THE UNITED STATES: 1990 (BY COUNTY AS A PERCENTAGE OF TOTAL POPULATION).* UNITED STATES MAPS, GE-90 NO. 6. [WASHINGTON, D.C.: U.S. DEPT. OF COMMERCE, BUREAU OF THE CENSUS, 1990.]

FIGURE 3.9

Isarithmic

Isarithmic maps use isolines to connect data points with equal values; hypothetically, although the isolines have been extrapolated between points of known and equal value, they have a continuous value along their entire length. The points on one side of the line will have a lower value than the points on the other side. Isolines are used quite a bit in depicting the natural world (Figure 3.10). Contour, or topographic, maps are one of the most common types of isarithmic maps. Contour lines, connecting spot heights of equal values, show the height about sea level; bathymetric lines do the same for the depth to the ocean floor. Other uses of isolines include rainfall, air pollution, average date of first frost, and barometric pressure. Users of isarithmic maps need to remember that the locations of the isolines are approximations.

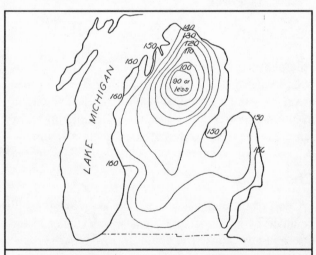

ISARITHMIC MAP SHOWING LENGTH OF THE GROWING SEASON IN DAYS FOR MICHIGAN'S LOWER PENINSULA. CONCENTRIC "CIRCLES" ARE NOT UNCOMMON ON THIS TYPE OF MAP. "THE INFLUENCE OF LAKE MICHIGAN UPON ITS OPPOSITE SHORES, WITH COMMENTS ON THE DECLINING USE OF THE LAKE AS A WATERWAY." RAY HUGHES WHITBECK. *ANNALS OF THE ASSOCIATION OF AMERICAN GEOGRAPHERS.* VOL. 10 (1920): 44.

FIGURE 3.10

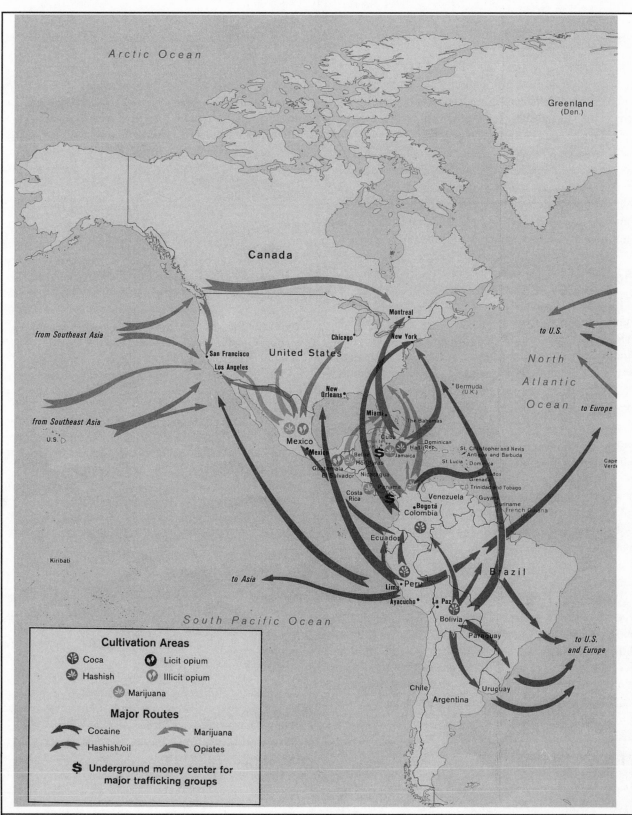

FLOW MAP SHOWING WESTERN HEMISPHERE DRUG TRAFFIC. ONLY DIRECTION OF FLOW AND KIND OF DRUGS ARE INDICATED. THIS MAP
CANNOT BE USED TO ESTIMATE EITHER VALUE OR TONNAGE MOVED. PORTION OF: *MAJOR NARCOTICS CULTIVATION AREAS AND
TRAFFICKING ROUTES.* SCALE NOT GIVEN. "707041 (545038) 2–86." [WASHINGTON, D.C.: CENTRAL INTELLIGENCE AGENCY, 1986.]

FIGURE 3.11

Cartograms

Cartograms distort area and distance to convey information about time and distribution of phenomena. Areas and distances are increased or decreased to reflect the relative size of the attribute being described by the map. For example, the sizes of states can be made proportional to the number of people over 65. Some do not consider cartograms to be true maps because they distort spatial accuracy so much. But cartograms show both geographical relationships and depict information tied to specific regions and, as such, need to be considered as viable options for conveying geographic information.

Flow

Flow maps connect places by showing the movement of goods, people, and ideas from the point of origin, possibly through intermediate locations, and finally the destination (Figure 3.11). Line thickness, or weight, commonly is used to represent the volume of flow. Sometimes different line-like symbols, for example, dotted, dashed, solid and double lines, are used to show ordinal relationships between flows. Lines can be colored differently to represent different cargoes or carriers. Because many flow maps are very small-scale, the flow lines do not represent actual routes and should be used only as a general indication of connectivity. Large-scale flow maps, such as commuter traffic maps, will show better approximations of actual travel paths. Migration and the movement of commercial goods are commonly shown by flow maps.

While maps need to lie in order to present information, the lies are developed selectively, systematically, and according to principles and practices developed during more than 500 years of cartographic production. An understanding of the constraints upon maps as tools for information display and decision making will assist users in making more appropriate interpretation and use decisions.

BIBLIOGRAPHY

An Album of Map Projections. John P. Snyder and Philip M. Voxland. U.S. Geological Survey Professional Paper 1453. Washington, D.C.: Government Printing Office, 1989. ISBN: 0-16-003368-3.

Cartographic Citations: A Style Guide. Suzanne M. Clark, Mary Lynette Larsgaard, and Cynthia M. Teague. MAGERT Circular no. 1. Chicago: Map and Geography Round Table, American Library Association, 1992. ISBN: 0-8389-7581-X.

Cartography: Thematic Map Design. 5th ed. Borden D. Dent. Boston: WCB/McGraw-Hill, 1999. ISBN: 0697384950.

Elements of Cartography. 6th ed. Arthur H. Robinson, [et al.]. New York: Wiley, 1995. ISBN: 0471555797.

Flattening the Earth: Two Thousand Years of Map Projections. John P. Snyder. Chicago: University of Chicago Press, 1993. ISBN: 0-226-76747-7.

Greenwich Time and the Longitude. Rev. ed. Derek Howse. London: Philip Wilson, 1997. ISBN: 0-85667-468-0.

How to Lie with Maps. 2nd ed. Mark Monmonier. Chicago: University of Chicago Press, 1996. ISBN: 0226534200.

The Illustrated Longitude. Dava Sobel and William J.H. Andrewes. New York: Walker, 1998. ISBN: 0-8027-1344-0.

The Language of Maps. 16th ed. Philip J. Gersmehl. Pathways in Geography Series, no. 1. Indiana, Pa.: National Council for Geographic Education, 1996. ISBN: 0-9627379-3-3.

The Map Catalog: Every Kind of Map and Chart on Earth and Even Some above It. 2nd ed. Joel Makower, ed. New York: Vintage Books, 1992. ISBN: 0-679-74257-3.

Map Use & Analysis. 4th ed. John Campbell. Boston: McGraw-Hill, 2001. ISBN: 0-697-22969-6.

Map Use: Reading, Analysis, and Interpretation. Rev. 4th ed. Phillip C. Muehrcke, Juliana O. Muehrcke, and Jon Kimerling. Madison, Wis.: JP Publications, 2001. ISBN: 0-9602978-5-5.

The Nature of Maps: Essays Toward Understanding Maps and Mapping. Arthur H. Robinson and Barbara Bartz Petchenik. Chicago: University of Chicago Press, 1976. ISBN: 0226722813.

On-line References

"Coordinate Systems Overview." Peter H. Dana. Geographer's Craft Project, University of Colorado at Boulder, 15 December 1999. <http://www.colorado.edu/geography/gcraft/notes/coordsys/coordsys_f.html> (14 October 2003).

"Decimal Degrees° <=> Degrees° Minutes' Seconds"." University of Illinois at Urbana-Champaign, Map & Geography Library, 18 February 2000. <http://web.library.uiuc.edu/asp/max/DD2DMS.asp> (14 October 2003).

"Degrees, Minutes, Seconds, and Decimal Degrees Latitude/Longitude Conversions." Federal Communications Commission (FCC), Audio Services Division, 2003. <http://www.fcc.gov/mb/audio/bickel/DDDMMSS-decimal.html> (14 October 2003).

"NGS Geodetic Tool Kit." NGS, NOAA, 2 April 2002. <http://www.ngs.noaa.gov/TOOLS/> (14 October 2003).

"What Is a Legal Description?" Wisconsin Department of Natural Resources, 10 April 2003. <http://www.dnr.state.wi.us/org/land/forestry/Private/PLSSTut/legaldesc.htm> (14 October 2003).

CHAPTER 4
Finding Place Names

TOPICS COVERED

Gazetteers
World and World Region Gazetteers
National and State Gazetteers
Older Gazetteers
Specialty Gazetteers
Government Place Name Agencies
Place Name Resources

MAJOR SOURCES DISCUSSED

Columbia Gazetteer of the World
Merriam-Webster's Geographical Dictionary
GEOnet Names Server
Getty Thesaurus of Geographic Names
Where Once We Walked and ShtetlSeeker
Geographic Names Information System
U.S. Census Bureau U.S. Gazetteer
Army Map Service/Board on Geographic Names
   Gazetteers

Gazetteer of the World
Stehiler's Hand Atlas
*Dead Countries of the Nineteenth and Twentieth
   Centuries*
Place-Name Changes, 1900–1991
GeoNative
   United States Board on Geographic Names
   United Nations Group of Experts on Geographical
      Names
*Place Names: How They Define the World—
   And More*
*Geographic Names & the Federal Government:
   A Bibliography*
*Bibliography of Place-Name Literature: United
   States and Canada*
*Gazetteers and Glossaries of Geographical Names of
   the Member-Countries of the United Nations and the
   Agencies in Relationship with the United Nations:
   Bibliography, 1946–1976*
American Name Society

Working with place names can be difficult because they are not permanently attached to the landscape. Names are fluid, changing to reflect changes in populations and power structures. New names can be re-spelled old names or can have no relationship to anything that has gone on before. People do not hear names of places pronounced the same way, causing confusion in completing important paperwork such as emigrant records. Nor is the relationship between places and objects always clear, especially to a person not familiar with a region or the conventions of the language spoken there.

The scientific study of names is called *onomastics,* and the specific study of place names is *toponymy.* Studying place names can help trace movements of people and cultures through geographic space. Standardizing place names, or at least agreeing on what to

call a place for specific purposes, aids in communication about the place and the activities occurring there. There are many lists of place names, some official and very inclusive and others short with a specific focus. These lists can help identify the location where a scientific specimen was collected or the name of an ancestor's home village that has changed three times in the past 100 years.

GAZETTEERS

A gazetteer is an alphabetical list of place names with information that can be used to locate the areas that the names are associated with. There are three basic styles of gazetteers with varying levels of inclusiveness: alphabetical list, dictionary, and encyclopedic.

The simplest gazetteer is the alphabetical list of place names and locations, information typically found in atlases or on state highway maps. In this context, the gazetteer is often referred to as an index. Each name in the list will minimally include an indication of where it can be found on the accompanying map or maps. Sometimes both map location and geographic coordinates are given. If a place name is used in multiple locations or at different administrative levels, such as county and town, the entry should include appropriate information to distinguish between uses. The list of place names will be constrained by the areas covered by the atlas or map; it will not include any places not visible in the maps being indexed although, hypothetically, all places named on the map should appear in the gazetteer unless the gazetteer is defined as including only specific kinds of locations. Depending on the size of the publication being indexed, these gazetteers can range in size from a few hundred to tens of thousands of locations. Many countries have separate volumes of gazetteers that list place name, place type, and location. These volumes often are extensive indexes to national medium- or large-scale sets of topographic maps.

Dictionary-style gazetteers include location information augmented by other kinds of information. Because the dictionary gazetteer is not created to index a specific cartographic product, location cannot be given using any kind of map designation. Location will be indicated using geographic coordinates or by describing spatial relationships to other places. Entries typically will be brief; pronunciation guides along with brief demographic, economic, and historic information may be included. Dictionary gazetteers need to be thought of as being somewhat abridged. They will not contain every place possible; the gazetteer preparer should include preface information describing how inclusion decisions were made.

Encyclopedic gazetteers will have many entries and more extensive entries than dictionary gazetteers. Place name entries are extended into articles and essays researched and written by area specialists. The same kinds of information as presented in dictionary gazetteers will appear (demographic, economic, historic, cultural, and physical), but greatly expanded. Although larger in scope than the typical dictionary gazetteer, the encyclopedic gazetteer will still be limited in its nature and the limitations should be explained within the publication.

Dictionary or encyclopedic gazetteers will be good places to begin learning about a place's history or current economic or political status. But to locate places, especially small villages or less important physical features, more exhaustive gazetteers that were compiled to index sets of maps will be much more useful.

Gazetteers can be found in library catalogs using two different subject searches: [Country/state name]—Gazetteers or Names, Geographical—[Country/state name]. These searches will result in lists of books devoted solely to place names. Subject searching for gazetteers will not yield lists of atlases that include place name indexes. These are best found by reading the description of the atlas in the library catalog carefully or by actually examining the atlas of interest.

Because the word *gazetteer* has been used by the DeLorme Map Company as part of the title of its state atlas series, such as the *Illinois Atlas and Gazetteer,* searching the Web for gazetteers can be tricky. Many of the results searching for "gazetteer Illinois" will be Web advertisements by book sellers for the DeLorme products. "Gazetteers" as a search produces a completely different set of results. Included in the list will be a list of links to gazetteers through Oddens' Bookmarks (http://oddens.geog.uu.nl/browsepages/Gazetteers.html). The links are arranged alphabetically by continent or country name, which need to be selected from a pick list. Selecting "United Kingdom" generates a list of Web sites, some general and others with specific geographical or chronological emphasis. Not all of the resources listed are strictly gazetteers; the United States results includes the National Park Service's National Register of Historic Places Web site, InfoSpace's Yellow Pages, and Map Blast, along with gazetteers for the entire nation and for more specific areas. The countries with only one resource listed are relying on a "Global Gazetteer" Web site hosted by Falling Rain Genomics (http://www.calle.com/world/). This Web site includes 2,880,532 cities and towns with links to maps showing where the communities are located. Selecting from a list of the first two letters of a town's name will display a second list with complete names and generalized latitude, longitude, and altitude. Selecting a specific place name displays specific latitude and longitude information in both decimal degrees and degrees/minutes/seconds, altitude in both feet and meters, links for weather and airport information, and maps. The latitude and longitude data in the "Global Gazetteer" is from the GEOnet Names Server hosted by the National Imagery and Mapping Agency; elevation data comes from GTOPO30, a global digital elevation model available through the USGS EROS Data Center.

The Map Collection at the Arizona State University Libraries in Tempe maintains a list of Web-based gazetteers that may be helpful (http://www.asu.edu/lib/hayden/govdocs/maps/geogname.htm). Links to standard gazetteers such as GNIS and GEOnet Names Server are maintained as well as links to a number of European national gazetteers.

WORLD AND WORLD REGION GAZETTEERS

The Columbia Gazetteer of the World

The *Columbia Gazetteer* is a core English-language gazetteer of the world and a classic among place name resources. It is based on two previous, and highly regarded, gazetteers, *Lippincott's Pronouncing Gazetteer* (1855) and *The Columbia-Lippincott Gazetteer of the World* (1952). The *Columbia Gazetteer* contains more than 165,000 entries in three weighty volumes. Encyclopedic in nature, the entries go far beyond merely listing place name and geographic coordinates. Depending on the nature of the place or feature described, entries include information on demography, physical and political geography, economic and industrial activities, cultural landmarks, transportation, and history. Location is described by geographic coordinates, elevation, and direction and distance from other relevant locations. Official and alternate place names and spellings along with pronunciations are also included. Some entries describing countries span multiple pages.

The locations described fall into three categories: political, physical, and "special places." Political locations vary from countries to neighborhoods. Physical features include continents and oceans, mountains and valleys, glaciers and volcanoes. "Special places" cover a myriad of locations and areas constructed by or identified as unique by humans including parks, airports, shopping malls, military bases, and trade routes.

The names assigned to locations are most often spelled following conventions established by the decisions made by the United States Board on Geographic Names, although alternate spellings are included "to reflect native pronunciations of names transliterated from native tongues" (*Columbia Gazetteer,* cgvii). Main entries are usually official names as used by national agencies, but English versions are used for places with widely known English names. The pronunciation guide is based on a scheme used by news broadcasters augmented to include sounds that are normally not found in American English.

The editors of the *Columbia Gazetteer* strove for maximal yet balanced coverage. Places included, except for in the United States, had to meet criteria such as population thresholds appropriate to the national situation, areal size, and cultural significance. With an American audience, it is not surprising that 40,000 entries, nearly a quarter of the total, are for sites in the United States, including "every incorporated place and country [*sic,* county] in the United States, along with several thousand unincorporated places, special-purpose sites, and physical features" (*Columbia Gazetteer,* cgv). The number of entries specific to other countries range from 6,068 for Russia to 21 for Andorra.

Although the *Columbia Gazetteer* will not answer all place name queries, especially those related to small villages, the entries included will illuminate the history of regions, perhaps explaining why place name research for a particular locale is difficult. Unlike the GEOnet Names Server or the Army Mapping Service country gazetteers (both discussed below), the *Columbia Gazetteer* does not require foreknowledge of the appropriate holding nation. The look and feel of the pages and entries will be familiar to anyone who has used a dictionary or a single-volume encyclopedia.

The *Columbia Gazetteer* is often an appropriate first step in locating a specific place or for doing background reading before moving to more specific information sources. There are no maps in the three volumes, but the verbal descriptions of locations relative to other places usually suffice to locate areas on separate maps.

The *Columbia Gazetteer* is also available through the Web (http://www.columbiagazetteer.org) as a fee-based service. The database can be searched by place name, much in the same way as using the printed version, or by type of place, or a full-text search that includes the text from all of the entries can be performed. The type-of-place search allows searching for locations such as lakes at elevations higher than 7,000 feet in South America or named gas fields in the Middle East. Using the full-text search can be tricky because not all phrases or geographical names are spelled in full. It would be worthwhile to do some directed browsing of entries using place name searches before attempting full-text searches. Search results are displayed as clickable lists that include place/feature name, type of feature, country/U.S. state, and, if appropriate, population or some other criteria (area, length, width, depth, elevation, and capacity).

Merriam-Webster's Geographical Dictionary. 3rd rev. ed.

In size and appearance, the *Merriam-Webster's Geographical Dictionary* strongly resembles *Webster's New Collegiate Dictionary* but it is not a dictionary of terms like *cold front, population pyramid,* or *cartouche.* This desk-sized gazetteer contains 48,000 place name entries and 258 maps along with extensive explanatory notes, a discussion of map projections, glossary, and a list of non-English geographical terms.

Entries tend to be brief, typically fewer than 10 lines except for country and major city descriptions. Potential information for inclusion is feature type, population, size, economy, and history. A pronunciation guide also is included along with alternate names. Cross-references lead from alternate name entries to full descriptions. Location is described through distance and direction from other places or general description. Some entries, in particular those for states and provinces, include tables of counties with their areas and populations.

Places described include both political entities and physical features. Physical features were selected for inclusion based on "significance"; towns were included based on general population guidelines. Towns in the United States and Canada with populations greater than 2,500 were included, while the threshold for towns in the United Kingdom was 10,000 and for Bangladesh towns 100,000, although places with lower populations, but of historical or cultural significance, are included. These decisions were made assuming that the vast majority of *Merriam-Webster's Geographical Dictionary* users would be interested in, or living in, the United States or Canada.

The black-and-white maps are of individual countries and U.S. and Canadian states and provinces. They typically are placed close to the appropriate entry and include a location map. City and country entries are not keyed to the maps, nor are the maps at a common scale so visual comparisons of size and distances can not be done using *Merriam-Webster's.*

While potentially useful for high school and lower-division undergraduate students, *Merriam-Webster's* will be disappointing to the serious genealogist because of its typically brief entries and generally high population inclusion thresholds. Still, this volume will be found at nearly every library reference desk to be enjoyed by casual map explorers.

A number of other inexpensive gazetteers are available in newer editions. *The Oxford Essential Geographical Dictionary, American Edition,* contains listings for more than 10,000 physical, political, and cultural places in only 425 pages. One-third of the entries are for locations in North America with expanded information on the states of the United States and the

provinces and territories of Canada and Mexico. The information included is basic, pronunciation, physical description, history, and population. Small maps, circa one square inch, illustrate most of the country entries. Some countries such as Germany and Mexico have larger maps. Appendices include lists of major rivers, volcanoes, mountains, and lakes along with oceans, continents, and major metropolitan areas. The paperback *Oxford Essential* might be just the right size to carry around in a briefcase or backpack for quick reference. *The Penguin Encyclopedia of Places,* 3rd ed., is heftier than the *Oxford Essential,* over 12,000 places in 1,031 pages. Most of the entries are longer but there are no accompanying maps. *The Penguin Encyclopedia* also has more of a British slant than the *Oxford Essential* in the choice and proportion of entries.

GEOnet Names Server (http://164.214.2.59/gns/html/index.html)

The GEOnet Names Server is hosted by the National Imagery and Mapping Agency (NIMA). According to the Web site, approximately 20,000 of the database's 3.88 million features (5.34 million names) are updated each month. The updates come from the Foreign Names Committee of the Board on Geographic Names. The database has its roots in the paper gazetteers published by the Army Mapping Service and the Board on Geographic Names beginning in the 1940s and covers the entire world except for the United States, its territories, and Antarctica, all of which are covered by the Geographic Names Information System (GNIS). These two databases are combined in the Alexandria Digital Library Gazetteer (http://fat-albert.alexandria.ucsb.edu:8827/gazetteer/).

Results of queries can be received as either normal gazetteer information or in a tab-delimited ASCII file for loading into GIS software applications. Extensive instructions are included at the top of the search form. A country or countries must be included as part of the search. Wild cards are allowed in searches, and users can indicate whether the characters input into the name field starts the feature name, must be matched exactly, is contained by the feature name, or ends the feature name. The database can also be searched using a bounding rectangle; for these searches no other search criteria should be used. The Web site will open a new browser window to display the search progress and results. Responses can be ordered by feature identifier, name, ascending latitude, or feature type. The feature identifier may be a meaningless sort mechanism; feature identifiers are unique numbers that identify the feature. The other three sort choices may be more understandable: alphabetical by name, ascending latitude, or grouping like features together. The results list includes basic gazetteer-type information: name and name type; region code corresponding to continental location; feature type designation; latitude and longitude in degrees, minutes, and seconds; area code indicating country and first-order administrative division; Universal Transverse Mercator coordinate grid; Joint Operations Graphics map number; unique feature and name identifiers; and populated place classification, which will indicate the relative importance of a place. The populated place classification is a new field and usually will not be completed.

Names for individual countries can be downloaded from the GEOnet Names Server Web site as zip files; the data will be tab-delimited. Some countries will require multiple files. The date given after the file name is not the edition date of the data but is the date when the data covering an individual country was "carved out of" the primary database.

For the most comprehensive results, GEOnet Names Server should be used in combination with other world and national gazetteers.

Getty Thesaurus of Geographic Names
(http://www.getty.edu/research/conducting_
research/vocabularies/tgn/index.html)
The Getty Thesaurus of Geographic Names (TGN) was developed to assist art historians and researchers in recording place names appropriate for art objects and their creators. The TGN is a global vocabulary of nearly 1 million place names identifying more than 900,000 political and physical places that was developed and is distributed through the Internet by the Getty Research Institute. TGN does not prescribe the correct name to be used for a particular chronological or political situation; it lists possibilities. All of the place names are placed into equivalence, hierarchical, and associative relationships with the other included terms. Equivalence relationships are multiple names for the same place such as Rome and Roma; the names have equal validity. Hierarchical relationships show how locations are contained by other entities either politically or physically. A typical hierarchy for an inhabited place in the United States would include continent, country, state, county, then town. Associative relationships create connections between places that are related for reasons besides hierarchy and will be indicated through notes in place entries. Springfield and Vandalia, Illinois, might be placed in an as-

sociative relationship because Springfield is the current state capital and Vandalia was the capital between 1820 and 1837. Other kinds of associative relationships include old and new town locations that need to be traced if settlements have been moved and absorbtion of small towns by larger nearby cities.

Searching the TGN is simple, merely type in the name of the desired place; however, interpreting the results can be complicated because of the great possibility of needing to examine multiple records as well as the structure and display of the records. The search mechanism is nothing more than entering a keyword or a complete place name into a search box. Searching for "Chicago" yields 96 matching records, including the expected large city in Illinois but also a large number of creeks, peaks, mines, and lakes. Each of the entries in the initial results list, sorted alphabetically by entry name, includes the place's name, type of place, abbreviated hierarchy, and a TGN record number. Multiple occurrences of the same name are secondarily sorted using the hierarchy. Clicking on the hot-linked place names displays one entry at a time; multiple entries can be selected for sequential display by clicking on the checkboxes that proceed each name. Clicking on the hierarchy icon in front of a place name will display only the full hierarchy. All levels of the hierarchy will be hot-linked to full records. The hierarchy is also displayed as part of a full record. A typical full record will include location coordinates in both degrees/minutes/seconds and decimal degrees, notes, hierarchical position, names, place types, and source materials consulted for each name. The location coordinates are usually a single pair representing the center of the named area or, in the case of streams, the location of the source. Notes may include settlement history, physical features such as climate and geology, and general information about ethnic groups and languages. After each name will be two single-letter codes inside a set of parentheses: C, current name; H, historic name; V, vernacular name; O, variant name in another language. The codes after United States are C and V while the codes following Estados Unidos de América are C and O.

A single record cannot be relied upon to trace a place completely. If "Fort Dearborn" is searched, two records are pulled up. The first is the "Chicago" record with the information about the 1816 fort construction. The second is a record specifically for Fort Dearborn, but the emphasis in this record is on the fort that had been at the site prior to 1816 and the War of 1812 battlefield surrounding the fort. The name is coded (C,V) in the record specifically on Fort Dearborn; in the Chicago record, Fort Dearborn is coded (H,V).

The TGN might not be the ideal gazetteer to use if nothing else is known about a place beyond its name. In the Chicago results list, there are eight entries for "Chicago Mine" in six different states plus a ninth entry for "Chicago Mine Hill." These particular entries do not include any historical or contextual notes beyond the hierarchical position. Many of the U.S. entries, including all of the Chicago Mine entries, are pulled from the United States Geological Survey's Geographic Names Information System (GNIS) without information from additional sources. For U.S. locations, GNIS might be a better first alternative because its entries also include appropriate topographic quadrangles, information that has been stripped from the TGN database. GNIS does not include connections to historic or alternative names or contextual notes.

Looking at non-U.S. locations, some inconsistencies appear. Egypt is treated only as a historic region, not as a nation. Detective work, using a list of African nations and regions that can be found by clicking on "Browse the World" and then examining the Africa hierarchy, will eventually lead to an entry for "Misr." Within this entry, "Egypt" is included as a current, non-vernacular name for the nation. The distinction may be that "Egypt" refers, according to TGN, to a smaller area than the current nation as commonly identified by North Americans; "Egypt" is not a nation but instead is the historical core of a country called "Misr."

TGN's big pluses are the huge number of names attached to specific locations and the references to other name resources. With persistence and creative thinking, TGN will assist in linking historic names to current sites.

Where Once We Walked
ShtetlSeeker (http://www.jewishgen.org/
  ShtetlSeeker)

Where Once We Walked is intended to be a gazetteer to Jewish communities in eastern and central Europe prior to the great upheavals caused by the two world wars. It is not tied to one specific country. But the place name researcher does not need to be Jewish to find valuable information in either this volume or the spin-off Web-based *ShtetlSeeker*. Jewish communities or enclaves were nearly ubiquitous throughout central and eastern Europe early in the twentieth century.

Where Once We Walked has two primary sections, an alphabetical listing of towns and a listing of towns by the Daitch-Mokotoff Soundex System. The alphabetical listing is similar to most listings of this kind; the information included for each entry includes country, description of location in relation to a primary or larger central town, latitude/longitude coordinates, and a source code referring to the resource in which the town was found. Some entries also include alternate names and a Jewish population figure. The primary entry names are the names listed in the United States Board on Geographic Names (BGN) gazetteers; alternative names come from other sources and include Yiddish names and any other distinct variants. The compilers of *Where Once We Walked* did considerable background work with an extensive list of resources beyond the BGN gazetteers to expand the data. All of these resources are described in the introductory material and may serve as additional information sources for place name research in central and eastern Europe.

A section titled "What To Do If You Cannot Find Your Town Listed" is also included in the introductory material and contains straightforward advice of how to work with the unlocatable place. Included are reminders of some basics: check spelling and consult maps. The authors' first suggestion is to spell the place name phonetically using a soundex system. They also acknowledge that some towns might not be listed.

The Daitch-Mokotoff Soundex System groups towns by how their names sound, not by how they are spelled. Names are encoded using a coding chart and then the sequence of numbers is matched to a list. Names that code the same way are listed together next to the code number. Generally, vowels are not coded, except if they are the first sound in a name. Double consonants, *ss* or *nn* as examples, are coded as a single letter, *s* or *n*. The system is easy to apply and quickly derives a list of alternate names and spellings. The soundex system will make it easier to interpret poor handwriting and regional dialects or accents.

The ShtetlSeeker has transformed *Where Once We Walked* into a free on-line database. Place names can be searched using either exact spelling or a Daitch-Mokotoff Soundex System algorithm. Latitude and longitude, along with direction and distance from the country's capital city, will be displayed. Neither alternate names nor source codes are displayed, but clicking on the coordinate display will generate a map centered on the town. The entire database covering 24 countries can be searched at once or specific countries can be selected. Because of being able to search all of the countries at the same time and the flexibility of the soundex system, the ShtetlSeeker can give more extensive results than the same basic data found in the GEOnet Names Server. ShtetlSeeker, or its paper counterpart *Where Once We Walked,* should be on the required resource list for anyone doing family or historical research centered on central and eastern Europe.

NATIONAL AND STATE GAZETTEERS

Geographic Names Information System (http://geo names.usgs.gov/index.html)

The Geographic Names Information System (GNIS) database is available at no charge through the Web. Data for place and feature names for all 50 states, the District of Columbia, U.S. territories, and Antarctica are included. Some states' data were also printed by the USGS as part of Professional Paper 1200 during the 1970s and 1980s. GNIS is described in the United States Geological Survey's "Data Users Guide 6," *Geographic Names Information System,* which is available in print and on the Web (http://mapping. usgs.gov/www/ti/GNIS/gnis_users_guide_toc.html). The system includes four databases: National Geographic Names Data Base (NGNDB), Antarctica Geographic Names Data Base (AGNDB), National Topographic Names Data Base (NTMNDB), and a Reference Data Base (RDB). The NGNDB includes nearly 2 million place names for all sorts of features including towns, rivers, mountains, glaciers, and in some cases specific buildings. The database was compiled in two phases. The first phase of gleaning place names from USGS 7.5-minute topographic quadrangles, Forest Service maps, NOAA nautical charts, and from other federal geographic data sources is complete for all states and territories. The second phase, enhancing and expanding the data collected during phase one by collecting current and historical place names from state and local documents, was complete in July 2002 for 35 states or territories with 11 others having begun. The feature name records fields include: official name; feature type; status of name; state and county in which the feature is located; geographic, and if appropriate source, coordinates in degrees, minutes, and seconds; and source of name. Other fields such as elevation and name history, along with variant names, might also be included.

At the GNIS Web page, users will need to choose between searching the U.S. states and territories database or the Antarctica database. Both databases are searched by completing a form with entry boxes for feature name, state or territory name, feature type, elevation range, county name, population range, and 7.5-minute topographic quadrangle name. The fields for state name and feature type are pick-list driven but all other fields are free-text. After filling in the search boxes and clicking on "send query," a table of features that match the search criteria will be displayed. The table will include official name, state, county, feature type, latitude and longitude, and the name of a 7.5-minute topographic map that includes the feature. Fuller information can be displayed by clicking on the feature name. The fuller information includes variant names, history, additional 7.5-minute maps covering the feature, and links to additional Web resources. Digital raster graphics (DRGs) and digital orthophotoquads (DOQs) showing the feature are available for viewing through Terraserver, general maps of the region produced through the Bureau of the Census's TIGER Map Server can be generated and zoomed in on, and information about the local watershed can be displayed through the Environmental Protection Agency's Surf Your Watershed Web site.

GNIS data can be downloaded via an anonymous FTP site. Data for individual states can be downloaded as well as four "thematic extracts." Each state or territory has two files listing feature names, one in columnar record format and the other in comma or quote delimited format. The data contained in the two files is identical. The four thematic extract files cross state boundaries. Populated places lists information about all cities, towns, and other kinds of smaller populated places. The concise file contains information about large features, both physical and cultural. The historical file describes features that no longer exist; these features will be marked "(historical)" in the entry. The Antarctica file includes only place names on the continent of Antarctica that have been approved for federal government use. The FTP files are updated daily as the phase two enhancement proceeds.

U.S. Census Bureau U.S. Gazetteer (http://www. census.gov/cgi-bin/gazetteer)

The Census Bureau's gazetteer is a much smaller data set than GNIS; it includes only incorporated places, counties, and county subdivisions such as townships. The database is searchable by place name or zip code. The initial results will include the place name and feature type, 1990 population, location in decimal degrees, zip code(s), and links to a TIGER map and the STF1A and STF3A tables for the area. The maps can be zoomed and panned and a variety of labels can be applied. The maps can also be downloaded as GIF images. The statistical tables allow the user to select data categories that can be displayed on the screen or downloaded for manipulation in statistical packages. The place name and zip code files that the application searches can also be viewed on-line and FTPed from the Web site as compressed files. The Census Bureau's product, although not as rich in place and feature names as GNIS, is a quick place to check for geographic coordinates and potential zip codes. Its true utility is as a gateway into deccenial census statistics.

Many states have available individually published gazetteers produced by state government agencies, historical and geographical societies, or university presses. These will vary greatly in age, comprehensiveness, and trustworthiness. Atlases with a single-state focus, in particular those that are primarily atlases of topographic maps, will also include gazetteer/index sections but normally only to populated places.

Army Map Service/Board on Geographic Names
  Gazetteers

The Army Map Service gazetteers were an outcome of the United States's entry into the Second World War and its increasing role in international affairs. Originally, the gazetteers indexed place names found on specific map sets such as the 1:500,000-scale set of Melanesia or the 1:100,000-scale sets for France. All of the earliest gazetteers were for places in the Pacific and European theatres. The volumes tended to be fairly small and straightforward; sometimes just a list of place names with an indication of the map sheet and location on the map sheet. Others include slightly expanded entries: name, feature type, administrative area, grid reference, and geographic coordinates. After the war, the program expanded to encompass the entire world, and the gazetteers were not as firmly tied to specific topographic map sets. The postwar gazetteers follow a standard format. They are all subtitled "Official Standard Names Gazetteer." Most include a black-and-white base map along with a foreword that describes the sources consulted to create the list of names and information on how to interpret the entries along with a glossary of generic terms, a code list of administrative areas, and a definition list of feature types. If necessary, the transliteration system used is also included. The entries include place name, designation or feature type, latitude and longitude to the nearest minute, and a code for the administrative area. Older volumes in the series also include a reference code for the map set that the name was drawn from. A listing of the BGN gazetteers available

for sale is available on the Web (http://mac.usgs.gov/mac/nimamaps/bgn.html). The publication dates of the catalogs available for sale vary between 1950 and 1998 and range in price from $5.00 to $295.00 per volume. Some countries require multiple volumes and can cost well over $500.00 for complete coverage. The seven-volume 1970 gazetteer of the Soviet Union will cost $1,535.00 in its entirety. With the availability of the cost-free GEOnet Names Server through the Web, there may be little reason for the AMS/BGN gazetteers to be purchased by individuals. Most major map collections and federal government depositories should have the volumes available for use. While they are becoming dated, the paper gazetteers still have some utility because it continues to be easier to browse a list of possible place names printed on paper than it is to browse a list of place names on the computer, especially if the exact spelling is not certain.

The Board on Geographic Names and the GEOnet Names Server are not the only options for non-U.S. place names. Many national governments publish national-level gazetteers. A number are available through the Web at the previously mentioned Oddens' Bookmarks gazetteer site.

OLDER GAZETTEERS

Older gazetteers are valuable for areas of historically fluid borders—especially eastern Europe—and are often used intensively for genealogical work.

Gazetteer of the World (1856)

This seven-volume gazetteer, edited by a member of the Royal Geographical Society, is similar to the *Columbia Gazetteer* in that its nearly 100,000 articles vary in length; some are just a few lines while others are as long as 25 pages. Woodcuts and steel engravings illustrate a number of the articles. The illustrations are of cities, localities, or natural objects that were deemed important in themselves or that had historical significance. The introductory material states that the illustrations are in styles imitating the prominent artists of the day. Maps also accompany some of the articles; some are full page, others embedded in the text. Many are keyed to the text so that the description can be read and the specific place located on the map. The information presented in the articles was drawn from "researches of recent travellers" and other original authorities. The articles may include descriptions of physical geography; political/statistical geography; "positions of place" (latitude, longitude, elevation); hydrography; orthography according to a "uniform system," especially for Oriental and African names; and ethnography. The seventh volume concludes with four appendices, including two that crosswalk between ancient and modern place names. The *Gazetteer* was designed for a British audience with prominent treatment of Britain and the British colonies along with former colonies and is a clear reflection of its time of creation and the attitudes of its creators. A number of opinions about people and places are expressed which at the beginning of the third millennium would not be considered appropriate for publication by a reputable scientific publisher. The *Gazetteer* makes for interesting reading and comparison to physical, social, and economic situations 150 years after its publication.

Older atlases that include place name indexes also are useful for finding noncontemporary names for locations and larger regions. The index in the back of *Stieler's Hand Atlas* is particularly valuable for place names in Eastern Europe late in the nineteenth and early in the twentieth century. From the first edition, published in 1817, to the 10th centenary edition, published in 1925, the atlas quadrupled the number of maps it contained. Generally, those published prior to 1890 lack an index. The indexes in the later editions are extensive, the 10th edition of 1925 has over 320,000 place names in its index, and reflect the times during which the atlases were produced, making them invaluable for tracing national and internal boundaries and for finding locations that no longer exist.

SPECIALTY GAZETTEERS

There will be many occasions when gazetteers that reflect the current political or toponymical situations are not appropriate. Gazetteers that focus on countries that no longer exist or on naming practices of minority peoples can help track down place names no longer remembered or rarely heard.

Dead Countries of the Nineteenth and Twentieth Centuries: Aden to Zululand

Dead Countries could be considered a dictionary gazetteer; the scope of the places included and their descriptions are quite limited. Although *Dead Countries* was written to supply philatelists with basic information about countries, colonies, and principalities that no longer exist but which had issued postal stamps during their existence, it contains information that may be useful to someone trying to locate or confirm the existence of a state. In order to be included, a place has to have had some kind of distinctive political

identity or independence that has since been lost. Some countries are included because of an identity loss due to a name change.

Dead Countries is arranged alphabetically into 15 subcontinental chapters containing 429 entries. Each chapter includes a map identifying where the defunct countries were located. The entries nearly all begin with an appropriate quotation and basic statistical information, area, capital, and population. This is followed by a paragraph or two describing the country's history, which often includes information on discovery and exploration, native or ethnic groups occupying the area, imperial claims and military campaign, and eventual absorption by another entity or other change to create the dead-country status. All of the entries are followed by citations to source material in the volume's bibliography.

Genealogists will find *Dead Countries* especially useful when tracing eastern and central European family members' locations during the nineteenth century. Prior to the two world wars, this region was comprised of many small principalities and duchies that eventually were united to form Prussia and the Austro-Hungarian Empire. These small areas no longer had autonomy with the creation of new nations after the First World War. Reallocations and the shuffling of boundaries before and after the Second World War have further confused ancient, or merely old, country identities.

For other regions of the world, *Dead Countries* provides a foundation to understanding how states and territories became bound together to form the nations we are familiar with early in the twenty-first century. The chapter on India and Central Asia includes the largest number of entries at 63, many of which help trace the incorporation of princely and feudatory states into the country of India. The five chapters on Africa trace the many holdings European imperial powers had in Africa prior to most of the current countries becoming independent in the 1950s and 1960s. Because of the large number of countries involved it would be difficult to create a map of the numerous changes of which *Dead Countries* gives an initial explanation.

Place-Name Changes, 1900–1991

Because of two world wars, innumerable local conflicts, and the disbanding of the great empires, place names changed throughout the twentieth century. Sometimes these changes were chronologically grouped immediately after a change in government or national structure such as the dissolution of the Soviet

Union. Other changes have occurred more gradually as local inhabitants establish local control more firmly. *Place-Name Changes, 1900–1991* attempts to track over 4,500 place name renamings, both official and unofficial. The changes documented may have occurred for a number of reasons: conquest, correction, change of official title, and occasionally spelling. Five kinds of situations are specifically not included in *Place-Name Changes:* alternate spellings, alternate names in different languages, new names for new territory configurations, new names created by merging of territories, and specialized or restricted-use renaming. Entries and cross-references are arranged in alphabetical order. Each entry has five parts: present name, type of place, location, former names, and years of renaming. The present name is the version that appears in standard name reference works such as the *Columbia-Lippincott World Gazetteer.* Many of the entries include a state or country as a location or a compass quadrant indicator, for example, northwestern Iraq. Former names are given in their standard English spellings, and if a place has been renamed more than once, the names are listed in chronological order. Places that no longer exist are marked with a dagger; place names that are being used for the first time are marked with an asterisk. All former names are cross-referenced to the current name. *Place-Name Changes* also includes a list, to 1993, of official country names and a bibliography of the resources used to compile the work.

Although there is sure to be overlap with *Where Once We Walked, Place-Name Changes* covers the entire world, not just an in-depth view of central and eastern Europe. *Place-Name Changes* includes an entry for the change from Upper Volta to Burkina, from Burma to Myanmar, and from Mount McKinley National Park to Denali National Park. The information in *Place-Name Changes* will help establish dates for documents and maps. But it will not help uncover why changes were made.

GeoNative (http://www.geocities.com/Athens/9479/welcome.html)

Ethnic place names can be important to help solidify a group identity. The GeoNative Web site has been up since 1996, a labor of love compiled by an ethnic Basque living in the Spanish part of the Basque Country. The premise of the Web site is that ethnic enclaves have names for places that are not used, recognized, or reflected in the language of the controlling ethnic or governmental group. More than 230 languages or dialects are included in the site. Tables list official place names with ethnic or local names within regions or countries and cover countries worldwide. There is a table of names in both English and Welsh for places in Wales and a table of French and corresponding Wolof place names for Senegal. The North American tables reflect "first peoples" naming practices and include tables for very specific areas (individual states) and specific tribes and tribal language groups. Some of the tables are surprising because they reflect not the original ethnic inhabitants but minority enclaves which are remnants of "colonization" by other groups such as Germans in the former Yugoslavia, Poland, or Russia. Also included are the beginnings of lists of place names in the former Soviet Union that have been changed from their Communist-based names, often back to an older name. This site has a lot to offer to the curious. But it also will serve genealogists and historians along with ethnic scholars.

GOVERNMENT PLACE NAME AGENCIES

Governmental agencies are instrumental in place name identification and in creating tools to list or inventory place names.

United States Board on Geographic Names (http://mapping.usgs.gov/www/gnis/bgn.html)

The United States Board on Geographic Names (BGN) is responsible for establishing and maintaining the list of place names used by U.S. federal agencies. By default, these names become the names used at state and local levels because of heavy reliance on U.S. federal cartographic products such as topographic quadrangles and nautical and aeronautical charts. The board is an interagency organization with representatives from departments and agencies that have an interest in, or need to use, geographic names. Departments represented include: Agriculture, Commerce, Defense, Interior, and State. Other agencies include the Central Intelligence Agency, the Government Printing Office, the Library of Congress, and the Postal Service. Each of these organizations produces, organizes, or is heavily reliant on geographic information, including place name data.

The board is organized into two primary decision-making committees, the Domestic Names Committee (DNC) and the Foreign Names Committee (FNC). Two special advisory committees also exist, one for undersea features and the other for Antarctica. These committees do not actually name features; they confirm and standardize place name use for specific locations working in different fashions.

The Domestic Names Committee reacts to and approves proposals from state and local agencies for new names and name changes at monthly meetings. Domestic naming in the United States is a grassroots, or bottom-up, activity. All of the states have their own boards on geographic names or agencies that include geographic names as part of their mission and work closely with the federal board. Names are typically funneled through county or state agencies to the board, garnering local support for proposed names. Strong local support is especially critical for commemorative name proposals. The Domestic Names Committee tests proposed names against five principles:

- The Roman alphabet is used as normally employed in the English language.
- Precedence is given to names in local usage.
- Names established by Act of Congress are official by law.
- Names of political subdivisions, bounded areas of administration, structures, and establishments—as determined by the appropriate, responsible public or private authorities—normally are recognized as official.
- One name, one spelling, and one application are authorized for each geographic entity.

The principles are further refined and defined by a number of policies that can be found in *Principles, Policies, and Procedures: Domestic Geographic Names* or at the portion of the USGS National Mapping Division's Web site devoted to the GNIS (http://mapping.usgs.gov/www/gnis/pppdgn.html). If a name meets the criteria, it will be approved and eventually will appear in products produced by the federal government, including maps, state-level gazetteers, and the Geographic Names Information System (GNIS). If a name is not approved it will not appear in federal products, but that does not preclude its use at state and local levels. Decisions are published annually in *Decisions on Geographic Names in the United States.*

The Foreign Names Committee is responsible for monitoring place name use outside of the United States and its territories. The committee does not actually name foreign locations; it assists the federal government by maintaining a list of standard names for all government agencies to use. Thus, the committee ensures that Moscow, not Moskova, is used by federal officials and documents. The Foreign Names Committee reacts to foreign events, searching out documents to support the use of names and attempting to confirm

changes and create a complete picture of an area's toponomy. The Foreign Names Committee also maintains official systems for the transliteration of non-Roman alphabets and characters such as Russian and Chinese. The database maintained by the United States Board on Geographic Names' Foreign Names Committee has been published as a series of national- and regional-level gazetteers and in the GEOnet Names Server. Recommendations and decisions are published in the *Foreign Names Information Bulletins,* available through the Web (http://www.nima.mil/gns/html/fnibs.html).

The Foreign Names Committee has traditionally worked closely with the Permanent Committee on Geographical Names for Official British Use and the Canadian Permanent Committee on Geographical Names. One of the products of collaboration with the British Permanent Committee was the 1994 publication of *Romanization Systems and Roman-Script Spelling Conventions,* which illustrates how 30 non-Roman script languages are to be Romanized. It also contains Roman-script spellings for some non-U.S. geographic names that are commonly written in non-Roman scripts. Besides Russian, the character sets include a number of eastern European and Asian scripts such as Bulgarian, Chinese, Greek, Hebrew, and Thai.

United Nations Group of Experts on Geographical Names (UNGEGN)

The United States Board on Geographic Names has also played a leading role in the United Nations Group of Experts on Geographical Names (UNGEGN), which meets every two years. Since 1967, eight conferences on geographic names have been hosted by the United Nations on a five-year schedule. Conference reports and technical papers are prepared for publication. One of the reasons the Foreign Names Committee plays a leadership role in cooperative work through the United Nations is that most countries do not have a formally recognized and dedicated place name authority similar to the BGN's Domestic Names Committee. Sometimes this work implicitly falls to a national mapping agency, but often there are many agencies assigning or regulating place names and their decisions do not always agree.

UNGEGN serves an advisory and facilitative role in the world of place name regulation. It promotes the work of national-level place name agencies and communication between national agencies. It does not mandate or prescribe any names but has developed principles to assist in name standardization by national agencies. UNGEGN assists countries in establishing place name agencies by supplying technical expertise and experience. Many of UNGEGN's tasks are educational. Information about the United Nations and geographical names is hosted on the Web by the Statistics Division of the United Nations Department of Economic and Social Affairs (http://unstats.un. org/unsd/geoinfo/default.htm). A brochure about UNGEGN can be downloaded from the United Nations Web site (http://www.un.org/Depts/Carto graphic/english/geoinfo/ungegn.pdf).

PLACE NAME RESOURCES

Place Names: How They Define the World—And More

The author of *Place Names,* Richard Randall, draws upon more than 20 years of experience with federal and international name agencies. Twenty chapters are grouped into six parts: The Nature of a Place Name; How Place Names Affect Us; Place Names Are Not Permanent; Efforts to End the Confusion; U.S. and International Names Programs during and after the Cold War; and Interesting and Unusual Names. Randall discusses what place names are, how maps are meaningless without place names, and place names used in commercial and social contexts. The most substantial portion of the book describes national and international work to standardize place name use and the agencies or organizations that focus or depend on standardized place names. The volume concludes with many appendices that serve as examples of results from gazetteers, procedures, and non-Roman scripts. Appendix I and Appendix J are especially valuable because they include access points for BGN-created data and sources for place name information. There also is a bibliography of cited sources and a brief list of other useful published sources.

Place Names will be a quick read; many of the chapters are brief and could be finished in a single sitting. Briefness should not be construed as being incomplete. Randall gets to the point quickly, with numerous illustrative and understandable examples. While *Place Names* will not be necessary for genealogists to read, it should be on hand for anyone needing to understand relationships among twentieth-century place name agencies.

Geographic Names & the Federal Government: A Bibliography

Geographic Names is the first time that a comprehensive listing of BGN publications has been compiled. The bibliography was prepared as part of the BGN's centennial celebration by reviewing the holdings of library collections at the (then) Defense Mapping Agency, the United States Geological Survey, the Library of Congress, and the National Archives. In addition to the listing of BGN publications, there is a selective list of place-name-related publications produced by BGN member agencies. The bibliography has three main sections: General BGN Publications (1890–1990); BGN Foreign Gazetteers (1943–1990); and Federal Agency Publications, Selected List. Many of the nearly 600 entries include short annotations, or like entries are grouped and preceded by explanatory text. The volume concludes with three indexes: authors, titles and place names. *Geographic Names* will be useful for exploring the BGN's history and publication patterns. It can also be used to track down older gazetteers and works on place name decision making.

Bibliography of Place-Name Literature: United States and Canada. 3rd ed.

This bibliography includes citations to journal and magazine articles about place names, including their history, distribution through the U.S. and Canadian landscapes, and how they weave their way into all facets of everyday life. Some of the articles focus on the derivation of a name of a single place while others discuss place names in a county, along a railroad line, or throughout a multistate region. The entries are divided into two major groups, United States and Canada, which are further divided into general sections and then alphabetically ordered sections of states or provinces. Some of the entries include brief annotations. Citations for gazetteers are included but most of the nation-level gazetteers are eighteenth- or nineteenth-century publications. The few state-level gazetteers that are included in the bibliography are also older, often reprints, not newer works. A few county-level place name lists are also included, many of which were published as a magazine or journal article or master's thesis. Two indexes are included: one for author and personal names, which also includes entries for corporations such as the National Geographic Society and government agencies, and the other for subjects. The utility of this work is the access it provides to older literature about place names. Newer articles can be accessed through online indexing services such as Geobase and America: History and Life. The sections that include the older national-level gazetteers can almost be used as checklists.

Gazetteers and Glossaries of Geographical Names of the Member-Countries of the United Nations and the Agencies in Relationship with the United Nations: Bibliography, 1946–1976

Gazetteers and Glossaries covers gazetteer production during a period of great change when the status of many countries was changing from colony to independent nation. The work is divided into five parts: lists of country and territory names; world, continental, regional, and oceanic gazetteers; country gazetteers; appendices; and supplemental lists of gazetteers being published from 1977 to 1982. The entries under each geographic region generally are divided by the kind of producing agency or publisher, international agency, national-level governmental agencies, and private individuals or companies. The country entries are divided into six different categories including official publications of the country, unofficial publications produced in the country, publications of other governments, publications of private individuals from other countries, indexes of atlases or maps produced by the country, and indexes of atlases or maps produced by other countries. This organizational scheme may seem redundant for entries that are easily read by English readers. Its real utility lies in assisting the user in determining what the official and unofficial publications are for countries where the language may be less accessible. Like all lists of this kind, *Gazetteers and Glossaries* is dated. Its contents can be supplemented by searching bibliographic utilities such as OCLC's WorldCat for gazetteers published after 1976 using *Gazetteers and Glossaries* as a guide to potential publishers.

American Name Society (http//:www.wtsn.binghamton. edu/ans)

The American Name Society was founded in 1951 to encourage the study of names, including place names. A section of the American Name Society, the Toponymy Interest Group—formerly the Place Name Survey of the United States (PLANSUS)—is specifically devoted to place name studies. Its members work closely with the BGN and UNGEGN to promote place name research methods and to distribute the results of place name research. Information about the interest group, including the roster of current officers is available through the Web (http://www.wtsn.binghamton. edu/plansus/). The society meets annually, and there are smaller regional meetings. Three publications are produced by the society: the *ANS Bulletin,* with current events and organization information (3 times per year); the *Ehrensperger Report,* which lists name research activities undertaken by members during the previous year, appears each December; and the quarterly journal *Names: A Journal of Onomastics. Names's* authors come from a number of different disciplines, including geography, history, librarianship, and sociology. Slightly less than one-quarter of its articles are on geographical place names, and occasionally special issues are devoted only to place names.

The importance of place names cannot be underestimated. Names demarcate territory, boundaries, and spheres of influence. They give us a means of navigation, a method of marking the extent of human knowledge, and a memorial to the aspirations and accomplishments of our predecessors. Without place names, maps are meaningless.

BIBLIOGRAPHY

ANS Bulletin. Binghamton, N.Y.: American Name Society. 3 per year.

Bibliography of Place-Name Literature: United States and Canada. 3rd ed. Richard B. Sealock, Margaret M. Sealock, and Margaret S. Powell. Chicago: American Library Association, 1982. ISBN: 0-8389-0360-6. On-demand printing: ISBN: 0-598-34913-8.

The Columbia Gazetteer of the World. 3 vols. Saul B. Cohen, ed. New York: Columbia University Press, 1998. ISBN: 0-231-11040-5.

The Columbia-Lippincott Gazetteer of the World. Leon E. Seltzer, ed. Morningside Heights, N.Y.: Columbia University Press, by arrangement with J.B. Lippincott Co., 1952.

Dead Countries of the Nineteenth and Twentieth Centuries: Aden to Zululand. Les Harding. Lanham, Md.: Scarecrow Press, 1998. ISBN: 0-8108-3445-6.

Decisions on Geographic Names in the United States. U.S. Board on Geographic Names. Washington, D.C.: U.S. Dept. of the Interior, 1963– . Annual. ISSN: 0363-6828.

Ehrensperger Report. Binghampton, N.Y.: American Name Society. Annual.

A Gazetteer of the World or Dictionary of Geographical Knowledge compiled from the most recent authorities, and forming a complete body of modern geography, physical, political, statistical, historical, and ethnographical. Edinburgh: A. Fullarton, 1856.

Gazetteers and Glossaries of Geographical Names of the Member-Countries of the United Nations and the Agencies in Relationship with the United Nations: Bibliography, 1946–1976. Emil Meynen. Wiesbaden: Franz Steiner, 1984. ISBN: 3-515-04036-6.

Geographic Names & the Federal Government: A Bibliography. Donald J. Orth. Washington, D.C.: Geography and Map Division, Library of Congress, 1990.

Geographic Names Information System. Data Users Guide 6. Roger L. Payne. Reston, Va.: U.S. Geological Survey, 1995.

Lippincott's Pronouncing Gazetteer. Joseph Thomas. Philadelphia: J.B. Lippincott, 1855.

Merriam-Webster's Geographical Dictionary. 3rd. ed., rev. Springfield, Mass.: Merriam-Webster, 1997. ISBN: 0-87779-546-0.

Names: A Journal of Onomastics. Potsdam, N.Y.: State University College, 1953– . Quarterly. ISSN: 0027-7738.

The Oxford Essential Geographical Dictionary. American ed. New York: Berkley Books, 1999. ISBN: 0-425-16994-4.

The Penguin Encyclopedia of Places. 3rd ed. John Paxton. London: Penguin Books, 1999. ISBN: 0-14-051275-6.

Place-Name Changes, 1900–1991. Adrian Room, comp. Methuchen, N.J.: Scarecrow, 1993. ISBN: 0-8108-2600-3.

Place Names: How They Define the World—And More. Richard R. Randall. Lanham, Md.: Scarecrow Press, 2001. ISBN: 0-8108-3906-7.

Principles, Policies and Procedures: Domestic Geographic Names. Donald J. Orth. Reston, Va.: United States Board on Geographic Names, 1989.

Romanization Systems and Roman-Script Spelling Conventions. U.S. Board on Geographic Names, Foreign Names Committee Staff. Fairfax, Va.: Defense Mapping Agency, 1994.

Stielers Hand-Atlas. Adolf Stieler. Gotha, Germany: Justus Perthes' Geographical Institute, 1925.

Where Once We Walked: A Guide to the Jewish Communities Destroyed in the Holocaust. Gary Mokotoff and Sallyann Amdur Sack. Teaneck, N.J.: Avotaynu, 1991. ISBN: 0-9626373-1-9.

On-line References

Alexandria Digital Library Gazetteer Server. Alexandria Digital Library, 31 May 2002. <http://fat-albert.alexandria.ucsb.edu:8827/gazetteer/> (14 October 2003).

American Name Society. Home page. Michael F. McGoff. ANS, 28 August 2003. <http://www.wtsn.binghamton.edu/ans/> (14 October 2003).

"BGN Gazetteers and Publications." U.S. Geological Survey, 31 December 2002. <http://mac.usgs.gov/mac/nimamaps/bgn.html> (14 October 2003).

Columbia Gazetteer of the World. Columbia University Press, 2003. <http://www.columbiagazetteer.org> (14 October 2003).

"Consistent Use of Place Names." United Nations Group of Experts on Geographic Names (UNGEGN), 1999. United Nations Cartographic Section. <http://www.un.org/Depts/Cartographic/english/geoinfo/ungegn.pdf> (14 October 2003).

Foreign Names Information Bulletins. 1992– . U.S. Board on Geographic Names, Foreign Names Committee. National Imagery and Mapping Agency, 14 August 2002. <http://www.nima.mil/gns/html/fnibs.html> (14 October 2003).

"Gazetteers." *Oddens' Bookmarks: The Fascinating World of Maps and Mapping.* Utrecht University. February 2002. <http://oddens.geog.uu.nl/browsepages/Gazetteers.html> (14 October 2003).

Geographic Names Information System. Data Users Guide 6. <http://mapping.usgs.gov/www/ti/GNIS/gnis_users_guide_toc.html> (14 October 2003).

Geographic Names Information System (GNIS). Developed by the USGS and the U.S. Board on Geographic Names (BGN). U.S. Geological Survey, 30 July 2003. <http://geonames.usgs.gov/index.html> (14 October 2003).

GeoNative. Luistxo Fernandez. 16 December 1999. <http://www.geocities.com/Athens/9479/welcome.html> (14 October 2003).

GEOnet Names Server. National Imagery and Mapping Agency (NIMA), 10 October 2003. <http://164.214.2.59/gns/html/index.html> (14 October 2003).

Getty Thesaurus of Geographic Names. J. Paul Getty Trust, 29 September 2003. <http://www.getty.edu/research/conducting_research/vocabularies/tgn/index.html> (14 October 2003).

Global Gazetteer. Falling Rain Genomics, 7 June 2002. <http://www.calle.com/world/> (14 October 2003).

The JewishGen ShtetlSeeker. JewishGen, Inc., 3 January 2003. <http://www.jewishgen.org/ShtetlSeeker/> (14 October 2003).

Official Standard Names Gazetteer. Various eds. Main title after the subject country, e.g.: *Denmark: Official Standard Names Gazetteer.* Washington, D.C.: U.S. Board of Geographic Names, 1943–1998.

"Place Name Servers on the Internet." Linda Zellmer. Arizona State University Map Collection, 29 August 2003. <http://www.asu.edu/lib/hayden/govdocs/maps/geogname.htm> (14 October 2003).

Principles, Policies, and Procedures: Domestic Geographic Names. On-line ed. Donald J. Orth and Roger L. Payne. Board on Geographic Names (BGN), U.S. Geological Survey, 29 December 1998. <http://mapping.usgs.gov/www/gnis/pppdgn.html> (14 October 2003).

Toponymy Interest Group of the American Name Society. 19 January 2003. <http://www.wtsn.binghamton.edu/plansus/> (14 October 2003).

United States Board on Geographic Names. U.S. Geological Survey, 4 January 2001.<http://mapping.usgs.gov/www/gnis/bgn.html> (14 October 2003).

U.S. Gazetteer. U.S. Census Bureau. Information from 1990 census. <http://www.census.gov/cgi-bin/gazetteer> (14 October 2003).

CHAPTER 5
Earth's Ups and Downs

Maps showing mountains were created as early as 3800 B.C. Relief, the shape of the land, has been depicted using a number of techniques, including pictures, landform drawings, hachures, shading, hypsometric tints, and isolines. Isolines on maps of the Earth's surface are called *contours,* and those showing the depths of water bodies are called *isobaths.* Although isolines began to be used sometime between the late sixteenth and the early eighteenth centuries, they were not extensively used on maps until the mid-nineteenth century. In the twentieth century, national surveys have made contours the preferred method of relief depiction.

Maps that show details of the land's surface form through contours are usually referred to as topographic maps because of their place (*topo-*) description (*-graphy*) attributes. Topographic maps show landforms and cultural features; they may also show bathymetry. Annually, national mapping agencies produce more topographic quadrangles than any other kind of map. Topographic quadrangles are individual map sheets that meet established accuracy standards, follow an established format and geographic coverage pattern (often a regular grid pattern), and together as an entire set provide cartographic coverage for a defined area such as a state or a country. Topographic maps have a widescale range, but even though they may be included on less detailed map, contours generally do not have much functionality on maps at scales smaller than 1:250,000.

Topographic maps could be considered general or reference maps because the kinds of information that they display is so varied. The uses for topographic maps also vary widely including: general landform studies; projecting of possible flood extents or plotting the potential pathways for the movement of volcanic mud flows; locating botanical specimen collection sites; discovering abandoned country schools and private family cemeteries; and hiking and camping. Topographic maps are often used as base maps for other kinds of data. Geologic and land use or land cover data can be mapped on top of a topographic base by government agencies as can data about hydrographic or drainage basins, 100-year flood plains, and soils. Individual researchers or private firms might elect to map information about phenomena such as land ownership, tree species, zoning, point-source pollution, and biking routes over topographic data. The topography recedes into the background and serves as a context for the data that is mapped over it. Topographic maps also provide base information for raised relief maps, three-dimensional representations of portions of the Earth's surface.

HISTORY OF TOPOGRAPHIC MAPPING

Changes in surveying and printing techniques, as well as colonial and military activities, are important to keep in mind when looking for and reading information about topographic maps. Changes in techniques influenced the kind of data collected and depicted. Military and colonizing activities influenced data collection and product format, along with publication availability, and also often established or influenced the agencies that would continue to be responsible for creating maps long after countries gained their independence from colonial powers. Information about the development of topographic mapping techniques and surveys is scattered through a number of different resources. Some journal titles to consider checking for information on the history of topographic mapping, in particular pre-twentieth-century developments, include *Imago Mundi, Mercator's World, Cartographica, The Cartographic Journal,* and *International Yearbook of Cartography.* The first chapter of *Cartographic Relief Presentation,* "Historical Developments," quickly surveys and illustrates a number of different techniques used to show relief, including molehills, fish scales, hachures, shading, and isobars. The chapter also includes a brief description of how changes in printing technologies impacted relief representation methods. There is very little discussion of specific national agencies. *Topographic Mapping of the Americas, Australia, and New Zealand* includes a two-chapter survey, with extensive references, of the development of topographic mapping methods. In the first chapter of the same title, a number of definitions of topographic maps are collected and common relief depiction techniques are described.

A recent report of the International Cartographic Association (ICA) Commission on the History of Cartography (ICA-CHC) to the ICA executive committee indicated that a small group is working on compiling a bibliography or guide to the history of national mapping organizations (http://www.stub.unibe.ch/ica-chc/reports/icaexec-2000.html). The bibliography is expected to be completed in 2003. This kind of work is important because, historically, most topographic maps have been produced under the auspices of national mapping agencies.

GENERAL STYLE SIMILARITIES AND DIFFERENCES

Although topographic quadrangles produced by different mapping agencies obviously have the same underlying purpose of showing a portion of the Earth's surface, they will differ in appearance as well as scale and size of area covered. Over time, many mapping agencies have developed a graphic style by consistently and constantly using the same line weights, type faces, color schemes, and pictorial symbols on most or all of their cartographic products. The consistencies will assist in building map-reading confidence because once an agency's set of symbols has been correctly decoded they will only need to be remembered—a new set of symbols will not need to be learned for each sheet in a topographic map set. Generally, although the shades may differ, green stands for vegetation and blue for water. Contour lines could be brown, black, or orange, and because they are isolines, they will never cross. Urban areas will look congested with many intersecting lines; some urban area depictions will include indications of many individual structures while others will only show large buildings, but the intersecting lines representing the basic street pattern will still be present. Topographic map readers should be able to transfer their experiences with one agency's products into being able to use most of the similar products produced by other mapping agencies.

THE IMPORTANCE OF A GOOD INDEX

The importance of index maps cannot be overemphasized. Without an index, maps in topographic as well as other kinds of sets are inaccessible. A map index does the same job as the index in the back of a book, but instead of listing page numbers where a particular topic is discussed, the map index graphically shows the name or, more commonly, the number of the map sheet that covers a particular geographic region. Each map set should have an index. Indexes go beyond indicating which map covers which area. Indexes can also be used to determine the designations for maps of adjoining areas, to show relationships between maps of different scales that cover the same or overlapping areas, and can even be used to track the progress being made toward complete cartographic coverage. Index maps are necessary for ordering topographic maps from dealers or for pulling maps from map library collections because catalog item numbers and filing sequences are often based on the topographic maps' names or numbers as shown on the index map.

Indexes generally are available from map producers and map vendors. They usually are on paper, but some agencies and dealers, along with some map libraries, are beginning to scan set indexes and make them available through the Web. Large sets will usually have an index published on a separate piece of paper. Smaller sets sometimes include an index as part of the information found in each map's collar or margin. Occasionally, maps that are part of a large set will include in their margin a partial index, sometimes referred to as a location diagram, that places a specific sheet into the context of the surrounding map sheets. In addition to individual index maps, there are a number of books that emphasize indexes: *Inventory of World Topographic Mapping; World Mapping Today;* and *Map Index to Topographic Quadrangles of the United States, 1882–1940.*

WHAT'S AVAILABLE FOR WHERE?

One of the most important things to remember about topographic maps is that the existence of maps covering the United States at 1:24,000 does not mean that the same product, or even similar products, will be available elsewhere. Each nation sets its own mapping priorities and projects and determines its own policies on access and acquisitions. Canada and Mexico are not part of the United States; they do not produce 1:24,000-scale topographic maps. The United States is unusual in the large-scale map coverage that is easily available for purchase without obtaining government permission and clearances. There are a number of countries, India being a notable example, that do not allow official purchase of topographic maps for coastal or border areas. Some countries will not permit the export or sale of maps with scales larger than 1:1,000,000. Finding out what might be available for purchase or review can be difficult. Fortunately, there is a small group of publications devoted to describing the history of mapping on a nation-by-nation basis

and listing the kinds of materials that were produced and could possibly be purchased.

Inventory of World Topographic Mapping

The *Inventory of World Topographic Mapping* is a neutrally compiled, detailed three-volume work describing topographic mapping country-by-country for the entire world. Countries are grouped into volumes by continent: volume 1—Western Europe, North America, and Australasia; volume 2—South America, Central America, and Africa; volume 3—Eastern Europe, Asia, Oceania, and Antarctica. Each country's entry follows the same pattern: the national mapping organization's name both in English and the native language and script if appropriate; a brief history of topographic mapping of the country; geodetic data for projections and ellipsoids commonly used; a list of map scales and series; a bibliography; and small samples from map series and indexes. While the entries follow the same general pattern because of information availability, levels of mapping activity, and agency cooperation, they are in no way all the same length. According to the third volume's introductory material, only four countries (Libya, Saudi Arabia, Malaysia, and Turkey) did not respond to the compiler's request for responses to drafts of country descriptions. These countries are included but the sections have not been checked or updated by the national agencies responsible for creating or distributing many of the maps described.

The "History in Brief" included in each country's section can be very important for understanding what agencies and other countries have played a role in creating topographic maps for the country of interest. Some nations still do not have vigorous national mapping programs, and the historical description will lead to the discovery of topographic maps produced by former colonial powers or countries with influence over a region along with helping to explain why maps are sometimes not available because of national security constraints or the absence of mapping efforts. The map samples, or extracts, are all fairly small, 2.5-by-2.5 inches. None are in color. They make possible a general comparison of detail levels available at different scales and give a vague sense of design look and feel. The set indexes are also black-and-white. Most are reduced reproductions of original indexes; they have not been redrawn for publication in *Inventory of World Topographic Mapping.* Because they are reduced reproductions, some of the indexes are more easily read than others.

Inventory of World Topographic Mapping was compiled during a period of great political upheaval that included the dissolution of both the Soviet Union and Yugoslavia and the resulting creation of many new independent states. Fortunately, these nations were slated to be included in the final volume. The set as a whole will age gracefully because topographic mapping is a long-term activity with relatively few completely new sets or projects appearing. While the information regarding set completion will become outdated the general descriptions will remain accurate.

World Mapping Today. 2nd ed.

World Mapping Today reviews the status of national mapping programs and available cartographic products. The second edition reflects the digital transformation of the cartographic process since the first edition was published in 1987 and pulls "together within a single cover as much as is possible of the variety of kinds of information needed for finding out about the acquisition and accessing of current mapping and spatial data" (*World Mapping Today,* 1). "Current" maps are those that are available (although that should not be interpreted as being easily available or acquirable), useful for current needs, and not superseded by other maps. The information for the volume was compiled by direct contact with the publishers; 1,500 questionnaires were sent to mapping organizations. Countries that never responded included some of the former Soviet nations, Marxist nations, Iraq, Libya, and North Korea. Areas that lacked a direct response or gave a less-than-full response were developed using map dealers' listings, unpublished reports, conference proceedings, and secondary sources such as *Inventory of World Topographic Mapping* plus follow-up by e-mail and through information available on the Web.

Because the nation-state is "one of the most significant influences on map style and content" (*World Mapping Today,* 4), the volume is organized in alphabetical order by country within continental groups. Maps that cover multinational areas are listed under the continent. There are 19 discussions of continent-sized areas and 230 country/nation-state or region chapters. Each country's entry includes five sections. The textual section discusses principal mapping agencies or companies and their policies and products, emphasizing contemporary mapping efforts, explaining variations in publications, describing materials no longer available and some materials that are not listed in the "cata-logue" section because they did not meet the criteria for inclusion. The history of national mapping is not specifically emphasized. The second section, "Further Information," is a list of references, publishers' catalogs, indexes, and Web sites that might helpful in locating materials or determining if specific sheets have been produced or are potentially available. The third section is a directory of mapping organizations and private publishers including contact information with, if appropriate, telephone and fax numbers, e-mail addresses, and URLs for Web sites. "Catalogue," the fourth section, lists available publications; each entry in the list follows a standard format making the individual entries easy to interpret. The publication listing should be used in the context established by the text description at the beginning of the country's entry. The final section is a set of graphic indexes that show map sheet organization for sets. The indexes do not show which sheets have been completed. The indexes were drawn specifically for *World Mapping Today;* they are not reductions of indexes published elsewhere. They are clean-looking and will photocopy clearly to serve as indexes for sets owned by libraries but may be difficult to interpret because of the sparseness of information provided by the base map.

World Mapping Today's emphasis is on single-sheet maps and topographic sets but other kinds of materials are included. The items listed in the catalogue section for each country might include, in order: atlases, gazetteers, general maps, image maps, topographic maps and data, bathymetric maps, aeronautical charts, maps showing earth sciences, maps of the environment and natural resources, administrative maps, maps of human activities, and urban maps. Each of these sections does not appear in every country description. Digital data sources are listed with paper maps that depict the same subject matter. Early maps are not included nor, generally, are historical atlases.

Atlases are not limited only to national atlases, particularly national atlases with multiple themes, but also include commercial road atlases in either print or electronic formats. The gazetteers listed include place name resources published in the country and the appropriate United States Board on Geographic Names publication. The general maps included tend to be smaller scale, for the most part 1:250,000 or less-detailed relief maps or road maps produced by governmental agencies or English-language commercial publishers. Image maps are true- or simulated-color poster images and map series that use images as their base. This section does not include unrectified aerial photographs or unprocessed satellite images. Throughout the volume, it seems to be the exception rather than the norm for image maps to be included; they are not a common product. Only the most significant topographic maps series, with scales between 1:20,000 and 1:1,000,000 and relief shown by contours, are listed. Digital data may be included in this section but only selectively. Bathymetric maps do not include nautical charts; instead small-scale overviews and thematic maps like general fishing charts are listed. Because nautical charts are not listed, many countries with extended coastlines, including island nations, possibly do not have any maps listed in the bathymetric section. Aeronautical charts include only national series that are en route charts, not international small-scale sets. The functions of the geosphere are the emphasis of the earth sciences section. A wide variety of single-sheet and set maps, usually produced by national geoscientific agencies, will be found here including coverage of geologic, geomorphic, volcanic, metallic, and magnetic phenomena. Environmental and resources maps also have a wide variety: soils, water quality, snow and ice cover, land capability, forests, and climate. There will also be a wide range of scales but most of the listed maps have been produced by national agencies. Administrative maps include boundaries for governmental divisions like states, provinces, or county equivalents, but also included in this section are maps of postal areas and federal election and representation districts. "Social, Cultural, and Economic" maps revolve around human activities with a wide variety of activities included: politics, manufacturing, population statistics, railroads, archaeological sites, power generation, immigration and emigration, and traffic volumes. The "Urban" section nearly always includes description for a map or atlas of the national capital, but occasionally other products that focus narrowly on city mapping are included.

World Mapping Today is packed with brief descriptions of national mapping programs, contact information for governmental and quasi-governmental agencies responsible for producing maps, and short citations of maps and map sets to help begin the search for items. The index maps are simple and photocopy cleanly. The volume concludes with two indexes, geographical and publisher. The information contained presents a more current view of possible map availability than *Inventory of World Topographic Mapping,* but *World Mapping Today* does not provide the same kind of references to source materials.

Topographic Mapping of the Americas, Australia, and New Zealand
Topographic Mapping of Africa, Antarctica, and Eurasia

These volumes on topographic mapping describe the history of topographic mapping, country-by-country, including colonial era mapping as well as native national mapping. The products included in the national entries are the official maps intended to cover the entire nation that are available publicly or were announced as having public availability. Foreign products are noted if no native mapping is available. In general, the map sets discussed are at scales of 1:250,000 or larger. The volumes are heavily referenced—some statements are supported by multiple references—and include extensive bibliographies.

Topographic Mapping of the Americas, Australia, and New Zealand includes 24 countries plus chapters on history of the topographic map from the fifteenth through the twentieth century. Topographic mapping activities are covered through the early 1980s. *Topographic Mapping of Africa, Antarctica, and Eurasia* includes countries with area of 4,000 square miles or larger; Monaco and San Marino are too small to be described. The lengths of the entries vary from just one or two pages to full chapters. All follow the same general pattern of chronological description followed by a list of brief references to relevant titles in the bibliography at the end of the volume. These works are not intended for pleasurable reading; they are meant to be used as reference sources for consulting with specific questions or needs in mind. The entries with their plethora of parenthetical references do not read easily, but regardless of reading ease, the information presented is fundamental to understanding national mapping history and trends in map availability. Both volumes of *Topographic Mapping* clarify why maps might not be obtainable and why some nation's mapping resembles mapping produced elsewhere.

Discovering what is available for purchase will require making contacts with map vendors. Some map vendors, such as MapLink (http://www.maplink.com) and Omni Resources (http://www.omnimap.com), will potentially be able to assist with locating topographic maps regardless of geographic area. Other vendors specialize in specific geographic regions. As examples, East View Cartographic (http://www.cartographic.com) specializes in materials produced in Russia and the former Soviet Union; and Treaty Oak (http://www.treatyoak.com), although selling materi-

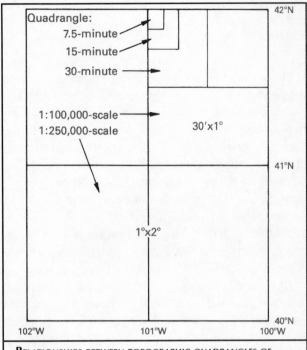

RELATIONSHIPS BETWEEN TOPOGRAPHIC QUADRANGLES OF DIFFERENT SCALES. 30-MINUTE SCALE = 1:125,000. 15-MINUTE SCALE = 1:62,500. 7.5-MINUTE SCALE = 1:24,000. *MAPS FOR AMERICA,* 22.

FIGURE 5.1

als with global coverage, has developed a specialization in maps from Mexico and Latin America. Some vendors have indexes scanned and available for viewing through their Web sites, and others will have lists of quadrangles available for purchase. All of the vendors should be able to assist in determining which topographic quadrangles will cover desired areas. The International Map Trade Association maintains a Web site (http://www.maptrade.org/index.cfm) that includes a listing of members and short descriptions of their services; this might be helpful in finding map vendors. Map libraries should also be able to provide contact information.

UNITED STATES GEOLOGICAL SURVEY

The United States Geological Survey (USGS) is the predominant civilian mapping agency in the United States. The conterminous United States and Hawaii are completely mapped at the 1:24,000 scale. Alaskan urban areas are mapped at 1:24,000 while the rest of the state will eventually be fully mapped at 1:63,360. The USGS has also prepared 1:100,000 topographic

quadrangles of the conterminous United States; some states have 1:100,000 topographic county maps that are produced from the same data sets as the quadrangles. Topographic coverage at 1:250,000 has been produced for the entire United States, and single- or two-sheet 1:500,000 topographic state maps (for Alaska, 1:2,500,000) are also available. It requires more than 57,000 1:24,000-scale quadrangles to cover the conterminous United States, 1,800 1:100,000 sheets, and 640 1:250,000 sheets. The United States is gridded-out following lines of latitude and longitude. The 1:250,000 sheets cover an area one degree tall (north to south) and two degrees wide (east to west); the 1:100,000 quadrangles are 30 minutes tall and one degree wide. The 1:24,000 topographic quadrangles are often called 7.5-minute quadrangles because they cover areas that are 7.5 minutes of latitude by 7.5 minutes of longitude, a mathematical although not physical square. There was a set of 1:62,500, or 15-minute, topographic quadrangles that was partially completed for the conterminous United States, but it was discontinued in the 1970s in favor of completing the 7.5-minute series and because it was largely being replaced by the newer 1:100,000-scale series (Figure 5.1 and Figures 5.2a–e).

These huge sets are accessible by using graphic indexes that show a base map of the United States or, for the 7.5-minute series, a specific state with the topographic map grid overprinted, complete with names of individual sheets. The USGS has produced indexes in a variety of styles during the last 50 years. Initially the indexes for the 7.5-minute state subsets were printed over a base map that included county boundaries and names, many town names, rivers and lakes, and major roads and railroads. The 7.5-minute quadrangles along with the 15-minute quadrangles, and, in some cases, the even older 30-minute quadrangles (1:125,000) were all indicated on the index map (Figure 5.3). In the 1980s, the USGS moved to a book-format index accompanied by a book catalog. Each "square degree" of latitude and longitude was indexed on a separate page; map numbers were assigned to sheets based on their row and column location within the square degree. The map numbers corresponded to catalog numbers. The United States is unique in that it is the only nation to identify maps through names (often after one of the more prominent locations shown on the map) instead of map numbers. In the 1980s, map numbers had to be artificially generated, based on whole-degree latitude, longitude, and location within the resulting square to facilitate computer-

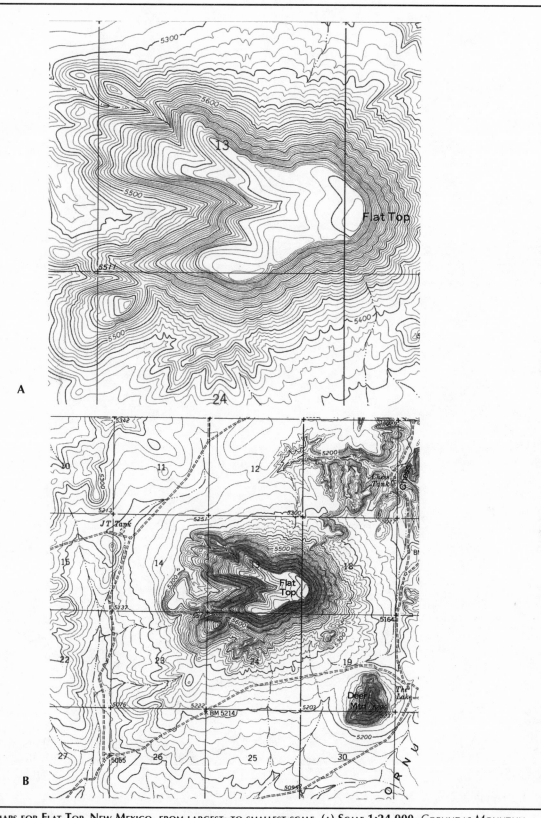

Topographic maps for Flat Top, New Mexico, from largest- to smallest-scale. (A) Scale 1:24,000. *Cornudas Mountain, New Mexico-Texas.* 1:24,000. 7.5 Minute Series. Reston, Va.: USGS, 1975. **(B) Scale 1:62,500.** *Alamo Mountain, New Mexico-Texas.* 1:62,500. 15 Minute Series. Washington, D.C.: USGS, 1959.

FIGURE 5.2

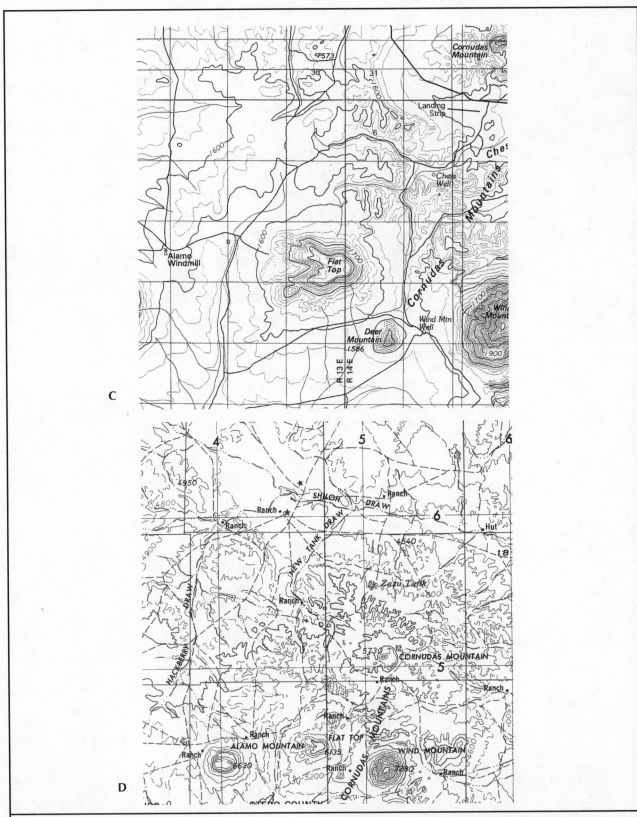

C

D

TOPOGRAPHIC MAPS FOR FLAT TOP, NEW MEXICO, FROM LARGEST- TO SMALLEST-SCALE. **(C) SCALE 1:100,000.** THE ELEVATIONS ON THIS MAP ARE IN METERS. *CROW FLATS, NEW MEXICO-TEXAS.* 1:100,000. 30 x 60 MINUTE SERIES. RESTON, VA.: USGS, 1979. **(D) SCALE 1:250,000.** CARLSBAD, NEW MEXICO; TEXAS. 1:250,000. WESTERN UNITED STATES, V502. SHEET NI 13-11. WASHINGTON, D.C.: USGS, 1972.

FIGURE 5.2 (continued)

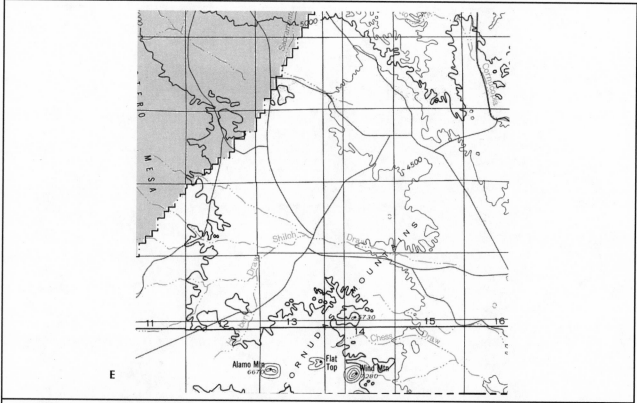

TOPOGRAPHIC MAPS FOR FLAT TOP, NEW MEXICO, FROM LARGEST- TO SMALLEST-SCALE. (E) SCALE **1:500,000.** *STATE OF NEW MEXICO: BASE MAP WITH HIGHWAYS AND CONTOURS.* 1:500,000. WASHINGTON, D.C.: USGS, 1985.

FIGURE 5.2 (continued)

assisted order placement and fulfillment. The book indexes were not easy to use, and the USGS bowed to pressures from libraries and users to continue to issue single-sheet index maps. Some of the index maps that were produced to accompany the book indexes and catalogs include a lengthy number printed in the center of each square degree. Generally this number can be ignored because it refers to the whole-number latitude and longitude that intersect at the southeast corner. The indexes produced during the 1980s and 1990s do not include information about 15- and 30-minute quadrangle maps. Nor does the base map include as many details, only county boundaries and names, major roadways, large lakes, urban extents of major towns, and the Public Land Survey System grid appear—although the very newest indexes are showing an increase in base map detail (Figure 5.4). Current indexes can be obtained without charge from the USGS. A fact sheet titled "United States Map Indexes" (http://mac.usgs.gov/mac/isb/pubs/factsheets/fs13401.html) is available through the USGS Web page devoted to fact sheets about the survey's Geogra-

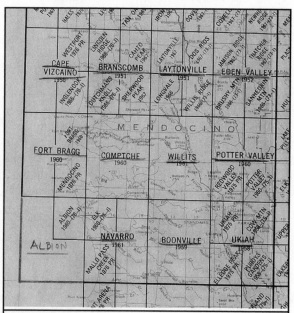

PORTION OF A TOPOGRAPHIC MAP INDEX DISPLAYING 7.5- AND 15-MINUTE QUADRANGLES. *INDEX TO TOPOGRAPHIC MAPS OF CALIFORNIA.* RESTON, VA.: USGS, 1979.

FIGURE 5.3

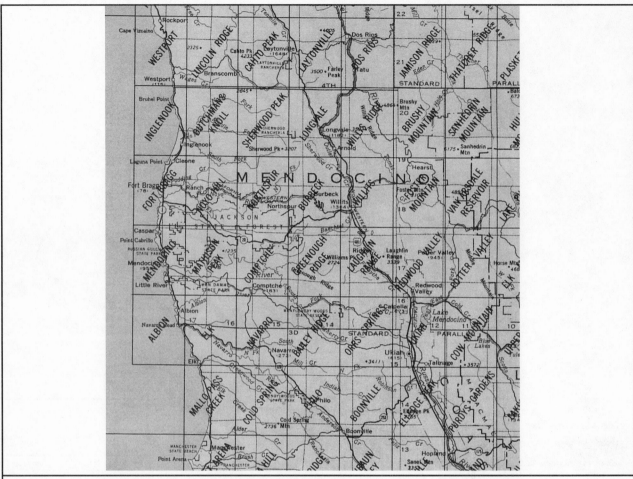

PORTION OF A TOPOGRAPHIC MAP INDEX DISPLAYING ONLY 7.5-MINUTE QUADRANGLES. *CALIFORNIA: INDEX TO TOPOGRAPHIC AND OTHER MAP COVERAGE.* RESTON, VA.: USGS, 1996.

FIGURE 5.4

phy Program (http://mac.usgs.gov/mac/isb/pubs/pubs lists/fctsht.html).

USGS topographic maps can be identified through a pair of Web-based search tools: GNIS (described in the gazetteers chapter) and EarthExplorer Map Finder (http://edcns17.cr.usgs.gov/finder/finder_main.pl?dat aset_name=MAPS_LARGE). Map Finder has three search mechanisms: input the name of a populated place (*i.e.,* village, town, city plus state name), input a zip code, or click on a map. Entering a name or zip code will display an index map centered on the 7.5-minute topographic quadrangle that contains the place name or zip code area. There will be no indication on the index map where the place name or zip code area actually is located. The clickable map for the conterminous United States will require two zooms/clicks to get to the level where 7.5-minute topographic quadrangle names are viewable. The index maps from all

three of the search methods can be recentered using arrows at the margins. Map Finder is intended to function as a sales outlet, complete with electronic shopping cart, for USGS. GNIS is not a sales outlet and has a more flexible and powerful search that will give more specific results.

Once the appropriate quadrangle has been selected from the index map and acquired, the business of interpretation begins. The USGS uses five standard colors to print its maps: black, red, blue, green, and brown. Each one of these colors is applied to specific purposes (Table 5.1). USGS color use is similar to color use by national mapping agencies elsewhere.

In some cases a sixth color, purple, might appear on a map. These are editions of maps that had been previously published and that have been *photorevised* by comparing the map with more recent aerial photography. Important changes are inscribed on a separate

TABLE 5.1

COMMON COLOR USE ON UNITED STATES GEOLOGICAL SURVEY TOPOGRAPHIC MAPS.

Color	Use
Black	Information in the margins such as map title, scale, compilation data; reference grids including latitude and longitude, state plane survey, and UTM; cultural features such as roads, highways, railroads, powerlines, buildings, and administrative boundaries; feature and place name labels
Red	Cultural features such as urban areas, interstate highways, grid produced by the Public Land Survey System and other surveys
Blue	Hydrography including fresh and salt water and isobaths and glacial contours
Green	Vegetation including woods, orchards, vineyards, and swamp
Brown	Contours

printing plate and printed in purple as an additional data layer. The changes might include additional roadways, extended urban areas, new administrative boundaries, new landforms created by massive earth-moving activities like open-pit mining, or new water bodies such as lakes created by dams or water treatment plants. The symbols will need to be carefully interpreted by examining not only the features' shapes but also their contexts. A new interstate highway will be easy to identify because of its linear nature and because it will be labeled with the appropriate interstate shield symbol and interstate number. Extended urban areas will be a solid light purple so new water bodies cannot be a solid light purple. Instead they have a very fine dot pattern, a pattern similar to, but not exactly like, the vineyard pattern. The lower right corner of a photorevised quadrangle will also have, printed in purple, "Photorevised [date]."

In low-lying areas with little variation in topography such as south Florida and portions of the coast of Georgia, the USGS has used aerial photography as the base layer for topographic mapping, creating orthophoto quadrangles (Figures 5.5a and b). Aerial photographs, black-and-white or natural color, are manipulated to reduce error and are formatted to fit the topographic map grid. A minimal amount of cartographic symbols and labels are overprinted on the photograph.

The provisional edition is another variation on USGS 7.5-minute topographic quadrangles. During the late 1970s, the survey was strongly encouraged to find a way to expedite completing coverage of the conterminous United States at 1:24,000. In 1980 approximately 12,000 7.5-minute quadrangles had not yet been produced. The provisional map program was designed to speed production of these maps with a target completion date of 1988. Coverage by 7.5-minute quadrangles eventually was completed in 1992, more than 50 years after beginning. Provisional maps look different from final-product maps. The most immediately noticeable difference is that the margin or collar information is printed in brown, not black, but the rest of the five-color scheme is the same as standard topographic quadrangles. The second visual difference is the appearance of some of the lettering and numbering and some of the line work; characters and line work generated by computers are not being replaced by typeface. The provisional maps meet national mapping accuracy standards and can and should be used just like all of the rest of the USGS products.

In 1993 the USGS and the United States Forest Service began cooperative, interagency work on *single-edition* quadrangle maps, reducing costs and duplication of effort. Prior to the beginning of the single-edition program, National Forest lands might have had two separate quadrangles produced by the two agencies. Now, the agencies are jointly responsible for producing and updating the topographic quadrangles that cover lands administered by the Forest Service. The Forest Service has taken on the responsibility for updating the maps while

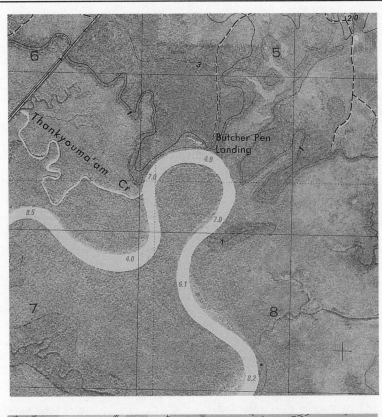

A

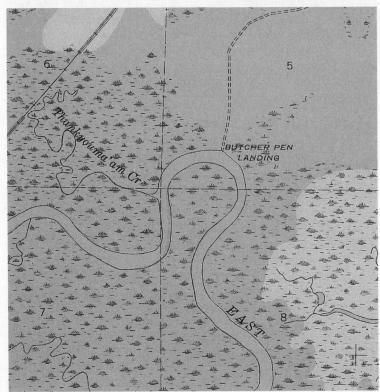

B

ORTHOPHOTOQUADRANGLE AND TOPOGRAPHIC QUADRANGLE FOR THE SAME LOCATION. (A) ORTHOPHOTOQUADRANGLE—RECTIFIED AERIAL PHOTOGRAPH WITH A SMALL AMOUNT OF OVERLAID CARTOGRAPHIC SYMBOLS. *BEVERLY, FLA.* 1:24,000. 7.5 MINUTE SERIES ORTHOPHOTOMAP (TOPOGRAPHIC-BATHYMETRIC). RESTON, VA.: USGS, 1981. **(B) TOPOGRAPHIC QUADRANGLE—USE OF ONLY CARTOGRAPHIC SYMBOLS POTENTIALLY INCREASES AMOUNT OF GENERALIZATION.** *BEVERLY, FLA.* 1:24,000. 7.5 MINUTE SERIES. WASHINGTON, D.C.: USGS, 1945.

FIGURE 5.5

USGS does the printing and distribution. The agencies estimate that by 2010 all Forest Service–administered areas will have single-edition maps, approximately 10,600 sheets. The single-edition maps look slightly different; there is an expanded symbol set, primarily focusing on road types, along with enhanced information about Forest Service-administered lands and private inholdings. The single-edition quadrangles meet appropriate national mapping accuracy standards just like the quadrangles in the regular topographic series. Unfortunately, when "single-edition topographic maps are revised, they might not be completely updated. Areas within National Forest lands may be completely checked and extensively revised while areas outside receive only basic checking and revision. The USGS has a fact sheet at its Web site that describes single-edition topographic quadrangles (http://mac.usgs.gov/mac/isb/pubs/fact sheets/fs09498.html).

Through the years, the USGS has done some redesign of its maps. Older 7.5-, 15-, and 30-minute quadrangles will not have solid blue water bodies; water bodies once were shown by concentric blue shapes or blue lines drawn parallel to the shore giving a feeling of waves and motion. More recently, the urban area or house-omission tint on 7.5-minute quadrangles has been changed from a bold pink to a more urban-appearing gray; a similar change was made on the 1:250,000 quadrangles for urban areas, from bright yellow to urban gray. Further information about the USGS's topographic map revision program is available through the Web (http://mac.usgs.gov/mac/isb/pubs/factsheets/fs04700.html). An additional survey site, "The Evolution of Topographic Mapping in the U.S. Geological Survey's National Mapping Program," may also provide answers to some frequent questions (http://mapping.usgs.gov/misc/evolution.html).

Beyond the fact sheets already mentioned that describe indexes or single-edition topographic quadrangles, the USGS has a number of other fact sheets and brochures available about topographic mapping that are available in online versions through the USGS map information Web site (http://mac.usgs.gov/mac/isb/pubs/pubslists/index.html) or printed on paper. Included are booklets titled "Topographic Mapping" (http://mac.usgs.gov/mac/isb/pubs/booklets/topo/topo.html) and "Topographic Map Symbols" (http://mac.usgs.gov/mac/isb/pubs/booklets/symbols/), both of which will assist in interpreting topographic maps. Other publications available include price lists and order forms, general information about using topo-

graphic maps in the sport of orienteering, and an assortment of teaching packets. Fact sheets are usually available for viewing in both HTML and PDF formats.

Information about new or revised topographic quadrangles is available through the "New Publications of the U.S. Geological Survey" (http://pubs.usgs.gov/publications/index.shtml) portion of the USGS Web site. These monthly lists include publications from all divisions (Geology, Biology, Water, and Mapping) of the survey. After selecting a year and a month to view, a list of different kinds of materials can be selected for display. The topographic maps list is in alphabetical order by state and quadrangle name. The online lists begin in 1995; to investigate publication or revision dates prior to 1995 the monthly print version of *New Publications of the U.S. Geological Survey* will need to be consulted. The print and electronic versions are cumulated annually in *Publications of the U.S. Geological Survey* but the lists of new topographic maps are not included in the cumulations. Lists of topographic maps can also be generated from the USGS Web site (http://mac.usgs.gov/mac/maplists/index.html) by selecting a state, by inputting a map name, or by selecting a latitude-longitude coordinate pair. The tables that are displayed include the USGS stock number and map name, the southeast corner coordinate pair for the area covered by the quadrangle, a currentness and a version year, and a short statement of map type (most will be "topographic map"). The two years listed have subtle but important differences. The version year is the large date printed underneath the quadrangle name at the lower right corner of the map sheet; if more than one date appears there, the version year will be the most recent date. The version year is usually the year in which the map was printed, while the currentness year is an indication of the age of the geographic information as the currentness year is the year in which the map was last corrected or verified. A currentness year could be older than the version year if the photographs or surveying upon which the map is based were completed in years prior to the printing year. Currentness years can also be later than the version year; this might occur if an older map is compared to more recent aerial photography and is found to still be correct.

Books about USGS Mapping

Maps for America. 3rd ed.

The first edition of *Maps for America* was published to commemorate the centennial of the founding of the United States Geological Survey (1879–1979). *Maps for America* is not intended to describe the mapmaking process from survey to printed map. Its objective is to educate the reader/map user about four broad areas: the meaning of lines, colors, images, symbols, numbers, captions, and notes that appear on maps; the possible errors and anomalies affecting the reliability and interpretation of maps; the different kinds of maps and map data; and the various sources of maps and related data. While the volume's primary focus is USGS products, products of other agencies are included, usually to establish the context of the USGS titles discussed. The U.S. mapping situation in 1987 is described; there is no attempt to forecast possible or probable changes. The volume includes 10 chapters, 2 appendices, an address list, a glossary, references, and an index. All of the chapters, along with the appendices, are extensively illustrated.

Chapter 1 is a survey of the history of U.S. federal agency mapping from the establishment of the Survey of the Coast in 1807 through the four great western surveys (King, Hayden, Powell, and Wheeler), the establishment of the USGS and its early work, and the impacts of the two world wars on civilian mapping techniques—a useful grounding in basic mapping history and common mapping terms. The second chapter briefly discusses kinds of maps and map data with short definitions embedded in the text and an extensive table of map products that identifies producing and distributing federal agencies.

Chapters 3, 4, and 5, "Characteristics of Geological Survey Maps," "Natural and Cultural Features on Topographic Maps" and "Boundaries, Names, and Marginalia," respectively, contain essential information for understanding and interpreting topographic maps. Chapter 3 discusses scale, how the Earth's surface is gridded-out into quadrangle sections, and (very generally) source materials. Chapter 4 illustrates how specific symbols are applied and makes clear how similar features are differentiated for appropriate symbol application. A large number of pages are devoted to buildings and urban areas including short descriptions of how different kinds of buildings are selected to be shown and how they are depicted. Chapter 5 on "Boundaries, Names, and Marginalia" covers essential cartographic and geographic information that often does not have a physical presence on the ground. A useful list of the states and their predominant survey system (public land system or not) along with a description of local subdivision methods (counties or their equivalents along with appropriate subunits) is

included. The section on the public land survey system provides basic information on the survey method and how its results are depicted on USGS products. The section on marginalia (all of the graphic and textual information outside of the map's neat line) will help in understanding source materials, coordinate systems, and mathematical information such as magnetic declination, contour interval, and scale.

Chapter 6 on "Map Maintenance and Accuracy Standards" illustrates the distinctions between different levels of revision and how revisions are added to topographic maps. USGS maps meet National Map Accuracy Standards for horizontal and vertical accuracy. The standards, and how maps are evaluated using the standards, may not be of interest to the casual topographic map user but more intense consumers should be aware of the standards and how they shape USGS products. Chapter 7 is an extended look at a variety of USGS products, in particular topographic maps at different scales, with many color illustrations. A table is included that compares different scales of topographic maps and the kinds of features that are depicted on them. This table could possibly assist a user in determining which scale might be appropriate for a specific need if particular features must be seen on or could be omitted from the map. Beyond topographic maps, there are sections on photoimage maps, coastal maps, geologic maps, hydrologic maps, land use maps, and maps generated from data collected by satellite.

The remaining chapters survey map products produced by other agencies, sources for obtaining cartographic products and data from the federal government, and a brief look at "recent" trends. The appendix presents foundation information on map projections, coordinate systems, and surveying. There also is a graphic that compares the five standard USGS topographic series. The definitions in the glossary are straightforward and easy to understand. A selected bibliography and index conclude the volume.

Even if the third edition of *Maps for America* is not readily at hand, the basic and essential information about map symbols and the history of topographic mapping in the United States can be accessed in either of the two previous editions. This volume, or its predecessors, is an essential primer in using basic USGS topographic map products. It assists with map interpretation while explaining the basic constraints that are placed upon both the topographic map and its users.

Map Index to Topographic Quadrangles of the United States, 1882–1940
A Cartobibliography of Separately Published U.S. Geological Survey Special Maps and River Surveys

Both of these works inventory the cartographic output, mainly topographic maps, of the United States Geological Survey. They are important because the survey was not consistent or comprehensive in recording the titles and scales of map sheets as they were produced. *Map Index to Topographic Quadrangles of the United States, 1882–1940* focuses on topographic quadrangles produced during the first 60 years of USGS quadrangle production. The volume is "a graphic bibliography of out-of-print topographic maps published from 1882 to 1940 in the 15-, 30-, and 60-minute series for all States except Alaska." (*Map Index,* t.p.) Topographic quadrangles were not created by the USGS prior to 1882. The year 1940 was selected as the volume's closing date because at the time of *Map Index's* preparation 99 percent of the pre-1940 small-scale quadrangles were out-of-print while most of the quadrangles from the 1940s and beyond were still in print. Also, after 1940 the 30- and 60-minute quadrangles were no longer produced by USGS.

Map Index opens with a foreword that sets the entire work into a historical context by briefly describing the sequence in which the USGS began producing different topographic map series. The introduction explains the problems of trying to identify or confirm the existence of specific small-scale topographic map sheets without a comprehensive or easy-to-use index. As the 7.5-minute series grew in size and came closer to completion, the survey began dropping information from its indexes and from the collar information on the map sheets that led users to older and smaller-scale quadrangles. The smaller-scale quadrangles were allowed to go out-of-print when the larger-scale maps that covered the same area were completed. The policy of removing index information that described out-of-print quadrangles decreased the ability to determine the availability of and access to older topographic maps and geographic information—such as one-room schoolhouses, previous drainage patterns, and older road networks—that they contained.

Map Index is intended for the typical map user who uses a graphic index, not a list, to determine maps appropriate for a particular use. Each state in *Map Index* has a two-part entry. The first page (or for large states, pages) of the entry is a two-color map. Blue state and county boundaries for the focus state, along with the same information for portions of the adjoining states, are used as the base map. A black grid of numbered rectangles representing quadrangles is overprinted. The largest rectangles represent 60-minute quadrangles, the mid-sized represent 30-minute quadrangles, and the smallest represent 15-minute quadrangles. The numbers refer to the alphabetical quadrangle listing that follows immediately after the index map. The entries in the list include quadrangle name, date of first publication, an indication of scale, and the southeast corner coordinates of the area that the quadrangle covers.

Map Index does not comprehensively index all USGS topographic quadrangles at scales smaller than 1:24,000. For quadrangles first published after 1940, map users will still need to rely on sheet indexes, if they are still readily available. Many map libraries will have retained old editions of topographic map indexes. In some instances, a state agency may have recently produced an index to topographic maps that indexes both the 7.5-minute series and the older 15-minute series. The old indexes, or newly produced indexes, are critical and important works because the USGS declared the 15-minute topographic map series as a whole as being out-of-print in 1994. Also, the sources that *Map Index* was compiled from may not have been complete. The information provided by *Map Index* can serve as an initial list. Other indexes or lists will be important to consult to create as full a list as possible. *Map Index* provides access to pre-1940 quadrangles; post-1940 coverage still may be difficult to confirm or locate

A Cartobibliography of Separately Published U.S. Geological Survey Special Maps and River Surveys describes USGS products that do not fit the mold of the typical quadrangle-based map, maps often referred to as *specials*. Specials do not conform to standard survey products because of their scale, the geographic scope of coverage, or the mapping technique employed. Geologic maps are not included in *Cartobibliography* nor are maps that appeared only in USGS book publications such as the Annual Report or Professional Papers series. The products included in *Cartobibliography* range from 6-minute, 1:20,000-scale topographic quadrangles of Los Angeles through a "Map of President Hoover's Camp, on the Headwaters of the Rapidan River, Virginia" to 1:500,000 shaded-relief maps of the state of Washington and multiple-sheet maps of the entire United States.

The author's introduction is, by necessity, lengthy because it sets the cartobibliography into historical and intellectual contexts, explains the scope of the work, and describes the methodology and sources used to compile the entries. The list of maps is divided into two parts; part one is titled "Special Maps" and part two is "River Surveys." The maps described in part one were published between 1882 and 1961; 1961 was selected as the final year of coverage so that the listing would correspond with the dates included in the first bibliography of USGS publications, *Publications of the Geological Survey, 1879 to 1961.* Each entry follows a standard format as illustrated on the first page of the section. All include an "accession number," the two-letter abbreviation for the state the map falls on plus a number. Other information included to fully describe the maps is: title, scale, compilation date(s), publication date(s), geographic coordinates, contour interval, number of sheets with size, and descriptive notes if applicable. Different editions of the same map are recorded in separate entries. If a map was reprinted, all of the reprint dates are included in the entry. The descriptive notes may include information about the engraver, use of color, kinds of information depicted, and geographic scope. Part one is nearly all textual entries but there are a few graphic indexes for sets of quadrangles that cover all of Alaska or parts of California, Michigan, and South Carolina. Part one concludes with two indexes: one to shaded-relief maps and the other to all other maps included in the list.

Part two focuses on river surveys. These generally are multiple-sheet maps that seem to include a lot of blank space because the map covers the course of a specific river and the land immediately to either side of its banks including mileage traveled upstream from the survey's origin. Often the river surveys include profiles, schematic drawings of a river's descent through its valley that show drops in elevation. Some of the river surveys might also include damsite maps. The chronological coverage of the river surveys is not terminated at 1961 as is the coverage of the special maps because, while he was compiling the section, the author was told that there would be no new river surveys issued thus there was no purpose in using a cut-off date.

The entries are similar to those in part one: accession number, short title, survey or compilation date, printing dates, number and description of sheets, sheet size, scale of maps including the vertical scale of the profile, contour intervals, description of the survey from the lowest point working upstream, and notes. Like part one, the river survey entries are arranged alphabetically by including state, then by river name. Part two concludes with an alphabetical river index.

Cartobibliography will help confirm that a specific map, that for some reason did not conform to standard USGS product lines, was in fact produced by the USGS. The compilation method points out the necessity of working with map collections that have a focus or depth for the region of interest. Although the initial list of maps was compiled from USGS sources, including microfilmed historic maps, additional information was gleaned from academic and government agency libraries nationwide.

Both *Map Index* and *Cartobibliography* should be considered jumping-off or starting points for locating old topographic quadrangles or maps that do not fit the normal USGS product pattern. Many of the specials have been cataloged separately and can be located through library catalogs. State natural history, resource, or geologic agencies might have internal collections of older materials specific to their regions. The Web is an increasingly rich resource for confirming that specific maps were published. The University of New Hampshire's Dimond Library has listed (with scans available through the Web) old 15- and 7.5-minute topographic quadrangles for six New England states plus some areas in New York State (http://docs.unh.edu/nhtopos/nhtopos.htm). The Illinois State Library has lists at its Web site of library holdings of superceded 7.5-, 15-, and 30-minute quadrangles for the six states surrounding Illinois (http://www.cyberdriveillinois.com/library/isl/ref/historical_topos.html) and 7.5- and 15-minute Illinois quadrangles (http://www.cyberdriveillinois.com/library/isl/ref/lstopo_quads.html). Historic topographic maps of the San Francisco Bay Area have been scanned and mounted on the Web by the University of California, Berkeley, Earth Sciences & Map Library (http://sunsite.berkeley.edu/histopo). Other sites with scanned historic topographic maps or information about historic topographic map collections can be found by searching the Web for "historic topographic maps," along with the state desired, if needed.

Digital Data Products

The USGS is producing three different digital data products related to the topographic quadrangles: digital raster graphics (DRGs), digital line graphs (DLGs), and digital elevation models (DEMs). Files of all three data types will have the same name as the 7.5-minute, 1:100,000-scale, and 1:250,000-scale topographic maps that cover the same area. DRGs are scans of the topographic maps that, when viewed using appropriate software, look just like the paper maps. Information about DRGs is available through a USGS fact sheet (http://mac.usgs.gov/mac/isb/ pubs/factsheets/fs08801.html). Additional information about DRGs, including how DRGs are created and how to order DRGs, is available through the USGS's Web page on digital maps and data (http://ask.usgs.gov/digidata.html).

DLGs do not reproduce an entire topographic map as one image. DLGs are produced by selectively digitizing specific kinds of data from the topographic map. Multiple files will be generated from the same map; each file contains data on specific, usually related, kinds of geographic features. The files currently divide up geographic features into these groups: political and administrative boundaries; hydrography; the Public Land Survey System and property boundaries; transportation systems; and significant manmade structures. Eventually, data about topography and both vegetative and nonvegetative surface cover will also be produced. DLG data are often used as base data in geographic information system (GIS) applications. A fact sheet along with some DLG samples and information about obtaining DLGs is available from the USGS digital data Web page (http://ask.usgs.gov/ digidata.html).

DEMs are a regularly-spaced grid of elevation data that can be used to generate representations of topography that in turn can be used in a wide variety of applications, including flight simulations, tracing pollution sources, and examining the course of rainstorm runoff. DEM data is collected from topographic maps, digital hypsometric and hydrographic data, and aerial photography. The previously mentioned USGS digital data Web page also includes information about obtaining and using DEMs.

For accessing digital data through the Web, the USGS has collected a number of links to projects developed with USGS business partners and through Cooperative Research and Development Agreements (CRADAs); the links can be found on the Web page "View USGS Maps and Aerial Photo Images Online" (http://mapping.usgs.gov/partners/viewonline.html). These links include sites that display DRGs such as Topozone (http://www.topozone.com), MapServer (http://mapserver.maptech.com/homepage/index.cfm), and Terraserver (http://terraserver-usa.com). Each of

these sites allows the user to put in a place name or zip code to display topographic maps through the Web. The maps can be zoomed, panned, and printed. The USGS also has a fact sheet about data available through the Web directly from the survey (http://mac.usgs.gov/mac/isb/pubs/factsheets/fs04600 .html).

OTHER NORTH AMERICAN TOPOGRAPHIC MAPPING

Topographic maps are produced nationally for Canada and Mexico by the Centre for Topographic Information of Natural Resources Canada (CTI) and the Instituto Nacional de Estadítica, Geografía e Informática (INEGI), respectively.

Currently, 1:50,000- and 1:250,000-scale topographic maps are produced by CTI; 1:50,000 quadrangles, which are 15 minutes of latitude by 30 minutes of longitude in size, have been bilingual since the mid-1970s. Other scales, including 1:25,000, 1:125,000, and 1:500,000, have been produced in the past and might be available for consultation in libraries even though they are no longer available for purchase. Although Canadian topographic quadrangles are named, most quadrangle identification revolves around sheet numbers based on the Canadian National Topographic System (http://maps.nrcan. gc.ca/topographic.html). This system is efficient because sheets that are in close geographic proximity often have proximal numbers and because the numbering system builds in an automatic relationship between a small-scale map and the larger-scale maps that provide details of the same area of coverage. Natural Resources Canada maintains a Web site that will assist in determining which topographic quadrangle is needed by clicking on an interactive map, searching by geographic coordinates, or searching for a place name (http://maps.nrcan.gc.ca/search/index.html). The Canada Map Office does not sell paper maps directly; those interested in purchasing maps must go to a map dealer (http://maps.nrcan.gc.ca/cmo/index. html).

Like Canada, INEGI (http://www.inegi.gob. mx/inegi/default.asp) topographic maps for Mexico are currently being produced at 1:50,000 and 1:250,000. The 1:50,000-scale quadrangles cover areas 15 minutes of latitude by 20 minutes of longitude in size. The 1:250,000-scale set has been used as the base map for a number of thematic sets including geology, land use and vegetation cover, surface and subsurface hydrology, and soils. Similar sets for a number of these topics are under development based on the 1:50,000-scale set. Similar to the Canadian topographic maps, Mexican topographic quadrangles are named but sheet numbers are the primary identification and organization tool. The numbering system takes advantage of the grid established for the 1:1,000,000-scale International Map of the World, each sheet number "nesting" inside of the designation for the corresponding 1:1,000,000-scale sheet. Mexican topographic mapping is sold by a number of different map dealers.

TOPOGRAPHIC MAP INTERPRETATION

Interpreting the data and information conveyed by topographic maps is a matter of both being able to determine what the symbols mean and understanding how the features being depicted interact with each other. This might be as simple as needing to remember that contour lines around streams often appear to be arrows pointing uphill or knowing that a railroad and a highway shown parallel on a map might be much closer in reality than measuring the distance between them on the map would indicate. Unfortunately, there are very few recent publications devoted solely to assisting map users in learning how to read or interpret topographic maps.

Interpretation of Topographic Maps

Interpretation of Topographic Maps is intended as a textbook for learning how to interpret the ways that physical features are represented by topographic maps, going well beyond map reading to being able to see features and aspects of landscape in context. Nine different feature types or mechanisms and processes that result in landscape forms are explored in 12 chapters. The first two chapters are devoted to basics and map interpretation generalities. The following nine chapters focus on specific features or feature-producing mechanisms, while the last two chapters cover feature types that do not neatly fit into one of the specific chapters or that examine complex landscapes. The appendix is titled "Getting Acquainted with Topographic Maps," and it might be a useful review of basic map-reading concepts. The volume also includes a list of references, a glossary, and answers to questions. *Interpretation of Topographic Maps* is problem-and-exercise-intensive. The volume concludes with 97 black-and-white partial reproductions of USGS topographic maps for use with the exercises that form the

majority of the text. Some knowledge of geological processes might be helpful in making the most of the information found in *Interpretation of Topographic Maps* as the text's emphasis is on physical, not cultural, features.

Cultural Geography on Topographic Maps

Cultural Geography on Topographic Maps is similar to *Interpretation of Topographic Maps* in that it uses exercises to acquaint the reader with methods of topographic map feature interpretation. The volume opens with color reproductions of parts of 30 topographic quadrangles; most of the maps are of portions of the United States but four represent diverse regions of Canada. Each map is accompanied by brief information about the region, such as historic, cultural, or economic context; noteworthy physical features; monthly average temperature and precipitation; periodic population figures; and the map's scale and contour interval. There is an index of cultural features that lists specific feature types and the sample map on which they appear and a bibliography with references that specifically focus on the areas shown on the sample maps or the regions in which the maps are located. The volume also includes information about aerial photographs that cover the same areas as the maps. A nine-section study guide follows the maps and contextual information. Each section concentrates on typical cultural features depicted on topographic maps, usually within an environmental or historical context, and how cumulatively the representation of features builds to an integrated description of the area.

Two of the chapters in *The Language of Maps* focus specifically on learning how to interpret topographic maps. The first focuses on fundamental elements: information found in topographic map margins; color conventions; elevation depiction along with slope calculations and contour interpretation for profile construction; route finding; and landforms. The second of the two chapters on topographic maps continues the examination of landforms and interpreting landform depictions, along with symbolization of cultural features, to infer a more complete picture of the world.

Cartographic Relief Presentation gives an advanced explanation of how to interpret many different kinds of relief depiction methods, well beyond contour lines, but does not discuss the depiction or interpretation of human-created or non-topographic features. Information about reading and using topographic maps is also scattered throughout the books *Map Use: Reading, Analysis, and Interpretation* and *Map Use & Analysis*.

Topographic maps, beyond being the most common type of map produced, are among the most important maps created by a mapping agency because they are so often used as base maps for other data types and because they have myriad and varied potential uses. While not always available at large scales such as 1:24,000 or 1:50,000, there will be topographic maps at smaller scales for nearly every place on Earth.

BIBLIOGRAPHY

A Cartobibliography of Separately Published U.S. Geological Survey Special Maps and River Surveys. Peter L. Stark. Western Association of Map Libraries Occasional Papers, no. 12. Santa Cruz, Calif.: Western Association of Map Libraries, 1990. ISBN: 0-939112-15-9.

Cartographica. Toronto: University of Toronto Press, 1980– . Quarterly. Former title *Canadian Cartographer.* ISSN: 0317-7173.

The Cartographic Journal. London: British Cartographic Society, 1964– . Semiannual. ISSN: 0008-7041.

Cartographic Relief Presentation. Eduard Imhof. H.J. Steward, ed. Berlin: Walter de Gruyter, 1982. ISBN: 3-11-006711-0.

Cultural Geography on Topographic Maps. Karl B. Raitz and John Fraser Hart. New York: John Wiley & Sons, 1975. ISBN: 0-471-70595-0.

Imago Mundi: The International Journal for the History of Cartography. London: Imago Mundi, 1935– . Annual. ISSN: 0308-5694.

International Yearbook of Cartography. Bonn: International Cartographic Association, 1961–1990. Annual. ISSN: 0341-0986.

Interpretation of Topographic Maps. Victor C. Miller and Mary E. Westerback. Columbus, Ohio: Merrill, 1989. ISBN: 0-675-20919-6.

Inventory of World Topographic Mapping. 3 vols. Rolf Böhme, comp. Vol. 1: *Western Europe, North America and Australia;* Vol. 2: *South America, Central America and Africa;* Vol. 3: *Eastern Europe, Asia, Oceania and Antarctica.* London: Elsevier Science, on behalf of the International Cartographic Association, 1989–1993. ISBN: 1-85166-357-6 (vol. 1); ISBN: 1-85166-661-3 (vol. 2); ISBN: 1-85861-034-6 (vol. 3); ISBN: 0-08-042414-7 (all 3).

The Language of Maps. 16th ed. Philip J. Gersmehl. Pathways in Geography, no. 1. Indiana, Pa.: National Council for Geographic Education, 1996. ISBN: 0-9627379-3-3.

Map Index to Topographic Quadrangles of the United States, 1882–1940. Riley Moore Moffat. Western Association of Map Libraries Occasional Paper, no. 10. Santa Cruz, Calif.: Western Association of Map Libraries, 1986. ISBN: 0-939112-12-4.

Maps for America: Cartographic Products of the U.S. Geological Survey and Others. 3rd ed. Morris M. Thompson. Washington, D.C.: Geological Survey, 1987. ISBN: 0-16-003363-2.

Map Use & Analysis. 4th ed. John Campbell. Boston: WCB McGraw-Hill, 2001. ISBN: 0-697-22969-6.

Map Use: Reading, Analysis, Interpretation. 4th ed., rev. Phillip C. Muehrcke, Juliana O. Muehrcke, and A. Jon Kimerling. Madison, Wis.: JP Publications, 2001. ISBN: 0-9602978-5-5.

Mercator's World: The Magazine of Maps, Atlases, Globes, and Charts. Eugene, Ore.: Aster Pub. Corp., ca. 1996–2001. 6 per year. ISSN: 1086-6728.

New Publications of the U.S. Geological Survey. United States Geological Survey. Reston, Va.: USGS, 1907–2003. Monthly until 1995, semi-annual in 1996, quarterly thereafter. ISSN: 0364-2461.

Publications of the U.S. Geological Survey. United States Geological Survey. Reston, Va.: USGS, 1948– . Annual.

Topographic Mapping of Africa, Antarctica, and Eurasia. Mary Lynette Larsgaard. Western Association of Map Libraries Occasional Paper, no. 14. Provo, Utah: Western Association of Map Libraries, 1993. ISBN: 0-939112-29-9.

Topographic Mapping of the Americas, Australia, and New Zealand. Mary Lynette Larsgaard. Littleton, Colo.: Libraries Unlimited, 1984. ISBN: 0-87287-276-9.

World Mapping Today. 2nd ed. R.B. Parry and C.R. Perkins. London: Bowker-Saur, 2000. ISBN: 3-598-11534-2.

On-line References

"Canada Map Office: Regional Distribution Centres." Natural Resources Canada, 14 July 2003. <http://maps.nrcan.gc.ca/cmo/index.html> (15 October 2003).

"Canadian Topographic Maps: The National Topographic System." Centre for Topographic Information (Ottawa), 3 January 2003. <http://maps.nrcan.gc.ca/topographic.html> (15 October 2003).

"Digital Maps & Data." U.S. Geological Survey, 10 July 2003. <http://ask.usgs.gov/digidata.html> (15 October 2003).

EarthExplorer Map Finder. U.S. Geological Survey, 28 August 2003. <http://edcns17.cr.usgs.gov/finder/finder_main.pl?dataset_name=MAPS_LARGE> (15 October 2003).

East View Cartographic. Home page. East View Cartographic, 2003. <http://www.cartographic.com> (15 October 2003).

"The Evolution of Topographic Mapping in the U.S. Geological Survey's National Mapping Program." U.S. Geological Survey, 26 January 1998. <http://mapping.usgs.gov/misc/evolution.html> (15 October 2003).

Geographic Names Information System (GNIS). Developed by the USGS and the U.S. Board on Geographic Names (BGN). U.S. Geological Survey, 30 July 2003. <http://geonames.usgs.gov/index.html> (15 October 2003).

Geography Program Fact Sheets. United States Geological Survey, 20 August 2003. <http://mac.usgs.gov/mac/isb/pubs/pubslists/fctsht.html> (15 October 2003).

"Historical Topographic Quadrangles of Indiana, Iowa, Kentucky, Michigan, Missouri, Wisconsin." Illinois State Library, 5 February 2001. <http://www.cyberdriveillinois.com/library/isl/ref/historical_topos.html> (15 October 2003).

"Historic Topographic Maps of California." University of California, Berkeley Earth Sciences & Map Library, 10 October 2003. <http://sunsite.berkeley.edu/histopo/> (15 October 2003).

"Historic USGS Maps of New England & New York." University of New Hampshire, Dimond Library Documents Department & Data Center, 10 October 2003. <http://docs.unh.edu/nhtopos/nhtopos.htm> (15 October 2003).

Instituto Nacional de Estadítica, Geografía e Informática (INEGI). Home page. INEGI, Mexico, 2003. <http://www.inegi.gob.mx/inegi/default.asp> (15 October 2003).

International Map Trade Association. Home page. International Map Trade Association, 2003. <http://www.maptrade.org/index.cfm> (15 October 2003).

"Large-Scale Topographic Quadrangles of Illinois." Illinois State Library, 27 January 2003. <http://www.cyberdriveillinois.com/library/isl/ref/lstopo_quads.html> (15 October 2003).

"Map Indexes Available from the U.S. Geological Survey." Fact Sheet 134-01. U.S. Geological Survey, 31 December 2002 <http://mac.usgs.gov/mac/isb/pubs/factsheets/fs13401.html> (15 October 2003).

Map Link. 2002. <http://www.maplink.com> (15 October 2003).

Maptech MapServer. Maptech, Inc., 2003.<http://mapserver.maptech.com/homepage/index.cfm> (15 October 2003).

New Publications of the U.S. Geological Survey. On-line version. Updated monthly. U.S. Geological Survey, 24 September 2003. <http://pubs.usgs.gov/publications/index.shtml> (15 October 2003).

"NRCan [Natural Resources Canada] Topographic Map Search." Natural Resources Canada, Centre for Topographic Information (Ottowa), 23 December 2002. <http://maps.nrcan.gc.ca/search/index.html> (15 October 2003).

Omni Resources. Home page. Omni Resources, 2003. <http://www.omnimap.com/> (15 October 2003).

"Online Map Lists." U.S. Geological Survey, 14 March 2003. <http://mac.usgs.gov/mac/maplists/index.html> (15 October 2003).

"Report to ICA Executive Committee ICA-EC (2000)." Christopher Board. Commission on the History of Cartography (ICA-CHC), 29 May 2003. <http://www.stub.unibe.ch/ica-chc/reports/icaexec-2000.html> (15 October 2003).

"Revision of Primary Series Maps." Fact Sheet 047-00, April 2000. U.S. Geological Survey, 31 December 2002. <http://mac.usgs.gov/mac/isb/pubs/factsheets/fs04700.html> (15 October 2003).

"Single-Edition Quadrangle Maps." Fact Sheet 094-98, August 1998. U.S. Geological Survey, 31 December 2002. <http://mac.usgs.gov/mac/isb/pubs/factsheets/fs09498.html> (15 October 2003).

Terraserver. Microsoft, 2003. <http://terraserver-usa.com> (15 October 2003).

"Topographic Mapping." On-line edition. U.S. Geological Survey, 9 October 2003. <http://mac.usgs.gov/mac/isb/pubs/booklets/topo/topo.html> (15 October 2003).

"Topographic Map Symbols." U.S. Geological Survey, 31 December 2002. <http://mac.usgs.gov/mac/isb/pubs/booklets/symbols/> (15 October 2003).

TopoZone. Maps a la carte, Inc., 2003. <http://www.topozone.com> (15 October 2003).

Treaty Oak, Map Distributor. Home page. Treaty Oak, 2003. <http://www.treatyoak.com/> (15 October 2003).

"US GeoData Available through the Internet." Fact Sheet Number 046-00, June 2000. U.S. Geological Survey, 31 December 2002. <http://mac.usgs.gov/mac/isb/pubs/factsheets/fs04600.html> (15 October 2003).

"USGS GeoData Digital Raster Graphics." Fact Sheet 088-01, September 2001. U.S. Geological Survey, 31 December 2002. <http://mac.usgs.gov/mac/isb/pubs/factsheets/fs08801.html> (15 October 2003).

"USGS Information Products about Mapping and Related Subjects." U.S. Geological Survey, 9 May 2003. <http://mac.usgs.gov/mac/isb/pubs/pubslists/index.html> (15 October 2003).

"USGS National Mapping Information: View USGS Maps and Aerial Photo Images Online." U.S. Geological Survey, 22 July 2003. <http://mapping.usgs.gov/partners/viewonline.html> (15 October 2003).

CHAPTER 6
Special Format Maps

TOPICS COVERED

Aeronautical Charts
  National Aeronautical Charting Office (NACO)
    Aeronautical Charts
  National Imagery and Mapping Agency (NIMA)
    Aeronautical Charts
Nautical Charts
  National Ocean Service (NOS) Nautical Charts
  National Imagery and Mapping Agency (NIMA)
    Nautical Charts
Geologic Maps
  United States Geological Survey—Geologic Division
  State Surveys
Fire Insurance Maps
Outline and Base Maps
Historic Land Records and Plat Maps
Weather Maps and Information

MAJOR SOURCES DISCUSSED

Nautical Chart Symbols Abbreviations and Terms, "Chart No. 1"
Geologic Map of the United States
National Geologic Map Database
New Publications of the United States Geological Survey
Publications of the U.S. Geological Survey
GeoRef
Main Types of Geological Maps: Purpose, Use and Preparation
Geological Maps: An Introduction

Geologic Maps: A Practical Guide to the Preparation and Interpretation of Geologic Maps
Fire Insurance Maps: Their History and Applications
Description and Utilization of the Sanborn Map
Fire Insurance Maps in the Library of Congress
Union List of Sanborn Fire Insurance Maps Held by Institutions in the United States and Canada
Central Intelligence Agency base maps
The World Factbook
World Eagle Today reproducible atlases
Illinois State Library list of Government Land Office collections
Bureau of Land Management land patents Web site
Weather Maps: How to Read and Interpret All the Basic Weather Charts
Air Apparent
Oxford Dictionary of Weather
Weatherwise
American Meteorological Society
Daily Weather Maps, Weekly Series
Climatic Atlas of the United States
Climate Atlas of the United States
UM Weather
The Weather Channel—Weather.com
USA Today Weather
National Oceanographic and Atmospheric Administration (NOAA) weather Web site
NOAA Weather Radio
National Weather Service Web site
National Climatic Data Center
Aeronautical Chart User's Guide
Understanding Aeronautical Charts

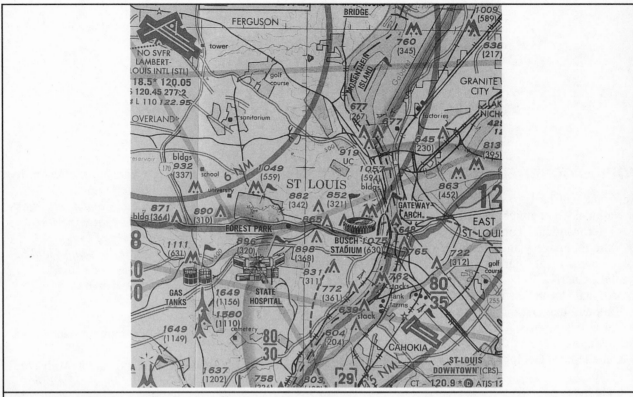

VISUAL FLIGHT RULES AERONAUTICAL CHART. NOTE THE PICTORIAL SYMBOLS FOR LARGE CONSTRUCTED LANDMARKS. *VFR TERMINAL AREA CHART, ST. LOUIS.* 1:250,000. 58TH ED. WASHINGTON, D.C.: U.S. DEPT. OF TRANSPORTATION, FEDERAL AVIATION ADMINISTRATION, NATIONAL AERONAUTICAL CHARTING OFFICE, 2002.

FIGURE 6.1

Some kinds of geographic data require specially formatted maps to meet specific display and analysis needs. These materials often are used under specific circumstances, but they have also been repurposed to meet unrelated or unforeseen needs. Many special format maps have a complex set of symbols or unique presentation styles that are not used on more general maps. The methods of depicting large amounts of information on special format maps may appear confusing at first, but with experience people interested in topics as diverse as the weather and historic urban buildings will find special format maps that help explore the natural and human-built environments.

AERONAUTICAL CHARTS

In the United States, aeronautical charts are produced by both civilian and military agencies. Generally, the civilian agencies create charts for domestic air and water while the military agencies, currently the National Imagery and Mapping Agency, create charts for nondomestic water and worldwide air.

National Aeronautical Charting Office (NACO) Aeronautical Charts

Since October 2000, domestic aeronautical charts have been created by the National Aeronautical Charting Office (NACO), part of the Federal Aviation Administration. Prior to October 2000, these charts were produced by the National Oceanic and Atmospheric Administration's (NOAA) Office of Aeronautical Charting and Cartography. A number of different aeronautical products are available ranging from 1:12,000-scale Airport Obstruction Charts to the 1:6,200,000-scale Gulf of Mexico and Caribbean Planning Chart. Each type of chart has unique features and specific intended uses as well as differing revision schedules. Some of the charts cover only specific areas such as individual airports, Airport Obstruction Charts, and Airport/Facility Directory entries, or regions with heavy air traffic, Terminal Area Charts (Figure 6.1), and Helicopter Route Charts. Other products provide complete quadrangle-based coverage of the United States, such as Sectional Aeronautical Charts and Instrument Flight Rules (IFR) EnRoute Low Altitude Charts.

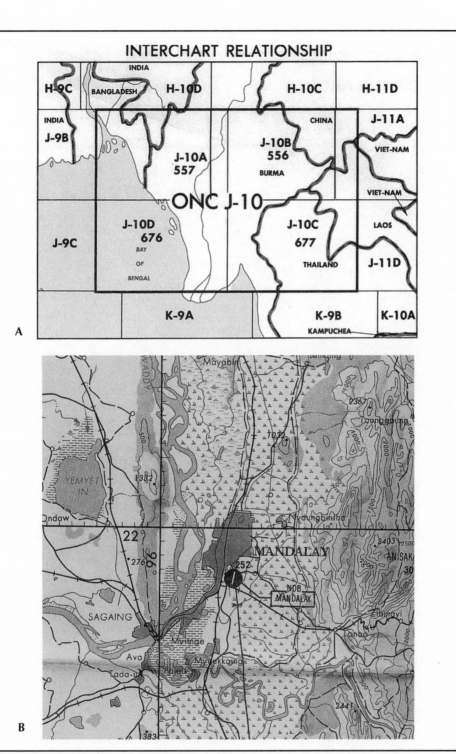

INTERCHART RELATIONSHIP

AN AERONAUTICAL CHART THAT ALSO COULD BE USED AS A SMALL-SCALE ROAD MAP. *TPC J-10A (Bangladesh, Burma, India).* 1:500,000. Ed. 4. St. Louis, Mo.: Defense Mapping Agency Aerospace Center, 1983. Reprinted by NIMA 8–97. **(a)** Sheet numbers for TPCs "nest" in ONC sheet numbers. **(b)** Road and railroad connections to Mandalay appear emphasized.

FIGURE 6.2

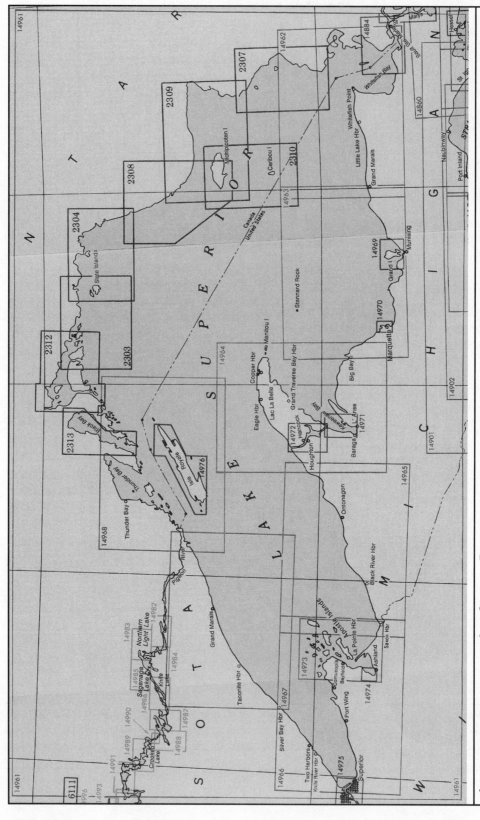

INDEX TO NAUTICAL CHARTS FOR LAKE SUPERIOR. EACH RECTANGLE REPRESENTS A SEPARATE CHART. *UNITED STATES GREAT LAKES AND ADJACENT WATERWAYS. CATALOG 4. 2000–2001.* WASHINGTON, D.C.: NATIONAL OCEANIC AND ATMOSPHERIC ADMINISTRATION, NATIONAL OCEAN SERVICE, OFFICE OF COAST SURVEY, 2000.

FIGURE 6.3

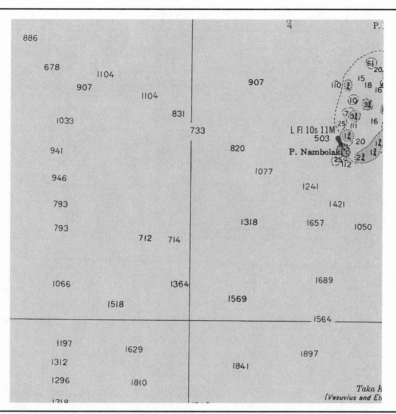

PORTION OF A NAUTICAL CHART SHOWING STRAIGHT LINE DATA COLLECTING PATTERN. *KEPULAUAN MACAN (KEPULAUAN BONE RATE) TO SELAT PELENG.* 1:747,750. 8TH ED. NIMA CHART 73008. 1996.

FIGURE 6.4

Descriptions of NACO's whole range of aeronautical chart products can be found on the Web (http://www.naco.faa.gov) by selecting "Catalog" from the left-hand navigation bar. Information about the latest editions of charts along with some digital products, mainly products that are heavily text-based, can be accessed through the Web site as well. NACO-produced aeronautical charts can be ordered directly from NACO via mail, in person, or by telephone, fax, or e-mail. NACO also has a network of authorized sales agents; a listing of these agents is available through the NACO Web site, as is a price list and other ordering information.

National Imagery and Mapping Agency (NIMA) Aeronautical Charts

The world coverage NIMA aeronautical products that are available for public use tend to be small-scale, generally 1:500,000 or smaller. Descriptions of NIMA products can be found in the free catalog available from NACO titled *National Imagery and Mapping Agency Public Scale Aeronautical Charts and Publications.* Some of the quadrilinear sets, such as the 1:500,000-scale Tactical Pilotage Charts (TPCs) (Fig-

ures 6.2a–b) and 1:1,000,000-scale Operational Navigation Charts (ONCs), can double as small-scale topographic maps for areas that have dated or difficult-to-locate topographic mapping. In fact, the description of TPCs in the NIMA public sales catalog says, "In remote areas of the world they can be substituted as road maps." Current price lists are maintained as part of the NACO Web site. NIMA aeronautical charts are available for purchase through NACO and through a network of authorized dealers.

The *Aeronautical Chart User's Guide,* an FAA publication, will serve as an introduction to aeronautical charts, explaining and illustrating symbols for visual flight rule charts, instrument flight rule charts, and instrument approach procedures. A printed guide can be purchased inexpensively, or it can be downloaded free-of-charge as PDF files from the web (http://www.naco.faa.gov/index.asp?xml=naco/online/aero_guide).

Understanding Aeronautical Charts provides a textbook-like description of aeronautical charts and other supplemental air navigation tools. The 10 chapters include 2 on the history of aeronautical charts and the basics of map reading, 3 covering visual charts, 3 on instrument procedure charts, and 2 on publications

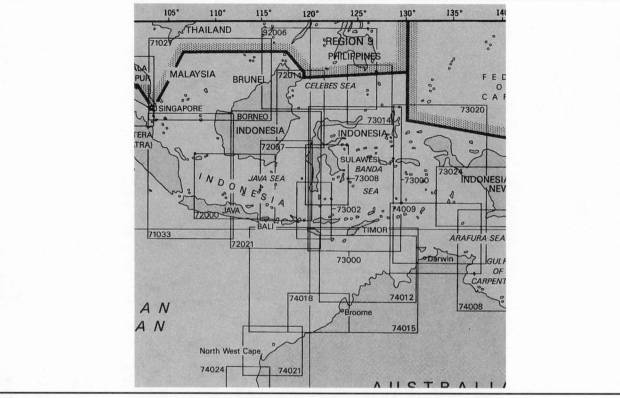

PORTION OF INDEX TO NAUTICAL CHARTS OF INDONESIA. EACH RECTANGLE REPRESENTS A SEPARATE CHART. "REGION 7: COASTAL CHARTS. FIGURE 7–1." P. 7–3 IN *CATALOG OF MAPS, CHARTS, AND RELATED PRODUCTS. NATIONAL IMAGERY AND MAPPING AGENCY PART 2- VOL. 1 HYDROGRAPHIC PRODUCTS, NAUTICAL CHARTS AND PUBLICATIONS.* 9TH ED. WASHINGTON, D.C.: DEFENSE LOGISTICS INFORMATION SYSTEM, 1998.

FIGURE 6.5

that supplement and support aeronautical chart use. Differences in the information presented by the charts and their uses are discussed. Black-and-white illustrations appear throughout the volume.

The *Aviator's Guide to Navigation* may also be of interest, especially for putting aeronautical charts into a use context, but it is intended for those who already have a basic understanding of aviation. Nineteen chapters describe and illustrate visual- and instrument-based navigation along with a variety of aids for navigation.

There are also nongovernmental aeronautical chart publishers. Commercially produced aeronautical training software, airport directories, "free flight" atlases for North America and Europe, as well as airfield manuals for European facilities and maps showing locations of European "aerodromes," are available from Jeppesen Sanderson (http://www.jeppesen.com/). National governments other than the United States also produce aeronautical charts.

NAUTICAL CHARTS

Like the aeronautical charts, nautical chart production occurs within a civilian agency, NOAA, and a military agency, NIMA, with the bulk of the military agency's public sales and distribution being handled by NOAA.

National Ocean Service (NOS) Nautical Charts

Domestic water charts are produced, within NOAA, by the National Ocean Service (NOS), specifically by the Office of Coast Survey (OCS). There are approximately 1,000 different charts of assorted types produced for domestic waters. Regardless of type (small craft, intercoastal waterway, harbor, coast, or general charts are most common), the fundamental purpose of a nautical chart is to facilitate safe navigation. Nautical charts are both road maps for marine areas and worksheets for developing safe routes. Information about nautical chart products is available through the OCS Web site (http://www.nauticalcharts.noaa.gov/). Besides paper, nautical charts are becoming available digitally in either raster or vector format. NOS nautical charts are indexed on four index maps that divide U.S. waters into four separate areas: Atlantic and Gulf coasts including Puerto Rico and the Virgin Islands; Pacific Coast including Hawaii, Guam, and Samoa Islands; Alaska; and the Great Lakes with adjacent waterways (Figure 6.3). (See Figures 3.3a–d for samples of NOAA nautical charts.)

Through the MapFinder (http://oceanservice.noaa. gov/mapfinder/), potential nautical chart users can identify the charts most appropriate for their use. The site also provides access to information about coastal photography and environmental maps. Scanned images of historical charts are available at the previously mentioned Office of the Coast Survey Web site.

NOS maintains a Web page about agency publication and products (http://www.nos.noaa.gov/pubs/welcome. html) that includes links to offices, programs, and projects along with links for ordering NOS-printed products or for accessing electronic products.

National Imagery and Mapping Agency (NIMA) Nautical Charts

NIMA nautical charts (Figure 6.4) are described and indexed in *Catalog of Maps, Charts, and Related Products*, Part 2, *Hydrographic Products: Nautical Charts and Publications*. The world's coastlines are divided into nine regions; each has a separate section in the catalog with index maps (Figure 6.5) that show the general extent of chart coverage as well as chart numbers and accompanying tables that include chart numbers, titles, scales, and price category. Sections two through nine show NIMA charts; section one, which covers North America, shows locations of NOS and Canadian Hydrographic Survey charts. The hydrographic products catalog is a necessary tool for determining chart coverage and ordering charts for purchase; many map libraries also use it as the index to their nautical chart collections. The *NIMA Hydrographic Products Catalog* is not available in its entirety through the Web, but the text in the catalog has been converted to a database that is searchable through the NIMA Maritime Safety Information Center Web site (http://pollux.nss.nima.mil/index/ index.html). This Web site also includes a number of different maritime calculators, PDF versions of *Notices to Mariners* that are used to update nautical charts, and other information sources for nautical travel. NIMA nautical charts, as well as the hydrographic products catalog, can be ordered through the U.S. Government Online Bookstore (http://book store.gpo.gov).

NIMA has also been working on a Digital Nautical Chart (DNC). Public access to the DNC is not yet widely available nor has DNC yet been authorized for civil navigation use. Distribution of the DNC will probably be done on CD-ROM. Background information about DNCs and viewing software are available through the NIMA Web site (http://164.214.2.53/ dncpublic/index.htm).

"Chart No. 1," produced jointly by NOS and NIMA *Nautical Chart Symbols Abbreviations and Terms*, is a nearly 100-page symbol key for charts produced by NOS and NIMA (as well as symbols specified by International Hydrographic Organization charts and some that appear on NIMA reproductions of foreign-produced charts). "Chart No. 1" is essential for using nautical charts. The symbols are divided into 21 lettered sections based on feature type, for example, "Rocks, Wrecks, Obstructions" and "Buoys, Beacons," grouped into four larger divisions: general, topography, hydrography, and aids and services. The index book also includes listings of abbreviations and is indexed. The contents of the current edition, the 10th, of "Chart No. 1" are available as PDF files—each file corresponding to a lettered section—through the "NIMA On-Line Navigation Publications" section of the NIMA Maritime Safety Information Center Web site (http://pollux.nss.nima.mil/index/index.html).

The *Nautical Chart User's Manual* expands on the information conveyed by "Chart No. 1," discussing different kinds of charts, the information presented on nautical charts, and how to interpret nautical chart symbols and use nautical charts for navigation. The author suggests that *Nautical Chart User's Manual* be read with "Chart No. 1" and a representative sample nautical chart nearby for easy reference. *Nautical Chart User's Manual* is available for free download from the OCS Web site (http://chartmaker.ncd.noaa. gov/staff/ncum/ncum.htm).

GEOLOGIC MAPS

Geologic maps and maps about geologically related phenomena like earthquakes, volcanoes, and subterranean aquifers are fundamental in understanding why the world looks and behaves the way it does. Geologic maps can be used to make initial decisions about which areas to examine more carefully for groundwater or petroleum resources. They can be used to site buildings in relationship to earthquake fault lines to potentially minimize earthquake-related damage. Geologic maps can also be used in the context of topographic maps to understand differences in landscape forms and patterns of weathering and erosion.

United States Geological Survey— Geologic Division

The lead U.S. federal agency for creating geologic maps is the Geologic Division of the United States Geological Survey (http://geology.usgs.gov/index.shtml). The division focuses attention on geologic hazards (earthquakes, volcanoes, landslides), geologic resources (mineral and energy), and geologic framework (bedrock geology, surficial geology).

Geologic maps are available at a wide variety of scales. The United States Geological Survey prepares geologic maps with areas ranging in size from the entire nation down to individual topographic quadrangles. The conterminous United States is covered by a 1:2,500,000-scale map, *Geologic Map of the United States (Exclusive of Alaska and Hawaii),* published on two sheets plus a separate legend sheet by the United States Geological Survey in 1974. Twenty years later, the map was reprinted and was reformatted for release on CD-ROM as part of the Geological Survey's *Digital Data Series.* At a Web site devoted to the *Geology of the Conterminous United States at 1:2,500,000 Scale* (http://pubs.usgs.gov/dds/dds11/), an image of the map can be viewed; map files compatible with ESRI's ARC/Info and ArcView software can be downloaded for free; and text from *Professional Paper 901,* which describes how the 1974 geologic map was compiled and the history of geologic mapping in the United States, can be read. The CD-ROM also includes the full text of *Professional Paper 901* in both PDF and HTML formats. The map is stored on the CD-ROM in a number of different formats and also comes with a map-viewing software package.

The United States Geological Survey has a number of "lettered" map series devoted to geologic mapping. The Geologic Quadrangle (GQ) series use 7.5- and 15-minute topographic quadrangles as base maps for multicolor maps showing bedrock, surficial, and engineering geology. Other series that include geologic maps on a variety of base maps and at a variety of scales are Miscellaneous Investigations (MI), called Geologic Investigations after August 1996, and Miscellaneous Field Studies (MF). Quite often, geologic maps have appeared in a "pre-publication" state as part of the Open File (OF) series. All geologic maps approved for publication by the United States Geological Survey after August 1996 are appearing in the Geologic Investigations series.

Beyond typical surficial, bedrock, and engineering geology maps, the United States Geological Survey has created a number of maps showing geologically-related topics such as the "ring of fire" surrounding the Pacific Ocean Basin, seismic-hazard maps for Alaska and the Aleutian Islands, maps showing coal-mining areas, and maps showing areas that could be affected by pyroclastic mudflows from Mount Rainier. Surprisingly, the Geological Survey also prepares maps of extraterrestrial areas like the Moon, Venus, and Mars for the National Aeronautics and Space Administration (NASA).

Information about geologic map coverage is available through the National Geologic Map Database (http://ngmdb.usgs.gov). Print and digital geologic maps and other geologic information resources can be searched for by data or information "theme," location, author, title, map number, scale, format, date, and publisher. The database includes citations to nearly all of the United States Geological Survey's geologic publications plus some state geological survey and geological society publications. The lists resulting from searches include full citations and purchase information. A few of the digital products, for example, the "Color Shaded Relief Map of the Conterminous United States," are available for free download through the Web. In these cases, there is a link in the citation information that leads directly to the download's Web page.

New Publications of the U.S. Geological Survey
 (http://pubs.usgs.gov/publications/index.shtml)
Publications of the U.S. Geological Survey
 (http://usgs-georef.cos.com/)
GeoRef

New Publications of the United States Geological Survey is available at no cost through the Web: once released monthly and then quarterly, it is no longer available on paper. The Web site's monthly updates include full citations often accompanied by brief abstracts or descriptions for all publications released by the Geological Survey. Some items are available through the Web, and the entries will include URL links to PDF documents or sites from which data sets can be downloaded.

Contents of *New Publications of the U.S. Geological Survey* can be searched on-line without cost through Publications of the U.S. Geological Survey, which is a subset of the American Geological Institute's *GeoRef* database. The reports and maps included in the database include USGS publications, non-USGS publications authored by USGS authors, and materials produced by the western surveys of

Hayden, King, Powell, and Wheeler prior to the founding of the United States Geological Survey.

GeoRef, the most comprehensive database on the geosciences with more than 2.1 million entries, combines four major print bibliographies plus additional specialized sources into one database covering publications since 1785 about North American geology and publications since 1933 for other areas of the world. Materials indexed, beyond all of the United States Geological Survey's publications, include journal articles, books, maps, conference reports and papers, and theses. All aspects of geology are covered by the database. Information about *GeoRef,* including a full list of topics and journals indexed, can be found at the *GeoRef* Information Services Web site (http://www.georef.org). *GeoRef* is not a free service; the database can be subscribed to through a number of different database service providers.

State Surveys

Each state has a state geological survey. The variety of scale and scope of materials published by state geological surveys augments and is similar to that of the United States Geological Survey. State surveys have produced maps covering entire states as well as maps using standard USGS topographic quadrangles as base maps. State geologic surveys, along with other state agencies, may also be responsible for working closely with the Mapping Division of the United States Geological Survey to update topographic quadrangles and to fly statewide aerial photography on a regular schedule.

Links to state geological survey Web sites have been collected by the Association of American State Geologists (http://www.stategeologists.org). The association also maintains links to a wide variety of other geological professional organizations and to geologic agencies of non-U.S. nations.

Main Types of Geological Maps: Purpose, Use and Preparation
Prepared under the auspices of the French Oil and Gas Industry Association, *Main Types of Geological Maps* includes straightforward descriptions of more than 40 kinds of geological and geophysical maps. The descriptions are presented in a standardized format: definition; research purpose; use, including both advantages and disadvantages along with other maps that the subject type could be used with; preparation method, including materials and techniques used; and

variant maps. Many of the descriptions include black-and-white diagrams and maps, and there is a small section of color plates at the end of the volume. The introductory material includes general information about geologic map preparation with an extensive section illustrating typical geologic map symbols. There also is a table that classifies all of the maps discussed by their objectives, serving as a functional or definitional table of contents to the book.

Main Types of Geological Maps, because of its formulaic definitional approach, does not rely on extended amounts of text to describe different types of geologic maps. Instead it relies on short, to-the-point, and somewhat technical descriptions that sometimes necessitate a previous understanding of geologic terms. This work will not necessarily be of assistance in reading and interpreting geologic mapping, but it may be useful to communicate with agencies that create geologic maps about information needs.

Geological Maps: An Introduction. 2nd ed.
Geological Maps, intended as a textbook for first-year British undergraduate students, covers fundamentals of geologic map reading and interpretation in 12 chapters. After the first chapter, which describes basics of topographic base maps and the kinds of information found on geologic maps, 10 chapters describe specific geologic aspects as shown on maps. Using geologic maps to develop geological histories; for activities that affect the environment, like waste disposal and construction; and for understanding landscapes are covered in the next three chapters. *Geological Maps* concludes with a chapter documenting the historical development of geologic mapping and a chapter about producing geologic maps.

Nearly all of the chapters are extensively illustrated with black-and-white maps and diagrams. Eight color maps with interpretative questions and text can be found in the middle of the volume. Throughout *Geological Maps,* key vocabulary is printed in bold type, and each chapter concludes with a numbered list of summary statements and a brief bibliography. Twenty-four map exercises are scattered throughout the volume. The volume concludes with a bibliography and index.

Geological Maps is highly readable. Although it is intended for a British audience, the examples and map exercises are drawn from throughout the world, with half from England or Wales. All of the maps necessary to complete the exercises are included in the volume. *Geological Maps* assumes that the reader has some

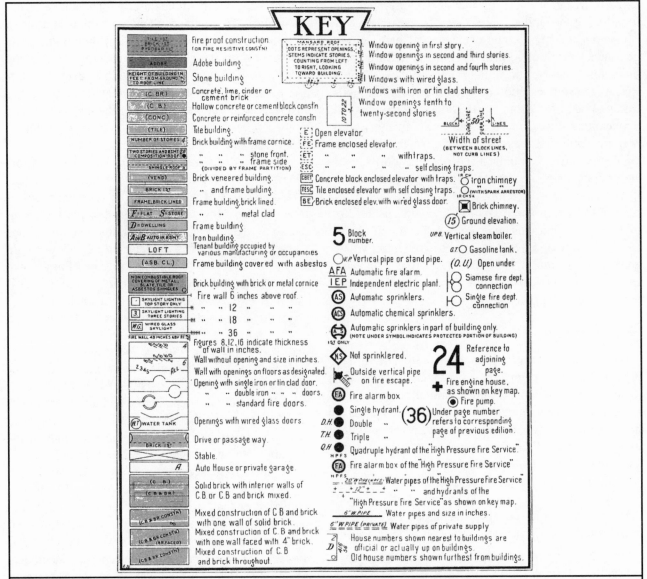

SYMBOL KEY TO SANBORN FIRE INSURANCE MAPS. *THE KEY TO SYMBOLS. DESCRIPTION AND UTILIZATION OF THE SANBORN MAP. NEW YORK: SANBORN MAP COMPANY, 1953. COPYRIGHT (1953) THE SANBORN MAP COMPANY, THE SANBORN LIBRARY, LLC. ALL RIGHTS RESERVED. FURTHER REPRODUCTIONS PROHIBITED WITHOUT PRIOR WRITTEN PERMISSION.*

FIGURE 6.6

basic level of map-reading ability along with a fundamental understanding of geologic terminology and periods, although the illustrations go a long way to assist in understanding the text.

Geologic Maps: A Practical Guide to the Preparation and Interpretation of Geologic Maps. 2nd ed.

Geologic Maps is a "work manual" with perforated pages intended to be used in courses on geologic map interpretation or field geology or as a self-instruction guide. The 12 short chapters describe maps and images used to study the Earth, maps used as base maps for geologic mapping, interpreting geologic maps and

aerial photographs, depicting common structures and rock types on geologic maps, and preparing geologic maps. All of the chapters include black-and-white illustrations, maps, and diagrams; 19 color maps are included as a "Geologic Map Reference Set" in the second appendix. The first appendix briefly covers a variety of topics essential for "Safety in the Field." *Geologic Maps* also includes a selected bibliography. All of the chapters, except for the first, include map exercises using materials included in the volume, and all of the exercises focus on features found in the United States. Unfortunately, answers for the exer-

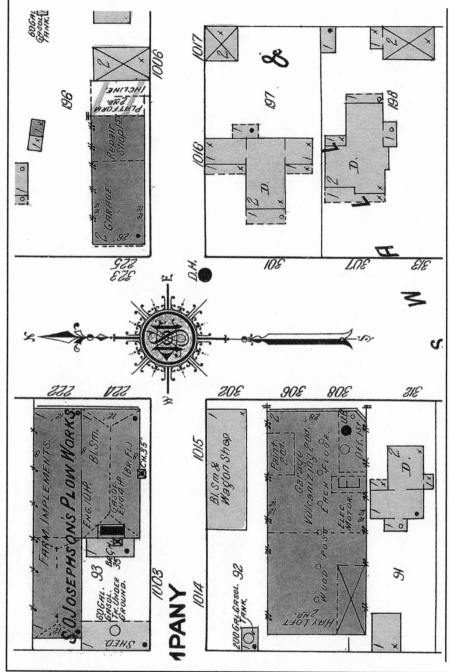

PASSAGE OF TWENTY YEARS MADE A LARGE DIFFERENCE AT THIS INTERSECTION. NOTE THE DISAPPEARANCE OF THE WAGON SHOP AT THE SOUTHWEST CORNER AND THE LARGE HOME ON THE SOUTHEAST CORNER REPLACED BY A FILLING STATION. (A) PRINCETON, ILL. SHEET 6. OCT. 1911. NEW YORK: SANBORN MAP COMPANY, 1911. *COPYRIGHT (1911) THE SANBORN MAP COMPANY, THE SANBORN LIBRARY, LLC. ALL RIGHTS RESERVED. FURTHER REPRODUCTIONS PROHIBITED WITHOUT PRIOR WRITTEN PERMISSION.*

FIGURE 6.7

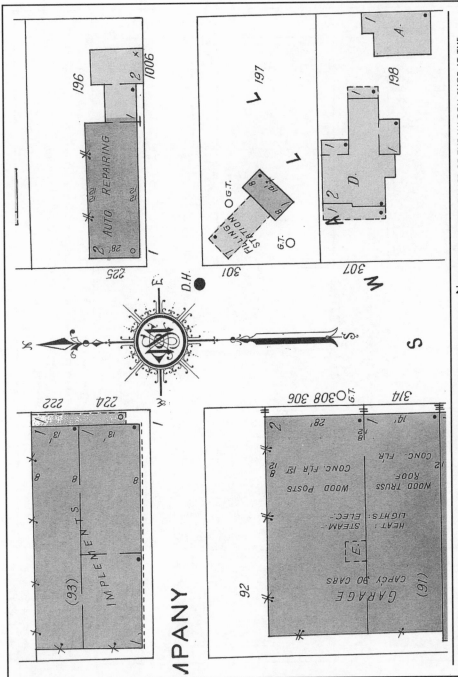

PASSAGE OF TWENTY YEARS MADE A LARGE DIFFERENCE AT THIS INTERSECTION. NOTE THE DISAPPEARANCE OF THE WAGON SHOP AT THE SOUTHWEST CORNER AND THE LARGE HOME ON THE SOUTHEAST CORNER REPLACED BY A FILLING STATION. (B) PRINCETON, ILL. SHEET 3. JAN 1931. NEW YORK: SANBORN MAP COMPANY, 1931. *COPYRIGHT (1931) THE SANBORN MAP COMPANY, THE SANBORN LIBRARY, LLC. ALL RIGHTS RESERVED. FURTHER REPRODUCTIONS PROHIBITED WITHOUT PRIOR WRITTEN PERMISSION.*

FIGURE 6.7 (continued)

cises are not included in *Geologic Maps.* An instructor's manual is available.

FIRE INSURANCE MAPS

Fire insurance maps of urban areas were produced from the mid-eighteenth until the mid-twentieth century to assist underwriters in determining the likelihood of a specific structure being destroyed by fire based on building structure, heating mechanism, use, and the characteristics of neighboring structures. Information on street and fire suppression systems was also included.

Historic fire insurance maps are being used by corporations and individuals interested in acquiring a particular piece of property to determine if there is a possibility of needing to invest in environmental remediation. Urban history studies can be enhanced by using fire insurance maps to track how particular plats of land or buildings were used; to establish a sequence of construction, demolition, and new construction; and to trace industrial growth. Family historians have used fire insurance maps to confirm details in family letters about places of both residence and employment and about transportation methods (foot, streetcar, or urban rail line) between home and work.

The first fire insurance maps for major towns in the "colonies" were produced in London between 1785 and 1792; unfortunately, these maps no longer appear to exist. After the War of 1812, the number of U.S. insurance companies began to increase. Small companies generally insured urban construction in their immediate area. Eventually small providers were aggregated to create larger companies, and centers of the insurance industry quickly developed in Hartford, Connecticut; Boston; and New York City. Large companies that insured structures scattered over a wide area had to rely on fire insurance maps, instead of personal field surveys, to describe the buildings they had contracted to insure. Map standards were developed in the mid-nineteenth century for color, symbols, size, and scale (Figure 6.6) and were closely followed by most fire insurance map producers for more than a century.

The Aetna Fire Insurance Company was an early and enthusiastic adopter of fire insurance maps. In 1866, Aetna hired David A. Sanborn to prepare maps of cities in Tennessee. In 1867, after finishing his work in Tennessee, Sanborn founded the D.A. Sanborn National Insurance Diagram Bureau in New York City. Eventually, the Sanborn Map Company became the overwhelming leader in preparing fire insurance maps and had a near monopoly by 1920. In 1926, on the occasion of the company's 60th anniversary a commemorative volume was printed that stated "that nearly every town with a thousand inhabitants and over in the United States and territories has been mapped." (*Sixtieth Anniversary,* p. 11) There were other companies that produced fire insurance maps, often focusing on a specific region, but because of Sanborn's large presence this specialized map format is often casually referred to as "Sanborns" in the same way that photocopying is often called "Xeroxing."

Sanborn fire insurance maps follow the stringent fire insurance map standard. The earliest maps are all at the scale of 1 inch = 50 feet, 1:600. Construction methods are shown by color: frame, yellow; solid brick, red; stone or masonry, blue; fireproofed or construction of noncombustible materials, brown. Wall thickness, the number of window openings on each floor, and building dimensions including height are all documented. Building use is recorded, often very simply such as "D" for dwelling or "A" for private automobile garage (Figures 6.7a–b). Commercial buildings are detailed with type of business, sometimes with specific firm names for larger structures. If a business used a heat source in part of its process (kilns, smelting furnaces, and smokehouses are all typical examples), the specific location is indicated as are any concentrations of flammable materials.

Multiple editions were published. Each edition built upon and corrected or updated the previous edition, and later editions usually cover more area than earlier ones. In some cases, particularly for later editions, updates and corrections have been made by pasting in correction slips that were available from the Sanborn Map Company through a subscription.

Each set has a graphic index, a simplified map of the community with colored and numbered rectangles overprinted to represent how individual sheets provide coverage. Conveniently, sheet numbers often remained consistent from edition to edition. Rarely is an entire town completely represented. It appears that commercial and industrial areas are usually completely covered but residential areas are not always fully represented. Sometimes an area will have been built but will not be included until a later edition. Users should not assume that they are without coverage until all possible editions have been inspected.

Often, especially for larger sets, a tabular index of streets, including block and house numbers keyed to map sheet numbers, is also included. Sometimes the tabular index does not point to the expected sheet. This is because the house and block number may have been changed since the time of map publication. Potential users are advised to know both house or block number and cross-streets. It also is imperative to already know, or to be willing to accept if discovered, alternative street names.

Fire Insurance Maps: Their History and Applications

Fire Insurance Maps: Their History and Applications describes the history of the Sanborn Map Company in detail along with brief coverage of other companies, which were sometimes competitors but often were later absorbed by Sanborn. This book is full of anecdotes that help illustrate the personalities that created the Sanborn maps. An entire chapter is devoted to describing how Sanborn maps were created and updated.

The history of fire insurance mapping in the United States is most fully covered by Walter W. Ristow in his 1968 article "United States Fire Insurance and Underwriters Maps, 1852–1968," which was first published in *The Quarterly Journal of the Library of Congress* and reprinted in *Surveying and Mapping*.

Description and Utilization of the Sanborn Map

Although most community sets include a symbol key, *Description and Utilization of the Sanborn Map* (1953) will be a useful guide to making fuller use of the maps. The booklet appears to have been produced for map users and, after a short company history and discussion of possible uses, includes extensive "narrative descriptions" interpreting two small sample maps, one of a commercial block and the other of a residential area. Each narrative works through each building in detail, describing how the symbols build to create a description of structure construction and use. Because the Sanborn Map Company's adherence to the fire insurance standards, ideas gleaned from these interpretive guides can be applied to any of the company's maps.

Fire Insurance Maps in the Library of Congress: Plans of North American Cities and Towns Produced by the Sanborn Map Company

The Library of Congress, Geography and Map Division holds the nation's most extensive collection of Sanborn-produced fire insurance maps, more than 12,000 cities covered by an excess of 700,000 map sheets. This coverage is listed in *Fire Insurance Maps in the Library of Congress: Plans of North American Cities and Towns Produced by the Sanborn Map Company*. The checklist includes the division's entire Sanborn collection: bound, unbound, or reproduced on microfilm. Cities are arranged alphabetically within state chapters. Each edition entry includes the month and year of publication, the number of sheets contained, and as needed, additional comments about other towns included in the set and any distinctive features or variations. Two indexes follow the entries, one a list of city entries by state and the other an alphabetical list of all towns covered by the maps. This second index is essential because occasionally one set provides details of multiple, adjacent villages or a set for a large city will include coverage for immediately adjacent suburbs. The entries are preceded by an extensive introduction to fire insurance maps and the history of the Sanborn Map Company. Because of the extensiveness of the division's collections, the checklist can be used as a guide to whether coverage for specific towns and years exists. It will help in accessing both the collection housed in Washington, D.C., and collections throughout the United States because between 1955 and 1978 the Geography and Map Division distributed duplicate Sanborn materials to universities nationwide. These institutions are listed in the preface to *Fire Insurance Maps in the Library of Congress*.

Union List of Sanborn Fire Insurance Maps Held by Institutions in the United States and Canada

A two-volume bibliography, *Union List of Sanborn Fire Insurance Maps Held by Institutions in the United States and Canada* (1976 and 1977), lists Sanborn maps held by 162 libraries, excluding the Library of Congress and the library at California State University, Northridge, which have their own lists. Like the list of the Library of Congress, Geography and Map Division, the *Union List* provides a state-organized alphabetical town list. Edition years with number of sheets and coding for owning libraries follow each town name. Although the Library of Congress has the most extensive collection, other libraries will have revisions that the Library of Congress does not have. The *Union List* may indirectly lead to smaller, less known collections through discussions with experts at the listed collections. The *Union List* does not include holdings from all possible organizations. It primarily focuses on large, well-established collections. There will be pockets of fire insurance maps at county and local historical societies and city and county offices. Another possible place to inquire would be at insurance agency offices with long-established ties to the local community. There is always the possibility that maps, although no longer used, have been secreted away in a forgotten closet.

Occasionally, journals published by map librarians and historical geographers have included union lists of fire insurance maps for specific states. These lists often focus on fire insurance map producers other than Sanborn. Local experts will be able to assist in tracking down such specialized publications.

The Sanborn fire insurance maps are available for purchase as black-and-white microfilm copies. Two companies have been involved in this endeavor: Chadwyck-Healey and University Publications of America (UPA). The Chadwyck-Healey product reproduced Sanborns at the Library of Congress while UPA reproduced maps in the Sanborn Map Company's archives. The advantage to these sets is that more people are able to view and use Sanborn maps. But the color-coded construction information is lost. Most recently, digital versions of the Sanborn fire insurance maps have become available for use through the Web by subscription from ProQuest Information and Learning. The digital Sanborns were produced from black-and-white microfilm copies of the Library of Congress collection. Paper copies of individual maps can be ordered from Environmental Data Resources (EDR), which purchased the Sanborn Map Company in 1996 (http://www.edrnet.com).

OUTLINE AND BASE MAPS

Outline, also called blank or base, maps are usually simple maps showing a country's or state's external boundaries and sometimes including water features, major cities, first-level administrative boundaries, or large landforms such as mountains. These simple maps can be used as the foundation (or base) layer for creating thematic maps. Some base maps include a sufficient amount of detail that they can stand as a "complete" map, while others are no more than a polygon enclosed by a single simple line. Base maps are available on paper and through the Web.

Geography About.com includes a number of links to "Blank & Outline Maps" (http://geography. about.com/cs/blankoutlinemaps/), some created by About.com and others housed at external sites. Additional sites can be found by searching "outline maps, "blank maps," or "base maps." Most often, the maps will be in either GIF or PDF formats. The GIF-formatted maps can be copied to graphics programs for editing and adding features, names, or color prior to printing, but the PDF-formatted maps can only be printed as they appear on the site.

Many outline map providers, including those linked to by Geography About.com, are educational textbook publishers. The Houghton Mifflin Social Studies Center (http://www.eduplace.com/ss/) includes a section of outline maps, scans of maps—some in PDF format—that have been published previously on paper. The selection includes maps of continents, hemispheres, the world, and nine that focus specifically on the United States, including a map with all of the states and their capitals labeled, a map of climate zones, and a political/physical map that includes (without labels) state boundaries, major rivers, and mountain chains. Unfortunately, the U.S. thematic maps do not necessarily display well; the climate map is particularly confusing because five types of climate are listed in the symbol key but on both the screen display and printed page only two shades of gray can be differentiated. The maps in PDF are formatted to make use of an entire 8.5-by-11-inch sheet of paper; the other maps use only one- to two-thirds of the sheet when printed, and the text may not be completely readable.

The Scott Foresman educators' Web site (http://www.scottforesman.com/educators/) section on cross-curricular activities includes outline maps with a predominant focus on the United States with seven regional maps. There are also continental maps and a world map. None of the maps have any text or relief features (mountain chains); some major lakes (Great Salt Lake, Yellowstone Lake, Lake Tanganyika) are shown. As with the Houghton Mifflin site, the maps print on the top half of an 8.5-by-11-inch sheet of paper.

The National Geographic Society's Xpeditions Web site (http://www.nationalgeographic.com/xpeditions/) contains a number of educationally related resources, including an extensive library of outline maps called "Xpeditions Atlas," which have been designed specifically for Web viewing and printing. World, continental, and national maps, plus maps focusing on individual states or provinces of the United States, Canada, and Mexico, can be displayed and printed with or without place names. Countries and states display within the context of surrounding areas. Surrounding areas are shown with the name of the state or country regardless of whether the place names have been turned off for the focus area. Place name details, if activated, are shown only for the focus area. The maps can be displayed both in GIF and PDF, with PDF the better printing option. The maps are all oriented 11-by-8.5 landscape, which does not always work successfully. States or countries that are wider east-to-west than they are tall north-to-south make better use of the page than areas that are taller in the north-south aspect.

The Central Intelligence Agency has produced a group of 8.5-by-11-inch maps of continents, regions, and individual countries. The country maps usually appear in two different versions: a planimetric version, which includes no indication of relief, and a shaded relief version. Both versions include major roads, rivers, and cities. The maps of continents and regions are usually political and show individual countries as solid colors, although recently the agency has been releasing shaded relief maps of regions. Generally, the CIA maps make good color overhead transparencies and slides. They do not copy well on standard black-and-white copiers because the blue that is used to depict rivers and coastlines (the boundary between land and ocean) is unable to be photocopied well; photocopied coastlines will be fuzzy and rivers will disappear.

Many of the CIA maps, including maps larger than the 8.5-by-11-inch base maps, have been scanned and are available through the Web. A small group of reference maps, primarily continents and regions, in two formats, JPG and PDF, can be found at the CIA's *World Factbook* site (http://www.odci.gov/cia/publications/factbook/). A much more extensive collection has been scanned and is being hosted by the Perry-Castañeda Library Map Collection of the University of Texas at Austin (http://www.lib.utexas.edu/maps/index.html). The maps are organized by continent and by country covered. Most of the files are JPGs with a few GIFs and PDFs. Many of the maps are larger than a single screen and will require multiple pieces of 8.5-by-11-inch paper to print.

It is unfortunate that the CIA's 8.5-by-11-inch base maps do not copy well on a self-service machine because they are ideal for including in reports or on posters. World Eagle Today has published a group of six reproducible loose-leaf atlases for Africa, Asia, Europe, Latin America, the Middle East, and North America. The last section in each atlas is comprised of black-and-white 8.5-by-11-inch copies of base maps from the Central Intelligence Agency, the United States Department of State, and the United Nations. Some of these maps have the potential to copy on a self-service photocopier more clearly than the color CIA maps. Beyond the map section, the *[Continent Name] Today: A Reproducible Atlas* includes statistical graphs and charts, comparative maps, maps of regions, thematic maps, and blank continental maps plus some descriptive text.

HISTORIC LAND RECORDS AND PLAT MAPS

The 13 American colonies were originally surveyed using a system called *metes and bounds,* which relied on lines plotted and described by referring to landmarks. Unfortunately, the landmarks were often impermanent, such as trees, fence posts, and river bends, and the descriptions could be quite lengthy and difficult to interpret. The surveys usually began at a specific landmark and described property boundaries in an almost conversational style with indications of compass direction and distance, bounding corner landmarks, and owners of adjoining property. The property boundary would be described in a sequence designed to encircle the entire property and close the description at the beginning point.

After the Revolution, the U.S. government owned a substantial amount of land that had been either confiscated from people loyal to the British crown or that had been ceded to the United States by other nations or by individual states. The confederation of states also had numerous debts to pay both to France and to the veterans of the Revolution. The debt to the soldiers dated to the signing of the Declaration of Independence when the Continental Congress offered bounties of land for enlistment. The United States had no ready stash of cash but it did have land. The rectangular land survey system, or Public Land Survey System (PLSS), was put into place in 1785 through an ordinance passed by Congress to facilitate the division of land for claims and sales. Surveying began in September 1785 on the north bank of the Ohio River at Pennsylvania's western boundary. Additional legislation was passed by Congress in 1796 that refined procedures for surveying. This act put into place the numbering scheme still used today to number sections within townships. The description of property was greatly streamlined from the laborious metes-and-bounds descriptions. Four sections in the center of the township, sections 15, 16, 21 and 22, were reserved for the government. Eventually, beginning in 1803, section 16 of each township was granted to the states to support schools. Some states sold the lands; others retained the lands and continue to support schools through rents and natural resources sales. An important piece of documentation procedure was enacted in May 1800 in which the Surveyor General was required to produce three copies of the plat maps—one for the land sales office, a second for the Secretary of the Treasury, and the original for the files of the Surveyor General.

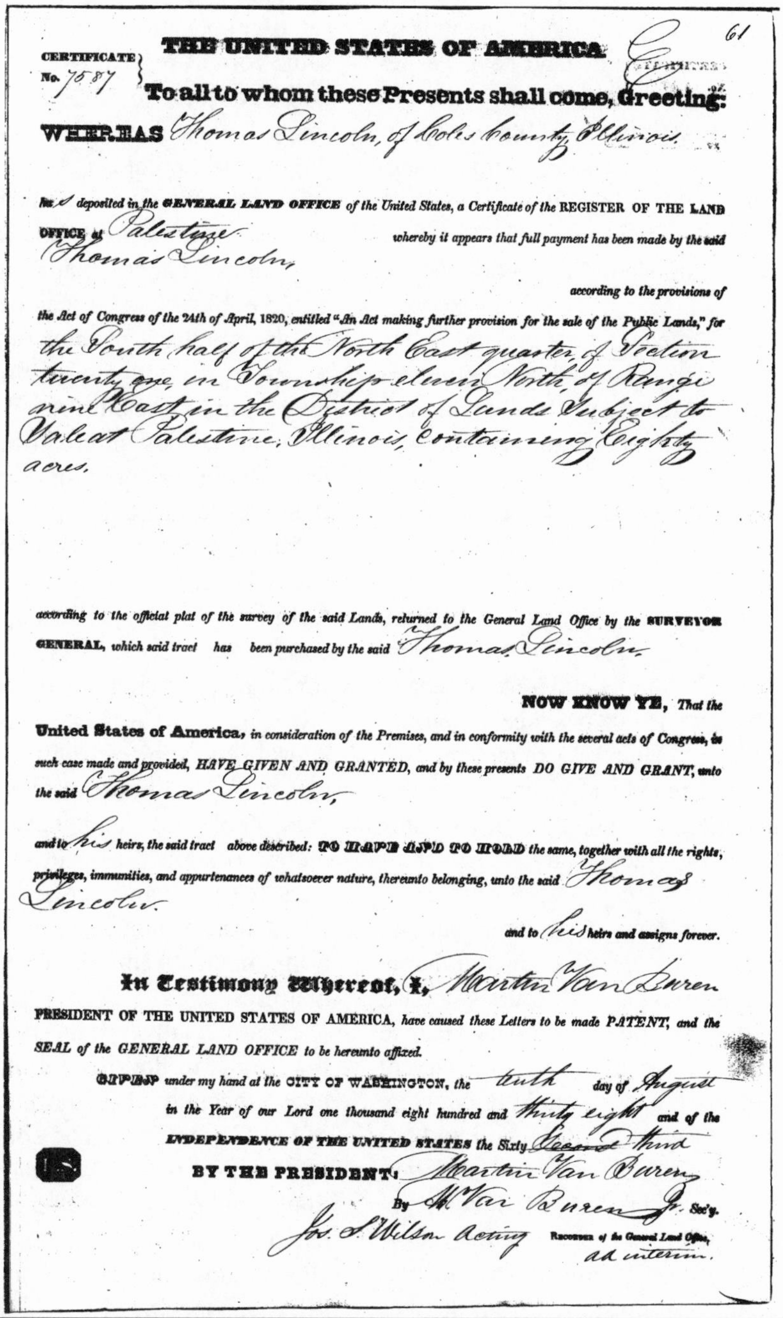

61

CERTIFICATE No. 7587

THE UNITED STATES OF AMERICA,

To all to whom these Presents shall come, Greeting:

WHEREAS Thomas Lincoln, of Coles County, Illinois

has deposited in the GENERAL LAND OFFICE of the United States, a Certificate of the REGISTER OF THE LAND OFFICE at Palestine whereby it appears that full payment has been made by the said Thomas Lincoln,

according to the provisions of the Act of Congress of the 24th of April, 1820, entitled "An Act making further provision for the sale of the Public Lands," for the South half of the North East quarter of Section twenty one in Township eleven North of Range nine East in the District of Lands Subject to Sale at Palestine, Illinois, containing Eighty acres,

according to the official plat of the survey of the said Lands, returned to the General Land Office by the SURVEYOR GENERAL, which said tract has been purchased by the said Thomas Lincoln,

NOW KNOW YE, That the United States of America, in consideration of the Premises, and in conformity with the several acts of Congress, in such case made and provided, HAVE GIVEN AND GRANTED, and by these presents DO GIVE AND GRANT, unto the said Thomas Lincoln,

and to his heirs, the said tract above described: TO HAVE AND TO HOLD the same, together with all the rights, privileges, immunities, and appurtenances of whatsoever nature, thereunto belonging, unto the said Thomas Lincoln,

and to his heirs and assigns forever.

In Testimony Whereof, I, Martin Van Buren

PRESIDENT OF THE UNITED STATES OF AMERICA, have caused these Letters to be made PATENT, and the SEAL of the GENERAL LAND OFFICE to be hereunto affixed.

GIVEN under my hand at the CITY OF WASHINGTON, the tenth day of August in the Year of our Lord one thousand eight hundred and thirty eight and of the INDEPENDENCE OF THE UNITED STATES the Sixty Second third

L.S.

BY THE PRESIDENT: Martin Van Buren

By M. Van Buren Jr. Sec'y.

Jos. S. Wilson acting Recorder of the General Land Office, ad interim.

THOMAS LINCOLN LAND PATENT ISSUED IN 1838. ABRAHAM LINCOLN NEVER LIVED ON THIS PROPERTY. HTTP://WWW.GLORECORDS.BLM.GOV/.

FIGURE 6.8

The Government Land Office (GLO) was created as a bureau within the Department of the Treasury in April 1812 and charged with overseeing public lands in the United States. The GLO was transferred to the Department of the Interior when it was formed in 1849. The Bureau of Land Management (BLM) published *A History of the Rectangular Survey System,* an extensive history of the work of the GLO from the early seventeenth century to 1946, when the GLO merged with a number of other agencies to form the Bureau of Land Management. A companion volume, *Initial Points of the Rectangular Survey System,* further discusses how the survey was applied to specific areas of the United States.

The GLO ultimately produced maps for 30 PLSS states. The field notes and original plat maps will be useful for constructing a picture of land cover, especially presettlement vegetation, early in the country's history. The original and (mainly) microfilm copies of the maps are still available for use along with surveyors' field notes; a list of their locations is available through a Web site hosted by the Illinois State Library (http://www.cyberdriveillinois.com/library/isl/ref/glo/glolocguide.html).

The Bureau of Land Management is making image files of GLO land patents, which document the transfer of land ownership from the federal government to individuals in public land states, available through the Web (http://www.glorecords.blm.gov). Land title records from 32 states plus Washington, D.C., are included thus far in the database. The original 13 colonies/states and their territories (Maine, Vermont, West Virginia, Tennessee, and Kentucky) are not included because none of the sale or distribution of land within their boundaries was overseen by the federal government.

The database can be searched by patentee or warrantee name, county name, legal land description, and date. Thomas Lincoln can be searched for in Illinois with one match, property purchased in 1838 in Coles County (Figure 6.8). Mark Twain's father, John Clemens, purchased property in Monroe County, Missouri, in 1837, two years after Twain was born. Scanned images of these and other patents can be viewed in three different formats and can be printed directly from the Web site. Certified copies can also be purchased. The General Land Office Records Web site includes a glossary of terms used by the General Land Office, descriptions of the kinds of records produced by the General Land Office, and a history and timeline of the office's activities. There are also a number of links to state-focused resources such as state archives and genealogy sites.

The General Land Office Records Web site will help identify when land was transferred from the federal government to private individuals, but it will not identify transfers of land between individuals. Landownership of specific areas, after the patent or warrant stage, can be tracked partially by using chronological sequences of plat books.

Current county plat books are published by a variety of publishers, both commercial and governmental. Commercial publishers often focus on a geographic service region (sometimes multistate), preparing and publishing plat books (often containing locally-based paid advertisements) within that region. Governmental bodies that produce plat books are often at the county level and produce a much more geographically limited set of publications. Plat books generally follow the same format regardless of publisher; a separate page will be devoted to each township. Sections, roads, railroads, bodies of water, and urban extent are all shown, but the focal point is rural property ownership with the size and shape of parcels indicated. Generally, the same kinds of information always will be found: township maps, county map, index to property owners. Some publishers also include a telephone directory to residents actually residing on the property. County plat books organized by township do not cover urban areas in any kind of detail; they only show the extent of the urban area. Plats for urban subdivisions can be located through city or county government agencies, but they only show lot location, shape, and size, not ownership.

Finding current or recent local plat books can be tricky because of the focused nature of the products. Calling the appropriate county agency, perhaps the county tax assessor or agricultural extension agent, for a recommendation may be a good first step. "Real property—[State]—[County]—Maps" is the appropriate subject heading to use when looking for plat books in library catalogs. Searching the Web for "plat book(s)," "landownership," or "landownership maps" produces a scattershot of results including sites for publishers or sellers of maps, information about library holdings, and a scattering of descriptions of pre-twentieth-century plat books or county histories.

Commercially produced county maps and atlases first began to flourish during the mid-nineteenth century, especially in the northeast and midwest sections of the United States and somewhat in the central and eastern portions of Canada. Typically, in the United States, the publishers took federally created plats, updated and augmented them with detailed information about roads and farms, and repackaged the maps to sell them specifically to inhabitants of and businesses in the represented county. Often, individuals and businesses became subscribers, taking out advertising in the published volumes. The advertising was not necessarily for businesses; subscribers also had biographical family sketches, portraits, and illustrations of homesteads, prized livestock, and grand homes appearing in the atlases. The period immediately before the Civil War through the late 1870s was the highpoint of illustrated county atlas production. Although county atlases continued to be produced later, the number of illustrations, either drawn or photographed, decreased substantially.

There are a number of works on county maps and atlases. *American Maps and Mapmakers,* a foundation title on nineteenth-century commercial cartography and publishing, includes two chapters specifically on county mapping with numerous references to this kind of activity throughout. This book includes numerous illustrations and extensive footnotes that will lead to other core readings.

The Cadastral Map in the Service of the State focuses less on the United States, instead giving attention to the historical development of property mapping in Europe and the resulting applications in colonial areas. This work will be especially useful for beginning research and reading about property mapping prior to the nineteenth century and for making connections and discovering similarities and differences between surveying and property ownership systems.

Journal literature should not be forgotten. "The County Landownership Map in America" traces county property maps from 1814, when the first county landownership map was published in the United States, to 1939. The 125 years covered are divided into five periods that revolve around the kinds of firms publishing the maps, the production technique or resulting products, and the uses to which the maps and atlases were being applied. Major publishers and technologies are highlighted, and the footnotes to the article are substantial, making it an ideal steppingstone to other reading.

Older, but no less important, is "The County Atlas of the United States," which was first published in 1960 and was republished the following year. This article follows the basic historic development of county atlases and contains information about production and sales techniques. The maps accompanying the article that show county atlas production by decade between 1860 and 1919 and the summary map showing the number of times counties were mapped between 1860 and 1950 highlight the midwestern nature of plat books.

County maps, atlases, and plat books are also included in bibliographies. Some focus on a particular library's holdings while others focus on atlases created to cover counties in a specific state. *Land Ownership Maps: A Checklist* highlights maps owned by the Library of Congress, Geography and Map Division.

WEATHER MAPS AND INFORMATION

The weather is a topic of conversation for nearly everyone. Everyday activities are affected by the weather, and everyday activities can culminate in changes to the climate. Information about the weather, climate, and meteorology is available through print media, radio, television, and the Internet.

Weather Maps: How to Read and Interpret All the Basic Weather Charts. 3rd ed.

In 45 very short chapters, readers are introduced to a wide assortment of weather-depiction graphics. Some, such as surface weather maps, may already be familiar, while others, like lightning-detection summary charts, might be familiar from television broadcasts, although in slightly different formats. Most of the chart types included in *Weather Maps* are rarely seen by television viewers or newspaper readers because they are used to prepare weather summaries and predictions, but they are becoming more available to the general public through the Web, necessitating a resource that describes them.

The longest chapter in *Weather Maps* focuses on surface weather maps and includes information on reading coded weather observations along with basics about high- and low-pressure centers, wind, and weather fronts, and finally putting all of the pieces together to interpret a surface weather map. Most of the other chapters describe one specific kind of chart with information about what the chart is used for, how it was created, how it might be used in the context of other information sources, and occasionally a description of the weather events that are responsible for generating the data described.

Each of the weather maps described is illustrated in black-and-white. Unfortunately, there is no glossary nor is there an index. Readers will not be able to look up "thunderstorms" in an index to find a list of all chart types that are used to either track thunderstorms or to forecast their formation. The table of contents lists each kind of chart specifically as a chapter title, but meteorological contexts are not given; there is no indication that "Lifted Index Chart" applies to thunderstorm forecasting until the text is read. If a reader already knows what the name of the chart-of-inquiry is, the table of contents will provide adequate guidance, but if the name of the chart is not known, the reader will need to browse through the entire volume.

Air Apparent: How Meteorologists Learned to Map, Predict, and Dramatize Weather

Air Apparent describes, in 12 chapters, both the development of scientific understanding of meteorological events and the tools developed to interpret, predict, and illustrate the weather. Through engaging prose, the reader is led through more than 200 years of intellectual and technical weather experience. Technology is not always strictly related to weather data gathering but also includes changes in communication and transportation methods. *Air Apparent*'s topical arrangement helps to show the links between forecasting the weather and technological change. The focus, though mainly on weather maps, also extends to using meteorological information to model the movement of air pollution and airborne contaminants. *Air Apparent* includes a list of Web site addresses for core weather sites. Black-and-white illustrations appear throughout the volume, and there is a section of color illustrations as well. There are extensive endnotes and an index. While *Air Apparent* is perhaps best read in its entirety, the chapters are compartmentalized enough that readers could read just the chapter on weather satellites or only the chapter on weather radar.

Oxford Dictionary of Weather

The more than 1,800 terms included in the *Oxford Dictionary of Weather* are those generally used by students, amateur meteorlogists, and the interested lay public when describing weather events. Definitions are not overly technical and should be understandable for most adult readers with basic science backgrounds. Some of the definitions are accompanied by black-and-white illustrations, and there also is a center section of photographs of different kinds of clouds. Four appendices follow the alphabetical definitions: Weather Records, Conversion Tables, British Climate Data, and World Climate Data. Fuller treatment of weather-related topics can be found in titles such as the two-volume *Encyclopedia of Weather and Climate*.

Weatherwise

Weatherwise is a glossy, commercially published magazine issued six times a year. Each issue contains four or five articles, illustrated with color photographs and other graphics, and regular columns and book reviews. One of the columns, "Weatherwatch," describes weather in specific regions of the United States and Canada for previous months; it is accompanied by maps showing the percent of normal precipitation received and the departure of the average temperature from the normal temperature. *Weatherwise*'s low-key articles will be easy entry points for reading about weather, climate, and meteorology. They are not written in scientific prose nor do they include footnotes, but basic concepts are explained using appropriate terminology and in such a way as to build a foundation of understanding. The *Weatherwise* Web site (http://

www.weatherwise.org/default.htm) includes an archive of articles that can be searched and then purchased on-line

American Meteorological Society (http://www.amet soc.org/)

The American Meteorological Society is the primary professional meteorological society in the United States. The society publishes nine scholarly journals, including *Journal of Applied Meteorology, Monthly Weather Review,* and *Weather and Forecasting.* The full text of articles from the society's *Bulletin,* along with abstracts of articles from the other journals, can be viewed without cost through the AMS Journals On-line page (http://ams.allenpress.com/). Also available through the society's Web site is a booklet about careers in meteorology, *Challenges of Our Changing Atmosphere,* plus information about educational projects undertaken and materials prepared by the society.

Daily Weather Maps, Weekly Series

The *Daily Weather Maps, Weekly Series* has been produced for more than 50 years by a variety of U.S. federal weather agencies affiliated with the Department of Commerce. Each paper issue, eight pages in length, seven pages of daily maps (Monday through Sunday) and a cover page (Figure 6.9). The maps viewed in sequence can be used to track weather events such as hurricanes and cold fronts. Each day of the week is depicted on four maps: Surface Weather Map and Station Weather at 7:00 A.M. EST; 500-Millibar Height Contours at 7:00 A.M. EST; Highest and Lowest Temperatures; and Precipitation Areas and Amounts. The cover page includes information about the times of day at which the mapped data were collected and a model weather station. There is no key on the printed *Daily Weather Maps, Weekly Series* to the symbols used in the weather station. Users will need to look elsewhere for a key; the New Jersey Department of Environmental Protection (http://www.state.nj.us/dep/seeds/wssym.htm) and the American Meteorological Society (http://www.ametsoc.org/dstreme/extras/wxsym2.html) are two possibilities.

Daily Weather Maps, Week Series is no longer being printed; current issues and a substantial archive file are available online through the NOAA Central Library U.S. Daily Weather Maps Project (http://doc.lib.noaa.gov/rescue/dwm/data_rescue_daily_weather_maps.html). This site also includes an explanation of the weather station and station symbols. As a cautionary note, the "Daily Weather Maps" available through the

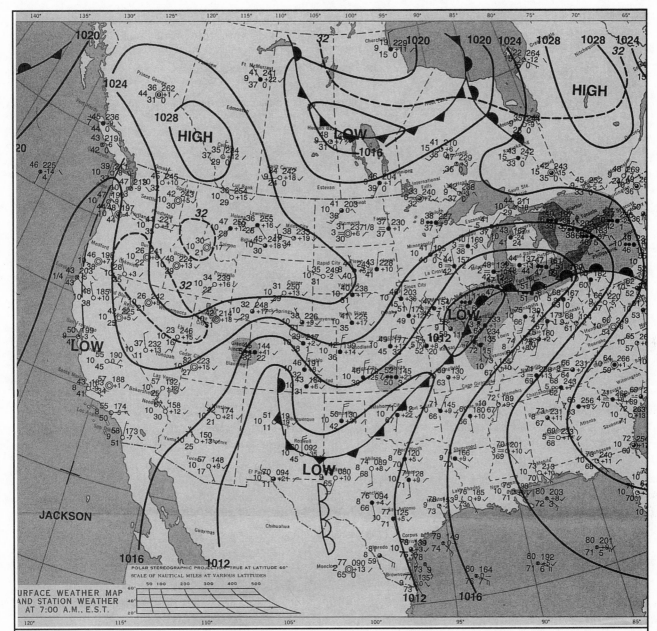

MOTHER'S DAY, 2002. "SUNDAY, MAY 12, 2002" FROM *DAILY WEATHER MAPS WEEKLY SERIES MAY 6–12, 2002*. CAMP SPRINGS, MD.: NATIONAL OCEANIC AND ATMOSPHERIC ADMINISTRATION, NATIONAL WEATHER SERVICE, NATIONAL CENTERS FOR ENVIRONMENTAL PREDICTION, HYDROMETEOROLOGICAL PREDICTION CENTER & CLIMATE PREDICTION CENTER, 2002.

FIGURE 6.9

Web at the National Center for Environmental Prediction, Global Modeling Branch Modeling Center Web site (http://wwwt.emc.ncep.noaa.gov/gmb/STATS/MAPS.html) are forecast maps, not records or interpretation of actual circumstances.

Climatic Atlas of the United States (1968)
Climate Atlas of the United States (CD-ROM, 2000)

The 1968 *Climatic Atlas of the United States* contains black-and-white monthly and annual maps showing mean or normal measurements of common climatic elements such as temperature, precipitation, humidity, sunshine, wind, and barometric pressure. The coverage includes multiple maps for different aspects of the same element. Some of the topical coverage includes tables or explanatory text. The data mapped were generally collected between 1931 and 1960 with some data sets focusing on smaller time spans within the 30-year period. Using these maps, the reader needs to remember that a large amount of data aggregation and generalization took place to produce the maps, most of which are very small-scale. A cautionary note to that affect appears on many of the maps.

In late 2000, *Climate Atlas of the United States,* a CD-ROM product, was published to "replace" the 1968 *Climatic Atlas of the United States.* On the disc, 737 color maps, over 500 more maps than available in the older print atlas, can be viewed through ESRI's ArcExplorer software, which comes on the CD-ROM. As with the previous print publication, the CD-ROM atlas's purpose is to show normal climate patterns. The data depicted are generally from 1961 to 1990. *Climate Atlas of the United States* relies on ArcExplorer to display maps. When the atlas is opened an atlas interface window appears with seven radio buttons: temperature, precipitation, snow, wind, pressure, days with, and other elements. After a user selects an element, then a specific parameter needs to be selected from a scrollable pick list. A new window will open to run ArcExplorer. Displays for a number of base map elements, such as weather station locations, state boundaries, city locations, county boundaries, climate divisions, interstates, and lakes and rivers, can be turned on and off. Under "Help" on the atlas interface window, information can be found about how the data were collected. The full text of *Using ArcExplorer* is included as a PDF file on the CD-ROM.

The maps in the 1968 *Climatic Atlas of the United States* include Alaska and Hawaii; they are not included on the 2000 CD-ROM. An additional CD-ROM product for Alaska and Hawaii is scheduled for release in summer 2002. The data on the *Climate Atlas of the United States* CD-ROM can be purchased through the National Climatic Data Center Web site (http://lwf.ncdc.noaa.gov/oa/ncdc.html) in either PDF format or ESRI ShapeFile format. Purchasers have the option to purchase specific data files individually or to purchase an annual subscription to all map data released.

Information about climate is often included in national and state atlases. There are also some atlases, beyond *Climate Atlas of the United States,* that focus solely on the climate or elements of climate for specific states.

UM Weather (http://cirrus.sprl.umich.edu/wxnet/)
The Weather Channel—Weather.com (http://www. weather.com)
USA Today Weather (http://www.usatoday.com/ weather/wfront.htm)

An overwhelming number of weather and climate resources, produced by both the commercial and government sectors, are available through the Web. Some provide analyzed data, similar to the weather reports broadcast on television or printed in newspapers, while others include photographs of weather events, information at a variety of levels about weather patterns and how data are collected, and data that can be viewed as maps on line or downloaded.

UM Weather is sponsored by the University of Michigan Weather Underground. This site goes far beyond being able to type in a zip code and get back a weather forecast—although that capability is available. UM Weather includes a list of links to nearly 400 North American weather sites, including commercial firms, academic departments, television and radio stations, and state and federal agencies, plus links to a number of "gophers." UM Weather also includes links to a large number of weather cams and has links to sites where weather software can either be downloaded or purchased. There is little explanatory text, just weather data and weather-related links.

The Weather Channel's Weather.com presents information about current weather conditions and forecasts for specific places through a city or zip code search. The site's emphasis on "lifestyle weather information" is highlighted by how the maps are organized for browsing by activity, geography, or map type. Under the activity browse, a list of activities and health concerns are linked to subsets of maps. Clicking on "Allergies" yields maps such as mold spore, ragweed, and wind forecast. "Construction" includes Doppler radar (rain) and lightning strikes in its group of maps, while "Financial" includes energy consumption forecasts and 30-day precipitation forecast maps. Browsing by geography brings up a list of regions, continental and subcontinental, worldwide. For non-U.S. areas, only satellite images, which can be put into motion, are available, but for the United States choices include current surface conditions, satellite, soil moisture content, and forecast maps. The map type browse provides access to all of the maps. When first viewed, the maps appear in a very small window but they can be enlarged. Each map has a "How to read this map" text block that will appear in a new window.

USA Today's Weather Web site places a greater emphasis on textual description of weather events and processes than the Weather Channel. It includes an extensive "Weather Basics" section with information and examples of a large number of different kinds of weather events, climate, predicting weather, and extreme weather along with suggested books about weather and climate. Forecasts can be searched for and basic maps of precipitation and frontal systems along with satellite imagery can be viewed. An almanac section includes information about normal weather patterns and average measurements. USA Today has published an introductory weather book, *The USA Today Weather Book*, which includes much of the same information as the Web site's "Weather Basics" section accompanied by extensive illustrations.

Weather About.com (http://weather.about.com) follows the same kind of format as the other About.com pages, with content authored by About.com experts and links to appropriate Web sites. Yahoo! Meteorology (http://dir.yahoo.com/Science/Earth_Sciences/Meteorology/) includes links to nearly 1,000 Web sites with weather- or meteorological-related content.

National Oceanographic and Atmospheric Administration (NOAA)

U.S. federal agencies, in particular offices in the National Oceanographic and Atmospheric Administration (http://www.noaa.gov/wx.html), provide much of the Web-based weather coverage available. NOAA's weather Web site provides links to the National Weather Service, the Storm Prediction Center, the Aviation Weather Center, the Marine Prediction Center, and the Space Environment Center, which monitors solar activities. News stories, weather warnings, and Web pages on "Hot Topics" like drought, La Niña, and radiation are available through the NOAA weather site. The NOAA weather site is also an entry point to hundreds of satellite images of large weather and environmental events during the past 30 years, including the 1993 Mississippi flood, side-by-side images allowing viewers to compare the sizes of Hurricane Floyd (1999) and Hurricane Andrew (1992), and images showing oil field fires during the Persian Gulf War. There are also a few sequences of images compiled to create "movies" of a solar eclipse, the eruption of Mount Saint Helens, and squall lines and tornadoes. Many of the images are false color or color enhanced. All of the still images are JPG files and can be downloaded from the site at no cost; prints can be ordered at reasonably low cost.

NOAA Weather Radio (http://www.nws.noaa.gov/nwr)

NOAA's Weather Radio "all hazards" network of more than 600 broadcasts current weather conditions and forecasts, watches and warnings, and information about natural and technological hazards such as earthquakes, volcanoes, and chemical spills. Current weather conditions and forecasts from National Weather Service offices are repeated on an ongoing basis twenty-four hours a day while other information is repeated as necessary or as it is updated. Weather Radio stations generally have a 40 mile broadcast area radius. Best-case scenario signal reception maps are located at the Weather Radio Web site under "Station Listing and Coverage." There are also lists of broadcast frequencies and transmitters by state as well as lists of counties with information about the appropriate transmitter and frequency to which to tune. Similar information for Canada can be found at Weatheradio (http://www.msc-smc.ec.gc.ca/cd/factsheets/wxradio/index_e.cfm).

National Weather Service (NWS)

The National Weather Service, "the sole United States official voice for issuing warnings during life-threatening weather situations," maintains a Web site (http://www.nws.noaa.gov or http://weather.gov) with maps and radar or satellite images, warnings, forecasts, statistical tables, and current conditions. The latest surface analysis chart can be easily selected and viewed as can maps showing 12-hour, 24-hour, and 7-day forecasts. Satellite imagery for different areas of the United States, including the "Atlantic Hurricane Sector," is available. Some of the imagery is black-and-white and some is color enhanced. United States, international, and marine weather conditions and forecasts can be read, radar composite images and animated loops can be viewed, and the most recent weather facsimile charts can be downloaded in TIFF format. The charts include surface analysis, barometric pressure, significant weather, radar summary, and forecasts. The charts will be in black-and-white.

National Climatic Data Center (http://www.ncdc.noaa.gov/oa/ncdc.html)

The National Climatic Data Center (NCDC) claims to be the "world's largest archive of weather data" with nearly 500 terabytes of data. One of the reasons that NCDC is so large is that it archives all but one percent of NOAA data. The data sets available are both national and global and have been collected by environmental satellites; from surface, marine, and upper-air observations; and through the Next Generation Weather Radar system (NEXRAD). Data can be ordered from NCDC through the Web but it is not free.

There are many other kinds of special format maps including: census tract maps, zoning maps, flood zone and flood insurance maps, parcel maps, and soil maps.

Map librarians will be an invaluable resource in finding the right kind of map to meet each geographic information need.

BIBLIOGRAPHY

Aeronautical Chart User's Guide. 5th ed. Greenbelt, Md.: U.S. Dept. of Transportation, Federal Aviation Administration, Aviation System Standards, National Aeronautical Charting Office, 2002. ISBN: 1-56027-192-2.

Air Apparent: How Meteorologists Learned to Map, Predict, and Dramatize Weather. Mark Monmonier. Chicago: University of Chicago Press, 1999. ISBN: 0-226-53422-7.

American Maps and Mapmakers. Walter W. Ristow. Detroit: Wayne State University Press, 1985. ISBN: 0814317685.

Aviator's Guide to Navigation. 3rd ed. Donald J. Clausing. New York: McGraw-Hill, 1997. ISBN: 0-07-011792-6.

BAMS: Bulletin of the American Meteorological Society. Boston, Mass.: American Meteorological Society, 1920– . Monthly. ISSN: 0003-0007.

The Cadastral Map in the Service of the State: A History of Property Mapping. Roger J.P. Kain and Elizabeth Baigent. Chicago: University of Chicago Press, 1992. ISBN: 0-226-42261-5.

Climate Atlas of the United States. CD-ROM. Ashville, N.C.: U.S. Dept. of Commerce, National Oceanic and Atmospheric Administration, National Climatic Data Center, 2000.

Climatic Atlas of the United States. John L. Baldwin. Washington, D.C.: United States Environmental Data Service, 1968.

"The County Atlas of the United States." Norman J.W. Thrower. *The California Geographer* 1960: 7–16. Republished in *Surveying and Mapping* vol. 21, no. 3 (September 1961): 365–73.

"The County Landownership Map in America." Michael P. Conzen. *Imago Mundi* 36 (1984): 9–31.

Daily Weather Maps, Weekly Series. Washington, D.C.: Climate Prediction Center, 1996–2002. ISSN: 0898-6592.

Description and Utilization of the Sanborn Map. New York: Sanborn Map Co., 1953.

Encyclopedia of Weather and Climate. 2 vols. Michael Allaby. New York: Facts on File, 2002. ISBN: 0-8160-4071-0 (set).

Fire Insurance Maps in the Library of Congress: Plans of North American Cities and Towns Produced by the Sanborn Map Company: A Checklist. Library of Congress, Geography and Map Division. Washington, D.C.: Library of Congress, 1981. ISBN 0-8444-0337-7.

Fire Insurance Maps: Their History and Applications. Diane L. Oswald. College Station, Tex.: Lacewing Press, 1997. ISBN: 0-9659698-0-0.

Geologic Map of the United States (Exclusive of Alaska and Hawaii). Philip Burke King, Helen M. Beikman, and Gertrude J. Edmonston. Denver, Colo.: United States Geological Survey, 1974

Geologic Maps: A Practical Guide to the Preparation and Interpretation of Geologic Maps: For Geologists, Geographers, Engineers, and Planners. 2nd ed. Edgar Winston Spencer. Upper Saddle River, N.J.: Prentice Hall, 2000. ISBN: 0-13-011583-5.

Geological Maps: An Introduction. 2nd ed. Alex Maltman. New York: J. Wiley & Sons, 1998. ISBN: 0-471-97696-2.

Geology of the Conterminous United States at 1:2,500,000 Scale: A Digital Representation of the 1974 P.B. King and H.M. Beikman Map. CD-ROM. Paul G. Schruben, et al. Release 1998 2 of U.S. Geological Survey Digital Data Series, DDS-11. Reston, Va.: United States Geological Survey, 1998.

A History of the Rectangular Survey System. C. Albert White. Washington, D.C.: Bureau of Land Management, 1983.

Initial Points of the Rectangular Survey System. C. Albert White. Westminster, Colo.: Produced for Professional Land Surveyors of Colorado, Inc., by The Publishing House, 1996.

Journal of Applied Meteorology. Boston, Mass.: American Meteorological Society, 1988– . Monthly. Previously titled *Journal of Climate and Applied Meteorology.* ISSN: 0894-8763.

Land Ownership Maps: A Checklist of Nineteenth Century United States County Maps in the Library of Congress. Richard W. Stephenson, comp. Washington, D.C.: Library of Congress, Geography and Map Division, 1967.

Main Types of Geological Maps: Purpose, Use and Preparation. Indira Kohli, trans., and Margaret Majithia, ed. New Delhi: Oxford & IBH Pub., 1997. ISBN: 2-7108-0622-3.

Monthly Weather Review. Boston, Mass.: American Meteorological Society, 1872– . Monthly. Previously published by U.S. Army, Signal Corps; U.S. Weather Bureau; and other U.S. government agencies. ISSN: 0027-0644.

National Imagery and Mapping Agency Public Sale Aeronautical Charts and Publications. 4th ed. (1998–2000). Washington, D.C.: U.S. Dept. of Commerce, National Oceanic and Atmospheric Administration, National Ocean Service, 1998.

Nautical Chart Symbols Abbreviations and Terms: Chart No. 1, United States of America. 10th ed. Department of Commerce, National Oceanic and Atmospheric Administration, National Ocean Service and Department of Defense, National Imagery and Mapping Agency. Washington, D.C.: U.S. Dept. of Commerce, National Ocean Service, 1997.

New Publications of the U.S. Geological Survey. United States Geological Survey. Reston, Va.: USGS, 1907–2003. Monthly until 1995, semi-annual in 1996, quarterly thereafter. ISSN: 0364-2461.

Oxford Dictionary of Weather. Storm Dunlop. New York: Oxford University Press, 2001. ISBN: 0-19-280063-9.

Sixtieth Anniversary, 1866–1926, Sanborn Map Company. New York: Sanborn Map Co., 1926.

Understanding Aeronautical Charts. 2nd ed. Terry T. Lankford. New York: McGraw-Hill, 1996. ISBN: 0-07-036467-2.

Union List of Sanborn Fire Insurance Maps Held by Institutions in the United States and Canada. 2 vols. Santa Cruz, Calif: Western Association of Map Libraries, 1976–1977. Vol. 1: *Alabama to Missouri.* R. Philip Hoehn. WAML Occasional Paper no. 2, 1976. Vol. 2: *Montana to Wyoming; Canada and Mexico.* William S. Peterson-Hunt and Evelyn L. Woodruff. WAML Occasional Paper no. 3, 1977. ISBN: 0-939112-16-7 (vol. 1); ISBN: 0-939112-03-5 (vol. 2).

"United States Fire Insurance and Underwriters Maps, 1852–1968." Walter W. Ristow. *The Quarterly Journal of the Library of Congress* vol. 25, no. 3 (July 1968): 194–218. Reprinted in *Surveying and Mapping* (1970).

Weather and Forecasting. Boston, Mass.: American Meteorological Society, 1986– . Bimonthly. ISSN: 0882-8156.

The Weather Book. 2nd ed., revised and updated. Jack Williams. New York: Vintage Books, 1997. Often referred to as the *USA Today Weather Book.* ISBN: 0-679-77665-6.

Weather Maps: How to Read and Interpret All the Basic Weather Charts. 3rd ed. Peter R. Chaston. Kearney, Mo.: Chaston Scientific, 2002. ISBN: 0-9645172-7-2.

Weatherwise. Washington, D.C.: Heldref Publications, 1948– . Bimonthly. ISSN: 0043-1672.

World Eagle *[Continent Name] Today: A Reproducible Atlas.* 6 vols. Littleton, Mass.: World Eagle, 1995–1997. Vol. 1: *Africa Today.* Rev. ed. 1996. ISBN: 0-903141-60-1. Vol. 2: *Asia & Oceania Today.* Rev. ed. 1995. ISBN: 0-930141-57-3. Vol. 3: *Europe Today.* Rev ed. 1996. ISBN: 0-930141-59-8. Vol. 4: *Latin America Today.* Rev. ed. 1997. ISBN: 0-930141-61-X. Vol. 5: *Middle East Today.* Rev. ed. 1997. ISBN: 0-930141-62-8. Vol. 6: *North America Today.* Rev. ed. 1995. ISBN: 0-930141-58-X.

On-line References

"About Geography: Blank & Outline Maps." About.com, 2003. <http://geography.about.com/cs/blankoutlinemaps/> (15 October 2003).

"About Weather." About.com, 2003. <http://weather.about.com> (15 October 2003).

American Meteorological Society. Home page. AMS, March 2002. <http://www.ametsoc.org/> (15 October 2003).

AMS Journals Online. American Meteorogical Society, April 2002. <http://ams.allenpress.com> (15 October 2003).

Association of American State Geologists. Home page. AASG, 8 October 2003. <http://www.stategeologists.org/>. (15 October 2003).

Aviation Systems Standards, National Aeronautical Charting Office—NACO. Federal Aviation Administration, 2003. <http://www.naco.faa.gov> (15 October 2003).

Bureau of Land Management, *General Land Office Records.* Bureau of Land Management (U.S.), 2003. <http://www.glorecords.blm.gov> (15 October 2003).

Daily Weather Maps. Environmental Modeling Center, Global Modeling Branch, National Center for Environmental Prediction, 2003. <http://wwwt.emc.ncep.noaa.gov/gmb/STATS/MAPS.html> (15 October 2003).

DNC: Digital Nautical Chart. National Imagery and Mapping Agency, 2003. <http://164.214.2.53/dncpublic/index.htm> (15 October 2003).

Environmental Data Resources, Inc. Home page. EDR, Inc., 1 October 2003. <http://www.edrnet.com> (15 October 2003).

Geology of the Conterminous United States at 1:2,500,000 Scale: A Digital Representation of the 1974 P.B. King and H.M. Beikman Map. Paul G. Schruben, Raymond E. Arndt, and Walter J. Bawiec. USGS, 25 February 2002. <http://pubs.usgs.gov/dds/dds11/> (15 October 2003).

GeoRef Information Services. Home page. American Geological Institute, 2003. <http://www.georef.org> (15 October 2003).

Houghton Mifflin Social Studies Center. Houghton Mifflin, 2003. <http://www.eduplace.com/ss/> (15 October 2003).

Jeppesen. Home page. Jeppesen Sanderson, Inc., 2002. <http://www.jeppesen.com> (15 October 2003).

"Leadership Letters: Issues and Trends in Reading." Scott Foresman, 2001. <http://www.scottforesman.com/educators/index.html> (15 October 2003).

"A Location Guide to the General Land Office (GLO) Survey Plats." Illinois State Library, 21 May 2000. <http://www.cyberdriveillinois.com> (15 October 2003).

Mapfinder. National Oceanic and Atmospheric Administration, National Ocean Service, 1 July 2003. <http://oceanservice.noaa.gov/mapfinder/> (15 October 2003).

NACO Aeronautical Chart User's Guide: Digital Aeronautical Chart User's Guide. FAA, 2003. <http://www.naco.faa.gov/index.asp?xml-naco/online/aero_guide> (15 October 2003).

NACO Aeronautical Products Catalog. National Aeronautical Charting Office, 2003. <http://www.naco.faa.gov/index.asp?xml-naco/catalog> (15 October 2003).

National Climatic Data Center. Home page. National Oceanic and Atmospheric Administration (NOAA), NCDC. 7 October 2003 <http://www.ncdc.noaa.gov/oa/ncdc.html> (15 October 2003).

National Geologic Map Database. U.S. Geological Survey, 21 October 2001. <http://ngmdb.usgs.gov> (15 October 2003).

National Imagery and Mapping Agency (NIMA) Maritime Safety Information Division. Home page. NIMA, 16 May 2003. <http://pollux.nss.nima.mil/index/index.html> (15 October 2003).

National Oceanic and Atmospheric Administration (NOAA) Weather. NOAA, 9 October 2003. <http://www.noaa.gov/wx.html> (15 October 2003).

National Weather Service. NOAA, NWS, 16 September 2003. <http://www.nws.noaa.gov> (15 October 2003). Mirrored at <http://weather.gov>.

Nautical Chart User's Manual. National Oceanic and Atmospheric Administration, Office of the Coast Survey, 11 March 2003. <http://chartmaker.ncd.noaa.gov/staff/ncum/ncum.htm> (15 October 2003).

"New Publications of the U.S. Geological Survey." U.S. Geological Survey, 24 September 2003. <http://pubs.usgs.gov/publications/index.shtml> (15 October 2003).

NOAA Central Library U.S. Daily Weather Maps Project. NOAA Central Library Data Imaging Project, 27 June 2003. <http://docs.lib.noaa.gov/rescue/dwm/data_rescue_daily_weather_maps.html> (15 October 2003).

NOAA Weather Radio. Home page. NOAA, National Weather Service, 18 December 2002. <http://www.nws.noaa.gov/nwr/> (15 October 2003).

Office of Coast Survey. Home page. National Oceanic and Atmospheric Administration, Office of the Coast Survey, 21 May 2003. <http://www.nauticalcharts.noaa.gov> (15 October 2003).

"Perry-Castañeda Library Map Collection." General Libraries, The University of Texas at Austin, 9 October 2003. <http://www.lib.utexas.edu/maps/index.html>. (15 October 2003).

"Publications." National Oceanic and Atmospheric Administration, National Ocean Service, 14 April 2003. <http://www.nos.noaa.gov/pubs/welcome.html> (15 October 2003).

"Publications of the U.S. Geological Survey." American Geological Institute, GeoRef database, 8 April 2003. <http://usgs-georef.cos.com/> (15 October 2003).

Selected DataStreme Atmosphere Weather Map Symbols. American Meteorological Society, 19 August 2002. <http://wwwametsoc.org/dstreme/extras/wsym2.html> (15 October 2003).

UM Weather. The Weather Underground, University of Michigan at Ann Arbor, 6 October 2002. <http://cirrus.sprl.umich.edu/wxnet/> (15 October 2003).

United States Geological Survey, Geology Discipline Home Page. USGS, 25 March 2003. <http://geology.usgs.gov/index.shtml> (15 October 2003).

"USA Today Weather." USA Today, 2003. <http://www.usatoday.com/weather/wfront.htm> (15 October 2003).

U.S. Government Online Bookstore. Superintendent of Documents, U.S. Government Printing Office, 1 October 2003. <http://bookstore.gpo.gov> (15 October 2003).

Weather.com. The Weather Channel Enterprises, Inc., 2003. <http://www.weather.com> (15 October 2003).

Weatheradio. Environment Canada, Communication Directorate. 28 December 2002. <http://www.msc-smc.ec.gc.ca/cd/factsheets/wxradio/index_e.cfm> (15 October 2003).

Weather Station Symbols. New Jersey, Dept. of Environmental Protection, 2001. <http://www.state.nj.us/dep/seeds/wssym.htm> (15 October 2003).

Weatherwise. Online selections from print magazine. Heldref Pub., 3 September 2003. <http://www.weatherwise.org/default.htm> (15 October 2003).

The World Factbook. Central Intelligence Agency, 2003. <http://www.odci.gov/cia/publications/factbook/> (15 October 2003).

Xpeditions. National Geographic Society, 2003. <http://www.nationalgeographic.com/xpeditions/> (15 October 2003).

"Yahoo! Meteorology." Yahoo! Inc., 2003. <http://dir.yahoo.com/Science/Earth_Sciences/Meteorology/> (15 October 2003).

CHAPTER 7
General Atlases

An atlas is a collection of maps that are often, but not always, bound together and are intended to be used together or have a connecting theme or geography. Atlases could be considered the "7–11" of geographic information because of the broad variety of information available in convenient, single-stop shopping. Comparison between similar titles is possible for world atlases but often there will be only one option available for a more geographically focused atlas at the national, state, or local level. The atlases described in this chapter are representative of a large and diverse universe of publications.

EVALUATING ATLASES

Time must be invested to properly evaluate an atlas title before use to ensure that the atlas selected will meet (without overpowering) information needs through quality cartography and indexing. A series of questions should be asked about any atlas under consideration, all of which can be summed up by "How will this atlas answer my questions?" The most important criteria to evaluate are: balance of map coverage, indexing, currency and accuracy, legibility or understandability, scale and projection, reputation of cartographic firm or publisher, other information included in the volume, and physical features of the volume. The largest or thickest volume is not always the best solution.

Balance of Map Coverage

All parts of the world are important. Hypothetically, the number of maps for an area should somehow be linked to the size of the area in relation to the total area. If strictly allocated in a world atlas, North America would receive slightly more than 16 percent of the map coverage because the continent contains 16 percent of the world's land mass. Unfortunately, this does not hold true in the atlas-production world. Atlases produced in North America have often tended to emphasize Europe and North America, slighting the other five continents. Approximately 25 percent of the maps in both the *Goode's World Atlas* and the *National Geographic Atlas of the World* provide North American coverage. European atlases may have a more balanced coverage; 17 percent of the maps in the *Times Atlas of the World* are of North America. Of course, this attention to geographically balanced coverage does not apply in the same way to non-world atlases. But there may be cases where geographical balance should still be considered, such as in continental atlases, or where the balance of thematic coverage is important.

Indexing

Without indexing, a volume of maps is useless. Imagine looking for a place named "Ditton" and having to scan all of the place names on 150 oversized, double-page atlas plates. The key to fast and efficient atlas use is the tabular index, or gazetteer, usually located in the back of the volume. At least 30,000 to 50,000 entries are required in a world atlas index for adequate, but not outstanding, coverage of place and feature names. (*Atlas Buying Guide,* 18) All of the places identified on the maps should appear in the index, and in reverse, all names in the index should be locatable on the maps.

Indexes will refer users to a page and a specific location on the page by either a latitude/longitude pair or a cartographer-created map-grid system. Entries should be sampled to check the accuracy of these location indicators.

Variant names should also be looked for. Place names change rapidly with new governments or changes in Romanization protocols. Indexes should either include cross-references from variant names or locate the place along with identifying the preferred name.

In addition to the tabular index, there may be a graphic index included on the endpapers. These will speed a browser to pages of interest, by passing the table of contents, which should list all plates included.

Currency and Accuracy

The 1990s were a decade of political and cartographic turmoil. From the unification of Germany to the dissolution of Yugoslavia, the renaming of Zaire, and the return of Hong Kong to China, cartographers have drawn, and redrawn, their maps. An atlas with a 1999 imprint date should include up-to-date information, not data from the situation in 1995 or earlier. Unfortunately, individual atlas maps are not supplied with a "date of situation"; it cannot be assumed that every map in an atlas shows data from the same year, let alone the year of publication. Select five or six recent political or name changes and check each one, being sure to check in all appropriate places. For example, in atlases published after 1997, Hong Kong should be shown as a Chinese possession on all the maps it appears upon.

Accuracy is of equal concern. The index must guide users to the correct page and specific location. Names must be correctly located and spelled. Countries should have the right shape and neighbors, rivers should flow out of the correct sources, and mountains should be given appropriate heights. Unfortunately, these are not always easy errors to spot, but if known information is displayed incorrectly there is a great likelihood that less familiar data are as well.

Legibility or Understandability

Cartographers and atlas designers have a difficult task in condensing or generalizing complex geographic situations for depiction on paper or screen. Choices of color, typeface and size, line weight, and symbols all affect how legible the resulting map will be. Maps, while potentially crowded, still need to be clear and consistent in their format. Placement of feature names can be especially problematic. Which dot, representing a town, belongs with which name? Can all of the letters in a river name that is placed to follow the course of the river be found? If the type is printed in black, can the letters be read when they have been placed on darker colored backgrounds?

Legibility can also be impacted negatively if color plates are not aligned or if colors, including shades of gray, have not been selected or proofread carefully. A university press published a group of black-and-white historical atlases for a number of states during the 1970s and 1980s. Unfortunately, a number of the choropleth maps were unusable because the grayscale values assigned to the counties to show levels of economic activity had not been printed correctly. On maps that should have been showing four or five shades of gray, only white and black (in place of the varied grays) appeared.

Scale and Projection

Atlases are often used to compare different areas or different activities. To make these comparisons easier and to facilitate moving from area to area within the atlas, a minimum of different scales should be employed. Clear scale statements should appear on each map. Missing scale statements should be a red flag for the atlas's integrity.

The appropriate use of projections may be difficult to judge. It is important, especially in world atlases where a variety of projections might be used, that the projection be identified on the map. It is especially helpful if the atlas includes a brief explanation and illustration of the projections used.

Reputation of Cartographic Firm or Publisher

Generally, an atlas prepared or produced by a reputable firm with an established track record in creating high quality cartographic products will be an acceptable atlas to use. Some publishers, such as Rand McNally and the National Geographic Society, have in-house cartographers creating their maps. Others, including Times Books, contract with such cartography firms as John Bartholomew. These contractual arrangements can be long-standing, which often, in some ways, can make a particular product synonymous with the cartography firm rather than the publisher. Occasionally, a publisher that has cartographers on staff will contract with a cartography firm to create entire works or supplemental materials.

Other Information Included in the Volume

There is a fine line between being an atlas with a clear emphasis on communication through cartographic items—such as maps, aerial photographs, satellite images, and images of three-dimensional objects (globes, relief models)—and a text with supporting cartographic graphics. Ideally, to be considered an atlas, a book should be more than 50 percent maps or maplike objects. In an atlas, maps should be supported and enhanced by text; they should not be subordinate to the text. Although the text is supportive, it should be clear, concise, and error-free. If needed, references to other works should be included. An essential non-map section, especially in general atlases, is the index to place names. Beyond maplike images, atlas compilers might include other graphics, tables, graphs, and illustrations. Again, these should not overwhelm the maps. They should clarify. Multitudes of non-map illustrations are not necessarily a good thing.

Physical Features of the Volume

If selecting an atlas to purchase, its construction should be considered. Large, oversized volumes must have sturdy bindings. Cloth-bound volumes will age more gracefully and withstand higher intensity use over a long term than paper-bound. This also holds true for sewn text blocks in comparison to glued. The precision of atlas bindings is of primary importance because so many maps extend across two pages. The binding should not be so tight that information is lost in the gutter but it should also not leave a gap of white space. Some atlases, in particular state or national atlases, include clear plastic overlays, which can be used to identify locations and features without printing them on each map. These are especially useful in atlases that repeatedly use the same scale or group of scales of base maps to display statistical data.

Kister's Atlas Buying Guide

Further guidance in evaluating world atlases can be found in *Kister's Atlas Buying Guide*. The greater part of this work is devoted to one- or two-page "Atlas Profiles" of world atlases available to North American users in the early 1980s. Each profile includes bibliographic and purchase information, an evaluation, and a list of review citations. Sadly, these evaluations are sorely out of date, but they may be useful in predicting what a new atlas title might look like based on past publisher practice. The chapter entitled "Finding the Best World Atlases" offers invaluable advice and ideas for evaluating atlases.

Atlas reviews appear in a number of different places, including journals published by such library and geography or cartography organizations as *Information Bulletin* (Western Association of Map Libraries), *Bulletin* (Association of Canadian Map Libraries and Archives), and *Cartographic Perspectives* (North American Cartographic Information Society). Key review publications of a more general nature include *Choice, American Reference Books Annual,* and *Booklist.* New atlases might also be listed in the new books listings of the Association of American Geographers *Newsletter, Cartography and Geographic Information Science, Base Line* (American Library Association, Map and Geography Round Table), and *Current Geographical Publications.* Additionally, some world atlases have been reviewed on the Amazon.com Web site.

WORLD ATLASES

World atlases vary considerably in size. The largest currently available are nearly five feet tall while the smallest are not quite eight inches. The depth of detail expands and contracts correspondingly as does the indexing and supplemental materials. World atlas users should expect to find geographically balanced map coverage and complete indexing of place names that appear on the maps. The maps should be easy to interpret and should have been cleanly produced. The gazetteer should be easy to use and accurate. A large number of atlases were issued in new editions timed to correspond with millennial celebrations

The Times Atlas of the World. 10th (comprehensive) ed.

The world atlas produced by Times Books has long been regarded as the best single-volume world atlas. Bartholomew, located in Edinburgh, has a solid history of fine cartographic craftsmanship, and the maps reflect their expertise. The 114 oversized, double-page plates contain finely detailed maps at scales generally between 1:1,000,000 and 1:5,000,000 with city details shown for 68 cities at 1:250,000 or 1:300,000. Topography and bathymetry are shown using gradient tints with spot heights for prominent peaks; heights are in feet while depths are in meters. The overall emphasis of the maps tends to be physical features and landforms rather than political and administrative details. Coverage is fairly well-balanced, although showing a European bias, with 35 maps of Europe, 34 of Asia, 12 of Africa, 20 of North America, 5 of South America, 7 of Australia/New Zealand/South Pacific, and 3 of oceans. Maps are arranged continentally with continental political overview maps at a smaller scale followed by larger-scale landform plates. All maps include a bar and relative fraction scale, projection statement, and elevation key.

The endpapers are graphic indexes with reference to appropriate plate, not page, numbers. The front endpapers index the entire volume except for larger-scale plates of North America and Europe, which are indexed in the back. The gazetteer section contains more than 200,000 names that follow the practices established by the British Permanent Committee on Geographic Names. Chinese places are in Pinyin with conventional English names indexed and displayed on the maps as room allows. The entry for each place includes both a page/map grid reference and an appropriate latitude/longitude coordinate pair in decimal degrees. Indexed places that are not villages, towns, or cities, such as mountains, counties, or rivers, are designated appropriately.

Eight thematic world maps displaying standard information about minerals, climate, vegetation, population, food and energy resources, and the political situation precede the geographic maps. These thematic maps all use the same base map and are at the same scale, allowing easy comparison and exploration of potentially related topics. A text section also precedes the geographic maps. The most useful material in this section is the statistical and geographic comparison sections. States and territories are listed alphabetically with areas in both square kilometers and miles and population figures along with the date to which the count corresponds. The geographical comparisons display continents, oceans, river basins, inland waters, and islands at constant scales with the size of each in kilometers and miles. This display drives home the facts that Africa is larger than North America and that the Mississippi River Basin is half the size of the Amazon River's.

If purchased, the *Times Atlas of the World* will require substantial financial and space investments; this is a big book at a large price. But the sizable index and generally high-quality cartography create a classic title with potentially years of use for many purposes.

National Geographic Atlas of the World. 7th ed.

Like *The Times Atlas,* the *National Geographic Atlas of the World* is built upon a long legacy of geographic publishing. The core of the atlas contains 131 continental or regional maps in the society's long-established style of pastel borders, red road networks, and place-name details. While topography is depicted by shading and spot heights, it is not the layer of information most easily seen. On many of the maps, the place names overwhelm landforms. Bathymetry is shown by gradient tints and soundings. The ocean maps also include information about major currents. Coverage is balanced but with less emphasis on Africa and Asia than in *The Times Atlas:* North America, 44 pages; South and Central America, 20 pages; Europe, 36 pages; Asia, 28 pages; Africa, 12 pages; Australia, 6 pages; Antarctica and the oceans, 22 pages. The National Geographic Society's atlas includes a large number of city detail maps; overwhelmingly, the maps are for North American cities (89) with 154 city maps divided unevenly among the remaining five continents.

The maps are arranged in continental sections following a pattern of a "natural color" remotely sensed image of the continent, a political map followed by a physical or land form map at the same scale, maps of portions of the continent at larger scales, and finally a group of city maps. The scales of the regional maps vary widely, between 1:1,000,000 and 1:11,000,000, with many in the vicinity of 1:3,000,000. Often regional maps for the same continent will have the same or similar scales, which eases transitions from one map to the next. Each continental section includes a set of pages of descriptive information about the countries with basic statistics and a sketch of the national flag.

The front endpapers include graphic indexes, and the gazetteer section contains more than 150,000 place and feature names, including names appearing on the map of the Moon, which is in the "Worlds Beyond" section. Gazetteer entries include only map-grid references, not latitude/longitude coordinate pairs. Names for nonpopulated places, if the name itself does not indicate the nature of the place, are identified with the appropriate feature type. The table of contents is sufficient but lacks details, such as a list of the cities included in the "Urban Regions" sections.

At the beginning of the atlas is an illustrated text section with suggestions of how to use the atlas, a description of changes in cartographic technologies, and an explanation of map projections followed by an extensive group of standard world thematic maps including: plate tectonics, landforms, climate, biodiversity, population, human cultures, economy, and food, energy, and mineral resources. The Moon, solar system, stars seen from Earth, the Milky Way, and the universe are illustrated in the next section, "Worlds Beyond." Three world maps, political, physical, and a satellite view, preceded the continental maps.

A set of "Geographic Comparisons," primarily lists of highest and lowest points, largest and longest bodies of water, and continental land areas and population sizes, concludes the map portion of the atlas. There also is an extensive table of monthly temperature and rainfall averages for selected locations worldwide as well as population figures for major cities of the world. The back endpapers are a graphical extension of the "Geographic Comparisons."

The *National Geographic Atlas of the World* is being kept up-to-date by the society through the Map Machine Web site (http://plasma.nationalgeographic.com/mapmachine). Along with a number of other resources, the site contains atlas updates with more than a dozen patches that can be previewed and then printed out using Adobe Acrobat.

Goode's World Atlas. 20th ed.

The *Goode's World Atlas,* titled *Goode's School Atlas* in earlier editions, is a portable alternative to large-format world atlases. This title is often assigned as a required or recommended text for introductory

college geography courses because of its inexpensive price and its interesting assortment of thematic maps. The atlas is divided into two main sections, world thematic maps and regional maps, accompanied by an introduction and a section of statistical tables. The introductory material places the atlas into the context of geographic education and inquiry with good, basic information on how data is manipulated and interpreted by cartographers to produce maps. Tools and techniques used by cartographers, such as map projections and remotely sensed imagery, are also discussed.

The editors continue to educate the atlas user in the introductory material to the world thematic maps by including a succinct discussion of what thematic maps are and how different kinds of data can be mapped. The 79 thematic maps, at two different scales, include basics such as landforms, vegetation, and major agricultural areas; but interesting specifics are often broken out of the overview maps and mapped separately. For instance, the agricultural regions map shows locations of agricultural methods (nomadic herding, plantation agriculture, commercial livestock, and crop farming as examples). Twenty-one maps showing the distribution of specific crops and agricultural products (wheat, coffee, cane sugar, beet sugar, beef) follow this overview. By using the agricultural overview map with the map of cane and beet sugar production, a user would be able to determine that cane sugar is produced in a plantation setting while beet sugar is a product of a crop farming system. Also included in the world thematic map section are three maps of ocean floors.

The regional maps, arranged in continental groups, follow the basic pattern of thematic maps, followed by an environment map and a political/landform map at the same scale then a group of more detailed reference maps. The continental maps are all at 1:40,000,000 and the regions are mapped at one of four specific scales to allow for comparisons. In addition, throughout the regional map section, there are 74 maps of urban areas, all at 1:1,000,000. The uniform scale will allow the user to compare area extent and development patterns without worrying that the areas are depicted at different generalization levels. Topography on the continental and regional maps is shown by gradient tints, shading, and spot heights; where appropriate, bathymetry is also shown using gradient tints. The thematic maps at the start of each continent show some of the subjects in the world thematic map section in greater detail. Energy, natural hazards, landforms, annual precipitation, population, and economic/minerals typically are shown. There is an extensive expanded thematic map section for the United States plus some additional thematic maps for Europe, the former Soviet Union, India, and China.

The gazetteer section includes approximately 30,000 place and feature names with generic terms for nonpopulated places, such as islands and rivers, or for sections of cities, such as neighborhoods. Page number and latitude/longitude coordinate pair in decimal degrees gives location within the volume. Many entries also include pronunciation guides. *Goode's World Atlas* follows a local name policy of including locally used names. On the maps, the Anglicized name will be included in parentheses after the local name; in the gazetteers, these names refer the user to the local name. There is no endpaper or other graphic index to the regional maps. The table of contents identifies the map and scale along with any inset maps and their scales.

The statistical section includes a table of national area sizes, populations, population densities, forms of government, capitals, and predominant languages. There are separate tables of national demographics; agricultural productivity; energy, minerals, and manufacturing; and environmental measures. Additionally, there is a page of comparisons of the sizes of landforms and features and an alphabetical list of principal cities and their populations. The included glossary of foreign geographical terms will be useful for atlas users not working on the United States. For users interested specifically in the thematic maps, there is a subject index that refers to world, regional, and country thematic maps following the gazetteer. The volume concludes with a partial list of information sources consulted to update or create the thematic maps.

World Atlas Comparison

The main purpose of a world atlas is to locate features worldwide. The *Times, National Geographic,* and *Goode's* atlases all perform this role, the *Times* and *National Geographic* with a greater level of detail, translating into more small places, than *Goode's*. The three titles differ in how directly they locate areas. Looking for Albania in the gazetteer sections leads to the European overview plate in the *Times,* a continental map of Europe and western Asia in *Goode's,* and a map of the Balkans in *National Geographic.* The *Times* and *Goode's* atlases expect the user to be able to narrow his or her focus to a more detailed page without assistance. The *Times* does provide the graphic endpaper index but *Goode's* forces the user to flip through pages or to refer to the table of contents. Once to the most detailed map showing Albania, the information shown seems to portray three different situations. The *Goode's World Atlas* locates only 15 cities or towns in Albania, a near ghostland, while the *Times* and *National Geographic* atlases place more than 60. The *Goode's* map not only looks empty, it *is* empty. This reflects both the relatively small scale of the *Goode's* map (1:4,000,000) and *Goode's* much smaller gazetteer size. *Goode's* provides a generalized landform overview; the larger-scaled *Times* allows users to see more specifics. Of the three atlases, the *National Geographic* has the least obstructed national boundaries because they are not competing with landform depiction.

Closer to home, perhaps reflecting their slightly greater emphasis on the United States, *Goode's* and *National Geographic* both index the Du Page River, west of Chicago, on Chicago-area detail maps. In fact, *Goode's* indexes both the east and west branches! The Chicago detail map in the *Times* is Chicago only, not the greater region, and does not extend far enough west. The Du Page River is shown on the *Times* Great Lakes region map, but it is unnamed.

Goode's is the hands-down "winner" in thematic map coverage. All three atlases include such basics as precipitation or climate, vegetation, and population, but only *Goode's* provides worldwide information on specific crops, minerals, and transportation networks. Both *Goode's* and *National Geographic* provide continental thematic maps; *Goode's* includes more. Another world atlas with an ample assortment of thematic maps is the *Peters Atlas of the World*. This atlas covers 46 topics in 246 maps. Regardless of source, thematic maps need to be read and interpreted carefully and in the context of statistical tables. Users must remember that thematic maps are displays of manipulated, grouped, and interpreted data, not raw, unprocessed statistics.

The *Goode's World Atlas* is intended for a different audience and purpose than the *Times* or the *National Geographic*. Its educational emphasis is clearly reflected in the abundance of thematic maps and more simple maps. *Goode's* will be ideal for young-adult and adult beginner map users. More seasoned map readers will appreciate *Goode's* straightforward style but will enjoy the details of *National Geographic* and the *Times*.

Electronic World Atlases

Some world atlases are available through the Web. Generally, they do not meet the graphical quality available from standard ink-on-paper atlases. Many include only basic political and physical maps, often scanned versions of the Central Intelligence Agency's maps along with facts from the Central Intelligence Agency's *World Factbook*.

World Atlas On-Line (http://www.fofweb.com)

Facts On File's *World Atlas On-Line* is a graphically cleaned-up and greatly expanded version of the popular three-ring binders *Maps on File* and *Outline Maps On File*. This on-line atlas, which is available by subscription—not for free, includes maps of the world, continents, countries, and states. Although the first map that is displayed is of the world, the core of the atlas are the "Fact Files" for continents, countries, and individual states and provinces of the United States and Canada. Each Fact File includes a political, outline, and elevation map. All three maps can be printed from PDF files on standard 8.5-by-11-inch paper oriented to best fit the shape of the area; black-and-white printers can produce adequate grayscale renditions of the maps, which display in color on the screen. The elevation maps print slightly smaller than the political and outline maps. The Fact File also includes the flag of the state, province, or country; a location map; and statistical data and descriptive information. The statistical and descriptive information is divided into four sections: Vital Statistics; Government & Politics; People & Demographics; and Chronology. The data has currency information included so that the reader will know how old the statistic is. There also is a bibliography of other resources, "On the Web" and "At the Library." There is no summary data, bibliography, or elevation map for the world.

Regions (primarily continents), countries, states, and provinces can be accessed through alphabetical lists. Each area has, as part of its Fact File, a drop-down pick list of adjoining areas or, in the case of the regions, countries contained in the region. The database can be searched by feature type—such as archipelago, lagoon, or river—or by specific place name. There are also clickable lists of capitals and cities. The searching and clickable lists lead back to the Fact Files for countries, states, or provinces. Sometimes the term that has been searched does not appear either on the maps or in the statistical and descriptive information. The core to the Facts On File *World Atlas On-Line* is statistical, not cartographic. For that reason, this product might not be a true atlas, but the consistent presentation style and depth of information available in the statistical and descriptive information make it well

worth remembering as a potential basic information resource.

New Millennium World Atlas Deluxe

The *New Millennium World Atlas Deluxe* CD-ROM claims to be the "first atlas to recognize that each person's view of the world is unique." There are three ways to install: complete includes 1.7 million place names on maps (Rand McNally's World Digital Database of 170,000 names plus 1.5 million names from other sources); standard displays 750,000 place names (Rand McNally's World Digital Database of 170,000 names plus more than 550,000 from other sources); and compact shows names only from Rand McNally's World Digital Database. Regardless of the installation level, the kinds of maps displayed will be the same. The maps can be configured, through the Preferences menu, to display physical features, political boundaries, and manmade objects and locations. There are also articles, statistical information, and some illustrations.

The initial screen displays a map with basic navigational tools across the top of the window (duplicated through menu options), scale bar, a button to display the legend, zoom and pan icons, and a group of eight information access menus at the window's left. Maps can be displayed using two projections, a "globe" (orthographic) projection and a "wall map" (Plate Carree) projection. There are a number of preformatted display options, some including shaded relief and hypsometric colors to depict landforms, while others include only shaded relief or no landform depiction at all. The "political" and "student" maps show countries as solid polygons. Some features can be turned on and off. If a preformatted display option is selected, such as "Physical," some kinds of features are automatically displayed. The Physical display will show or name features like mountains, islands, highest points in countries, undersea trenches, and glaciers. It will not show political boundaries, city locations, or transportation networks, but these can be added to the display, potentially creating a new map style that can be named and saved by the user for access at another time. As maps are zoomed from smaller- to larger-scale displays, the amount of detail, including coastline intricacies, boundaries, transportation methods, and place names, shown increases.

The map display can be moved using standard zoom-and-pan tools to position the center of the map on the area of interest. The "Global Find" option gives the user the opportunity to search on place names using a dynamic search that scrolls to the appropriate part of the listing as each character is typed. Three different kinds of entries are indexed by the Global Find list. Place names preceded by globe icons will take the user to a map with the selected place name highlighted. Some larger cities, generally large national capitals and economic centers, have a globe icon and a second entry with an icon that resembles a city profile. City profile icons lead to maps of city centers; a list of city center maps can be found in the Find menu. There are many more city center maps listed than there are separate maps because some points of interest have been specifically listed so that maps will display centered on them or with their location highlighted. The full city center map probably will not display on standard desktop-sized monitors but it can be panned using either a "grab hand" icon or scroll bars. There is an option when printing city center maps to print the entire map or to print only the section displayed on the monitor. Printing the full city map on 8.5-by-11-inch paper yields a map on which not all location names are readable but the network of major streets will still be clear.

A third kind of information is available through the Global Find search; articles are indicated by an icon that looks like lines of text with a small illustration. Articles include country profiles similar to the information available through the Central Intelligence Agency *World Factbook;* there also are a number of city profiles. Not all of the choices in the Global Find list are geographic. Some are historical figures (Anne Boleyn, Benjamin Franklin) or events (Martin Luther King, Jr., and the March on Washington, Martin Luther Nails 95 Theses to Church Door). A full list of articles is included in the Find menu. The articles include links to other articles and appropriate maps. They also include links to a fourth kind of information, "Explorations." Explorations are marked by an icon of a hiking person seen in profile. These are somewhat simplistic graphics with images that provide links to very brief descriptive texts, images, or maps. The list of Explorations, available through the Find menu is quite varied, but the information presented is disjointed and the user is not given any guidance in navigating and Exploration graphic.

Seventeen different prepackaged world thematic maps and cartograms, broadly grouped into four categories (physical, economic, health, and social) can be displayed. These maps can be displayed at two different scales with the larger scale displaying a slightly higher level of detail than the small map. Textual explanations of the graphics can be listened to or read.

The Comparison–Compare Maps option splits the screen into two frames to allow the display of two different areas of the world or the same area using two different map styles. The map styles, political, classic or physical, cannot be manipulated. Both of the frames will display at the same scale. There is no way to display a large-scale and a small-scale map centered on the same location.

Statistical facts about countries can be compared through the Comparison–Compare Facts option. Four different kinds of graphs along with rankings can be displayed. The two styles of bar graphs are used to show data for a single year. The line graphs can show data for multiple years. The data are grouped into four broad areas: resources, business, people, and transportation and communication. Each area has two or three subareas that include multiple topics. Up to four countries can be compared on the graphs at once. The ranked list shows the selected kind of data for all countries from high to low. The group of Comparisons options also includes "World of Records," standard top-10 statistics about area, elevation, population densities, highest and lowest temperatures and rainfalls, and a variety of natural disaster impacts.

The Guidebook, Heritage, and Nature navigation options are all tied to the map being displayed. Guidebook will list links to articles specific to the displayed area, such as country and city profiles and travel information. Heritage focuses on articles and Explorations about historic events and people related to the area displayed, while Nature links to articles and Explorations about the physical nature of the area. As the area displayed in the map changes scale, becoming either larger or smaller, the lists of articles also change.

The Help menu includes a glossary, a list of translations of non-English terms, and a bibliography. Unfortunately, there are no citations included with the articles so, unless a user wants to scan the bibliography, which is arranged by author, there is no direct way of knowing what resources have been tapped to compiled the information.

Straight-line distances can be calculated, latitude and longitude at the cursor location can be displayed, text can be placed, polygons can be drawn, and "map pins" can be applied. The *New Millennium World Atlas Deluxe* is also configured to facilitate connection to the Internet.

Encarta Interactive World Atlas 2001

Microsoft's *Encarta Interactive World Atlas* is part of the *Encarta Reference Suite.* The editors intend that "navigating through Encarta World Atlas [will be] like thumbing through a paper atlas with more than 20,000 pages, all seamlessly connected." According to the "letter from the editors," the maps show more than 1.8 million places. Beyond the political and physical maps that show place names and feature locations, the atlas includes articles, photographs, and statistical data and maps.

The first, or home, screen display presents four basic navigational methods: Find; Dynamic Map; Country List; and Multimedia Features. A toolbar displays across the top regardless of the screen display, making the basic navigation methods always available. "Find" allows the atlas's entire contents, regardless of information type, to be searched at one time using "Pinpointer technology." Typing a place name into the search box and selecting "everything" for the types of information to be located generates two lists: maps (place names) and articles and media, which includes text, images with captions, maps locating points of interest with short explanatory text, and Web links. The list of place names changes as each character is typed into the search box to assist in locating places with uncertain spellings. Inputting "Camchaka" instead of Kamchatka results in a place name list that begins: Chamacha, Portugal; Camacha Theodosiopolis [Turkey]; Kamchatka (administrative division), Russia; Kamchatka Sea. There are no matching articles. Retyping Kamchatka spelled correctly yields both a list of places named Kamchatka and an extensive list of articles and images about Kamchatka or containing the word Kamchatka. Selecting one of the places from the list will display a map with the place name highlighted. There is a catch to displaying locations of towns; the "map style" that is selected from the menus at the far left of the screen must be either "comprehensive" or "political." Towns located through the find search box do not display on any of the other styles although the maps will be centered on the desired location.

Selecting "Dynamic Map" from the home screen will display the entire world using an orthographic (globe view) projection. Basic screen navigation tools at the bottom of the display will allow zooming and panning. The globe can be dynamically panned to display any area although it will not allow turning the image so that north is at the bottom of the screen or to either the right or left. There are seven zoom levels; each displays an increasing amount of detail. The globe view is especially striking when displaying such environmental data as average temperatures and rain-

fall; the globe view makes connections in worldwide circulatory systems easy to see. The entire world can also be viewed as a "flat map" using the Miller cylindrical projection. The flat map is seamless and, like the globe view, can be panned to center on any location. There are two different kinds of zoom. Using the "magnifying glass" will zoom to specific levels always centered on the original map center. The bounding box tool will zoom and center on the area enclosed by a drawn rectangle.

Statistical maps can be displayed along with bar charts of national comparisons. The more than 350 measures fall into 12 groups: Basic Indicators; Agriculture; Communications; Economy; Education; Energy and Minerals; Environment; Geography; Health; Population; Trade; and Transportation. After selecting a statistical measure, the map will display with a dynamic graph that can be used to determine a country's value or compare values; the graph can display the data either linearly or logarithmically. A nice feature is the details button, which displays a definition of the measure currently mapped, the source of the information, and why that particular measure is important. Unfortunately, only one map can be displayed at a time.

Beyond the maps, there are 55 broad articles arranged in five general categories in "Geography in Depth." These articles, along with the articles about specific places found using the "Find" search box have links to definitions, other topics, appropriate maps, video clips, still images, and related statistics. Words with definition links are blue and geographic links are green. Video clips have accompanying audio that can be turned down because the spoken text appears underneath the images. Still images all have captions; some are quite lengthy and usually include links to maps and definitions.

While the idea of a world atlas on CD-ROM is quite attractive, these products are not necessarily intuitive to use. The CD-ROM atlas's clear advantage over a print atlas is that more textual and non-map graphical information can be included in the publication, giving a wider range of information options and potentially a greater depth and breadth to the information. But cartographically, print atlases are more likely to contain clearer- and cleaner-looking maps, as well as being able to display larger areas than can be viewed at a similar level of detail on screen. Print atlases also may be easier and faster for some users to navigate through. It can be time-intensive to have to draw and redraw bounding boxes or use grab-hand tools and scroll bars to adjust the map display. But the ability to center a map on an area of interest instead of having to work around a publisher's map configuration is the boon of bounding boxes and other electronic navigation tools. Electronic atlases and print atlases could be used side-by-side or selectively depending on the exact information need or geographical situation.

REGIONAL ATLASES

If more specific information or a greater amount of detail is needed than what is available in world atlases, then atlases that focus on specific areas may need to be consulted. There will probably not be multiple publications from which to choose as there is at the world scope. Because atlases generally are expensive to compile and publish, for-profit publishers will not duplicate another publisher's efforts.

The regional atlases, those that are continental or subcontinental in scope, not subnational, vary in size and scale. Unfortunately, there may not be an up-to-date atlas for each continent.

The Atlas of Africa
An Atlas of African Affairs. 2nd ed.

Unfortunately, being nearly 30 years old, *The Atlas of Africa* is quite dated. Nevertheless, the fundamental information it contains is still useful, and it should be kept in mind as a potential resource for anyone interested in generalities about the African continent or for someone who needs a quick introduction to a country's history and resources. The first part of the atlas includes maps and text descriptive of the entire continent. Many of these maps, such as those for vegetation zones and geology, and the historical maps remain useful. The second part describes each nation, country by country, grouped by geographical region. Each region's section begins with two pages of text and an economic overview map of the region, which uses a very generalized shaded relief map as its base. The national descriptions all follow a similar format: a text description, usually three or four pages long, which includes a physical description; historical summary and economic overview; and two maps, one a physical map using gradient tints and the other a map of economic activities showing agriculture, fishing, mineral resources, industrial activity, and tourism. The atlas concludes with bar graphs of economic statistical data and an index and short glossary.

The Atlas of Africa was undertaken by a private company. Because of the expense involved in producing a large-format atlas like *The Atlas of Africa* with full-color maps and data drawn from a number of different sources, it is unlikely that a similar title will be published again. Stepping into the breach is *An Atlas of African Affairs.*

An Atlas of African Affairs is a much smaller volume, a normal-sized book in comparison to *The Atlas of Africa.* The volume is arranged in five sections: environmental, historical, political, economic, and the south. Each section is made up of a number of very short chapters, each with text, a single black-and-white map, and occasionally a table. All of the sections include a bibliography, and the volume concludes with a number of chronological and statistical tables, an additional bibliography, and an index. The amount of text included in *An Atlas of African Affairs* is extensive, perhaps tipping the scale away from an atlas-like presentation of information toward text with accompanying maps, but it works well as a digest to update some of the information presented in the much older *The Atlas of Africa.*

Atlas of Eastern Europe
The Former Yugoslavia

Atlas of Eastern Europe and *The Former Yugoslavia* were both produced by the U.S. Central Intelligence Agency. Both are slender, slightly oversized volumes with the colors, line weights, and typefaces that typically appear on CIA maps released for public consumption. Both of the atlases are organized with a section that covers the entire area geographically and historically, followed by a section that details the individual nations within the area. The Central Intelligence Agency atlases are good overviews that will support information gained from other sources. Because of the side-by-side presentation of close-to-the-same scale thematic maps, connections and conclusions might be easier to reach. For example, *The Former Yugoslavia* contains a shaded relief map of eastern Europe and a map at close to the same scale of ethnic groups. Comparing the terrain to the ethnic group dispersion could assist in explaining connections between the groups.

Both of these atlases were published at times when the political situation was still not clear or concrete. The *Atlas of Eastern Europe* includes "in transition to unification" at the start of the East Germany section. When consulting any kind of atlas, regardless of the area covered, the time frame of the background research and compilation must be kept in mind.

*Atlas of Eastern and Southeastern Europe (Atlas Ost-
und Südousteruopa)*
Tübinger Atlas of the Middle East (Atlas des
Vorderen Orients)

Regional atlases have also been published as individual map sheets, each with a unique theme. The Austrian *Atlas of Eastern and Southeastern Europe* began publication in 1989. The atlas thus far has focused primarily on social and economic topics and the effects of human activities on the physical environment. More than 20 sheets have been published, some covering all of eastern and southeastern Europe and others only specific regions or countries. Each map sheet is accompanied by a substantial booklet of text. The *Tübinger Atlas of the Middle East* has an even longer history of publication, beginning in 1977 and closing in 1993. The sheets are arranged in two sections. Part A is geography with maps devoted to the physical environment (relief, climate, hydrology, geology, vegetation) and economic and social topics (population, economics, transportation). Part B focuses on historical geography, arranged chronologically, from prehistory through the First World War. Atlases published over a period of time as separate map sheets can be found in library catalogs and collections treated in two different ways. Either each map will be cataloged separately with appropriate specific subject headings or the maps will be grouped together as an atlas with more general subject headings that may not necessarily reflect the precise topic of interest. Individual map sheets grouped under an atlas title umbrella can be difficult to identify and locate, but they often provide detailed information available nowhere else.

NATIONAL ATLASES

National atlases are often undertaken by national governmental agencies or quasi-governmental agencies. Some national atlases have been published in multiple editions, while others have appeared only once. National atlases are often large, if not oversized, volumes. Most national atlases cannot be used to locate specific places because they do not always include general geographic maps with indexes. National atlases tend to focus on the physical, cultural, social, economic, and historical environments of the country.

National Atlas of the United States

The *National Atlas of the United States,* published in 1970, is a big book with 335 pages of maps and an index section containing 41,000 place names. At the time of its publication, the *Atlas* was sold for $100 and was generally only purchased by government agencies and libraries. The *Atlas* "was designed to be of practical use to decision makers in government and business, planners, research scholars, and others needing

to visualized country-wide distribution patterns and relationships between environmental phenomena and human activities." Twenty two-page "general reference maps," containing the 41,000 places indexed in the gazetteer section along with five pages of larger-scale urban area maps begin the atlas. The bulk of the atlas is devoted to thematic maps, "Special Subject Maps," showing the distribution of a wide variety of natural and human themes divided into five broad sections: physical, history, economic, sociocultural, and administrative. There also is a section that discusses and illustrates different kinds of maps, and some of the steps that go into creating maps, and a very small group of world maps including maps showing U.S. relations with other parts of the world. Some of the sections also include explanatory text. The data mapped generally was collected during the mid-to-late 1960s. The *National Atlas of the United States* was never completely revised or updated. The United States Geological Survey distributed additional maps as separate sheets, some of which contained completely new content or were revisions of the maps published in the *Atlas.*

The 1970 *National Atlas of the United States* has been scanned by the Library of Congress, Geography and Map Division and is available through the Web (http://memory.loc.gov/ammem/gmdhtml/census.html). The introductory text and all of the text included within the thematic map section is included but the gazetteer is not. Also at this Web site are scans of three statistical atlases that were created using census data from 1870, 1880, and 1890. Navigation through all four atlases is done in the same way. Bibliographic information and small clickable images of the title page display after the atlas of interest is selected. Clicking on the title page displays the first set of 12 thumbnail images. Clicking on a thumbnail image displays the image larger. Images can be zoomed and panned using the server-based MrSID compression software. The scanned images from these four atlases are static, merely electronic copies of the original ink-on-paper publications.

The newest version of the *National Atlas of the United States* is much more interactive and less static. The United States Geological Survey, with a number of other cooperating federal agencies and private companies, began work on a new edition in 1997 that includes interactive and multimedia maps presented through the Web as well as individual maps printed on paper. The Web-based *National Atlas of the United States* (http://www.nationalatlas.gov) is "designed to provide a reliable summary of national-scale geographical information." The *Atlas* is intended to serve both the general public with a broad spectrum of interests and federal scientists and policy makers, and the atlas was specifically designed for users of "powerful home computers." From the *National Atlas* Web site, maps can be assembled interactively from data layers, multimedia maps can be viewed, map data layers can be downloaded, links can be made to other Web sites, and information can be accessed about ordering printed maps from either the digital atlas or the 1970 edition. The Web site also includes information about the *Atlas, Atlas* partners, recent developments, a FAQ list, and a customer survey/feedback form. All of the textual information at the Web site is available in either graphics or text mode but the interactive mapping and multimedia maps are, of course, only in graphics mode.

The interactive maps module allows the user to select from more than 400 data layers. Layers are displayed by checking boxes next to the layer names in the upper-right frame. This frame is also where the map legend will display and where three kinds of place name related queries can be performed. The map displays in the left frame, which will fill slightly more than half of the screen. Buttons below the map display allow zooming, panning, and clicking on counties to identify them by name and display specific selected statistics for the county. The frame in the lower-right corner contains either a map showing where the geographic area is that has been zoomed to or statistical information from the identify request.

The full help document is invaluable because it explains the order in which data layers display or cover each other. This is important because there is no way to change the order of the map layers. For example, if both annual average precipitation and time zones are selected, data layers that cover 100 percent of the United States, only one will display—time zones. Knowing the display order of the data layers will not only remove the mystery of where the data went but also will make it easier to know which data layer is currently displayed. There is a limited, set color palette so the same colors will be used to show aspects of multiple layers.

The data that create the map display can be downloaded free of charge through the Web site using FTP. Some of the files are quite large, although compressed using standard tools, and could take a long time to download. Metadata meeting Federal Geographic Data Committee standards can be viewed prior to downloading and will be automatically downloaded with the data layers. Data layers can also be purchased on CD-ROM; the prices of the files vary.

The National Atlas of Japan. Rev. ed.

The National Atlas of Japan is an exemplary example of how national atlases can evoke a sense of national culture. An oversized volume with 211 pages of maps and a 7-page list of administrative areas, *The National Atlas of Japan* covers all of the basic areas that could be expected of an atlas of this magnitude: physical features; climate; land development and conservation; population; agriculture, forestry, and fisheries; mining, manufacturing, and construction; transportation and communication; foreign trade; commerce, banking, and insurance; politics and finance; social conditions; and education and culture. It is the content of specific maps that help build a picture of important aspects of the Japanese culture. On the same page as maps of maximum and minimum temperatures, there are maps of the mean dates of the first flowering of the Japanese cherry trees and the first sighting of the cabbage butterfly. The importance of rice is pointed out by mapping the areas harvested for rice on one map and areas harvested for wheat, barley, and other grains combined on a second map. Education is highlighted by nine maps, only three of which are about colleges or universities; the others show the number of schools and children enrolled at a variety of education levels including "day nurseries" and kindergartens.

While *The National Atlas of Japan* does include a general, non-thematic, map of the nation, there is no index to places. Some other source, such as a road atlas, will be needed to locate specific places. *The National Atlas of Japan* is rich with a diverse set of physical, social, and cultural data.

National Atlas of Sweden

The *National Atlas of Sweden* is 18 volumes, each focusing on a different aspect of Sweden's physical or human geography. The text in the volumes is extensive, much more than found in other national atlases. There are also many photographs, graphs, and tables. Each of the volumes is indexed and includes a list of references.

The multivolume, extended approach to developing a national atlas allows for more in-depth discussion of specific events, ideas, or issues. For instance, the section on snow cover in *Climate, Lakes, and Rivers* (volume 14) describes why snow forms, how observations about snow depth are made, how snow on the ground responds to warming, and why snow is important for runoff. There are 15 maps in the section, one of which is "Percentage of White Christmases, 1931–1980." Similarly, in *The Population* (volume 3), each of the political parties is treated with a one- or two-page description that includes the name of the party with its symbol, a description of the party's history and aims, maps showing votes for the party in recent elections, and often a chronological list of party leaders and illustrations of election posters.

The *National Atlas of Sweden* is being published in both an English- and a Swedish-language edition. A CD-ROM version containing the data used for atlas map production is available but only in Swedish. The *National Atlas of Sweden* Web site (http://www.sna.se/se_index.html), again in both English and Swedish, contains over 1,000 thematic maps and general maps along with basic data about counties and municipalities. A gazetteer is also included in the Web site.

There are a number of other extensive, although not necessarily multivolume, national atlases that have been published by or on behalf of a national governmental agency including *National Atlas of Hungary, Atlas of Israel, Atlas del Peru, Atlante Thematico d'Italia,* and *Nuevo Atlas Nacional de Cuba. Atlante Thematico d'Italia* was distributed as loose fascicles intended to be housed in four boxes. Unfortunately, there have been few national atlases produced recently in African nations. Similar to the publication pattern of some regional atlases, there have been a few countries that have published over a long time period separate maps with similar formats and including a national atlas series title. *The Republic of Zambia Atlas* is being produced this way; a group of maps was produced between 1966 and 1976 and a second group, with no overlap of information with the first, began production in 1986.

Versions of national atlases, or portions of their contents, are beginning to appear on the Web. Searching just "national atlas" leads to an overwhelming number of links to the national atlases of the United States and of Canada. The National Atlas of Canada (http://atlas.gc.ca) includes scans of maps from the current, fifth, and fourth editions in a "Quick Maps" section. The current edition, designated as the sixth, is intended to be Internet-based. Some of the maps are in PDF format, some in HTML, and some in both. The "Make a Map" section creates thematic maps with the option to turn on and off base-layer information like provincial boundaries and water bodies. There also is

a substantial text section, "Facts about Canada," and a link to the cooperative "Canadian Communities Atlas Project," which is geared toward school use.

Locating atlas-like Web sites for other countries may be possible by searching for the country with "atlas" or "maps." But an easier, and perhaps faster, method would be to rely on the Oddens' Bookmarks site (http://oddens.geog.uu.nl/index.html) and, through the "browse" page, search for electronic and on-line atlases. The retrieved links vary widely in their contents and implementations. Some include only scans of maps while others allow the viewer to make some display and compilation choices. Not all of the national atlases displayed through the Web are official publications of federal level governments. Some have been created by private individuals and might not even be hosted on a server within the country depicted.

STATE ATLASES

State atlases that contain thematic maps, surprisingly, seem to be produced most often by universities, not directly by a state agency. As with national atlases, state atlases are an opportunity to showcase or highlight features and activities that make a state unique. In the United States, much of the demographic and economic data displayed in state atlases comes from the United States Bureau of the Census and is augmented by locally collected data.

Alaska in Maps: A Thematic Atlas

Alaska in Maps was a cooperative project of a number of organizations, including the Alaska Geographic Alliance, the Alaska Department of Education, the University of Alaska-Fairbanks, and the Alaska Pacific University. Funding was provided by a grant from the Alaska Legislature. The atlas, while useful as a general atlas of the state, was intended for school use. There is an elementary school textbook that complements the atlas's contents, *Alaska: A Land in Motion.*

The spiral-bound atlas contains 49 numbered single-topic page-size maps, most at 1:10,000,000, along with text, photographs, charts, graphs, and a number of smaller maps. These materials are organized into four sections: Perspectives on Alaska, Physical Geography, Human Geography, and Environment and Society. The table of contents is arranged in three columns that list the maps, figures, and broad topics within each section. The spacing of the entries in the columns will assist in making quick connections between the numbered maps and the supporting figures because the titles of the maps and figures are not spaced in strict even arrangement but are placed so that the titles of figures that will enhance understanding specific maps are printed on the same line as the appropriate map title. The spacing of the table of contents does not reflect the physical arrangement of the atlas.

Within the text at the beginning of the sections, each map is discussed, sometimes within the context of the information presented by other maps and graphics. The page-size maps follow the sectional text. Each of the four sections is color-coded. When maps are referenced by number within the text, the number is printed in a box the color for the section in which the map is located. Because many of the maps are at the same scale and projection, it is easy to compare the geographic distribution of different topics. For instance, an atlas user might want to think about the creation of Alaska Native Regional Corporations in the contexts of language groups, major mountain ranges, and land ownership. Sometimes the text assists in making appropriate connections between map topics.

The atlas includes a fifth very important section, "Uses of Geography." The section illustrates seven real-life examples of how geography and maps are used to explore or protect the environment, discover the past, direct new uses of land and the search for usable natural resources, and identify specific places. The atlas concludes with a resource list arranged by section. Some of the resources included are print and others are available through the Web.

As with national atlases, *Alaska in Maps* presents some topics, such as brown bear density and subsistence harvests, that might not appear in other state atlases; these kinds of topics help build a more specific understanding of the state and its inhabitants. That two of the four sections of topical information, "Physical Geography" and "Environment and Society," focus on the physical nature of Alaska and the impacts that nature has on humans or humans have on nature illustrates the great amount of consideration given to the natural environment in the regular course of life in Alaska. *Alaska in Maps* is the kind of straightforward atlas that will provide a general overview of a state's geographic qualities. Because Alaska is such a large landmass, the 1:10,000,000-scale maps can only give a taste of Alaska's qualities. *Alaska in Maps* could be used as a quick source of information but not as a resource for doing any kind of research.

The Atlas of Pennsylvania

The depth and breadth of topical coverage in *The Atlas of Pennsylvania* is much greater than *Alaska in Maps*. The atlas was intended to "be of direct relevance and utility to the economic development of Pennsylvania." Its audience is government agencies, private businesses, along with schools and colleges. The atlas's contents are divided into four topical sections, "Land and Resources," "Pennsylvania's Past," "Human Patterns," and "Economic Activity." There also is a very brief introductory section, "The Pennsylvania Mosaic," and a section that focuses on Philadelphia and Pennsylvania. Each of the topical sections includes a number of different topics, each authored or edited by an expert. Six different map scales are used to portray the entire state, and while many of the maps are choropleth, other techniques for indicating quantitative information, such as dots, graduated symbols, and proportional symbols, are used. *The Atlas of Pennsylvania* is one of the very few atlases that acknowledges nonstandard use of choropleth-like maps to depict absolute quantities, not ratios. Each specific topic has a page or two of coverage that includes maps, text, and supporting graphs or charts. Data and information sources are listed at the end of each topic. The atlas concludes with a small reference map section with maps of legislative and administrative districts, an eight-page shaded relief map of the entire state, and information about USGS medium-scale mapping of Pennsylvania. There also is a gazetteer, a short list of recommended readings, and an index.

The Atlas of Pennsylvania is a good example of a "full-service," or full-coverage, state atlas. It does a good job of balancing coverage of natural resources with human activities with fairly consistent scales enabling comparison between topics throughout the atlas. The data depicted varies in age; most topics include information from the early to mid-1980s. But there are also a number of topics that include historical data so that development patterns can be examined. The depth of data depicted is astounding, as it includes specifics about topics like retail sales by sector (food, automotive, building materials), value added by specific manufacturing activities along with information about the number of employees between 1950 and 1983, and seasonal wind power. With an atlas like *The Atlas of Pennsylvania,* users will be able to begin exploring a state's resources from a solid foundation.

Some publishers, such as DeLorme and Benchmark, are specializing in state atlases that have a road and recreational focus, although the atlases can be used for a number of other purposes. These are discussed in the "Thematic Atlases" chapter under "Road Atlases."

As with national atlases, searching on the Web for "[state name] atlas" may be problematic because many of the results will be booksellers' Web advertisements for the *DeLorme Atlas and Gazetteer* series (described in the "Thematic Atlases" chapter). Again, the links available through Oddens' Bookmarks (http://oddens.geog.uu.nl) could save time and reduce searching frustration. Some on-line atlases, like the *Interactive Florida County Atlas* (http://www.freac.fsu.edu/InteractiveCountyAtlas/Atlas.html), are selections from more extensive CD-ROM products. The *Massachusetts Electronic Atlas* (http://hcl.harvard.edu/maps/massatlas.html) has all of its contents, 250 different data layers, available for selection and viewing through the Web.

LOCAL ATLASES

Local atlases for counties, cities, or regions smaller than states are produced by a variety of agencies. Sometimes a community or special-interest group produces a title; other local atlases have been published by local governments and commercial firms. Atlases produced by community-based agencies or special-interest groups are often compiled for specific reasons, such as economic boosterism or natural resources preservation. Finding atlases produced by local groups and agencies can be difficult and may necessitate a number of personal contacts before finding the right source.

Atlases produced for towns and cities by commercial firms are usually easier to identify and locate than those produced by local groups. They often tend to be bound versions of, or have content very similar to, road and street maps produced by the firms, not atlases that display many different attributes for the area. Further descriptions of some common street atlases can be found in the "Road Atlases" section of the "Thematic Atlases" chapter.

FACSIMILE ATLASES AND ATLASES OF REPRODUCTIONS

Facsimiles are reproductions of old maps that look exactly like the original but have been printed using modern printing techniques. Facsimiles are not printed using the original printing plates but are copied, often using a photographic technique. The size of the copy should be the same size as the original, and often facsimile publishers use cream-colored paper stock to approximate the color values of the original paper.

A facsimile atlas could either be a facsimile of an entire atlas or a volume of facsimiles that have been drawn together from dispersed places because they have a common theme or tie. The introduction to *DK Atlas of World History* refers to its maps of noncontemporary time periods as "portraits of an alien world." Facsimile atlases could be considered reproductions of self-portraits drawn in an alien world.

During the 1960s and 1970s, an Amsterdam publishing house, Theatrum Orbis Terrarum, published a substantial number of facsimile atlases. Each volume includes a complete reproduction of an important historic item plus introductory material written by some of the foremost historians of cartography. These volumes also clearly credit the collection from which the original material was used. Harry Margary, a British publishing company, has specialized in producing facsimiles of atlases of Great Britain with occasional branching out to other areas. As with the Theatrum Orbis Terrarum publications, these include an introductory section placing the atlas into its historical context along with information about the original work and any supplemental pieces that were created to aid in using the facsimile.

The Theatrum Orbis Terrarum and Harry Margary publications are not in color. They are printed on cream- or buff-colored paper with black ink and reproduce a single atlas. Other facsimile atlases gather related items or reproduce selected portions of atlases. *Blaeu's The Grand Atlas of the 17th Century World* is a selection of maps from a nine-volume world atlas published in 1662. The maps are reproduced in color, slightly reduced from the original size, and are printed on white semigloss paper almost giving the volume the appearance of a coffee table book.

LESS-THAN-NEW ATLASES

Atlases should not be disregarded or discarded simply because they are outdated. Older atlases can be invaluable resources for boundary, place name, and statistical data from earlier eras. They can also be used to track changes in a publisher's standard design and even to examine changes in society and social awareness. Older atlases are good sources for chronological materials that examine the same economic aspect. The maps could be used as a visual progression showing change. Looking at three recent editions of *Goode's World Atlas* shows subtle yet potentially significant differences on a number of the thematic maps, such as the number of physicians, steel production, and exports and imports.

Older atlases can also be used to follow the changes in colonial influence in Africa and parts of Asia after the Second World War. Atlases from the 1980s may be useful for comparison with atlases published after 1991 to examine changes in eastern Europe as Communism began to wane and the Soviet Union eventually dissolved.

Finally, it needs to be remembered that the less-than-new atlases of today will be antiquarian materials in a century or less. Scholars of the future will be as interested in the broad cornucopia of information about the late twentieth and early twenty-first centuries presented in atlases as early twenty-first century scholars are interested in atlases of the eighteenth, nineteenth, and early twentieth centuries.

BIBLIOGRAPHY

AAG Newsletter. Washington, D.C: Association of American Geographers, 1967– . 12 per year. ISSN: 0275-3995.

Alaska: A Land in Motion. Nancy Warren Ferrell. Fairbanks, Alaska: University of Fairbanks, 1994. ISBN: 1-887419-00-4.

Alaska in Maps: A Thematic Atlas. Roger W. Pearson and Marjorie Hermans, eds. Fairbanks, Alaska: University of Alaska-Fairbanks, 1998. ISBN: 1-887419-02-0.

American Reference Books Annual. Littleton, Colo.: Libraries Unlimited, 1970– . ISSN: 0065-9959.

Atlante Tematico d'Italia. 4 vols. Touring Club Italiano. Milan: Touring Club Italiano, 1989–1992. ISBN: 8836504140.

Atlas del Peru. 1a ed. Lima: Instituto Geográphico Nacional (Peru), 1989.

The Atlas of Africa. Regine Van chi-Bonnardel. Paris: Editions Jeune Afrique, 1973. ISBN: 0-02-901070-5.

An Atlas of African Affairs. 2nd ed. Ieuan L. Griffiths. New York: Routledge, 1994. ISBN: 0-415-05488-5.

Atlas of Eastern Europe. Washington, D.C.: United States, Central Intelligence Agency, 1990. ISBN: 999145506X.

Atlas of Israel: Cartography, Physical and Human Geography. 3rd ed. Survey of Israel. New York: Macmillian, 1985. ISBN: 0-02905950-X.

The Atlas of Pennsylvania. David J. Cuff, ed. Philadelphia: Temple University Press, 1989. ISBN: 0-87722-618-0.

Atlas Ost- und Südosteuropa: Aktuelle Karten zu Ökologie, Bevölkerung und Wirtschaft (Atlas of Eastern and Southeastern Europe: Up-to-date Ecological, Demographic, and Economic maps). Wien: Österreichisches Ost- und Südosteuropa-Institut, 1989– . Number of maps issued per year varies.

Base Line: A Newsletter of the Map & Geography Roundtable. Golden, Colo.: Map & Geography Roundtable, American Library Association, 1981– . Bimonthly. ISSN: 0272-8532.

Blaeu's The Grand Atlas of the 17th Century World. John Goss. New York: Rizzoli, 1991. ISBN: 0847813002.

The Booklist. Chicago: American Library Association, 1969– . Semimonthly. ISSN: 0006-7385.

Bulletin. Ottawa, Ont.: Association of Canadian Map Libraries and Archives, 1968– . Triannual. ISSN: 0840-9331.

Cartographic Perspectives: Bulletin of the North American Cartographic Information Society. University Park, Penn.: The Society, 1989– . Triannual. ISSN: 1048-9053.

Cartography and Geographic Information Science. Bethesda, Md.: American Congress on Surveying and Mapping, 1999– . Quarterly. Formerly *Cartography and Geographic Information Systems* and *American Cartographer.* ISSN: 1523-0406.

Choice. Chicago: Association of College and Research Libraries, American Library Association, 1964– . Monthly. ISSN: 0009-4978.

Current Geographical Publications. American Geographical Society. Milwaukee, Wis.: University of Wisconsin, Milwaukee Library, 1938– . Monthly except July and August. ISSN: 0011-3514.

DK Atlas of World History. Jeremy Black, ed. London: Dorling Kindersley, 1999. ISBN: 0-7513-0719-X.

Encarta Interactive World Atlas 2001. Microsoft Corporation. Redmond, Wash.: Microsoft, 2000.

The Former Yugoslavia: A Map Folio. Washington, D.C.: United States, Central Intelligence Agency, 1992.

Goode's World Atlas. 20th ed. John C. Hudson, ed. Chicago: Rand McNally, 2000. ISBN: 0-528-84336-2.

Information Bulletin. Sacramento, Calif.: Western Association of Map Libraries, 1970– . Triannial. ISSN: 0049-7282.

Kister's Atlas Buying Guide. Kenneth F. Kister. Phoenix, Ariz.: Oryx Press, 1984. ISBN: 0-912700-62-9.

Maps on File. New York: Facts on File, 1981– . Annual. ISSN: 0275-8083.

National Atlas of Hungary. Hungarian Academy of Sciences, Geographical Research Institute. Budapest: Cartographia, on behalf of the Hungarian Academy of Sciences and the Ministry of Agriculture and Food, 1989. ISBN: 9633515084.

The National Atlas of Japan. Rev. ed. Geographical Survey Institute. Tokyo: Japan Map Center, 1990.

National Atlas of Sweden. 18 vols. Stockholm: SNA Publishing, 1990– . ISBN: 91-87760-04-5.

The National Atlas of the United States. Arch C. Gerlach, ed. Washington, D.C.: U.S. Dept. of the Interior, Geological Survey, 1970.

National Geographic Atlas of the World. 7th ed. Washington, D.C.: National Geographic Society, 1999. ISBN: 0-7922-7528-4.

New Millennium World Atlas Deluxe. CD-ROM. Rand McNally and Company. Skokie, Ill.: Rand McNally, 1998.

Nuevo Atlas Nacional de Cuba. 1a ed. Havana: Instituto de Geografia de la Academia de Ciencias de Cuba y el Instituto Cubano de Geodesia y Cartografia, 1989. ISBN: 84-7819-007-4.

Outline Maps on File. New ed. New York: Facts on File, 2002. ISBN: 0816049963.

Peters Atlas of the World. Arno Peters. Harlow, Eng: Longman, 1989. ISBN: 0-06-016540-5.

The Republic of Zambia Atlas. Lusaka: Surveyor General, Ministry of Lands and Mines, Republic of Zambia, 1966–1976, 1986– . Sheets issued irregularly.

The Times Atlas of the World. 10th comprehensive ed. New York: Times Books, 1999. ISBN: 0-8129-3265-X.

Tübinger Atlas des Vorderen Orients (Tübinger Atlas of the Middle East). Wiesbaden: Reichert, 1977–1993. ISBN: 3-88226-610-4.

On-line References

Atlas of Eastern Europe. Central Intelligence Agency. University of Texas at Austin General Libraries, Perry-Castañeda Library Map Collection, 4 September 2002. <http://www.lib.utexas.edu/maps/atlas_east_europe/atlas_e._europe.html> (16 October 2003).

Interactive Florida County Atlas. Florida State University, 29 January 2001. <http://www.freac.fsu.edu/InteractiveCountyAtlas/Atlas.html> (16 October 2003).

Map Machine. National Geographic Society, 24 June 2003. <http://plasma.nationalgeographic.org/mapmachine/> (16 October 2003).

Massachusetts Electronic Atlas. Harvard College Library, Harvard Map Library, 2003. <http://hcl.harvard.edu/maps/massatlas.html> (16 October 2003).

National Atlas of Canada. Natural Resources Canada, 2003. <http://atlas.gc.ca/site/english/index.html> (16 October 2003).

National Atlas of Sweden. SNA Publishing, 25 October 2002. <http://www.sna.se/e_index.html> (16 October 2003).

National Atlas of the United States. U.S. Geological Survey. Library of Congress, 22 February 2001. <http://memory.loc.gov/ammem/gmdhtml/census.html> (16 October 2003).

National Atlas of the United States. U.S. Geological Survey, 28 February 2003. <http://www.nationalatlas.gov> (16 October 2003).

Oddens' Bookmarks: The Fascinating World of Maps and Mapping. Utrecht University, 24 July 2002. <http://oddens.geog.uu.nl/index.html> (16 October 2003).

World Atlas On-Line. Facts on File, Inc. By subscription. <http://www.fofweb.com> (1 March 2002).

The World Factbook. Central Intelligence Agency, 5 August 2003. <http://www.cia.gov/cia/publications/factbook> (16 October 2003).

CHAPTER 8
Thematic Atlases

TOPICS COVERED

Historical Atlases
Bible Atlases and Atlases of Religion
Demographic and Statistical Atlases, Including Those
    Derived from U.S. Censuses
Road Atlases
    Continents and Countries
    States
    Counties and Cities
Environmental Atlases
Imagery Atlases

MAJOR RESOURCES DISCUSSED

Thematic Atlases for Public, Academic, and High
    School Libraries
Shepherd's Historical Atlas
The Times History of the World
The Times Atlas of World History
DK Atlas of World History
Historical Atlas of Africa
A Historical Atlas of South Asia
Historical Atlas of the United States
Historical Atlas of Canada
Concise Historical Atlas of Canada
Wisconsin's Past and Present
Atlas of the Year 1000

The Times Atlas of the Bible
Holman Bible Atlas
Atlas of the World's Religions
New Historical Atlas of Religion in America
Atlas of American Religion
Rand McNally Commercial Atlas and Marketing
    Guide
We the People: An Atlas of America's Ethnic Diversity
Atlas of the 1990 Census
The Atlas of Ethnic Diversity in Wisconsin
The Rand McNally Road Atlas
National Geographic Society Road Atlas
DeLorme *Atlas and Gazetteer* series
Benchmark *Road & Recreation* atlases
Rand McNally *StreetFinders*
Thomas Bros. Maps *Thomas Guides*
MapArt *Street Guides*
The New State of the Earth Atlas
World Atlas of Desertification
The Great Lakes: An Environmental Atlas and Re-
    source Book
Chicago Wilderness: An Atlas of Biodiversity
The Cartographic Satellite Atlas of the World
The Atlas of Global Change
Earth from Above
Atlas of North America: Space Age Portrait of a Con-
    tinent

Thematic atlases focus on depicting the spatial nature of a specific theme or group of related themes. There are thematic atlases about climate, environmental concerns, history, ethnicity, agricultural production, human health, and many other topics. Some atlases are wide-ranging; for instance *Women in the World: An International Atlas* includes maps on birth rates, access to contraception, literacy rates, employment opportunities, and crimes committed by women. Others, such as the *Agricultural Atlas of the United States,*

focus on a specific industry or economic sector within a single country.

Thematic atlases can be tricky to find. "[Topic]— Atlases or" [Topic]—Maps" as subject searches in library catalogs, with or without a geographic region, will either yield very little, in the case of the first, or, from the latter, potentially way too many options. Searching library on-line catalogs or OCLC's World-Cat for thematic atlases may take some creative thinking. A combination of subject terms and keywords might be necessary. *Atlas of Women and Men in India* includes no forms of either "atlas" or "map" in its subject headings, yet it can be found in WorldCat by using "atlas" as a keyword and "women" as a subject phrase to pick up from "Women—India—Social conditions" and "Women—India—Economic conditions." Unfortunately, this technique does allow some inaccurate results to appear. Searching "atlas" as a keyword and "monkey" as a subject word in WorldCat results only in titles similar to *A Stereotaxic Atlas of the Monkey Brain,* an anatomical atlas of the Rhesus monkey. This kind of result could be disconcerting if the seeker was not prepared for it.

In fact, there are no atlases that focus only on the geographical distribution of monkeys or, more broadly, nonhuman primates. Sometimes searches for topical information in thematic atlases need to be broadened. Maps showing the locations of monkeys might be found in more general atlases showing animal distribution throughout the entire world or in atlases that focus on just a specific country.

*Thematic Atlases for Public, Academic, and High
  School Libraries*

Thematic Atlases for Public, Academic, and High School Libraries provides extensive descriptions, evaluative comments, and citations to published reviews for 100 English-language thematic atlases. The atlases included are not necessarily geographic in nature; the author includes *Atlas of Human Anatomy* and *Visible Human Body: An Atlas of Sectional Anatomy.* Nor are all of the atlases rooted in reality, as illustrated by *Atlas of Middle-Earth,* which maps the fictional world depicted in the novels of J.R.R. Tolkien. Many of the atlases described are either national in scope or historical in nature.

Thematic Atlases begins with an extensive introductory section that discusses the inclusion and exclusion decisions that had to be made, how the atlases were located, and primary considerations in creating the entries. The entries are organized alphabetically; each is approximately two pages in length and includes a full bibliographic citation, a physical description of the atlas including section pagination, a list of topics covered, a brief table of contents, "Noteworthy Qualities," potential Library of Congress, Dewey Decimal, or Superintendent of Documents classifications, and brief citations for up to six reviews. The volume concludes with a brief (19 entries) gazetteer and three indexes to publishers, names/titles, and subjects.

HISTORICAL ATLASES

Historical atlases most often are published by for-profit or university presses. They require a large amount of intense research before map themes are decided upon, let alone mapped. The history of a place or of a group of people is a complex and very rich topic. Some historical atlases take a strictly chronological view while others organize around themes and trends.

Shepherd's Historical Atlas. 9th ed.
Shepherd's Historical Atlas was first published in 1911. The ninth edition, published in 1964, was reprinted most recently by Barnes and Noble in 1980. *Shepherd's* strength lies in the maps of Europe, especially central Europe, for centuries prior to the First World War. The maps convey intense amounts of information and accordingly can be visually very complex. Maps of central Europe, even if details cannot be fully understood, clearly show how kingdoms and duchies splintered the landscape into many small holdings with confused and possibly overlapping boundaries. *Shepherd's* will also be useful for people researching family history during the nineteenth century because it can be used as a tool to track, at an undetailed level, boundary and state name changes. There is virtually no text in *Shepherd's Historical Atlas,* nor are there any supporting photographs, tables or graphs; it is packed with maps and a place name index. The maps mainly are in chronological order with a group of maps focusing on the United States near the end of the main section of maps. A small group of "Maps Since 1929" has been added with overviews of the Second World War, the Cold War, the decline of European colonialism, and a map of Europe in 1964. The index of place names is also in two parts; the longer index corresponds to the maps in the main section and the supplement to the "Maps Since 1929" section.

While there might be other newer world historical atlases, *Shepherd's Historical Atlas* should be remembered as a core source of historical geographic information. Older historical information does not necessarily "go out of style." Although more recent research may add details or change how information is displayed, *Shepherd's Historical Atlas* has stood the test of time as a resource for foundational information.

The Times History of the World. New [5th] ed.
The Times Atlas of World History. 6th concise ed.

Previously titled *The Times Atlas of World History,* the new edition of *The Times History of the World* follows in the footsteps of four earlier editions with a view of world history that is global instead of being centered on Europe and European expansion. World history is depicted through maps and accompanying text and illustrations grouped into seven broad chronological sections. Prior to the historical sections is a 12-page "Chronology of World History," a time-line that allows cross-continental comparisons or conjunctions of events to be made. Each two-page spread in the chronological sections depicts a place, a time period, and pivotal events that define the period. A consistent format is used throughout the volume that includes a small chronological chart targeting the theme and time period of the spread, a quotation from significant writings about the period, pictures of appropriate artifacts, and references to other places within the volume where related events or peoples are discussed. The final four sets of pages summarize world political, economic, communications, and environmental situation at the end of the twentieth century. *The Times History of the World* concludes with a bibliography that includes historical atlases and textual materials, a glossary of individuals, nations, events, and treaties, and an index of place names. Although the maps in *The Times History of the World* were completely redrawn for the new edition and the design of the pages has been changed and updated, this volume will feel familiar to anyone who has used one of the previous editions of *The Times Atlas of World History*.

The sixth concise edition of *The Times Atlas of World History* is based largely, but not wholly, on larger atlases of the same title, those atlases that were the predecessors of *The Times History of the World*. *The Times Atlas of World History,* sixth concise edition, has smaller pages and fewer maps than *The Times History of the World,* making it more portable. The editor's goals were the same as for the large volume, to present a balanced, non-Eurocentric representation of civilizations, relations, and interactions. The 150 thematic- or event-based two-page map spreads are grouped into four parts. Most of the spreads include multiple maps along with explanatory text. As with the larger editions, *The Times Atlas of World History,* sixth concise edition, includes a bibliography and an index to place names. There is no glossary of people or events.

DK Atlas of World History

DK Atlas of World History is similar to many other DK publications: full of maps, graphs, and illustrations in a visually interesting package. *DK Atlas of World History* attempts to balance world chronological coverage with regional specifics. Slightly more than half of

the maps are regional in focus. Part one, "Eras of World History," is made up of 51 double-page spreads that focus on specified chronological periods. Part, two, "Regional History," depicts important periods for continents and subcontinents. There are nearly equal numbers of double-page displays for Europe and Asia (divided among three subcontinents), 22 and 27, respectively, and 11 for North America. There are only five to seven for South America, Africa, or Australasia and Oceania. All of the regional sections begin with a map showing the region 18,000 years ago, an interesting period of glaciation and lower sea water levels.

Most of the time periods or specific sequences of events are drawn over shaded relief base maps. A variety of scales, orientations, and projections are used, so it may be difficult to specifically compare events or distributions for the same region between different time periods. All of the two-page spreads include multiple maps, short caption-like text, and a variety of photographic illustrations. Some of the illustrations are images of maps that were produced during the time period under discussion, while others are photographs of artifacts or landmarks as they appear now.

DK Atlas of World History does not include an extensive introductory section or suggestions/cautions about use. There is a subject index/glossary and a gazetteer. The volume's bibliography is divided by region of coverage, listing atlases and other sources of information and making it useful for finding related materials.

Historical Atlas of Africa

Although nearly 20 years old, the *Historical Atlas of Africa* is still a reliable source of historical information about Africa from prehistoric times to 1980. The atlas contains 72 full-color maps, each with accompanying text and sometimes illustrations on the facing page and arranged in rough chronological order. The first five maps cover basic contextual topics, such as relief and rainfall, vegetation and soils, geology and natural resources, languages, and trypanosomiasis and livestock. The remaining 67 maps track human development and events from human origins to the movement toward decolonization and independence that followed the end of the Second World War.

The atlas contains three primary map types: event, process, and quantitative. Event maps will help locate towns or settlements, trade routes, tribal territories, gold mining areas, and other specific sites. Event maps need to be used within the context established by the accompanying text. These maps often have broad temporal bounds such as "Eastern and Southern

Africa 1200–1500" and "West Africa in the Nineteenth Century." Process maps show changes in an area ("before-and-after"), geographic integration or overlap of causally related features at a specific time, and geographic distribution of ideas or objects by using graphics such as arrows or isolines. A typical before-and-after map takes the form of two small maps about government expenditure for education, part of a group of maps titled "Education in the Twentieth Century." One of the government expenditure maps is subtitled mid-1930s and the other mid-1970s. Causal relationships can be seen on a number of the contextual maps such as the map of "Present Day Distribution of Cattle," which includes an indication of the extent of the Tsetse fly infestation. Maps showing language distribution, population movements, or trade routes are scattered throughout the atlas. The editors warn in the introductory material that these maps in particular should be considered schematic, not exact, representations of flows and connections. Quantitative maps depict numerical data, most often economic data. The editors also caution that the data used to create the maps potentially could be either incomplete or inaccurate, even though they worked toward obtaining reliable base data. In some cases, data are incomplete because the editors preferred to work from sole sources of information instead of combining data gathered from multiple sources. There also were space constraints within the volume that do not allow for explicit descriptions of how data would have been augmented from other sources.

The atlas begins with a preface and a "Cartographic Introduction"; both should be read to understand the constraints under which the atlas was produced and the compromises that had to be made. The atlas concludes with a small notes section and an index to place names. There is no topical index.

The text in *Historical Atlas of Africa* is often key to understanding the maps. The strong chronological arrangement will assist the user in locating maps showing appropriate time periods, but the lack of a topical index hinders the user's ability to find references to specific groups of people or activities throughout the atlas. Historical geography is more than just places at different times; it also is events and connections made by individuals and groups to places through time.

Because the *Historical Atlas of Africa* was published in 1985, with much of the work having been completed well before then, some of the content for more recent events may be slightly dated or nonexistent. *The New Atlas of African History,* a much smaller

volume with two-color maps, might be an appropriate supplement because it includes events and connections from prehistory through 1990, although there is only one map that is clearly post-1980, "Africa, Politics and Population, 1990."

A Historical Atlas of South Asia

A Historical Atlas of South Asia could be considered the seminal atlas on the history of the part of Asia currently known as India, Pakistan, Bangladesh, Afghanistan, Nepal, Bhutan, Sri Lanka, the Maldives, and Burma (until 1948). Its 149 pages of three- and four-color maps are followed by 131 pages of explanatory text, tables, charts, and graphs. The numbered maps are grouped into 14 sections, the first 9 sections primarily by historical period and the last 5 sections by topic, primarily social and demographic attributes from the second and third quarters of the twentieth century. The very first section contains contextual maps, world maps centered on Delhi, physiography, climate, and vegetation. The following historic period sections vary in both temporal length and map count. The historical sections begin with prehistory and follow through to depicting the situation in the third quarter of the twentieth century. More than half of the atlas covers events after 1857. Earlier periods include very little economic and demographic information because the data are not available. Throughout the atlas, emphasis is placed mainly on political history with some attention to social and cultural events. Generally, all of the map pages contain multiple maps on each page or plate. Many of the maps cover broad time periods, for instance "Religious and Cultural Sites of the Mughal period, 1526–1707." The table of contents lists all of the maps on each page. All of the map plates have a correspondingly numbered section in the text.

The introductory material at the beginning of the atlas is lengthy but goes far in explaining constraints of both atlas construction and use. People intending to use *A Historical Atlas of South Asia* should take the time to read the introduction because the editor explains some of the compromises that need to be made in historical atlas compilation, especially for depicting state or kingdom boundaries. The introduction to the atlas concludes with a bibliography. The individual sections in the text all include brief citations to source material. An extensive bibliography, organized by publication type, follows the text. There also is an index to place names. A number of important separate pieces are distributed with the atlas in a pocket in the back cover, including chronology charts and two overlay maps, physiography and administrative divisions, that fit over many of the maps in the atlas that have a common scale of 1:12,700,000.

A Historical Atlas of South Asia has been distributed in two impressions. The second impression includes some additional text, citations to new sources at the ends of some of the text sections, new bibliography sections, and a new place name index that extends the old index. There were no changes or additions to the maps.

Although *A Historical Atlas of South Asia* is intended for a broad audience, scholars and more advanced readers of South Asian history will be far more comfortable with the level at which the information is presented than will neophytes.

Historical Atlas of the United States. Rev. ed.

Historical Atlas of the United States was originally compiled, in part, to celebrate the centennial of the founding of the National Geographic Society. The atlas is full of different graphic presentation techniques: maps, remotely sensed images, photographs, timelines, sketches, paintings, graphs, and reproductions of historic works. Maps are placed in appropriate historical contexts through photographs of artifacts and of principal players. All of the maps and illustrations have extensive captions; much of the textual content of *Historical Atlas of the United States* is contained within the captions. Two kinds of sections alternate throughout the volume, thematic and chronological. There are six thematic sections: The Land, People, Boundaries, Economy, Networks, and Communities. The chronological sections divide recorded United States history into five uneven chunks, 1400–1606, 1607–1788, 1789–1860, 1861–1916, and 1917–1988, using such watershed events as King James I's patents granted to the Virginia and Plymouth companies (1606) and the beginning of the Civil War (1861) to determine dividing years. Maps and other graphics that apply to a specific situation could appear in either a thematic section or a chronological section.

The atlas concludes with a bibliography arranged by pages containing full citations for maps and illustrations, as well as sources for additional reading and acknowledgments to consultants. There also is an index to events, people, and places.

Historical Atlas of the United States is a complex volume depicting a complex history and multiple sequences of events. But it is highly browsable and will open the door to further exploration.

Historical Atlas of Canada
Concise Historical Atlas of Canada

The *Historical Atlas of Canada,* from which the *Concise Historical Atlas of Canada* was compiled, is a massive three-volume, beautifully produced set with a multidisciplinary focus. Each of the volumes covers a different time period: From the Beginning to 1800; The Land Transformed, 1800–1891; and Addressing the Twentieth Century, 1891–1961. Each of the volumes has a slightly different organizational scheme. The first volume is somewhat geographical with a "Prehistory" section that depicts a number of topics nationwide, followed by four sections focusing on large areas of Canada. The other two volumes are organized around economic and social processes. Scholars and researchers who were considered experts in their fields were invited to work with cartographers to develop the maps. Clearly, the maps in this atlas are the main emphasis. Each section begins with an introduction that sets the context for the maps historically and in context with each other. The maps are double-page plates that display intense amounts of data. The layout of the plates, the scales of the maps, the mapping techniques, and the use of other graphics such as graphs, tables, and illustrations varies from topic-to-topic. The plates include a small amount of text specifically illuminating the topic mapped, but there is never so much text that the maps become secondary.

The volumes conclude with notes about each map plate that contain citations to source materials and sources for further reading. The volumes are not indexed, but the tables of contents are sufficiently detailed to enable finding appropriate plates. The entry for each plate includes the titles of the maps included on the plate, along with those for any graphs and illustrations. In all three volumes, except for the pages of text at the beginning of each map section and the pages of notes at the end of the volumes, there are no page numbers. Location within the volumes is indicated by plate number.

The *Concise Historical Atlas of Canada* is a single volume, but that volume is as large as one of the volumes in the full *Historical Atlas of Canada*. Sixty-seven plates, and the appropriate endnotes, were selected from the full three-volume work to summarize Canadian history from prehistory to the 1960s. The maps are arranged in three groups: National Perspectives, Defining Episodes, and Regional Patterns. The emphasis of the committee that selected the plates was on what ordinary people would have experienced in Canada, not the heroes or extraordinary events.

Wisconsin's Past and Present

Wisconsin's Past and Present was prepared to coincide with the celebration of Wisconsin's sesquicentennial. The cartographers, authors, and editors were inspired by the *Historical Atlas of Canada* to find a way of merging history and cartography to tell the state's story through maps. Maps, text, and accompanying illustrations are arranged in three sections: Peoples & Cultures, Land & Economy, and Society & Politics. Through the atlas could be read cover-to-cover, the content's arrangement makes browsing and comparison between topics feasible and easy. Each topic is covered in a two-page spread; within the sections the topics are arranged somewhat chronologically. References to other topics tie the atlas together. The topics generally include main text and a central map with smaller maps and secondary text that provides depth by discussing a specific aspect of the topic. There is an extensive bibliography and a list of sources arranged by topic along with an index at the end of the volume.

Wisconsin's Past and Present was intended for use by the general public and in schools. The Wisconsin Cartographers' Guild also prepared a teacher's guide, *Mapping Wisconsin History,* to assist in integrating the atlas and its contents into the curricula. *Mapping Wisconsin History* includes color overhead transparencies, black-and-white maps that could be made into transparencies or photocopied for student work, and suggestions for activities and discussion. Although specific to Wisconsin, *Mapping Wisconsin History* could serve as a model for depicting ideas about other geographic areas.

Atlas of the Year 1000

Historical atlases do not only focus on changes in a particular place through time. *Atlas of the Year 1000* illustrates conditions worldwide during the year 1000 and a few years before and after. Following an introduction that discusses the significance, or insignificance, of the year 1000, six geographically based sections highlight the events, territorial extents, and general geographic situation of 43 different cultures. Each of the sections begins with an introductory essay. The volume concludes with a gazetteer, bibliography, and index.

Atlas of the Year 1000 does not strictly meet the "atlas test" of being 50 percent, or more, maps. Much of the text does not directly touch on the specific elements presented by the maps. In the discussion of Japan, "Japan: The Rise and Rise of Michinaga," one of the two maps, "Japan," shows major highways, the changing northern frontier, fortress sites, Ainu hillfort sites, and locations of private estates held by the imperial and Fujiwara families, Todaiji monasteries, and others. The other map, titled "Pilgrimages," shows

temple, shrine, and other pilgrim sites, the pilgrim route from Heian, and provincial boundaries. Michinaga was a member of the Fujiwara family and became regent in 995 to Emperor Ichijo. The text briefly discusses Michinaga's machinations along with the land ownership system so the first map has some textual context but the map of pilgrimages has no appropriate context at all. This kind of disconnect is not uncommon in *Atlas of the Year 1000,* especially when there were not large spatial changes during the time period being discussed or the principal players in important events do not have an overt geographical connection.

Other period-focused historical atlases include titles such as *Mapping the Great Irish Famine, Historical Atlas of the Vietnam War,* and *Atlas of the Roman World.* Each is bound by specific time constraint based on some kind of event or organization. The presentation methods used by the atlases differ, but all authors or compilers of the volumes found that maps were important to explain situations and to assist in the discovery of connections.

BIBLE ATLASES AND ATLASES OF RELIGION

The Times Atlas of the Bible
Holman Bible Atlas

Atlases of the Bible could be considered a kind of historical atlas. They are hybrids of archaeology, anthropology, and interpretation of texts in combination with historical cartography and landscape depiction methods including sketches and photographs. Because much of the geographic information being conveyed by Bible atlases is either inferred or conjecture, many atlases rely heavily on photographs of current Middle Eastern landscapes, people, and activities, with the assumption that similar activities were undertaken in similar manners 2,000 years or longer ago, to fill geographic and cartographic gaps. As with other historical atlases, atlases showing Biblical events are the cartographers' best attempt to depict often less-than-adequately detailed data. Symbols in Bible atlases, especially those showing movement, dispersal, or territorial control always should be understood to be approximations and probably are grossly simplified.

The Times Atlas of the Bible acknowledges the necessary intersection of archaeology and interpretation; "Our aim in this atlas is to show the features of the land and to locate ancient places by making use of the most recent explorations and discoveries. In addition to these objectives, shared by others who draw historical maps, we have sought to impose upon the maps information in the Bible and other texts about important events." (*The Times Atlas of the Bible,* 6) The maps and text, along with other accompanying graphics, are arranged in three groups: Old Testament, Inter-Testamental Period, and New Testament. Within the groups, topics are further subdivided into somewhat chronological sections, such as "Emergence of Israel: Patriarchal Traditions" in the Old Testament group and "Palestine under the Romans" in the New Testament group. Most topics are covered in one double-page spread. The title of the topics will appear at the top of the spread, along with a brief introductory paragraph or synopsis of the topic's context. The box that the title and synopsis are printed in will have a background color coded to the group that the topic is in, purple or taupe for Old Testament, gold for inter-testamental, and dark gray for New Testament. Most of the maps in *The Times Atlas of the Bible* are shaded relief with colors, which lack a legend, that indicate elevation ranges. Some of the city and building-complex plans are three-dimensional renderings. The scale and extent of area covered vary greatly and are clearly topic-driven. Maps of areas larger than cities usually include a coordinate grid and north arrow because not all of the maps are printed with north toward the top of the page. Unfortunately, none of the maps or city plans include scale statements so there is no way to estimate areas or distances.

Like *The Times Atlas of the Bible,* the *Holman Bible Atlas* is arranged in three parts: The Biblical Setting, The Old Testament Period, and The New Testament Era: The World of Jesus and the Early Church. The first part, comprised of three chapters, establishes the geographical, physical, and cultural stages in which the other two parts are set. The remaining 18 chapters, 11 covering the Old Testament and 7 covering the New, are arranged chronologically with Biblical accents. The considerable text is often keyed to specific Biblical passages, which are referenced so that the reader can read the texts in their entirety. Most of the maps are on shaded relief bases; some of the city plans also include topography. All of the maps are oriented with north toward the top of the page. A timeline appears at the top of all of the pages in the second and third parts, placing the text, maps, and photographs into an approximate chronological context. Some of the text is specifically keyed to the numbered maps. Throughout the atlas, there are sidebar descriptions of places along with a number of charts that assist in establishing connections between rulers and their periods of reign. The atlas concludes with a short

glossary; a bibliography organized by broad topics, not in the order of the atlas's presentation; and two indexes, one to people and places and the other to place names appearing on the maps.

Atlas of the World's Religions
New Historical Atlas of Religion in America
Atlas of American Religion

Atlases of religion often provide information about multiple denominations, although some focus on a single faith. Many atlases of religion take a historical approach for exploring a denomination's geographical distribution and influence, as well as for building an understanding of how denominations have developed out of other faiths or denominations and how different faiths have impacted each other.

Atlas of the World's Religions places a very strong emphasis on historical developments and connections. After a very brief "Religion Today" section and a section on the historical geography of religion, there are 10 chapters in the section on specific religions or religions in named geographical regions: The Hindu World; Buddhism; East Asian Traditions; The Pacific; The Ancient Near East and Europe; Judaism; Christianity; Islam; Africa; and Indigenous Religions. All of the chapters begin with some general text and a double timeline that helps to put developments from a particular faith or region into a world context. Nearly all of the maps and accompanying text are historical in nature. *Atlas of the World's Religions* includes a glossary arranged by the faith or region to which the terms apply; a bibliography, again organized by chapter; and an index that combines topics and locations. Because of the atlas's scope and the generally small-scale of the maps, *Atlas of the World's Religions* should be considered a general introduction to religious historical geography.

More specificity can be found in atlases like the *New Historical Atlas of Religion in America* and the *Atlas of American Religion.* Both of these atlases map distribution of denominational membership on county-level base maps for over 300 years of European influence in the geographic area now known as the United States. *New Historical Atlas of Religion in America* begins its cartographic coverage of the Colonies in 1650, while *Atlas of American Religion* begins with 1776. Most of the other chronological distributions are from approximately the same time periods: 1850, 1890, 1950, and 1990. The statistics mapped are slightly different. The maps in *New Historical Atlas of Religion in America* tend to be of the number of churches, temples, societies, or meetings in a county; each statistical year is mapped separately. *Atlas of American Religion* maps the number of total adherents by county and the geographic change in distribution of adherents between 1850 and 1990. These maps of geographic change between 1850 and 1990 are difficult to interpret. Bibliographic references appear at the end of each denominational section in *New Historical Atlas of Religion of America* and at the end of the volume in *Atlas of American Religion*. Both of the atlases' maps are in color: *Atlas of American Religion* in two colors and *New Historical Atlas* in full color. *New Historical Atlas of Religion in America* is a bigger volume. It also includes groups not included in *Atlas of American Religion,* specifically Eastern and Middle Eastern religions. The religions included in *Atlas of American Religion* all have their foundations in the Judeo-Christian traditions. *New Historical Atlas of Religion in America* has another feature not included in *Atlas of American Religion:* case studies of how three different faiths, Lutheran, Mormon, and Roman Catholic, developed geographically and organizationally from the nineteenth century to the present. These case studies could serve as examples for people interested in doing similar work on other faiths. Overall, *New Historical Atlas of Religion in America* is more robust and inclusive than *Atlas of American Religion*. Both atlases present fundamental information about the development and distribution of religious groups and affiliations in the United States. Coupled with information gained from other sources about ethnic groups, economic well-being and other social indicators, both atlases will help create a multifaceted picture of the population of the United States.

DEMOGRAPHIC AND STATISTICAL ATLASES, INCLUDING THOSE DERIVED FROM U.S. CENSUSES

Rand McNally Commercial Atlas and Marketing Guide. 133rd ed.

The *Rand McNally Commercial Atlas and Marketing Guide* is published annually, presenting maps, tables, and charts to "[combine] maximum demographic coverage of the United States with an authoritative interpretation of business data" (*Commercial Atlas,* 6). The *Atlas* is a large volume of more than 575 oversized pages divided into six sections: metropolitan area maps; transportation and communications data; economic data; population data; state maps; and an index of places and statistics organized by state. The volume opens with a map of the United States showing major metropolitan areas and counties, and a brief glossary of terms follows the short preface. The glossary is essential for understanding how population data have

been aggregated and includes terms used by the United States Bureau of the Census and terms developed by Rand McNally to define geographic areas and specific kinds of economic data.

Fourteen metropolitan areas are mapped at 1:300,000, each with an index to towns and localities appearing on the map. The maps are very similar to the metropolitan area maps that appear in Rand McNally's road atlases but with a decreased emphasis on the road networks. Because the maps are all at the same scale, they could be an easy way to compare metropolitan area extents. "Transportation/Communication" includes information on highways, airlines, railroads, telephones, and the postal service. A number of basic maps are included: major highways, highway mileage and driving times, passenger (Amtrak) railroads, railroad lines, telephone area codes, and zip codes. The highway maps are the same as the general U.S. highway maps in the Rand McNally road atlases. The text and lists included in the transportation and communication section are as important, if not more important, as the maps. There is a list of cities with the airlines that provide service to them, an alphabetical list of railroads with a brief description of length and location, a table of railroad distances between major centers, alphabetical and numerical listings of telephone area codes, information on postal rates and regulations, and a numerical listing of zip code "roots" with general statistical data for the area covered. The statistical, specifically economic, data continue in the next section, which includes five maps (trading areas, retail sales, manufacturing, major military installations, and metropolitan statistical areas) with extensive tables of economic data arranged by "trading area," state, metropolitan statistical area, counties, or "principal business centers." This section also includes a list of Fortune 500 companies. The population section is also statistics-heavy, containing four maps of population or population change and 30 pages of statistical lists such as population trends and college populations.

The section of state maps is indexed by the index section that follows, which includes 128,765 places. In some ways, the index section, half of the *Atlas'* total page count, is more important than the maps because of the statistical and descriptive data contained in each location's entry. It is arranged alphabetically by state; each state section begins with basic data about the state, a list of principal towns by population, and a table of basic data for the counties. The alphabetical place entries include information on county; map location; codes for the presence of a post office, college (with population), hospital, prison (with population), or bank; codes for railroads or airlines that serve the community; zip code; population from the most recent census; and a Rand McNally estimate of the population in the year of publication. If a location does not have its own post office, the town where the post office that serves the community is given. There also will be an indication if the town is a county seat. Interestingly, not all of the locations listed are incorporated areas, and some no longer exist officially. The maps in the *Rand McNally Commercial Atlas and Marketing Guide* are not works of great cartographic beauty. They are four color (blue, black, red, and green) with green being overwhelmingly predominant. Relief is shown inconsistently; the Rocky Mountains in only Montana and Idaho are shown using inelegant hachures. None of the other states include indications of mountain ranges beyond scattered peak locations. The scales of the maps vary greatly because most of the maps are spread across two pages; thus Alaska and New Hampshire occupy the same amount of "page real estate" even though Alaska has 63 times the land area of New Hampshire.

Although the maps in the *Rand McNally Commercial Atlas and Marketing Guide* may be a disappointment, they are not the intended central focus of the atlas. The atlas's strength is in the intense presentation of basic economic and demographic statistical data. The index to locations will serve well as a quick way to locate small places—including unincorporated areas and large shopping centers, as well as locales that no longer exist—and basic information about specific places.

We the People: An Atlas of America's Ethnic Diversity

We the People is based on 1980 census data, in particular the questions on race, Spanish/Hispanic origin, and ancestry. The question on ancestry allowed the respondents to describe themselves, while the other two questions had specific categories from which to select answers. These questions appeared on both the short and the long form of the questionnaire. From the statistics, the authors created maps for nearly 70 distinct ethnic groups. The maps are arranged in nine chapters by geographic area of origin. Each chapter contains subsections for the separate groups with brief summary statistics, text placing the group's arrival and dispersion into a historic and economic context, and often two maps, one showing ancestry in 1980 aggregated to the county level and the other showing the percent of each state's population that claims the ethnic group's language as its "mother tongue." Some

groups' descriptions also include maps showing net migrations within the United States, if a pattern could be established. The first three chapters are essential reading to understand how the maps were compiled and the limitations placed on the maps by the data collected through the 1980 Census. The final chapter synthesizes and generalizes the data with summary text and maps of "Predominant Ethnic Population," "Ancestries of State Populations," and "Racial and Hispanic Minorities in Large Metropolitan Areas." There is an extensive section of references to Bureau of the Census publications, reports of the Immigration Commission, and books and articles. Many of the books and articles listed could serve as entry points into the literature that describes specific ethnic groups and the American experience. Three appendices conclude the volume: Ancestries of State Populations, Ethnic Population Data for States and Counties, and Reference Maps: United States Counties. There also is an index to ethnic groups and a short index to places specifically mentioned in the text.

Although *We the People* is becoming dated, it remains a fundamental source of introductory information on the diverse ethnic background of the population of the United States. *We the People* can assist in identifying patterns of ethnic geographic dispersion and co-location of similar and dissimilar groups. Although the maps can stand alone, the text sets them into context and helps explain why people move to particular locations and the social structures that subsequently established or reinforced.

Atlas of the 1990 Census

Like *We the People*, *Atlas of the 1990 Census* is based on data collected by the U.S. Bureau of the Census, but *Atlas of the 1990 Census* is more general in nature than *We the People*. The atlas is divided into six parts: population, households, housing, race and ethnicity, economy, and education. Each part begins with a page of introductory text, including some gross or summary level statistics, somewhat arranged in the same order as the maps that follow. The maps first show the data for a topic aggregated to the state level, then the United States is divided into six regions to display the same topic aggregated to the county level. Although the classifications remain consistent among the six regional maps, the color schemes differ; for example, maps cannot be quickly compared just by looking for the same color that was seen on the midwest region map on any of the other five maps. The color palate consistency is between maps of the same region. All of the maps of the northeast range in color from gray to dark green and all the maps of the northwest from gray to dark blue regardless of topic. As with any set of maps, the legend must be read carefully and applied to the correct map. Many of the national maps present the 1990 situation with an accompanying map that shows the change between 1980 and 1990, but some show only the change between two economic censuses instead of showing the results from a specific census.

The atlas begins with a foreword and introduction that briefly describe the importance of *Atlas of the 1990 Census* as a supplement to and tool for understanding the census. The volume concludes with a section of base maps for the regional maps that will help in identifying specific counties as, throughout the atlas, the names of counties do not appear on any of the thematic maps. There also is a statistical table for cities, arranged by size beginning with New York City, and containing total population and percentages of whites, blacks, American Indians, Asians, Hispanics, and people over 65. The final item in the atlas is a short glossary.

Atlas of the 1990 Census provides a quick graphic overview of population characteristics of the United States in 1990. It will enable basic comparisons of fundamental data between regions and may assist in discovering some causal relationships.

The Atlas of Ethnic Diversity in Wisconsin

Demographic atlases do not need to cover entire nations. *The Atlas of Ethnic Diversity in Wisconsin* maps 1990 census data for 62 different groups. Nearly all of the groups have a two-page set of graphics. The first page includes a page-size map of Wisconsin with inset maps of Milwaukee County and the entire United States. There also is a list of counties with highest percentage population of the ethnic group. The second page has a group of bar and pie charts showing place of residence (central city, rural, or suburban), nativity and year of entry to the United States, household income, educational attainment, and employment of industry, plus an age-sex pyramid showing population composition. The ethnic groups are arranged in 10 chapters by broad region of origin such as African, Asian and Pacific Island, and southern European. Each chapter begins with text discussing the individual ethnic groups; the maps follow at the end of the text section. The atlas concludes with a number of comparative bar graphs, statistical tables, and a group of reference maps. There is a bibliography and an index. This atlas would work nicely with the historical atlas *Wisconsin's Past and Present.*

It will be interesting to see what kinds of print and electronic atlases are derived from the 2000 U.S. census data. With free or relatively inexpensive GIS software, many more individuals, agencies, and companies will be able to produce their own statistical maps than ever before.

ROAD ATLASES

Road atlases are available covering different sizes of areas including continents, countries, states, and such small areas as counties and cities. Quite often atlases of this type will appear in new editions nearly annually, or on a very regular schedule. Publishers also will use the same general format as a template for atlases of many different places.

Continents and Countries

Rand McNally Road Atlas. 2002 ed.
National Geographic Road Atlas. 2001 ed.

The *Rand McNally Road Atlas,* with coverage of the United States and, to a lesser level of detail, Canada and Mexico, has been published annually since the 1920s. Its format is familiar to many who have planned or taken extensive automobile trips. Each state is depicted on two or four oversized pages accompanied by small maps of urban areas and national parks. Each state map has its own bar scale, mileage chart, and a small group of state trivia such as state nickname, land area, and largest city. There is a map of the entire United States close to the front of the atlas and, at the back, a gazetteer of town names arranged by state, a nationwide mileage chart, and a map showing interstate mileage and drive times. *The Rand McNally Road Atlas* may also include information about road construction, typical temperatures, and sources for tourist information. Rand McNally's *Road Atlas* is published in a number of other related editions, including a business traveller's version, a large-scale edition, a deluxe edition, and a motor-carriers' version. The extended publication history of Rand McNally's *Road Atlas* creates an opportunity to track changes in the United States' highway network.

The National Geographic Society began publishing its *Road Atlas,* in direct competition with Rand McNally's atlas, in 1998. Unfortunately, the 2001 edition appears to be the last published. The basic elements of the *National Geographic Road Atlas* are the same as the *Rand McNally Road Atlas,* maps on two or four pages with small city and national park maps, town names alphabetized under the appropriate states, small mileage charts for each state and a national mileage chart near the end of the atlas, a highway map of the entire United States near the front, and a map of interstate driving distances and times at the back. The *National Geographic Road Atlas* was published in both a standard and a deluxe edition.

Both of these atlases are somewhat oversized but slender books. The major difference between the two atlases is in color choice and the depiction of terrain. Except for national parks, terrain in the *Rand McNally Road Atlas* is shown by spot heights for major peaks; the Rand McNally maps look flat. *The National Geographic Road Atlas* uses shading throughout the atlas and both shading and tinting on the highway map of the entire country making it easier to predict when a route might encounter major hills.

The American Automobile Association also publishes a road atlas that covers the United States, Canada, and Mexico, as do Hammond and the American Map Company, but the Rand McNally road atlases are the biggest sellers by far.

Road atlases are also available for other countries. Michelin has published atlases for France; Italy; Spain and Portugal; Great Britain and Ireland; Europe; and Germany, Austria, Benelux, Switzerland, and the Czech Republic. Most of Michelin's road atlases are spiral bound. They will include a place name index and plans for larger towns. The *ADAC Maxi Atlas: Deutschland* has an especially extensive gazetteer section, along with readable maps, which makes this road atlas invaluable for locating smaller communities. The publisher, ADAC Verlag, has also published a road atlas of Europe, but nearly all of the rest of its publications are city street maps and highway maps. Guia Roji has published a road atlas for Mexico. This company also publishes a number of road maps for Mexican states and cities. A limited number of road atlases for Africa have been published by Lonely Planet, AA Publishing, and Map Studio. Lonely Planet has also published road atlases for Australia, Southeast Asia, Portugal, Turkey, and Chile.

Because of how subject headings are created for library catalogs, road atlases can be tricky to find using standard subject searching. A road atlas for Great Britain and Ireland will have the subject heading "Roads—British Isles—Maps." The *Rand McNally Road Atlas* will probably have three subject headings: Roads—United States—Maps; Roads—Canada—Maps; and Roads—Mexico—Maps. Unfortunately, "atlas" is not used as part of a subject heading in the way that "maps" is, so "Roads—[Place name]—Maps" subject heading is used for both road atlases

and road maps. There are a few ways of working around the problem of less-than-specific subject headings. If a likely publisher is known, such as Rand McNally, Michelin, or Lonely Planet, then the corporate name can be used in combination with keywords like "atlas" or "road atlas" to look in library catalogs and OCLC's WorldCat for items that are more likely to be book-format.

On-line vendors, in particular places like Amazon.com, are not constrained by subject heading rules. Subject headings are assigned but they include words that will help limit results much more easily than library-based subject headings. In Amazon.com, "atlas south africa" results in nearly 50 matches for titles with a wide range of topics; *The Atlas of Changing South Africa* and *Atlas for Lesotho* are two of the results. Adding "travel" to the search, "atlas south africa travel," reduces the results list to only six, all of which include words like "touring," "road," or "motoring" in their titles. Using "road" instead of "travel" in an Amazon.com search can produce inconsistent results because "road" is not part of Amazon.com's subject terms. Searching "road atlas Japan" produces one match; searching "travel atlas Japan" produces five matches. But doing the same two searches for Ireland, including "road" results in 31 matches and "travel" only 20. Of course, Amazon.com can also be searched using a known publisher's name.

States

State atlases that focus on roads often have an amazing amount of other information included so that they often become much more general or multipurpose. Major state road atlas publishers, those with more than one or two titles, have created products that are similar in format from state-to-state. Quite often, state road atlases are close to the Rand McNally and National Geographic Society atlases in size.

DeLorme *Atlas and Gazetteer* series
Benchmark *Road & Recreation* atlases

DeLorme originally specialized in maps and atlases for the New England states but now the *Atlas and Gazetteer* series is available for all of the states in the United States. The atlases show paved and unpaved roads plus trails, often include topography or spot elevations, and indicate locations for a wide variety of sites of potential interest for outdoor recreation and travel in general. The atlases usually have a map index on the back cover and on the first page inside the atlas. There is a gazetteer of town names and a number of tables or lists of recreational and cultural sites such as parks, wilderness areas, beaches, wildlife areas, wineries, scenic drives, museums and science centers, historic sites, tours, natural features, campgrounds, fishing and hunting opportunities, and areas for specific kinds of sports including skiing, biking, or golfing. Public lands are usually clearly marked. Depending on the size of the state covered by a specific atlas, map scales generally range from 1:65,000 to 1:300,000. All of the map pages in a state atlas, except for Alaska, will be at the same scale, which allows for easy movement from page to page while traveling through the state. The newest editions of the state atlases include tick marks at one-minute intervals of latitude and longitude so that the atlases can be used with GPS receivers.

DeLorme has also begun a regional street atlas series; thus far, only regions and cities in New England are available. Plus, the company has street atlas software available. DeLorme atlases can be found at many general bookstores, on-line map and book sellers, retailers specializing in outdoor recreation, and through the DeLorme Web site (http://www.delorme.com).

Benchmark Maps atlases, though similar in size to the DeLorme atlases, take a slightly different approach to road atlas production. Benchmark specializes in mapping the western states and is a collaboration of three companies specializing in cartography: Allen Cartography, Eureka Cartography, and Map Link. The results of this collaboration are clearly seen in Benchmark's use of base maps that show relief by gradient tints and shading. The look of these atlases is very similar to the 1:500,000-scale relief maps produced by Allen Cartography for individual states. The atlases completely map the focus state more than once; each group of maps has a specific emphasis. The *Arizona Road & Recreation Atlas* is typical of Benchmark's publications. It is divided into six sections, four of which are devoted to maps. "Regional Maps" sets the focus state into context with a map of U.S. highways; a relief map centered on the state and showing the surrounding states with major roadways and physical features; a map of the entire state that includes county boundaries, highways, rail lines, national forests, and towns; and, if appropriate, maps of distinctive regions within the state. The atlas for Arizona includes a topographic, shaded relief map of the Grand Canyon. The "Recreation Guides" section is a group of indexed lists of various kinds of features and facilities that might be of interest to outdoor recreationalists. These might include campgrounds, boating, golf, and recreational vehicle parks. "Land-scape Maps" is one of the main map sections. The state will be divided into multiple two-page spreads that show highways, towns of different sizes, waterways, and a number of different kinds of other locations on a gradient tint, shaded relief base map. The base map helps emphasize what the landscape is like. The same scale maps and grid are used in the next major map section, "Public Lands." The same kinds of features are shown as on the landscape maps but instead of emphasizing relief or landforms, the Public Lands maps show federal and state ownership of land. In western states, this is of particular interest because so much of the land is controlled by government agencies. Relief is still shown by using shading and occasional spot heights. The next section contains maps of metropolitan areas showing highways, surface streets, and major urban landmarks such as hospitals and colleges. The final section, "Index," includes contact information for recreational sites and map location information for towns and other places.

Benchmark currently has six atlases available with others in production. The company also produces a street atlas for Albuquerque–Santa Fe and a four map regional series for Arizona. The company's Web site (http://www.benchmarkmaps.com) describes all of the atlases. They can be purchased through the company or through normal atlas outlets such as bookstores, on-line sellers, map vendors, and recreational retailers.

Looking at a DeLorme atlas and a Benchmark Maps atlas side-by-side further emphasizes the differences between these products. The DeLorme *Arizona Atlas and Gazetteer* takes 53 pages of maps at 1:250,000 to map the entire state while the Benchmark Maps *Arizona Road & Recreation Atlas* uses 30 pages of maps at 1:400,000. The greatest difference in scale between the two companies' products is for California; DeLorme takes two atlases to cover the entire state, both at 1:150,000, while Benchmark Maps' single atlas is primarily at 1:300,000. The number of town name entries in the index sections of the Arizona atlases is approximately the same. The indexing for other kinds of features is very different. The Benchmark atlas lists feature names with map location, codes for facilities, and telephone number. DeLorme provides similar information but for a greater diversity of features and for some kinds of attractions also includes a brief verbal description. The DeLorme atlas does not include the same kind of regional maps as Benchmark, but it does include a Grand Canyon map at a slightly smaller scale than the Benchmark map. The Benchmark map of the Grand

Canyon emphasizes the contours of the land while the DeLorme map uses softer colors to show relief so that the road and trail networks, especially on the south side of the Canyon, are more prominent. Because of their larger scale, the DeLorme maps covering the state appear fuller; they include more local roads, more details of small and intermittent waterways, and townships. While topography appears on the maps, it has been subtly downplayed through the entire atlas, giving precedence to the road network and feature locations. The DeLorme maps show federal and state land ownership on the 1:250,000 map pages but only the Bureau of Land Management and Arizona state lands are color-coded. Boundaries of lands controlled by other agencies, for instance national park or reservation land, are shown but the areas are not colored. The DeLorme atlas user needing an overview of the variety of governmental land holders will need to consult the 1:1,500,000-scale in the middle of the atlas, "Publicly Owned Lands Locator Map."

The smaller scale and use of elevation tints to emphasize landforms in the Benchmark Maps atlas for Arizona decreases the emphasis on roads, especially local roads, and also does not allow for including as many small waterways. The Benchmark method of showing topography is much more dramatic and striking than DeLorme's. Towns, even a large urban area like Phoenix, also are de-emphasized by using light colors for street networks and not showing urban extent with a color that contrasts with the colors to show landforms. The DeLorme atlas highlights urban areas using a nonlandscape color and a red street network. Through its use of color, the Benchmark will give readers a much clearer picture of land ownership and control, a very complex issue in western states. Beyond the group of regional maps that DeLorme does not include, the Benchmark Arizona atlas also has metropolitan area maps for Phoenix and Tucson at scales of 1:123,000 and 1:150,000, respectively. Street names, and occasionally direction of one-way travel, are clearly marked as are the names of landmarks and locations of interest.

If a choice is available, either between DeLorme and Benchmark or DeLorme and some other publisher, a potential atlas user will need to consider needs carefully when comparing titles. In the case of DeLorme and Benchmark, someone considering travel in areas with unpaved roads might find DeLorme more useful. But a user who is more interested in land ownership and metropolitan area maps would be more pleased with Benchmark.

Counties and Cities

County and city street atlas producers often create similar products for many different places. Some publishers specialize in atlases for counties and cities in a specific region while others distribute atlases that cover cities nationwide.

Rand McNally *StreetFinders*

Rand McNally has more than 300 titles in its *StreetFinders* series. These standard-sized, approximately 11 by 8 inches, spiral-bound atlases are highly detailed Rand McNally street maps in a more convenient book form. Most focus on a major metropolitan city and the surrounding vicinity but some, such as the *Cape Cod, Southern Massachusetts StreetFinder,* cover discrete regions not centered on a larger city or provide details on a group of specific counties. Typically, the front cover of a *StreetFinder* atlas will fold out so that the index map for the atlas can be seen even when the atlas is opened to the map pages. The index map assists in locating the correct map for an area if the desired place's location is known. An alphabetical index to streets with an indication of which town the street is in, along with map page number and a grid designation to locate the specific map on the page, follows the map pages. Numbered state, U.S., and interstate highways are also indexed, as are golf courses, parks, cemeteries, schools, colleges and universities, named subdivisions, and other places of interest, including city halls, shopping centers, hospitals, and museums. Zip codes appear on the maps.

The Rand McNally *StreetFinder* atlases inexpensively provide fairly up-to-date and conveniently packaged street-level maps of areas that have complex road and street networks. Searching for *StreetFinder* at the Rand McNally Travel Store, part of the Rand McNally Travel Site (http://www.randmcnally.com), will yield a list of *StreetFinders* currently available directly from Rand McNally. A number of map dealers and bookstores also sell *StreetFinders*. Searching OCLC's WorldCat using "*StreetFinder*" and "Rand McNally" as search terms will display bibliographic records for *StreetFinders* published between the mid-1990s and the present and cataloged by libraries. It is important, in a WorldCat search, to include Rand McNally because *StreetFinder* has been used by Bartholomew, a British publisher, to identify some of its street map-related products.

Thomas Bros. Maps *Thomas Guides*

Thomas Bros. Maps is a California-based mapping firm. The company is best known for its *Thomas Guides,* spiral-bound standard-sized (8 by 10 inches) map books for urban areas. Those who have lived on the U.S. west coast will be saddened to learn that most of Thomas Bros. Maps' products are west coast–centered. It was not until 1997 that the firm expanded its coverage beyond California, Washington, Arizona, Oregon, and Nevada to begin producing coverage of Washington, D.C., Maryland, and Virginia. Thomas Bros. Maps was acquired by Rand McNally in 1999, not an uncommon happening in the U.S. map publishing industry, and has been operated as a subsidiary of Rand McNally since then.

The standard *Thomas Guide* is usually divided into multiple sections. The first section will contain large-scale maps of central metropolitan areas or downtowns. The other sections will be maps of the region at two scales; less-densely built, more rural areas will be at a smaller scale and the city and surrounding suburbs will be at a larger scale. The inside back cover usually includes a fold-out highway map that doubles as a graphic index to the atlas. Graphic indexes are also included in the first group of maps within the volumes. An alphabetical street index completes the volume. If multiple counties are included in the volume's coverage, the street index will be divided into counties. Besides streets, the alphabetical index includes map locations of cemeteries, chambers of commerce, city halls, colleges and universities, courthouses, golf courses, hospitals, hotels, libraries, motels, parks, points of interest, schools (divided by type of school), shopping centers, and transportation.

Thomas Bros. Maps *Thomas Guides* can be purchased through the Rand McNally Web site. Thomas Bros. Maps also has a Web site (http://www.thomas.com/) that describes the company's history and explains the Thomas Bros. Maps "Page and Grid System." One of the company Web site's features is a free "Points of Interest Online" map service. After selecting an urban area from a brief index list, the user will need to select the kind of features that are being specifically sought, such as airports, hotels, performing arts, or shopping malls. Clicking on one of these choices displays a list of links to specific sites of the selected type; clicking on the desired location displays a printable map, which looks just like part of a *Thomas Guide* printed map, showing where the site is located.

Other companies providing street atlases for towns in the United States include: American Map Company, throughout the United States; Universal Map, throughout the United States but focused on the southeast; Trakker, primarily Florida but also North and South Carolina; Arrow Map, New England, in particular Massachusetts, Connecticut, and Rhode Island but also the other states; Hagstrom Map, New York and New Jersey; and Alexandria Drafting Company, Middle Atlantic and southern seaboard states.

MapArt *Street Guides*

Canadian cities are covered by MapArt's *Street Guides.* Cities throughout Canada are covered, and some of the atlases are available annually in new editions. Most of the *Street Guides* are smaller than 9 by 7 inches; the deluxe editions are 11 by 8.5 inches. These publications, all with bright yellow on their covers, present easy-to-read city street maps. Depending on the area covered, some cities may require multiple pages dividing the cities into grids. Smaller communities in the region covered might be mapped in their entirety on one or two pages. Different sections within each *Street Guide* have color-coded edges making it easy to find the desired group of maps quickly. The volumes include both graphic and alphabetical street indexes. As appropriate, some of the *Street Guides* include text in both English and French. MapArt *Street Guides* can be ordered directly from MapArt through their Web site (http://www.mapart.com). They are also available from a number of map dealers and bookstores.

Beyond North America, city street atlases can be found for cities in a number of countries. As with the United States and Canada, specific companies have specialized in particular countries. Bartholomew has produced and published, often through HarperCollins, atlases for cities in England, Scotland, and Ireland. The Automobile Association has published an atlas of *Town Plans,* which is now in its third edition. By far and away, the most prolific publisher of city street atlases for England, Wales, and Scotland is Geographer's A-Z Map Company. The company's products are described on its Web site (http://www.azmaps.co.uk); maps can also be ordered through the Web site. Geographer's A-Z maps can also be ordered through map dealers in the United States.

ENVIRONMENTAL ATLASES

Environmental atlases either cover multiple environmental aspects of a specified area or describe particular environmental realms and processes.

The New State of the Earth Atlas. 2nd ed.

The New State of the Earth Atlas is typical of a number of Simon & Schuster and Penguin atlases by Michael Kidron (*The State of the World Atlas* and *The War Atlas*); it is a smaller, easily portable atlas with brightly colored maps and graphically complex symbols that present complex topics in a simple way. The author takes a global view, both geographically and topically, and presents a myriad of topics, some of which on the surface may not necessarily be environmental. The author intends readers to discover for themselves how "it is becoming increasingly evident that social, environmental, and economic issues are intertwined." The maps are divided into six parts: Worlds Apart; Modern Living; Energy; Industry and the Military; Ecosystems; and Politics. Most of the maps have evocative titles, and all have captions, which appear on both the map and the table of contents, that help to frame the questions that the map readers should pose. Each topic is illustrated in a double-page map that nearly always contains more than one map along with other graphics. Quite often, multiple facets of the same theme are displayed on the same map using different techniques. Brief descriptive text and a list of sources for each map are at the end of the atlas after all of the maps.

The maps in *The New State of the Earth Atlas* are eye-catching and thought-provoking. Many of the maps are at the same scale and use the same projection so it is easy to compare different aspects of the Earth's condition. *The New State of the Earth Atlas* is more of an idea sparker than an answer resource. Like other atlases with similar titles (*The State of the World Atlas, The War Atlas,* and *Women in the World*), *The New State of the Earth Atlas* shows that statistical information does not always need to be presented in a formal (and potentially boring) way.

World Atlas of Desertification. 2nd ed.

World Atlas of Desertification takes both a world and a regional view of the ongoing degradation of productive, yet susceptible, drylands. The atlas, intended to serve global, regional, and national governmental information needs as well as school educational missions, is a product of the United Nations Environment Programme and illustrates how fragile drylands, which at the time of publication were home to more than 1 billion people, are being eroded by natural and human-driven causes.

Information about desertification is presented in four sections: "Global," "Africa," "ASSOD: The New Assessment of Soil Degradation in South and South-East Asia," and "Desertification Studies and Issues." Each of the first three sections discusses specifically soil degradation, erosion and deterioration, and causes of soil degradation. The fourth section uses case studies and specific examples to highlight desertification databases and monitoring, links that desertification has with other environmental issues, and social and economic aspects of desertification.

As with many works rooted in research and written for a scientifically based audience, *World Atlas of Desertification* requires that its text be read in order to understand the complex situation that the maps and supporting graphics present. The extensive bibliography will help lead to general and specific sources for further exploration of the causes and impacts of desertification.

The Great Lakes: An Environmental Atlas and Resource Book. 3rd ed.
Chicago Wilderness: An Atlas of Biodiversity.

These two titles focus on specific regions. *The Great Lakes* is a federal government—specifically Environmental Protection Agency in cooperation with Environment Canada—publication, while *Chicago Wilderness* was published by a consortium of agencies and organizations with interests in the greater Chicago area's natural resources (http://www.chiwild.org). There is a difference in emphasis between the two atlases both in content and potential target audience. *The Great Lakes* appears to be intended for scientifically literate, but not necessarily expert, readers. All aspects of the environment are included: basic underpinnings of the Great Lakes system, natural processes, human uses and impacts on the lakes, areas of environmental concern, jurisdictional management of the Great Lakes, and suggestions for the future. The atlas includes 13 maps along with text, photographs, a number of diagrams, and tables. There also is a glossary, a brief list of references, and a list of source materials used to compile the maps. This type of atlas could serve as either an introduction or as a summary description of the Great Lakes and their environmental problems.

Chicago Wilderness, while scientifically grounded, paints a word picture of species (plant and animal) and the environments in which they live. The maps included are generally small and not very detailed. The text and photographs of species play the primary role in this publication, with maps generally serving as supporting graphics. After a basic introduction, six different kinds of environments are described; the atlas also includes some information about human habitation of the area and environmental conservation efforts. There is a list of member organizations of the Chicago Region Biodiversity Council with contact information, a bibliography, and two indexes, one for topics and the other for species. An atlas like *Chicago Wilderness* will introduce environmental and species-related concerns but will not necessarily go to great depths. This is not the work to consult if looking for detailed information about species distribution. Other atlases and data resources, both print and on-line, will provide greater details.

IMAGERY ATLASES

A number of volumes of Earth imagery are available; some are atlases and some are landscape photograph albums.

The Cartographic Satellite Atlas of the World
The Atlas of Global Change
Earth from Above

The Cartographic Satellite Atlas of the World is a thin volume in comparison to other volumes of imagery. Data collected by Landsat satellites were processed and analyzed to create a natural-color land relief map for a world atlas. Data from the National Oceanographic and Atmospheric Agency's (NOAA) ETOPO-5 files (generated from a variety of digital databases on a 5-minute latitude/longitude grid) were used to display ocean floor relief. The map/image portion of the atlas begins with seven large-scale images of metropolitan areas and alpine and Antarctic ice forms. Fifty-one maps cover the world with portions ranging in scale from 1:2,080,000 to 1:40,740,000. The endpapers include images of the world centered on the Atlantic (front) and the Pacific (back). A place name and feature index concludes the atlas. *The Cartographic Satellite Atlas of the World* will not stand alone as a world atlas. Other more traditionally formatted atlases do a better job of presenting place names, national and internal boundaries, and topical information. *The Cartographic Satellite Atlas of the World* could be used side-by-side with more traditional, fully cartographic atlases to enhance an understanding of landscape, land forms, location, and connections between locations, as well as climate, vegetation, and cultures.

The Atlas of Global Change uses remotely sensed data in the form of photographs along with oblique photographs of landscape features to illustrate a variety of environmental conditions, natural and human influenced or created. Images vary in scope from the entire Earth to individual coral reefs. The full Earth images illustrate worldwide patterns such as contours, plate tectonics, cloud and precipitation distribution,

temperatures, and vegetation. Some of the worldwide topics are also illustrated with images of smaller areas; "Earthquakes and Volcanism" is illustrated by two full Earth image maps plus an image of the Mount Saint Helens area and one of the Alenuihaha Channel in the Hawaiian Islands. Many of the worldwide topics have more specific images drawn from areas outside of Europe. These provide balance for the images in the final section of the volume that focus solely on Europe. The images are most often derived from Landsat or NOAA-AVHRR (Advanced Very High Resolution Radiometer) data but there also are images based on other remotely sensed data sets and on digital topographic data models. Information about data sources is included at the end of the volume following a glossary and index. *The Atlas of Global Change* is primarily images with accompanying text. The smaller, area-specific images are all accompanied by a location map, with the image area indicated by a red rectangle. This volume could serve to jump-start thoughts about case studies on the environment and climate change.

Earth from Above is not truly an atlas; it more closely resembles an Earth photograph album, photographed by one person, with little cartographic content, consisting mostly of images accompanied by explanatory text. *Earth from Above* has many large-scale, close-to-the-ground images that show details of hedge mazes and shadows cast by animals. Very small maps are used to pinpoint image locations. For a feeling of differences in visual textures, *Earth from Above* would be an ideal starting place.

Atlas of North America: Space Age Portrait of a Continent

Although the *Atlas of North America* is more than 15 years old, it still serves as a good introduction to how remotely sensed data can be tied into other data sources to present a fuller picture of the environment and human activities. The atlas is divided into 16 geographic chapters. The short introductory section provides a basic overview of remote sensing. Each of the geographical chapters opens with a remotely sensed image followed by text, maps, and, in the chapters focusing on regions of the United States, more images of subregions. Although there are chapters on Canada and Central America, the overwhelming emphasis of *Atlas of North America* is on the United States. All of the images are accompanied by a location map and an explanatory caption that gives the viewer some ideas of what to look for in the image.

Atlas of North America includes a number of different image types: false- and true-color images; infrared images; images that have been manipulated to emphasize relief by shading deep valleys and slopes that face away from "the sun"; images that have been mosaicked together to create a larger panorama; thermal images of water bodies; high- and low-altitude aerial photographs; handheld camera images from the space shuttle; images from Landsat; images comparing the same area through four seasons; images that include cloud cover; and classified (specific kinds of land cover have been grouped together and assigned a color code) and unclassified images. The atlas primarily displays views of cities, regions, and states. Different kinds of land uses and landforms can be compared. The final pages of images before the place name index is a set of six map strips showing how different kinds of maps look; a similar group of four strips appears with the foreword at the beginning of the book. The beginning group may be more effective because the four maps are all of exactly the same area and at the same scale. The atlas also includes a "Key to Views from Space," information about where the National Geographic Society obtained data, and how the data were manipulated. One of the final, remote-sensing-related features of *Atlas of North America* is a graphic on the back endpaper showing the electromagnetic spectrum with information about wavelengths, camera and sensor systems, and the aircraft and spacecraft in which the camera and sensor systems are mounted.

Just as in the previous chapter ("General Atlases"), the titles described in this chapter are only a small sampling of the published possibilities. Thematic atlases bring to light different views of the world, highlighting specific kinds of data, illuminating problems, and showing new ways of seeing. Some thematic atlases, such as the historical atlases and road atlases, can be used in many different ways. Other thematic atlases have such a narrow scope as to limit their audience and usage to very special arenas. As with general atlases, thematic atlases are best used in appropriate contexts and with an understanding of the limits of both the maps and the underlying data that the maps depict.

BIBLIOGRAPHY

1992 Census of Agriculture. Vol. 2, Part 1, *Agricultural Atlas of the United States.* Washington, D.C.: U.S. Dept. of Commerce, Economics and Statistics Administration, Bureau of the Census, 1994.

ADAC Maxi Atlas Deutschland 2002/2003. Munich: ADAC Verlag, 2002. ISBN: 3-82641-038-6.

Arizona Atlas and Gazetteer. 4th ed. Freeport, Maine: DeLorme Mapping, 2000. ISBN: 0-89933-325-7.

Arizona Road & Recreation Atlas. 2nd ed. Berkeley, Calif.: Benchmark Maps, 1998. ISBN: 0-929591-31-3.

Atlas for Lesotho. New enlarged ed. Johannesburg: William Collins (Africa) (Pty) Ltd., 1978. ISBN: 0003601773.

Atlas of American Religion: The Denominational Era, 1776–1990. William M. Newman and Peter L. Halvorson. Walnut Creek, Calif.: AltaMira Press, 2000. ISBN: 0-7425-0345-3.

The Atlas of Changing South Africa. 2nd ed. A.J. Christopher. London: Routledge, 2001. ISBN: 0415211786.

The Atlas of Ethnic Diversity in Wisconsin. Kazimierz J. Zaniewski and Carol J. Rosen. Madison: University of Wisconsin Press, 1998. ISBN: 0-299-16070-X.

The Atlas of Global Change. 1st U.S. ed. Lothar Beckel, ed. New York: Macmillan Reference USA, 1998. ISBN: 0-02-864956-7.

Atlas of North America: Space Age Portrait of a Continent. National Geographic Society. Washington, D.C.: The Society, 1988. ISBN: 0-87044-605-3.

Atlas of the 1990 Census. Mark T. Mattson. New York: Macmillan, 1992. ISBN: 002897302X.

Atlas of the Roman World. Tim Cornell and John Matthews. New York: Facts on File, 1982. ISBN: 0-87196-652-2.

Atlas of the World's Religions. Ninian Smart, ed. New York: Oxford University Press, 1999. ISBN: 0-19-521449-8.

Atlas of the Year 1000. John Man. Cambridge, Mass.: Harvard University Press, 1999. ISBN: 0-674-54187-1.

Atlas of Women and Men in India. Sarawati Raju, et al. New Delhi: Kali for Women, 1999. ISBN: 90-5727-024-2.

Cape Cod, Southern Massachusetts Streetfinder. 2002 ed. Chicago: Rand McNally, 2002. ISBN: 0528992848.

The Cartographic Satellite Atlas of the World. WorldSat International Inc. Los Angeles: Warwick Publishing, 1997. ISBN: 1-895629-99-3.

Chicago Wilderness: An Atlas of Biodiversity. Jerry Sullivan. Downers Grove, Ill.: Chicago Region Biodiversity Council, 1997.

Concise Historical Atlas of Canada. William G. Dean, et al., eds. Toronto: University of Toronto Press, 1998. ISBN: 0-8020-4203-1.

DK Atlas of World History: Mapping the Human Journey. Jeremy Black, ed. New York: DK Inc., 2000. ISBN: 0-7894-4609-X.

Earth from Above. Yann Arthus-Bertrand. New York: Harry N. Abrams, 1999. ISBN: 0-8109-3267-9.

The Great Lakes: An Environmental Atlas and Resource Book. 3rd ed. Government of Canada and United States Environmental Protection Agency, joint producers. Chicago: Great Lakes National Program Office, U.S. E.P.A.; Toronto, Ont.: Government of Canada, 1995. ISBN: 0662151895.

Historical Atlas of Africa. J.F. Ade Ajayi and Michael Crowder. London: Longman, 1985. ISBN: 058264335X; 0-521-25353-5.

Historical Atlas of Canada. 3 vols. Geoffrey J. Matthews. Toronto: University of Toronto Press, 1987–1993. *Volume*

1: From the Beginning to 1800. R. Cole Harris, ed. 1987. *Volume II: The Land Transformed, 1800–1891.* R. Louis Gentilcore, et al., eds. 1993. *Volume III: Addressing the Twentieth Century, 1891–1961.* Donald Kerr, et al., eds. 1990. ISBN: 0-8020-2495-5 (vol. 1); ISBN: 0-8020-3447-0 (vol. 2); ISBN: 0-8020-3448-9 (vol. 3); ISBN: 0-8020-0691-4 (set).

A Historical Atlas of South Asia. 2nd impression, with additional material. Joseph E. Schwartzberg, ed. New York: Oxford University Press, 1992. ISBN: 0-19-506869-6.

Historical Atlas of the United States. Rev. ed. National Geographic Society. Washington, D.C.: National Geographic Society, 1994. ISBN: 0-87044-970-2.

Historical Atlas of the Vietnam War. Harry G. Summers, ed. Boston: Houghton Mifflin Co., 1995. ISBN: 0-395-72223-3.

Holman Bible Atlas: A Complete Guide to the Expansive Geography of Biblical History. Thomas C. Brisco. Nashville, Tenn.: Broadman & Holman, 1999. ISBN: 1-55819-709-5.

Mapping the Great Irish Famine: A Survey of the Famine Decades. Liam Kennedy, et al., eds. Dublin: Four Courts Press, 1999. ISBN: 1-85182-353-0.

Mapping Wisconsin History: Teacher's Guide and Student Materials. Wisconsin Cartographers' Guild. Madison: Office of School Services, State Historical Society of Wisconsin, 2000. ISBN: 0-87020-318-5.

National Geographic Road Atlas: United States, Canada, Mexico. 2001 ed. Mountville, Pa.: MapQuest.com, Inc., 2000. ISBN: 1572625473.

The New Atlas of African History. G.S.P. Freeman-Grenville, ed. New York: Simon & Schuster, 1991. ISBN: 0-13-612151-9.

New Historical Atlas of Religion in America. Edwin S. Gaustad and Philip L. Barlow. New York: Oxford University Press, 2000. ISBN: 0-19-509168-X.

The New State of the Earth Atlas: A Concise Survey of the Environment Through Full-Color International Maps. 2nd ed. Joni Seager. New York: Simon & Schuster, 1995. ISBN: 0-671-89103-0.

Rand McNally Commercial Atlas & Marketing Guide, 2002. 133rd ed. Chicago: Rand McNally, 2002. ISBN: 0528853244.

Rand McNally Road Atlas: United States, Canada & Mexico, 2002. 78th ed. Chicago: Rand McNally, 2001. ISBN: 0-528-84431-8.

Shepherd's Historical Atlas. 9th ed., revised and updated. William R. Shepherd. Totowa, N.J.: Barnes & Noble, 1980. ISBN: 0-389-20155-3.

The State of the World Atlas. Dan Smith. 6th ed. New York: Penguin Books, 1999. ISBN: 0-14-051446-5.

A Stereotaxic Atlas of the Monkey Brain: Macaca mulatta. Ray S. Snider and John C. Lee. Chicago: University of Chicago Press, 1961.

Thematic Atlases for Public, Academic, and High School Libraries. Diane K. Podell. Metuchen, N.J.: Scarecrow Press, 1994. ISBN: 0-8108-2866-9.

The Times Atlas of the Bible. James B. Pritchard, ed. London: Times, 1987. ISBN: 0723002959.

The Times Atlas of World History. 6th concise ed. Geoffrey Barraclough, ed. London: Times Books, 1997. ISBN: 0723009066.

The Times History of the World. New [5th] ed. Richard Overy, ed. London: Times Books, 1999. Previous editions titled *Times Atlas of World History.* ISBN: 0723008949.

The War Atlas: Armed Conflict—Armed Peace. 2nd ed. Michael Kidron. New York: Simon & Schuster, 1983. ISBN: 0-671-47249-6.

We the People: An Atlas of America's Ethnic Diversity. James Paul Allen and Eugene James Turner. New York: Macmillan, 1988. ISBN: 0-02-901420-4.

Wisconsin's Past and Present: A Historical Atlas. Wisconsin Cartographers' Guild. Madison: University of Wisconsin Press, 1998. ISBN: 0-299-15940-X.

Women in the World: An International Atlas. 2nd ed. Joni Seager. New York: Simon & Schuster, 1997. ISBN: 0-14-051374-4.

World Atlas of Desertification. 2nd ed. Nick Middleton and David Thomas, eds. New York: J. Wiley & Sons, 1997. ISBN: 0-340-69166-2.

On-line References

A–Z Map Company Ltd. Home page. Geographers' A–Z Map Company, Ltd., 2003. <http://www.azmaps.co.uk> (16 October 2003).

Atlas of Biodiversity. Chicago Wilderness, 1999/2002.<http://www.chicagowilderness.org/pubprod/atlas/index.cfm> (16 October 2003).

Benchmark Road & Recreation Atlases. Home page. Benchmark Maps, 17 June 2003. <http://www.benchmarkmaps.com> (16 October 2003).

Census of Agriculture. U.S. Department of Agriculture, National Agriculture Statistics Service, 10 October 2003. <http://www.nass.usda.gov/census/> (16 October 2003).

Chicago Wilderness: A Regional Nature Reserve. Home page. 1999/2002. <http://www.chiwild.org> (16 October 2003).

DeLorme. Home page. 2003. <http://www.delorme.com> (16 October 2003).

The Great Lakes: An Environmental Atlas and Resource Book. U.S. Environmental Protection Agency, 11 June 2003. <http://www.epa.gov/glnpo/atlas/> (16 October 2003).

MapArt Publishing Corporation. Home page. 2002. <http://www.mapart.com> (16 October 2003).

Rand McNally. Home page. Randmcnally.com, Inc., 2003. <http://www.randmcnally.com> (16 October 2003).

Thomas Bros. Maps. Home page. 2003. <http://www.thomas.com> (16 October 2003).

CHAPTER 9
Antiquarian Maps and the History of Cartography

Old maps are exciting. They show sea monsters, unexplored mountain ranges, or the piece of land that an ancestor claimed, cleared, and settled. Often old maps look substantially different from our current-day understanding of the world, its shapes, and relationships. California might or might not be an island. A Northwest Passage is possible. North America is attached to Asia's eastern shore, or Brazil is an island off the coast of Ireland. Old maps can show sequences of events such as the development of current state and county boundaries in the United States or the construction of a national road network. Old maps connect the present with the past and may lead to thoughts of how today's present is tomorrow's past.

Many people collect old maps. Some collect antiquarian maps; more than merely old, these items are generally older than 100 or 150 years. The idea of *an-tique* or *antiquarian* is a moving target. There would be general agreement that a world map from 1647 produced by Blaeu was an antiquarian item; some might not agree that a map of Illinois published in 1895 by Rand McNally was also antique. As we chronologically move farther away from the nineteenth century, the items produced during the nineteenth century are aging, sometimes not gracefully, and are becoming more widely desired by collectors and decorators.

Collectors have a focus, perhaps looking for items produced by a specific cartographer or publisher, in a specific location, during a particular time, or showing a special place. Some collectors add items to their collection because they show how boundary changes were depicted or how the shape of one of the Great Lakes changed as knowledge of the area increased.

Others are not interested in the cartographic content but select pieces because they use an interesting technique, are early examples of a developing technology, or have a particular decorative element in the cartouche or the border area. Other possible collection focuses are types of maps, such as nautical charts, strip maps or globes, and thematic content, such as road maps or geological maps.

Knowing about the history of cartography helps the collector be a better judge of a piece's importance, to evaluate its authenticity, and to place it into the context of the collection. The history of cartography is about people as individuals and about how they influence the work of others, national and world events, technological developments, and the increasing knowledge or understanding of the world.

COLLECTING GUIDES

Books on collecting maps can be found in library collections by searching "Early maps—Collectors and collecting" or "Maps—Collectors and collecting."

Collecting Old Maps
Collecting Antique Maps. Rev. ed.
Antique Maps. 3rd ed.

Collecting Old Maps, Collecting Antique Maps, and *Antique Maps* present complementary views and information about the history of cartography and collecting antiquarian cartographic items. All three are surveys of the area and contain basic information that will provide initial grounding for novice collectors and scholars while referencing core information resources for further exploration.

Of the three publications, *Collecting Old Maps* has the clearest emphasis on evaluating and acquiring maps for personal collections. This work is intended for a U.S. or North American audience and conveys the message that building a personal collection of old maps does not necessarily need to be an expensive undertaking. *Collecting Old Maps* is divided into three parts: "Collecting Old Maps," "The Maps Collected," and "Appendices." The eight chapters in "Collecting Old Maps" give fundamental guidance in what needs to be known or considered about antiquarian maps in general or about a specific piece that might be under consideration for purchase. Basic map parts, kinds of maps, and production techniques are defined and compared. Real maps are used as case studies to help integrate the information; some of the case studies even illustrate clever forgeries and demonstrate some of the telltale signs of forgery that should be looked for. Also

discussed are the different physical conditions of old maps, how physical conditions are described by dealers and in catalogs, what should or should not be done to stabilize or improve a piece's condition, and how physical condition and previous restoration and mending methods affect price. Different ways to find a collecting focus are described as are how to purchase maps, responsibilities that the collector and dealer must carry, and tips on how to sell a collection. Important ideas about working with antiquarian dealers are highlighted—including selecting appropriate dealers to work with based on collecting interests. Reading the first section of *Collecting Old Maps* will not give the novice collector instant expertise; much of the information should be considered advisory, cautionary, and way-finding. The need to consult with experts and to ask a lot of questions, plus to use common sense, are repeated often.

The second section of *Collecting Old Maps,* "The Maps Collected," is largely a pictorial, chronological, and egalitarian essay showing 500 years of printed maps, "selected to provide visual demonstration of the way the overall appearance of maps has changed through this time" (*Collecting Old Maps,* 121), without emphasizing trophy maps. One hundred thirty maps are reproduced in black-and-white, each with an extensive caption that includes full bibliographic and physical descriptions and contextual explanation.

The appendix section of *Collecting Old Maps* includes a brief listing of major cartographers with some of their works, a "Map Collector's Reference Library" bibliography with citations to both journals and books, eight pages of color illustrations (all with extensive caption information) that are referenced in the first part of the book, a guide to reading Roman numerals, a glossary of non-English map terms, essays about the materials that maps are printed on and about basic chemistry with an emphasis on acidity and buffering, a list of information sources such as the Web and collecting organizations, and finally a glossary and an index. For the beginning collector, *Collecting Old Maps* will provide a practical guide to collecting maps inexpensively and with a successful plan.

Collecting Antique Maps is a British publication that, while intended for the beginning collector or scholar, follows the more traditional path of displaying and discussing landmark or important pieces. *Collecting Antique Maps* is divided into five chapters: "Looking at Maps," "Mapping the World and Its Countries," "Globes, Curiosities and Miniatures,"

"Nineteenth Century Cartography," and "Map Collecting Today." There is considerably less text than in *Collecting Old Maps.* Throughout *Collecting Antique Maps,* the text is almost subservient to the extensive, and mainly color, illustrations and their lengthy captions and sidebars.

"Looking at Maps" includes short sections on collection, evaluation, important periods, pieces, and individuals in the history of cartography, and surveys of world maps, sea charts, and town plans. The middle chapters follow the historic development of cartography as illustrated by maps grouped by regions and continents or publication type. The final chapter speaks specifically to private map collecting with a short bibliography and some ideas for contacting experts in the field. *Collecting Antique Maps* concludes with an index.

Collecting Antique Maps could be considered a "romp" through 500 years of cartographic production. It is a fine overview and provides the viewer color, although greatly reduced, images of striking and important historic cartographic items. The text, by and large, is general; important details about specific pieces are contained in the illustration captions. *Collecting Antique Maps* will be a good starting place but will not satisfy the need for in-depth information about either the items that are available for collection or how to go about collecting them.

Antique Maps takes a third approach to antiquarian maps. There is little direct emphasis on map collecting; the bulk of the volume surveys mapmakers and their outputs. *Antique Maps* is arranged in three parts: Map Making, Map Makers, and Map Collecting. Map Making's 10 chapters include a short broad-brush survey of the history of cartography from 6100 B.C. to A.D. 1791. The second chapter discusses production techniques, such as woodcuts and lithography, along with technical terms related to printing and publishing. The next seven chapters describe either specific items with geographic content, the Hereford Mappi Mundi and the Nuremberg Chronicle, or groups of cartographic items arranged by type: road maps and atlases, sea charts and atlases, town plans, topographic maps, and playing cards. The chapters describing cartographic genres generally follow the same pattern of historical and developmental overview followed by a list of example pieces arranged by cartographer. Although these chapters are somewhat international in scope, the emphasis is overwhelmingly British. The final chapter of part one is titled "'Here be Dragons...' Myths & Legends on Old Maps." A number of myths and legends as depicted on antiquarian maps are surveyed, including Prester John, Hy Brazil, Gog and Magog, El Dorado, and the Northwest Passage.

Part two, Map Makers, is a nation-by-nation survey of cartographic development and individuals involved in map production. Each chapter begins with a survey of events and developments through the eighteenth century. This is followed by a list of cartographers with their years of birth and death and a very select bibliography. Some entries also include brief biographical information. Reflecting the British emphasis of *Antique Maps,* there are separate chapters for England and Wales, Scotland, Ireland, and the British Isles. Maps and atlases covering the United States are covered in the world and continents chapter section on the Americas. Because the focus of *Antique Maps* is strongly pre-nineteenth century, there are few maps listed that show the United States alone.

Part three includes a very short chapter on "Buying Maps & Forming a Collection." This is followed by a "Biographical Supplement" of 70 biographies that were added for the third edition of *Antique Maps.* The presence of these additional biographical sketches and selective bibliographies is indicated in the chapters of the second part by asterisks. The volume concludes with three appendices: Editions of Ptolemy's Geographica; Blaeu/Jansson Maps of the English and Welsh Countries; and Historical Chart-Map Making 600 B.C.–A.D. 1800. The volume also includes a short bibliography with annotated entries and is indexed. *Antique Maps* has black-and-white illustrations throughout. There is a section of eight color plates reproducing in reduction maps of England, the world, and the Americas.

The structure of *Antique Maps* will make this volume a quick place to gain a basic grounding in the pre-1800 maps of a specific country. Collectors of North American, African, or Asian materials will probably find little of interest. Collectors focusing on Europe will best be able to make use of the information presented to begin placing their items or cartographers of interest into context. The text of *Antique Maps* can be read through the Web (http://www.antiquemaps.co.uk/book).

HISTORIES OF CARTOGRAPHY

Histories of cartography will help collectors put potential purchases in context or even create an initial theme around which to focus a new collection. There are many histories that cover a wide spectrum of time and cartographic production. A number of scholars also are researching more specific aspects of the history of cartography and publishing narrowly focused works.

The Mapmakers. Rev ed.

The Mapmakers tells the story of cartography's development from prehistoric and ancient periods through the end of the twentieth century. Twenty-six chapters divided into four parts explore critical moments in the history of cartography, including attempts at measuring the Earth; developments in transforming a three-dimensional spheroid into a two-dimensional representation; advances in calculating time, distance, and location; systematic programs to map large expanses of territory; techniques used to survey map areas and attributes that are difficult to see; and mapping locations not of the Earth. *The Mapmakers* will engage the reader through lively prose; this is not textbook-style writing. *The Mapmakers* could be the ideal first choice for anyone who thinks that the history of cartography is too daunting for someone not formally trained in the field. The chapters are not footnoted but the prose clearly indicates its sources that can then be specifically pinpointed through the chapter-by-chapter bibliographical notes section. Because *The Mapmakers* is not strictly chronological or geographical in its arrangement and because it is such a broad survey of 5,000 years of cartographic endeavor, the index is an essential entry point. Black-and-white illustrations appear throughout; they are not always clear enough to show details but will give the reader an initial feel for the objects being discussed.

History of Cartography. 2nd ed.

History of Cartography, often referred to conversationally as "Bagrow," was originally published in Germany in 1951 as *Geschichte der Kartographie.* The English translation was first published in 1964 by Harvard University Press. The 1985 edition was enlarged to include additional monochrome and color illustrations. Although out of print, *History of Cartography* is considered a core or seminal work and appears on many bibliographies of essential titles to have read or be acquainted with when studying the history of cartography.

Bagrow's scope is from the earliest maps of primitive peoples to the second half of the eighteenth century, "the point where maps ceased to be works of art, the products of individual minds, and where craftsmanship was finally superceded by specialized sci-

ence and the machine" (*History of Cartography,* 22). Bagrow does not focus on the contents of individual maps or on the technologies that produced them. Instead he highlights the "externals" of map production, primarily the individuals and family firms that created and published maps and atlases, the web of connections among map producers, and the historic time periods of creation. *History of Cartography* contains 16 short chapters that highlight either specific kinds of maps or maps that depict specific geographic areas (often countries). Each chapter is packed with information, making for complex reading. If using Bagrow for the first time, the foreword should be read because it sets the bounds of the work and illuminates Bagrow's specific interests. Black-and-white illustrations appear throughout the volume, plus there is a section of black-and-white plates after the text and a group of color plates inserted between chapters 9 and 10. The plates are all numbered and referred to from the text. The illustrations, most much reduced from the original size, are not intended to show details but rather to give a feel for what the pieces look like. *History of Cartography* is not heavily endnoted. The volume concludes with a "List of Cartographers (to 1750)," a "Select Bibliography of the History of Cartography," and an index.

Bagrow is central to the study of the history of cartography because it touches on so many map formats, individuals, families, and schools of cartographic production. It is a lodestone for the field, sequencing essential events and providing framework that connects more specialized works with each other. The density of information presented in quick succession may be initially confusing or overwhelming to the novice scholar, but because of the centrality of this work, anyone with aspirations for pursuing work in the history of cartography must have an understanding of the information contained in Bagrow's *History of Cartography.*

The History of Cartography.

The History of Cartography is an interdisciplinary, multivolume work being published by the University of Chicago Press. Each volume is made up of commissioned chapters by an international group of subject specialists. The work is expected to be at least eight physical volumes (with some tricky numbering). The materials covered by volume two were so extensive that three books were required. Thus far, volumes one and two, all three books, have been published. Each volume is slated to focus on a different time period or society with a particular emphasis on the societal context: volume 1, *Prehistoric, Ancient, and Medieval Europe and the Mediterranean;* volume 2, book 1, *Traditional Islamic and South Asian Societies;* volume 2, book 2, *Traditional East and Southeast Asian Societies;* volume 2, book 3, *Traditional African, American, Arctic, Australian, and Pacific Societies;* volume 3, *European Renaissance and Reformation;* volume 4, *European Enlightenment;* volume 5, *Nineteenth Century;* volume 6, *Twentieth Century.* Publication of the set began in 1987.

The first volume, *Prehistoric, Ancient, and Medieval Europe and the Mediterranean,* sets the tone for the entire series with a chapter describing the development of the study of the history of cartography. The remaining 20 chapters are divided into three parts: prehistoric cartography, cartography in ancient Europe and the Mediterranean, and cartography in medieval Europe and the Mediterranean. All of the chapters are heavily referenced, containing both footnotes and a bibliography. The volumes conclude with a "Bibliographical Index." Full citations to the works referenced throughout the volume are arranged alphabetically by author, and the pages where the works are specifically referenced are listed. There is also a general topical index.

The first volume was awarded the 1987 "Best Book in the Humanities" award from the Professional and Scholarly Publishing Division of the Association of American Publishers. Volume two, book one, and volume two, book three, also were given awards, the R.R. Hawkins Award for Best Scholarly Book (1992) by the Association of American Publishers and the James Henry Breasted Prize (1999) by the American Historical Association, respectively.

The History of Cartography is intended to be scholarly and comprehensive. The chapters are the synthesis of deep research and immersion in the topics. Although the information presented is rich in details, the chapters have been carefully edited for readability. *The History of Cartography* perhaps is not the first work for a beginning scholar in the area to read but it should be on the list of required readings. The footnotes and references point to core materials in very specialized areas, materials that might not appear on standard bibliographies. More advanced readers could use the "Bibliographical Index" at the end of the volumes to quickly see where the ideas of the contributing scholars overlap or come from the same source materials.

The History of Cartography is being undertaken by the History of Cartography Project at the University of Wisconsin-Madison. The project has also arranged and curated an exhibit called "Windows on the World: A Selection of Historical Maps" and has sponsored conferences that have grown out of the work undertaken to research and produce *The History of Cartography* series. A virtual version of the exhibit, along with information about individual volumes, conferences, and electronic versions of the project's quarterly newsletter, can be viewed at the project's Web site (http://feature.geography.wisc.edu/histcart/).

Bringing together an international group of experts and including information well beyond the European cartographic experience, *The History of Cartography* is one of the most important works on the history of cartography, even though it is less than halfway completed.

Maps & Civilization: Cartography in Culture and Society. 2nd ed.

Maps & Civilization, by Norman J.W. Thrower, is a very readable "social and cultural survey" of the history of cartography. It focuses on maps in the context of the societies that produced them and devotes little space to the technologies of cartography. Unlike Bagrow's *History of Cartography, Maps & Civilization* treats cartographic items through to the end of the twentieth century, including information about government agency and organizational mapping. This volume, originally intended as a supplemental text for university students in courses on cartography, remote sensing, and the history of discovery, moves from maps produced by preliterate societies (chapter 1) to maps produced using computer software packages in nine chapters. There are some examples of non-Western cartography in chapters two and three, "Early Maps of East and South Asia" and "Cartography in Europe and Islam in the Middle Ages." The remaining five chapters focus on European and North American cartography with emphasis on the Renaissance, Scientific Revolution, the expansion of the cartographic industry during the nineteenth century because of scientific and technical revolutions, and the work of official governmental agencies during the late nineteenth century through the twentieth century. Much of the last three chapters focuses on cartographic events and developments in the United States accompanied by highlights of European milestones. The volume concludes with a table of map projections with their properties and appropriate uses, a list of isograms, a glossary, extensive endnotes, and an index. Black-and-white illustrations, primarily of maps, but also map legends and diagrams, appear throughout. *Maps*

& Civilization is readable and portable yet packed with information that will make easy the task of selecting the next title to explore.

A number of other history of cartography surveys often appear on bibliographies or in dealers' catalogs, including *The Story of Maps* (Brown) and *Maps and Their Makers* (Crone). While these are older publications—1949 and 1978 (5th edition), respectively—both are highly readable and portable, and both include references and bibliographies. Older histories of cartography should not be dismissed out-of-hand because of their age and perceived outdatedness. If anything, they should be considered context for reading newer histories to trace the increasing understanding of the history of map production and mapmakers and of the societal context of cartography.

Beyond the general surveys of the history of cartography there are numerous more specialized books that focus on specific areas, periods of production, cartographers, and content. Additionally, numerous journal articles, with very specific focuses, can be found through the many bibliographies that have been compiled.

BIBLIOGRAPHIES

Bibliographies will help focus reading and may also point a collector to works that need to be in a personal reference library. Older bibliographies may include older works not picked up by newer bibliographies; although bibliographies may become dated, they rarely become completely obsolete.

Concise Bibliography of the History of Cartography
 (http://www.newberry.org/nl/collections/conbib.html)
 The *Concise Bibliography of the History of Cartography* was compiled in 1997 by Robert W. Karrow, Jr., Curator of Special Collections and Curator of Maps at the Newberry Library in Chicago. This bibliography is not as concise as the title indicates; 312 works, many of which have been found to be useful by the Newberry Library's map reference staff, are described, including bibliographies and cartobibliographies, directories, technical guides, journals, general works, and catalogs. Generally, the works selected for inclusion are newer, in English, and of potential usefulness for people working on the history of cartography in either North America or the United Kingdom.

The bibliography is divided into two sections, "General Literature" and "Map Catalogs and Cartobibliographies." General Literature, the first 196 items in the bibliography, includes a wide range of items. Although some are bibliographies, most are textual

works such as Bagrow's *History of Cartography*. Not all of the titles are strictly on the history of cartography. This bibliography will also point to works on caring for maps, map projections, and biographies of map producers. The second half of the bibliography, Map Catalogs and Cartobibliographies, lists works that in a systematic fashion describe items depicting specific places. The catalogs included are not dealers' sales catalogs. Most of the catalogs give an inventory of holdings at particular libraries, while the bibliographies may be compiled from information housed at numerous locations.

Concise Bibliography of the History of Cartography will be useful as a signpost to high quality and reputable information resources. Bibliography users are not steered to odd or rare information resources; most of the items listed are mainstream titles and should not be difficult to find at bookstores or libraries.

Information Sources in Cartography
Keyguide to Information Sources in Cartography

Although not focusing on the history of cartography, both *Information Sources in Cartography* and *Keyguide to Information Sources in Cartography* include descriptions of resources to consult about the history of cartography. *Information Sources in Cartography* groups three chapters about general sources; area studies; and map types, design, and production methods into "Part 2: The History of Cartography." The chapters, written by subject specialists, are primarily composed of context-setting text and bibliographic references. Most of the entries are not annotated.

Keyguide to Information Sources in Cartography begins with a highly generalized survey of the history of cartography. A substantial annotated bibliography with 333 entries forms the second part of the book. The entries are divided into broad categories, many of which are subdivided further: General Sources, Individual Mapmakers, The Map Trade, Discovery and Exploration, The Developing World Map, Regional Mapping, Urban Plans, Hydrography and Nautical Charts, Survey and Surveying Instruments, Symbols, Ornamentation and Calligraphy, History of Map Reproduction, Identification of and Dating, Early Maps, Special Types of Map, Thematic Mapping, Unconventional Map and Cartographical Curiosities, Tapestry Maps, Globes, Map Collecting, and Facsimile Reproductions of Early Maps. The items in the bibliography are monographs, journals, book chapters, and articles.

Both of these works will point readers to foundational and fundamental materials, scholars, and ideas in the history of cartography. Because of their publication dates (1990 and 1986) they do not contain the newest literature but they can still be relied on for citations to classics in the literature.

Guide to the History of Cartography: An Annotated List of References on the History of Maps and Mapmaking

Walter Ristow, formerly Chief of the Geography and Map Division of the Library of Congress, is highly regarded and widely read in the history of cartography field. His *Guide to the History of Cartography* is firmly rooted in his knowledge of the field and is an expansion and revision of a bibliography that was published by the Library of Congress in 1960. The 1973 *Guide* is an annotated bibliography of 398 items arranged alphabetically by primary author. Most of the items are books; very few articles are included. The work concludes with an index to subjects and geographical areas along with secondary authors and other contributors. Ristow's *Guide* perhaps could be considered a classic, and it appears on a regular basis in other bibliographies and in dealer's catalogs. It is an essential work for identifying older core literature in the history of cartography.

JOURNALS

A limited number of journals focus on the history of cartography. Occasionally, history of cartography articles will be published in broader cartography or geography titles.

Imago Mundi

Imago Mundi advertises that it "is the journal of record for the history of cartography and the only international scholarly journal solely concerned with the study and interpretation of maps and mapmaking in any part of the world, at any period." For serious investigations into the history of cartography, *Imago Mundi* should be considered a core information resource.

Imago Mundi began publication in 1935 in Berlin. Because of the turmoil of the Second World War, it did not become a regularly published annual until 1947. Since then, like clockwork, a single issue has been published each year containing 8 to 10 full-length refereed articles, a handful of shorter articles, book reviews, a chronicle of the previous calendar year's events, an extensive bibliography of recently published works on the history of cartography, and reports and notices. *Imago Mundi's* current subtitle is *The International Journal for the History of Cartography,* and it is international in article coverage, author and editorial affiliation, and sources of information in the chronicle and bibliography. The first issue was almost exclusively in German, but since then most of the articles have been in English. Abstracts in French and German are included. Black-and-white illustrations have been included since the first issue; a section of color illustrations was first included in volume 49 in 1997.

Beyond being international in scope, *Imago Mundi* also takes an interdisciplinary perspective on the history of cartography. Recent issues have included articles by geographers, cartographers, librarians, political scientists, architects, art historians, and a theologian. The chronological scope of the articles in the past has tended to be pre-nineteenth century but there is a noticeable trend toward including more articles on the nineteenth century through the mid-twentieth century.

Imago Mundi has a Web site (http://www.map history.info/imago.html), part of the much larger History of Cartography Web site. The Web site includes general information about the journal such as details on submitting articles and purchasing either a subscription or previous issues. Tables of contents for all issues are included along with abstracts for volume 48 (1996) through the current volume.

Imago Mundi contains articles of solid scholarship. Because of the high level of scholarship, some articles may necessitate introductory or background reading from elsewhere to fully appreciate or understand the information conveyed. The notes and references, often very extensive, for the articles will lead readers deeper into the appropriate literature. For individuals interested in exploring "big name" historic cartographers, *Imago Mundi* will be a source of great riches. Those who are interested in non-Western cartography will also find that *Imago Mundi* holds information of interest.

Beyond the annual publication, the Imago Mundi Ltd. Board of Directors coordinates the biennial International Conferences on the History of Cartography. The scope of the papers, many of which are later published in *Imago Mundi,* presented at the conferences can range from ancient cartography to the twentieth century, including discussions about the theoretical foundations of the study of the history. Information about the biennial conference can be found on the Web (http://www.maphistory.info/confs.html).

The Map Collector

The Map Collector was published quarterly from 1976 to 1996. It appealed to a wide audience: collectors, scholars, librarians, and dealers. Each issue included four to six articles, shorter articles, a news section, book reviews, a "Collectors' Barometer" that listed recent auction prices, and a section of classified advertisements along with many advertisements scattered throughout each issue. Each issue was lavishly illustrated, initial issues in black-and-white only and later issues extensively in color.

As the articles do not tend to be as long as those in *Imago Mundi,* they may serve the needs of readers less experienced in reading about the history of cartography for introductory materials. On the surface, the articles appear to be popularized but they are firmly grounded in robust scholarship. Many of *The Map Collector*'s authors are or were highly regarded experts in the field. The topics covered by the articles tend to be pre-twentieth century cartographic materials or producers with a North American and European emphasis occasionally spiced with articles on maps or atlases of the Holy Land or Australia and less often on Africa or Asia.

Mercator's World

Mercator's World picks up where *The Map Collector* leaves off, beginning publication in 1996 and ceasing in 2001. Unlike *The Map Collector, Mercator's World* was published in the United States. It followed a format similar to *The Map Collector. Mercator's World* was published bimonthly, was interdisciplinary, and had a broad scope "[focusing] on the art, history, culture, and technology of cartography, geography, and exploration." Readership extended beyond the United States and Canada.

The content of *Mercator's World* is similar to *The Map Collector* but with a more rounded geographic balance. *Mercator's World* can be relied upon to have an interesting mix of articles; some will include suggestions of further reading. The scope of the articles that have been published extends into the twentieth century. In fact, news of contemporary events and products can be found in at least two places, "Mercator's Log," which usually includes four very short (half-page) pieces, and a regular section titled "Multi-Media." The author of MultiMedia varies but the emphasis is always on a fairly new CD-ROM product or a Web-based information resource. Mark Monmonier's regular column "All Over the Map" also often features twentieth-century items or technologies. *Mercator's World* usually includes five substantial feature articles, all lavishly illustrated in color, in each issue. There also often is a lengthy article about a map aficionado and his or her map collection. Be-

yond Mercator's Log and MultiMedia, there are a number of other regular sections: "Auction Block," which describes (often with illustrations) items that have recently been sold at auction; book reviews; an events and an auction calendar; and "Collector's Barometer," which lists (without detailed descriptions) items that have recently been sold at auction or listed in dealers' catalogs.

All issues of *Mercator's World* are extensively illustrated in full color. Many map dealers, from the United States and elsewhere, take out advertising in *Mercator's World,* making the magazine an ideal place to begin the search for a firm to meet particular collecting needs. Other advertisements for recently released books on the history of cartography may also be useful for keeping an eye on new publications.

WEB RESOURCES

Resources available through the Web, while excellent places to begin searching for information, should not necessarily be considered the best or only information source, especially if detailed or specialized information is needed.

MapForum.com: A Periodical for Antique Map Collectors (http://www.MapForum.com/index.htm)

MapForum.com is available only on-line. This webzine's mission is "to promote interest in & study of old maps, catering for the novice and the experienced collector," and the editors are principals in an antiquarian map dealership in London. Generally, each issue follows the same pattern of an editorial, a major article, a biography of an important cartographer often accompanied by a bibliography of work, a collation describing the plates in an antiquarian atlas, a checklist of maps produced for a specific place, auction information, book reviews, letters to the editor (some of which receive very lengthy replies), and a list of advertisers. Most of the articles, biographies, bibliographies, and checklists appear to be written by "in-house authors." Many of the advertisements link directly to dealers' Web sites. Although *MapForum.com* is produced in London, its coverage is not limited to European cartographic items. Unfortunately, individual issues have not been released with an attached date; this lack may make it difficult to reference the specific issues. *MapForum.com*'s substantive articles and atlas collations are indexed by the Map History/History of Cartography Web site and by Oddens' Bookmarks (both described below).

Map History/History of Cartography
(http://www.maphistory.info/)

The Map History/History of Cartography Web site, self-advertised as "THE Gateway to the Subject," is maintained by Tony Campbell, the Map Librarian at the British Library in London. The site includes more than 100 pages grouped into 20 categories intended to help guide Web users to information about collecting antiquarian maps and the history of cartography. Included are links to calendars of events, Web articles, image sites, information about fellowships and other kinds of awards, information about discussion lists, and bibliographies. Some of the links are accompanied by explanatory text. The site is updated regularly. Because of the vast amount of information contained, Map History/History of Cartography will require patience to use. But the diligence of the site's webmaster makes the Map History/History of Cartography site truly the premier entry point for finding information about the history of cartography available on the Web.

Oddens' Bookmarks (http://oddens.geog.uu.nl/index.html)

Oddens' Bookmarks does not have the specific focus on the history of cartography found at the Map History/History of Cartography site. But among the more than 21,500 site links there are a number of links associated with the history of cartography. The best way to find them might be to use the site's browse function. Links are divided into 13 thematic categories. Selecting "Maps and Atlases" brings up a basic search interface that, through drop-down pick lists, allows for the selection of "Maps and Atlases—Old" and a country or continent of interest. Browsing "Sellers of Cartographic Materials" works the same way—use a drop-down pick list to select "Antiquarian" and a country in which the dealer should be located. In "Literature," selecting "History of Cartography" results in more than 400 links listed by the regions that they cover. The links on this Web site are not quite as up-to-date as those at the Map History/History of Cartography. Nor is there the same kind of context established, but searching Oddens' Bookmarks will yield lengthy lists of clickable links of interesting Web sites. Its value lies in the extensive number of the sites it has indexed and makes available through very simple search mechanisms.

MapHist-L

MapHist-L is a listserv discussion group open to anyone interested in antiquarian maps or the history of cartography. It focuses on historical maps, atlases, globes, and other cartographic formats. Collectors, dealers, librarians, and museum curators all would find the content of the distributed messages interesting. They include information about publications, new library acquisitions, alerts about thefts, and announcements about conferences and programs, along with information about progress on current research projects and requests for assistance in identifying specific items. The list's membership is international in scope, with more than 650 individuals and organizations signed on. The listserv began running in 1994, and a CD-ROM containing an archive of all traffic from 1994 through 2001 is available for purchase. MapHist-L has a Web site (http://www.maphist.nl) that describes the mission of the listserv, includes a list of subscribers, and contains subscription instructions and links to discussion papers and related Web sites.

Map Collections: 1500–2002
(http://lcweb2.loc.gov/ammem/gmdhtml/)
David Rumsey Map Collection
(http://www.davidrumsey.com)

Just as facsimiles bring to hand reproductions of important, beautiful, and antiquarian maps, the Web is being used to disseminate scanned images of older maps that have a wide appeal. Map Collections: 1500–2002 is the Geography and Map Division's portion, focusing on Americana and cartographic treasures, of the Library of Congress's American Memory project. The maps on the site are divided into seven groups: Cities and Towns; Conservation and Environment; Discovery and Exploration; Cultural Landscapes; Military Battles and Campaigns; Transportation and Communication; and General Maps. Currently, each of these groups has one or two focuses; "Military Battles and Campaigns" includes two subgroups of maps on the American Revolutionary period and the Civil War plus a third subgroup of "additional" items. The items included in "Cities and Towns" are largely panoramic (or bird's-eye) views of nineteenth-century U.S. towns. Some of the subgroups include essays that place collection items into context and suggest other resources. Digital files can be freely downloaded from Map Collections: 1500–2002; download instructions are available at the site. The site also includes information about ordering printed reproductions and about how the items were scanned and cataloged.

The David Rumsey Map Collection contains nearly 9,000 images of eighteenth- and nineteenth-century maps. The collection focuses on the Western Hemisphere but does include some coverage of Africa,

Asia, and Europe. The maps in the collection go beyond single-sheet maps; they are from atlases, school geographies, books, nautical chart sets, government reports of official exploration expeditions, and globes. A database can be searched by country, state, author, or keywords. Search results display as thumbnail images that can be clicked on to open as larger images in new windows. The large images can be zoomed and panned. More than one image can be displayed on the screen at a time. Complete items have been scanned. If an atlas is searched for, all of its pages will display as thumbnails in proper order. Maps from volumes have not been cropped so that only the map can be seen; instead the edges of the pages underneath the map are visible giving an impression of where in the volume the map is located. The covers for folded maps that were distributed in paper, cloth, or leather are included in the database. Full descriptive (cataloging) data are available for each image. The images, which were scanned at a minimum of 300 dots per inch, can be printed directly from the Web site.

DICTIONARIES AND DIRECTORIES

Who's Who in the History of Cartography: The International Guide to the Subject (D9).

Who's Who in the History of Cartography is published approximately every four years and tracks ongoing history of cartography research and publication internationally. The guide is divided into two sections: "What's What in the History of Cartography" and "Who's Who in the History of Cartography." What's What includes brief citations to and descriptions of core monographic and journal literature, bibliographies and cartobibliographies, dictionaries, directories, electronic resources, and contacts for organizations. Who's Who lists alphabetically, with addresses and other contact information, 630 scholars worldwide working in the history of cartography arena. Also included are descriptions of their specific areas of research and citations to publications that appeared since the previous edition of the guide. The personal entries are indexed by institution, geographical area of research, topical area of research, and country. *Who's Who in the History of Cartography* is being partially updated through a Web site hosted by the Map History/History of Cartography Web site (http://www.maphistory.info/research.html). *Who's Who in the History of Cartography* will assist in making connections with researchers and in finding newer publications.

Cartographical Innovations

The Commission on the History of Cartography, established by the International Cartographic Association in 1976, undertook *Cartographical Innovations* as its first project. The editors, Helen Wallis and Arthur H. Robinson, are recognized experts on cartography and the history of cartography. *Cartographical Innovations* is intended to describe ideas, concepts, and techniques that led to the advancement of mapmaking in the four millennia prior to 1900. The scope of the included ideas, concepts, and techniques is broad, covering types of maps, reference systems, symbols, technologies, and media. The introduction is a broadly sweeping survey of the history of cartography and development of cartographic techniques. Throughout the introductory text, the reader is referred to appropriate entries in *Cartographical Innovations*.

Cartographical Innovations includes 191 entries divided into eight sections or chapters: Types of Maps; Maps of Human Occupation and Activities; Maps of Natural Phenomena; Reference Systems and Geodetic Concepts; Symbolism; Techniques and Media; Methods of Duplication; and Atlases. Each entry is numbered, and the index refers to these numbers, not page numbers. A list of entry terms, along with their numbers, follows the introduction.

Most of the entries have three parts, labeled A, B, and C. Part A is usually a short or fairly brief and straightforward definition; *fan map* is defined as "Map drawn or printed on folding fans." Part B puts the definition into a historical, social, and technological context. Part B for *fan maps* describes the use of fan maps in Japan and how the form was brought to Europe by Portuguese traders in the sixteenth century, concluding with a description of fan maps in the eighteenth and nineteenth centuries and their gradual disappearance from popular Western culture. Part C is a bibliography of references on the entry's topic; each entry has at least one reference and most have many more than one.

A list of contributors is included but none of the entries are signed so it is difficult to attribute any one entry to a specific author. Although *Cartographical Innovations* is not heavily illustrated, the black-and-white illustrations were selected with care, and nearly all are referenced to the appropriate entries.

Tooley's Dictionary of Mapmakers. Rev. ed.

Tooley's Dictionary of Mapmakers is an A-to-Z listing of cartographers, publishers, printers, engravers, globemakers, and lithographers, in short all possible aspects of the cartographic production cycle. The individuals, firms, and families included were active primarily prior to the twentieth century. The entries, in alphabetical order, are usually brief; name, life span dates, profession, location, publications, and publication dates are possible included data but most entries do not include all of them. Families of cartographers and cartography firms receive longer entries as do cartographers with more extensive publication lists.

Tooley's has been published in three different versions. The first version, 10 installments published between 1965 and 1975 by Map Collectors' Circle in *Map Collectors' Series,* included cartographers with names beginning with the letters A through P. The second version, published in 1979 with a 1985 supplement, includes a complete alphabetical sequence. The third version, the revised edition, began publication in 1999. Two volumes have been released, A–D and E–J, and the last two volumes are in the compilation stage.

The 1979 edition includes a list of works consulted but none of the titles in the bibliography are ever cited in the entries. Some of the entries in the revised edition have been expanded from the 1979 version, and new entries have been added. Occasionally the entries in the 1999/2001 edition include references to information sources that speak specifically to the subject of the entry but there is no separate bibliography listing the sources; the bibliography for the entire edition will appear in the final volume.

Tooley's should be used as a quick reference to check names, dates, and family or firm relationships. It will not give details but will confirm that the individual being researched existed and that the name is being spelled correctly. *Tooley's* will also be useful in clarifying confusion between individuals with the same or similar names.

Antique Map Price Record and Handbook

Sixteen volumes and 2 CD-ROMs have been produced in the ongoing *Antique Map Price Record and Handbook* biennial series, often called "Jolly" after the series' first publisher. More than 86,000 cartographic items, primarily maps and atlases, have been described. The items described are pieces that have been sold at auction or offered through dealers' catalogs; the information comes directly from catalogs and auction records. *Antique Map Price Record and Handbook*'s purpose is to record the prices that have been asked or received for cartographic items, not to assist in pricing items that will be sold in the future or to guide in determining an appraisal value.

The introductory material in *Antique Map Price Record and Handbook* is extensive and focuses on changes to the publication, effects of electronic communication, and future plans for the series. A short list of "Resources on the Web" is included. The authors also make very clear the differences between dealers and auctions. "Dealers maintain an inventory that is available over time. The objective of an auctioneer is to liquidate a stock of merchandise at a point in time." Readers are cautioned that prices advertised in dealers' catalogs should not be compared with auction selling prices because the circumstances of the sales are completely dissimilar.

The introduction is followed by "How to Use the *Price Record,*" essential reading for anyone intending to use this resource. Entries follow a standard form with information about the mapmaker, title, date, source, commentary, dimensions, color, condition, references, illustrations, catalog code, and price. Each of the parts of the entry are explained in detail, some with examples. There also is a list of "Factors Affecting Value" with explanatory text: historical importance, region depicted, the mapmaker, age, size, aesthetic qualities, color, and condition.

The core of the *Price Record* is made up of seven sections: directory of map dealers; cumulative frequency distribution of mapmakers; main price listing; references; title index to main price listing; geographical index to main price listing; and currency conversion table and catalog codes. The names of 360 map dealers with addresses, telephone numbers, and, if appropriate, Web sites and e-mail addresses are included in the map dealer directory. Entries also include how sales stock can be seen, such as shop hours, mail order, map or book fairs, catalogs, or by appointment, and for some of the dealers an indication of the geographical area or time period of specialization. The directory was compiled using a questionnaire, and the 2001 questionnaire is included immediately before the dealer directory. The authors make it very clear that neither inclusion nor exclusion in the dealer directory is an endorsement or nonendorsement. The dealers directory is in three sections: an alphabetical listing of dealers in the United States with contact information, a chart of U.S. dealers arranged by state and city, and a listing of non-U.S. dealers with full entries arranged alphabetically by country.

The "Cumulative Frequency Distribution of MapMakers" lists the number of times that a cartographer or map publisher has appeared in *Price Record* and in which volumes. The table, alphabetical by cartographer's name, shows the total number of entries and then breaks the entries down by specific volumes. The volumes published since 1993 each have their own column while the volumes published between 1983 and 1992 are grouped together. This table will be useful in reducing the amount of browsing needed to find appropriate volumes to inspect. For instance, five maps produced by Daniel Djurberg have been listed in various volumes of *Price Record,* two in 1995, two in 1996, and one in 1997–1998. None of the other volumes would need to be examined. The cumulative frequency chart works well for cartographers that have not appeared often in *Price Record.* More prolific cartographers or publishing firms tend to appear in each volume; in these cases the cumulative frequency chart could be used as a informal measure of interest in a particular cartographer.

The central core of *Antique Map Price Record and Handbook* is, of course, the map price list. The entries, in alphabetical order by cartographer, follow the format laid out in the "How to Use the *Price Record*" section. Reading the entries takes patience and an eye for detail, especially if attempting to compare the entries to other descriptions or to a map at hand. In some cases, multiple copies or "states" (similar to editions) of a map have been sold or advertised for sale during the same year. These entries for seemingly duplicative items must be read especially closely to differentiate the differences between the copies. Often the differences are no more than slight staining or a different color treatment.

The "References" following the map list are standard resources that dealers refer to when compiling catalog entries; these works are often cartobibliographies or histories of cartography. The entries are brief, no more than author's name, title, and publication year. The alphabetized bibliography has a short tabular "Index of Specialized References" that will assist in quickly determining which title focuses on a specific region or topic.

The title and geographical indexes are entry paths to the map list. The title index lists all of the included items alphabetically by their title, giving the cartographer and dimensions, and the geographical index lists items by the areas they cover. *Price Record* concludes with a currency conversion table and a list of codes keyed to the catalogs and auction reports from which the map listing entries are drawn.

Beginning with the 2001–2002 volume, *Antique Map Price Record and Handbook* is being published as a CD-ROM product. The CD includes all of the data from the first 16 volumes plus 10,000 additonal, more recent records. Information about *Antique Map Price Record and Handbook* is available through the publisher's Web site (http://www.maprecord.com).

Also available at this site are up-to-date listings of U.S. and international map dealers and a link to the International Antiquarian Mapsellers Association (IAMA) Web site (http://www.antiquemapdealers.com).

Antique Map Price Record and Handbook will be of interest to map collectors and investors but also to someone who suddenly receives a map as a gift or inheritance. Its entries will be an indication of the amount of "traffic" in a particular cartographer's work. The accompanying materials, especially the reference section and the dealers directory, will be helpful in taking the first steps in acquiring antiquarian maps and atlases and in understanding these historic materials.

DEALERS

Finding map dealers is no longer as difficult as it once was because of on-line telephone directories and information available through the Web. Many dealers purchase advertisement space in *Imago Mundi* or *Mercator's World* as well as submitting information for the dealers' directory section of *Antique Map Price Record and Handbook.*

Additionally, there are antiquarian book and map fairs at which dealers can be contacted. The Miami International Map Fair, hosted by the Historical Museum of southern Florida (http://www.historical-museum.org), is held each year for three days in February. Dealers, primarily from North America and Europe, along with map collectors and historians of cartography attend. The program includes lectures, a keynote address, and time to meet dealers to make purchases or inquire about the availability of specific items.

Sheppard's International Directory of Print and Map Sellers. 4th ed.

The fourth edition of *Sheppard's International Directory of Print and Map Sellers* contains more than 1,600 self-reported entries describing print and map dealers. Some of the entries are quite short, no more than firm name and street or post office box address. Full entries include firm name and the name of the proprietor, address and telephone number, e-mail address and Web URL, establishment data, kind of business (shop, by appointment, by mail), size of stock, specialization, and catalog availability. The entries are arranged alphabetically by the country and city in which they are located. Five indexes are included: Index of Businesses, Index of E-Mail Addresses,

Index of Web Sites, Index of Proprietors, and a Specialty Index. The Specialty Index is divided into two parts, for prints and for maps; the map index includes entries under country names and map types. The introductory material includes an address list of trade associations, a short bibliography of works about maps, and address lists of auctioneers and of "Colourers, Framers, Cleaners of Prints and Maps." Richard Joseph, the publisher of *Sheppard's,* also produces a number of similar publications describing antiquarian and secondhand book dealers. *Sheppard's* will help locate dealers who do not yet have a Web presence.

Antique Map Reproductions

Antique Map Reproductions is not a volume of reproductions, it is a directory to companies and individuals that produce or sell facsimiles or reproductions of antique, pre–First World War maps and other cartographic items. The directory includes slightly more than 200 alphabetical entries with contact information and a brief description of available cartographic reproductions. Cartographic representations of historic viewpoints and knowledge do not always have to be "real" antiquarian items. There may be many occasions when a finely produced facsimile will serve intended purposes better, and less expensively, than a truly old piece.

International Map Collectors' Society (IMCoS)
(http://www.harvey27.demon.co.uk/imcos)

The International Map Collectors' Society includes map collectors, dealers, librarians, and scholars among its members. The society, founded in 1980, is a nonprofit organization based in London with two-thirds of its membership living outside of the United Kingdom. Many of the society's events, including an annual meeting in January and a map fair in June, are held in London, but there is an annual international symposium sponsored by the society in either September or October that has been held in other countries including Cyprus, Finland, Israel, Australia, Japan, Turkey, and (approximately every five or six years) the United States. Annual memberships are fairly inexpensive; in 2001, $50 for one year. The only membership requirement is an interest in maps and map collecting. The society publishes a quarterly journal, distributed as part of the membership benefit, and has begun a series of 10 bulletins that will be about map collecting. Although dealers belong to IMCoS, the society's Web site is not necessarily the most direct way to locate dealers.

A list of links to map societies worldwide (http://www.csuohio.edu/CUT/MapSoc/index.html) is maintained at the Cleveland State University Library. International, national, and regional societies are listed with contact information and links to Web sites. The regional societies in the United States may be especially helpful in locating dealers or collectors with specific geographic interests.

A number of map dealers belong to the Antiquarian Booksellers' Association of America (ABAA). To belong, booksellers must be "of good character, reputation and credit rating who have been in business for four continuous years and whose principal place of business is in the United States." Potential members must be sponsored by current members, and the application process is rigorous. The association's Web site (http://abaa.org) includes a "Find a Bookseller" search option. To find map dealers, select "Maps & Atlases" from the "Specialty" drop-down list on the search form. The alphabetical results list will include firm name, proprietors, areas of specialization, hours, and address, telephone and fax numbers, along with e-mail address and Web URLs.

The number of dealers and the amount of information available about antiquarian maps through the Web is staggering. Browsing the worldwide list of sellers of cartographic materials who specialize in antiquarian items through Oddens' Bookmarks gives over 300 links to scroll through. The Map History/History of Cartography Web site links for map collecting include Web sites for larger map dealers, some with on-line catalogs.

Becoming involved in the world of antiquarian maps and the history of cartography does not need to be expensive financially, but becoming an educated consumer will take time for study and a close attention to details.

BIBLIOGRAPHY

Antique Map Price Record and Handbook. Jon K. Rosenthal. Amherst, Mass.: Kimmel Publications, 1993–2001. Formerly *Antique Maps, Sea Charts, City Views, Celestial Charts & Battle Plans.* Continued by *Antique Maps Price Record* (CD-ROM). ISBN: 0-9638100-5-7.

Antique Map Reproductions: A Directory of Publishers & Distributors of Antique Map, Atlas & Globe Facsimiles & Reproductions. Gregory C. McIntosh, comp. Lakewood, Colo.: Plus Ultra Publishing, 1998. ISBN: 0-9667462-0-1.

Antique Maps. 3rd ed. Carl Moreland and David Bannister. London: Phaidon, 1993. ISBN: 0-7148-2954-4.

Cartographical Innovations: An International Handbook of Mapping Terms to 1900. Helen Wallis and Arthur H. Robinson, eds. Tring, England: Map Collector Publications in association with the International Cartographic Association, 1987. ISBN: 0906430046.

Collecting Antique Maps: An Introduction to the History of Cartography. Rev. ed. Jonathan Potter. London: Jonathan Potter Ltd., 1999. ISBN: 0951157760.

Collecting Old Maps. Francis J. Manasek. Norwich, Vt.: Terra Nova Press, 1998. ISBN: 0-9649000-6-8.

Guide to the History of Cartography: An Annotated List of References on the History of Maps and Mapmaking. Walter W. Ristow, comp. Washington, D.C.: Library of Congress, 1973. Reprint, Mansfield, Conn.: Martino, 1997. ISBN: 1-57898-035-6.

History of Cartography. Leo Bagrow. 2nd ed., revised and enlarged by R.A. Skelton. Chicago: Precedent, 1985. ISBN: 0-913750-33-6.

The History of Cartography. 2 vols. to date. David Woodward, ed. Chicago: University of Chicago Press, 1987– . ISBN: 0-226-31633-5 (vol. 1); ISBN: 0-226-31635-1 (vol. 2, book 1); ISBN: 0-226-31637-8 (vol. 2, book 2); ISBN: 0-226-90728-7 (vol. 2, book 3).

Imago Mundi: The International Journal for the History of Cartography. London: Imago Mundi, 1935– . Annual. ISSN: 0308-5694.

Information Sources in Cartography. C.R. Perkins and R.B. Parry, eds. London: Bowker-Saur, 1990. ISBN: 0-408-02458-5.

Keyguide to Information Sources in Cartography. A.G. Hodgkiss and A.F. Tatham. London: Mansell Publishing, 1986. ISBN: 0-7201-1768-2.

The Map Collector. Tring, England: Map Collector Publications, 1977–1996. Quarterly. ISSN: 0140-427X.

The Mapmakers. Rev. ed. John Noble Wilford. New York: Alfred A. Knopf, 2000. ISBN: 0-375-40929-7.

Maps & Civilization: Cartography in Culture and Society. 2nd ed. Norman J. Thrower. Chicago: University of Chicago Press, 1999. ISBN: 0-226-79971-9.

Maps and Their Makers: An Introduction to the History of Cartography. 5th ed. G.R. Crone. Hamden, Conn.: Archon Books, 1978. ISBN: 0-208-01724-0.

Mercator's World: The Magazine of Maps, Geography and Discovery. Eugene, Ore.: Aster Pub. Corp., ca. 1996–2001. 6 per year. ISSN: 1086-6728.

Sheppard's International Directory of Print and Map Sellers. 4th ed. J. Snelgrove, ed. Farnham, Surrey, England: Richard Joseph Publishers, 1999. ISBN: 1872699626.

The Story of Maps. Lloyd A. Brown. Boston: Little, Brown and Co., 1949. Reprint, New York: Dover, 1979. ISBN: 0-486-23873-3.

Tooley's Dictionary of Mapmakers. Rev. ed. Josephine French, et al., eds. Vol. 1: A–D. Tring, England: Map Collector Publications, 1999. ISBN: 0-906430-14-3.Vol. 2: E–J. Riverside, Conn.: Early World Press, 2001. ISBN: 0-906430-19-4.

Who's Who in the History of Cartography: The International Guide to the Subject (D9). 9th ed. Mary Alice Loenthwal. Tring, England: Map Collector, 1998. ISBN: 0906430186.

On-line References

Antiquarian Booksellers' Association of America. Home page. ABAA, 2003. <http://abaa.org> (16 October 2003).

Antique Maps. Carl Moreland and David Bannister. David Bannister, 20 January 2002. <http://www.antiquemaps.co.uk/book/> (16 October 2003).

Concise Bibliography of the History of Cartography. Robert W. Karrow, Jr., 1997. Newberry Library, 5 January 2000. <http://www.newberry.org/nl/collections/conbib.html> (16 October 2003).

David Rumsey Map Collection. Cartography Associates, 2003. <http://www.davidrumsey.com> (16 October 2003).

Historical Museum of Southern Florida. Home page. 9 September 2003. <http://www.historical-museum.org> (16 October 2003).

The History of Cartography. Home page. History of Cartography Project. David Woodward, 19 August 2003. <http://feature.geography.wisc.edu/histcart/> (16 October 2003).

Imago Mundi: The International Journal for the History of Cartography. Tony Campbell, 30 August 2003. <http://www.maphistory.info/imago.html> (16 October 2003).

International Antiquarian Mapsellers Association. Home page. IAMA, 2002. <http://www.antiquemapdealers.com> (16 October 2003).

International Conferences on the History of Cartography. (ICHC). Tony Campbell, 23 August 2003 <http://www.maphistory.info/confs.html> (16 October 2003).

International Map Collectors' Society. Home page. IMCoS, 28 September 2003. <http://www.harvey27.demon.co.uk/imcos/> (16 October 2003).

Map Collections: 1500–2002. Library of Congress, Geography and Map Division. Library of Congress, 13 March 2003. <http://lcweb2.loc.gov/ammem/gmdhtml/> (16 October 2003).

MapForum.com: A Periodical for Antique Map Collectors. MapForum.com, 2003. <http://www.MapForum.com/index.htm> (16 October 2003).

MapHist-L: Map History Discussion List. Home page. Hosted by the Faculty of Geographical Sciences, Utrecht University, The Netherlands. Peter van der Krogt, 12 March 2003. <http://www.maphist.nl> (16 October 2003).

Map History/History of Cartography. Tony Campbell. 5 October 2003. <http://www.maphistory.info/> (16 October 2003).

Map Record Publications. Home page. 1 September 2003. <http://www.maprecord.com> (16 October 2003).

"Map Societies around the World." Cleveland State University Library, 19 April 2000. <http://www.csuohio.edu/CUT/MapSoc/index.html> (16 October 2003).

Oddens' Bookmarks: The Fascinating World of Maps and Mapping. R. Oddens. Utrecht University, March 2003. <http://oddens.geog.uu.nl/index.html> (16 October 2003).

Researchers in the History of Cartography. Tony Campbell, 18 August 2003 <http://www.maphistory.info/research.html> (16 October 2003).

CHAPTER 10
Aerial Photographs and Remotely Sensed Images

Broadly defined, remote sensing is collecting data about an object without touching it. In practice, remote sensing of the Earth uses equipment such as cameras and a wide variety of other electromagnetic sensors to collect data for processing and interpretation, both of which usually happen at a later time and in a different location than the target location. Remotely sensed data of the Earth are captured by instru-

ments mounted on platforms at a variety of altitudes above the Earth's surface—from the height of a crane to the distance of satellites orbiting outside of the Earth's atmosphere. Remote sensing collects more than visible light. Sensors have been developed to passively collect from the ultraviolet portion of the electromagnetic spectrum, slightly shorter wavelengths than visible light, through visible light and infrared ra-

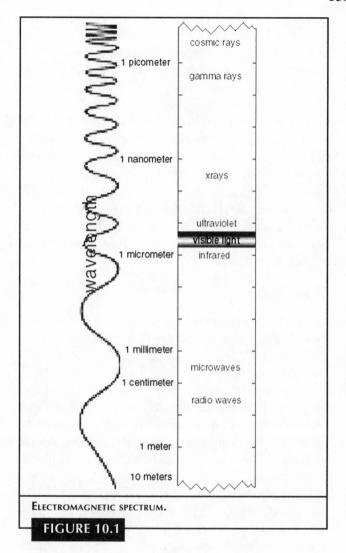

ELECTROMAGNETIC SPECTRUM.

FIGURE 10.1

on computer disk. The resulting images can be viewed directly on a computer screen instead of having to go through the photographic development process first, although prints can still be made. Aerial photography produced this way should be identified by the producer as "digital aerial photography." Aerial photography does not include sensing anything along the energy wavelength spectrum except for visible and near-visible light.

In contrast, satellite imagery is collected from outside of the Earth's atmosphere. Satellite imagery data are not collected using a humanly driven photomechanical method but by unmanned satellites with repeating orbits. Their sensors respond to wavelengths beyond the visible and near infrared portions of the electromagnetic spectrum and enormous amounts of data are sent in digital streams to receiving stations on the ground. The data group into different spectral bands, each band well-suited for displaying specific kinds of data. Panchromatic sensors collect data analogous to what can be seen by the human eye. Multispectral or multiband sensors collect data about reflected and emitted radiation in a number of different parts of the electromagnetic spectrum, near ultraviolet, visible, reflected infrared, thermal infrared, at the same time. Combining data from different bands aids in performing different types of analysis. Data are processed and classified using computers. A printed image is not always the final output. Some analyses result in graphs or images displayed on a computer monitor.

IMAGING HISTORY

The first aerial photograph was taken by Gaspard Felix Tournachon in 1858 near Paris; he attached a camera to a hot air balloon. James Black did the same for Boston in 1860; these photographs are the earliest surviving aerial photographs. Balloon- and kite-mounted cameras assisted the mapping of Confederate emplacements during the Battle of Richmond and the extent of earthquake and fire devastation in San Francisco in 1906. Although Wilbur Wright took the first photographs from an airplane of Centrocelli, Italy, in 1909, cameras constructed specifically for mounting in airplanes were not built until 1915. Aerial photography began to take off as a tool to collect reconnaissance information during the First World War. After the war, photography began to be used for civilian needs, primarily to produce land use and soil maps. The Tennessee Valley Authority was an early adopter of aerial photographs, followed quickly by the

diation to the shortest wavelengths of the microwave portion of the spectrum (Figure 10.1). Aerial photographs are photographs of portions of the Earth's surface taken from the air. The camera might be in an airplane but it could also be in a balloon, helicopter, glider, or even mounted on a pigeon's chest. Aerial photographs are taken from within the Earth's atmosphere. There are a few exceptions—namely handheld photographs taken by astronauts. Because the photography is taken closer to the ground, it may be easier for a nonexpert to interpret and will probably include more details than images collected from space. Traditionally, a photographic process, exposing and developing film, is involved in creating aerial photographs, although the final photograph might not always be printed on paper. Recently, some aerial photography has begun being collected digitally by exposing light-sensitive sensors instead of film and recording results

Soil Conservation Service. There were no major technological advances in aerial photography until the Second World War when Kodak developed color infrared film for detecting camouflaged targets. Healthy vegetation reflected red while dead vegetation or non-vegetation look-alikes appeared blue. As after the First World War, military technologies of the Second World War, including use of color infrared film for photography, made their way into civilian use. The Cold War and space race created a new focus for image collection: satellites as sensor platforms.

The 1960s brought the launch of the first meteorological satellite (TIROS-1), the first military reconnaissance satellite program (CORONA), and three U.S. manned space programs (Mercury, Gemini, and Apollo). Not until the early 1970s was there a civilian satellite project—first called ERTS-1 (Earth Resources Technology Satellite) but later renamed Landsat. During the 1980s, the Space Shuttle program took off, and the French began launching a series of satellites in the SPOT (Système Pour l'Observation de la Terre) commercial system. Russia has had a satellite program, in particular for military needs, in place as long as the United States. In the past decade, Canada launched its first satellite. A number of other nations have become active in using the equipment and data of these established programs.

AERIAL PHOTOGRAPHY

Aerial photography is used by governmental agencies, corporations, and private individuals to investigate natural and cultural phenomena. Because the information shown on aerial photographs has not been classified or generalized by the representation of objects using symbols, aerial photography is a potentially less biased source of primary information than maps. There are some difficulties in using aerial photographs. Unless rectified to correct directional and geographic distortions, some kinds of measurements, in particular of distance, direction, and area, cannot be made directly from aerial photographs. Nevertheless, aerial photographs are a powerful tool in analyzing landscapes and land uses. People and agencies interested in distribution of objects through the landscape and in how objects are related to each other use aerial photography; these might include city planners, real estate developers, transportation and utility planners, and environmental scientists. Aerial photography can be used to trace changes in land use including cropping patterns and urban growth. It is used as a tool in siting new commercial ventures as a way to examine the current situation and to review former land use. Many prospective property purchasers are interested in viewing the historic use of their area of interest because of legislation in place that determines who will be responsible for correcting environmental problems caused by previous uses. Aerial photographs also have applications in tracking the changes in landscape shape, both natural and human caused, such as movements of riverbeds, expansion of open pit mines, and creation of landfill. Soil and agricultural specialists can track erosion and loss of topsoil by examining aerial photographs. Aerial photographs are the primary resource in creating topographic and land use/land cover maps.

Film Types

Aerial photography can be taken in both black-and-white and color (Figure 10.2). Black-and-white panchromatic film is the most common because it is the least expensive to produce and the most flexible, with many kinds of users able to benefit. The wavelengths of light that the film responds to is in the same range as human eye response, although the resulting print includes many more shades of gray than human eyes can differentiate. This generally makes the photographs very crisp.

Color photography is usually "natural" color, meaning objects appear on the photograph the same color that they are on the ground; the wavelengths of light are in the human viewable range. Color photography can be easier to interpret than black-and-white but color photography is not always as crisp as black-and-white because of difficulties in correctly exposing the film. Color photographs will also be slightly more expensive than black-and-white to purchase.

Color infrared (CIR) photography is sometimes called "false color infrared" because the colors produced do not mimic natural world colors. CIR film captures wavelengths of energy shorter than eye-viewable red. CIR is used to monitor vegetation health and stress and can be used to differentiate between types of vegetation. Healthy vegetation generally is bright red while stressed vegetation is pink. Roads, roofs, and clear water are black; silty water will be light blue or greenish. Black-and-white infrared film is sometimes used. Like the color film, it picks up on vegetation health but can also be used to differentiate between dry and wet soils. Infrared film is a powerful tool for landscape

PEORIA, ILLINOIS. NOTE THE GOLF COURSE, GRID-LIKE STREET PATTERN, MANMADE WATER BODY NEAR THE PHOTOGRAPH CENTER, AND DIFFERENCE IN WATER DARKNESS. *BXF-5H-36, PEORIA COUNTY, ILLINOIS.* 1:20,000. WASHINGTON, D.C.: U.S. DEPT. OF AGRICULTURE, PRODUCTION AND MARKETING ADMINISTRATION, 1951.

FIGURE 10.2

and vegetation analysis, but it does require some experience or training to produce successful interpretations.

Obliques vs. Verticals

There are two basic types of aerial photographs: oblique and vertical. Vertical photographs are taken with the camera nearly parallel to the part of the Earth's surface directly below so that the optical axis of the camera is approximately 90° from the surface. The optical axis of oblique aerial photographs is deliberately set at an angle other than 90° from the surface, usually between 20° and 80°. Oblique photographs can be identified as low oblique, showing only the Earth's surface, or high oblique, showing the surface, horizon, and sky. Vertical photographs work well for measuring changes in land use and are the type of photograph rectified to produce orthophotomaps (discussed below). There will be some distortion of size and shape at the edges of the photographs because of platform tilt and the natural "fall away" of the Earth from the camera. Most aerial photography, in particular the photography produced by the U.S. federal government, is of the vertical type. Oblique photographs work well to examine specific features such as individual farms or city skylines. Just as eye-viewing landscape, distance and perspective distort the sizes of objects; things far away appear much smaller than objects nearby. Small independent aerial photography companies may be more apt to specialize in oblique photography.

Principles of Interpretation

Aerial photographs need to be examined with seven different aspects in mind. Together the aspects help build an appropriate interpretation of the current ground situation. Some of these aspects can be seen in Figure 10.2.

Pattern—Many manmade objects have easily recognizable patterns: curvy 1960s suburban subdivisions; 1-mile grid of country roads in the midwest and western United States; straight lines of soybean rows, vineyard trellises, or fruit trees in orchards; oval sporting tracks. Nature also creates patterns: oxbow lakes near rivers with moving beds, straight streams following geologic fault lines, parallel lines of hills or mountain ranges. Although an interpreter may not always know what causes a pattern, he or she should be able to explain what the differences in patterns are.

Shadow—Shadows assist in determining both object size and shape. Sometimes shadows are necessary to identify objects with relatively small "foot prints" such as transmission towers and smokestacks. Shadows can also assist in identifying tree species; many have distinctive shapes and silhouettes from branch configurations. Aerial photographs are usually flown at times during the day conducive to minimizing, but not completely eliminating, the possibility of shadows obscuring other features unless shadows are necessary for seeing details of subtle differences in the landscape or for locating objects of low relief such as archaeological sites.

Shape—Human-created objects tend to have regular, geometric shapes with well-defined corners; natural objects usually have irregular, nongeometric shapes. Shape is fundamental to an initial identification of an object. Athletic fields surrounded by tracks, baseball diamonds, airports, and interstate interchanges are readily identified because of their shapes. Natural objects with common shapes include alluvial fans, atolls, and volcanic cinder cones.

Site and Association—Sometimes many objects and aspects need to be put together to determine what the area of interest is. A large rectangular yet thin object with parallel arcs on one side in an area with few surrounding structures and no trees between the arcs might be a drive-in movie theater. An area of scattered trees, many of which appear to be conifers, with winding roads and small scattered structures or objects could be a cemetery. Curved patches of bright areas with a small scattering of trees in an otherwise open area may help locate a golf course.

Size—Size can be calculated if the scale of the photograph is known or if an object of known size is shown on the photograph. But even without a specific depiction scale, relative size is an important tool to use to differentiate between similar objects. A horseracing track will be much larger than a college or high school track-and-field track. An interstate highway will be wider than a county highway. Older trees may have larger crowns than younger. Tributary streams typically are smaller than the streams or rivers they flow into.

Texture—The appearance of texture is created by differences in color and shading. Pastures will appear smoother than forests; lava fields are rougher or courser than sand dunes. Depending on the scale of the photograph, the same object may appear to have different textures; as the scale increases the perception of roughness also increases.

Tone and Color—Tone and color refer to the number of shades or colors that can be differentiated on a photograph. Humans see fewer shades of gray than unique colors, so color photography may assist in identifying plant species, in particular trees and field crops, more easily than black-and-white. Both tone and color can be affected by the angle and intensity of sunlight.

Of course, having prior knowledge about the area that the aerial photography covers, such as type of terrain or typical tree species and cropping patterns, so that interpretations can be "ground truthed" is essential.

Basic Photo Interpretation

Basic Photo Interpretation was created as instructional materials for personnel in the USDA Soil Conservation Service. It includes 10 chapters with learning activities, some of which use a set of photographs and plastic overlay grid that accompany the text. Many of the chapters revolve around basics of map (and aerial photograph) reading and interpretation and would be of interest to nonusers of photographs. The text is straightforward and the illustrations are clear and concise. *Basic Photo Interpretation* would be ideal reading for a beginning aerial photograph user with an intense interest in interpretation. Working through *Basic Photo Interpretation* will also provide solid grounding in basic concepts and vocabulary before tackling remote sensing textbooks. Using the text successfully will require some additional equipment including a stereoscope. Though there is a glossary, there is no index, which makes searching for quick answers difficult, and unfortunately there are no answer sets for many of the learning activity questions. It appears that *Basic Photo Interpretation* may be out of print and neither a newer edition nor a similar but new publication are forthcoming.

United States Federal Programs

The United States has had a number of organized aerial photography programs. The Agricultural Adjustment Administration, later the Agricultural Stabilization and Conservation Service (ASCS), Soil Conservation Service, and Tennessee Valley Authority were early adapters of aerial photography as an inventory and survey tool. ASCS flights were flown beginning in 1935 over predominantly agricultural counties nationwide, producing photographs that were intended to forecast crop yields and to assist in mapping soil types. The Soil Conservation Service was interested in soil erosion and other problems of soil conservation and produced photography predominantly in the west and southwestern United States during the late 1930s. The Tennessee Valley Authority had, and still has, a much narrower focus, the area impacted by its dam building and power generating operations.

The National High Altitude Photography Program (NHAP) began in 1980 as a cooperative federal program coordinated by the United States Geological Survey. The program's specifications were modified in 1987, and its name was changed to National Aerial Photography Program (NAPP). The cooperating agencies include the Farm Service Agency (formerly Agricultural Stabilization and Conservation Service), Forest Service, National Agricultural Statistics Service, National Resources Conservation Service (formerly Soil Conservation Service), Bureau of Land Management, United States Geological Survey, and Tennessee Valley Authority. State agencies such as departments of natural resources, transportation, environment, and planning often contribute funding to be sure that flights will go forward as planned. The programs are intended to collect aerial photography at a consistent scale nationwide in such a way that it can be used for multiple purposes by multiple agencies. NHAP photography flightlines and centerpoints were centered on USGS 7.5-minute topographic quadrangles. Two photographs were taken, each covering the entire quadrangle, black-and-white at 1:80,000 and CIR at 1:58,000. Under the current NAPP program, photography is quarter-quadrangle centered, four photographs are required to completely cover the geographic area covered by a 7.5-minute topographic quadrangle. Black-and-white and CIR are both acquired at the same scale of 1:40,000. Flightlines for both programs run north-south. Generally, when aerial photography is flown for a state, the entire state is completed in the same year or, for large states or in case of difficulties because of technical or atmospheric problems, photography will be completed in the following year. NHAP/NAPP photography was originally slated to be acquired on a five-year cycle. This cycle is under modification and many areas are being changed to a seven-year cycle. NHAP/NAPP photography is available for purchase through the Farm Service Agency's Salt Lake City office, the Tennessee Valley Authority Map Store, and the USGS EROS Data Center in Sioux Falls, South Dakota. NHAP and NAPP are two of the aerial photography programs described at the EROS Data Center's aerial products Web site (http://edc.usgs.gov/products/aerial.html).

Aerial Photographs (http://ask.usgs.gov/photos.html)

The ESIC Web site has an extensive number of links to USGS information about aerial photography. This is a one-stop information site with information about aerial photography in general along with specifics on the NHAP/NAPP programs and digital orthophoto quadrangles (DOQs) and a link to Terraserver. The site includes a list of frequently asked questions; a page leading to scanned photographs available from the EROS Data Center; and fact sheets on a number of topics such as how to obtain aerial photography, how to search for older photography, and how to interpret color infrared photography. PDF files of order forms to send to ESIC offices can be printed. This site may be the ideal place to begin exploring the number of options available from the USGS for photography, but it also works well as an informational tool.

Format

Standard aerial photography prints are 9-by-9 inches. Some of the older ASCS photographs may be 6-by-9 inches. Aerial photographs typically have triangular markings in the center of each side and in the corners. These are fiducial marks that are built into the camera and are photographed each time along with the Earth's surface. If the fiducial marks are connected in pairs, each one with the mark directly across the photograph, the intersection of the connecting lines is the precise center of the photograph, the principal point. Knowing the location of the principal point is important because it depicts the nadir, the location on the ground that is exactly beneath the airplane on a vertical line from the camera to the center of the earth. The principal point is essential in calculating heights of objects.

Enlargements of standard-sized prints can be professionally produced photographically or by using photocopiers. Photographic enlargements will be crisper; photocopied images will be faster and less expensive to obtain. The federal agencies that sell photographs make the same images available for purchase at different sizes/scales. These images are all made directly from an original negative. Photographic reproductions and enlargements can be made from positive prints after first shooting the print to produce a negative. Caution should be used in interpreting the resulting image because it is at least three generations away from the first negative and distortions may have been incorporated.

Standard aerial photograph prints include distortion of distance, size, and angle. These distortions are "removed" through rectification, correcting for the tilt of the camera, differences in terrain relief, and the curvature of the Earth, to create orthophotographs. Newer photography can be rectified to meet very high accuracy standards because all of the required information is readily available. Unfortunately, older photography cannot be fully rectified because the information about the camera and specifics about the flight process are no longer available. Until the mid-to-late 1980s, this work was done using analog technology. Now all orthophotographs are produced digitally from NAPP photography and tend to be aligned with either USGS 7.5-minute quadrangles or with quarter-quadrangles (which creates digital orthophoto quarter-quadrangles, DOQQs). Digital orthophoto quadrangles (DOQs) are often identified by the same name as the topographic quadrangle that they collocate with. Nearly all DOQs are grayscale (black-and-white). The process is largely mathematical and needs specific kinds of information to be successful for an image: a minimum of three clearly identified positions on the photograph, camera calibration information such as the camera's focal length, a digital elevation model (DEM) for the area, and a high-quality digital image of the photograph. A brief description of the process is available through the USGS Web page about DOQs (http://edc.usgs.gov/products/aerial/dog.html).

DOQs can be used to measure distance, direction, and area. Sometimes, in areas of especially low relief such as the Everglades in Florida, DOQs are used as a base image upon which cartographic representations of boundaries, roads, and other cultural features are placed. They are used heavily for environmental and resource management but are not yet available for all locations in the United States. The Digital Orthophoto

Quadrangle home page (http://www-wmc.wr.usgs.gov/doq/) includes links to status graphics showing which DOQs have been completed and are for sale and which are in progress. The status graphics are updated quarterly. The images viewed through Terraserver (http://www.terraserver-usa.com) are DOQs, although they have been converted to the JPEG format for Web compatibility and will not be as crisp as the original images. DOQs and DOQQs are available for sale from the USGS for incorporation into geographic information systems applications.

Indexes

Indexes to sets of aerial photography generally take one of three different forms. Photomosaic indexes are much-reduced photographs of the entire set (Figure 10.3). A complete set of prints is placed on a table or board in their correct positions, overlapping where the photographs provide duplicative coverage. The photographs are placed so that the edge with the identifying information is completely visible. Then a photograph of the mosaic is taken and printed. Photomosaic indexes do not include any textual information; there are no city or river names and there is nothing to assist the viewer in determining if a straight line is a railroad or a highway. Users of photomosaic indexes need to be already very familiar with their study area or be able to consult reference materials such as county highway maps or small-scale topographic maps. Sometimes users of these indexes end up resorting to "driving" from a landmark to their study site on the index using the same written directions they would use in their car. Once the right place has been located on the mosaic, it is usually easy to identify the specific photographs required.

Line indexes show photograph center points connected by lines representing the flight line of the airplane. The lines and dots are usually superimposed on some kind of map. While these indexes make it easier to find a specific location, sometimes it is difficult to determine which photographs will include the study area because line indexes do not always show the footprint of the photographs, just the center points. Spot indexes are similar to line indexes except that the center points of the photographs are not connected by the flight lines. Again, spot indexes do not necessarily indicate the footprint of the photograph. The detail level of the maps that the line and spot indexes are printed on can vary greatly, from using a USGS 1:100,000 topographic map to using an outline of a county's

PHOTOMOSAIC INDEX, PEORIA COUNTY, ILLINOIS. PEORIA COUNTY'S USDA ASSIGNED CODE IS BXF. BECAUSE THIS IS NEAR THE COUNTY BOUNDARY, SOME OVERLAP WITH TAZEWELL COUNTY, CODE BXI, CAN BE SEEN. *INDEX, PEORIA COUNTY, ILLINOIS.* SCALE CA. 1:63,360. WASHINGTON, D.C.: U.S. DEPT. OF AGRICULTURE, PRODUCTION AND MARKETING ADMINISTRATION, 1951.

FIGURE 10.3

shape with an indication of the locations of major towns.

Regardless of its format, an index should yield all of the information necessary to completely identify a unique photograph so that it can be located in a collection or ordered from the producer.

Tips for Using Aerial Photograph Indexes

• Depending on the producing program, indexes cover different areas: counties, small-scale topographic maps, entire states.
• Each year of coverage for an area may necessitate a separate index; generally the same index cannot be used to request photographs for multiple years.
• Check the north arrow on the index to be sure that the index is oriented in a logical manner.

• If the index has multiple sheets, there often is overlap between the sheets; when laying the index sheets out, follow the assembly diagram and be sure to have all sheets oriented in the same direction.
• Consider using "assisting graphics" such as small-scale topographic maps, county plat books, or county highway maps to "drive" your fingers to their final destination, being sure to orient assisting item in the same direction as the index.
• Working with chronological coverage may be easier if the most current indexes are inspected first, moving backward to the oldest coverage; this could assist in mentally "removing" development, especially in highly urbanized areas.
• Correctly record all information required by the photograph provider including, but not limited to, county and state, year, producing agency, film roll or can, flight line, and photograph number.

Stereopairs

Vertical photographs are often produced as part of a large set covering a specified area such as a county or state. Photographs are flown in a regular pattern of flight lines that trace back and forth over the area until complete coverage has been acquired. If complete geographic coverage is all that is required, then only alternate photographs within a flight line need to be consulted. But if heights need to be measured or terrain needs to be examined in depth, then photographs that adjoin and overlap each other will be needed. Three-dimensional viewing is important in aerial photograph interpretation; without it hills and mountains only appear rough, but in stereopairs their relative height differences are readily apparent. This also applies to cityscapes.

Typical vertical aerial photography, if stereopairs are required, is flown with a 55–65 percent overlap between photographs in the same flight line and a 20–30 percent sidelap between photographs in adjoining flight lines. The camera is a monocular device, and by itself a single vertical photograph will not give a feeling of depth or three dimensions. But two overlapping aerial photographs from the same flight line placed next to each other and viewed through a stereoscope will mimic the biocular vision produced by two eyes. This is because the same object is photographed from two different angles as the plane advances along the flight line, just as eyes focus on the same object at slightly different angles because of their separation by a nose. The stereoscope lines up each eye on a separate photograph, and the viewer's brain combines the images to create the three-dimensional effect. There are a number of different kinds of stereoscopes. Not all are appropriate for viewing aerial photography, for example, a child's Viewmaster. The least expensive, and smallest, of the aerial photography stereoscopes is the lens or pocket stereoscope with 2× to 4× magnification and easy portability because its legs fold in so that the entire device could easily fit into a shirt pocket. Plastic pocket stereoscopes can be purchased for less than $10, and metal pocket stereoscopes retail for $30 to $40 depending on the magnification level. Due to its small size, the pocket stereoscope allows the user to see a much smaller portion of the photography overlap areas than the other kinds of stereoscopes. Mirror stereoscopes allow viewing a much larger expanse of the overlap. A system of four sets of mirrors is employed, and magnifying binoculars, with 3× to 8× magnification, may or may not be included.

Using a magnifying binocular will reduce the area visible. Mirror stereoscopes are much larger and much less portable than pocket stereoscopes and they have a correspondingly higher price tag of $375 to $2,000 or more. Laboratories and offices with heavy usage of stereopairs may have available a zoom stereoscope or a zoom transfer scope.

Tips for Using Stereopairs

• Work with photographs so that the shadows in the photograph fall toward yourself. Viewing a photograph with the shadows falling away can cause topographic inversion (rivers will appear to be on ridgelines instead of in valleys).
• Use two consecutive photographs from the same flight line.
• Limit intense stereopair viewing to less than 20 minutes. This kind of work is very hard on the eyes.
• If using a stereoscope with an adjustable-width eyepiece, be sure that the eyepiece is at the same width as the distance between your eyes.
• Remember to remove the plastic protective covers that might be over the mirrors on a mirror stereoscope. If they are not removed, the photographs cannot be seen.
• Reduce the amount of shadow falling on the photograph from the stereoscope or viewer.
• To quickly set up a stereopair for viewing, overlap photographs so that object of interest in both is aligned one on top of the other. Hold the lower photograph still while sliding the upper photograph away in a straight line so that the object of interest can be seen through both lenses of the stereoscope. While looking through the eyepiece, adjust the upper photograph while holding the lower photograph stationary. There may be an unfocused feeling or vertigo as the two images of the object come closer and closer to junction. Suddenly, often with a minute adjustment, the object will appear in three dimensions.
• Using stereopairs takes practice and patience. Practice using photographs that have well-defined changes in elevation—either from actual ground relief or from different kinds of ground cover such as vegetation or buildings.
• If you normally wear glasses, wear them when using a stereoscope.
• Not everyone can see aerial photographs in stereo.

Sources of Aerial Photography

Looking for information about aerial photographs in a library catalog may require multiple subject searches depending on the aspect required. For general materials and the broadest set of results, search

"Aerial photography." "Aerial photographs" may also find a limited number of items. Aerial photography as applied in specific disciplines can be found by searching "Aerial photography in [blank]," filling in the blank with an appropriate area such as archaeology, city planning, forestry, geology, or traffic engineering. To find materials on reading aerial photography, search for "Photographic interpretation."

"Photographic interpretation" also leads to some interesting results as a Web search, although not all are strictly about aerial photography. Because the Web does not use a common list of terms, both "aerial photography" and "aerial photographs" should be searched for as well as any other variations that can be thought of, including "air photo" and "airphoto." Results will include links to aerial photography firms and government agencies, a limited amount of aerial photography available through the Web, and course notes and other course-related materials.

The Aerial Photo Sourcebook

The Aerial Photo Sourcebook is intended to be "a centralized clearinghouse of information about and sources of U.S. aerial photography" (*Aerial Photo Sourcebook,* vii). After a brief introductory chapter, which includes an interesting table of aerial photography uses, and a short chapter overviewing aerial photography interpretation, the remainder of the book primarily is devoted to listing sources from which to obtain aerial photography. The chapter on U.S. federal agencies includes information about the kinds of photography available and the information necessary for communicating with the producing agency, but the chapters on state and regional resources and commercial dealers are only address and telephone lists. Half of the book is an extensive and chronologically diverse bibliography about aerial photography that is divided into subject sections reflecting aspects of photography production and areas of application or use. A glossary, a list of acronyms, and a list of journals round out the volume. *Sourcebook* is not the title to consult to learn how to use aerial photography or to view examples of aerial photography. The works described later in this chapter as well as the previously described *Basic Photo Interpretation*, would be better choices for becoming acquainted with how to interpret aerial photography. *Sourcebook*'s primary value will be in helping to make connections with aerial photography producers or agencies that have substantial collections of aerial photography available for use while the bibliography will guide nonexpert users into appropriate literature.

FEDERAL AGENCIES

United States Department of Agriculture

Information about obtaining photography produced by agencies of the United States Department of Agriculture is most easily found at the Web site for the USDA Aerial Photography Field Office (http://www.apfo.usda.gov/). The Field Office sells photography produced by three agencies, the Farm Service Agency, the Forest Service, and the Natural Resources and Conservation Service. The Field Office also sells photographs from NAPP and NHAP, which are multi-agency projects. The USDA began flying aerial photography in 1935 to assist in measuring farm acreage. The Field Office does not hold the negatives for the earliest flights (they are at the National Archives), but currently can provide photography from 1955 to the present. The catalog of flights available through the Web site will not assist in identifying specific aerial photographs; its purpose is to display, on a county-by-county basis, general information about flight years, scale, and percentage of county covered (Table 10.1).

After determining the year of flight for a county, then the potential aerial photography user submits, via surface mail, a combined photography search and order form, which is available through the Web site, as is a price list. Photographic prints range in size from 10-by-10 inches to 38-by-38 inches and in price from $3, for a black-and-white film negative, to $70 for the largest paper prints of color photography. Line and photomosaic indexes can also be purchased.

National Archives and Records Administration—Cartographic and Architectural Records

Obtaining older photography through the National Archives is not a straightforward or easy proposition. Photography users not located in Washington, D.C., need to be aware that the Cartographic Archives responds only to written or e-mail requests, not to telephone inquiries. The Archives holds pre-1955 USDA photography (Agricultural Stabilization and Conservation Service, Soil Conservation Service, and Forest Service) as well as early photographs from the USGS, the Bureau of Land Management, and military photography flown between the 1940s and the 1960s. In particular, the Cartographic Archives has an extensive collection of World War II photography taken by the United States and its allies, Germany, and Japan.

TABLE 10.1

TYPICAL COUNTY ENTRY FOR HOOD RIVER COUNTY, OREGON, FROM THE USDA AERIAL PHOTOGRAPHY FIELD OFFICE FILM CATALOG.

HOOD RIVER

41027 (BAZ   )   Square Mile Land Use: 536

PROG   %COV YEAR SCL FILM INDEXES RECT REMARKS

PROG	%COV	YEAR	SCL	FILM	INDEXES	RECT	REMARKS
FSA	(P)	1965	20	BW	PI	2	N	8962
FSA	(P)	1980	40	BW	PI	2	N	8963
NHAP1	100	1981	60	CIR		2	N	
NAPP1	10	1990	40	BW	SI	2	Y	PART USFS/CONTRACT
OTHER	(P)	1989	40	BW	LI	2	Y	USFS
NAPP2	100	1994	40	BW	DI	1	Y	PARTIALLY RECTIFIED
NAPP3	87	2000	40	BW		1	N	

The (P) under % COV indicates that only part of the county was photographed; note that there is no specific indication of which part. Hood River County, Oregon, includes Mount Hood National Forest; the partial coverage titled "Other" flown by the USFS probably includes coverage of just that forest. The NAPP3 with 87% coverage in 2000 will most likely have been completed in 2001.

There are two basic tools to begin exploring the Archives' aerial photograph holdings.

Aerial Photographs in the National Archives (Special List 25)

Special List 25 was published in 1971 and reissued in 1973; it is a guide to aerial photography of the United States. It contains an alphabetical list of states and counties with information about the photography years available, number of index sheets required, and the flying agency. Scale of photographs is not included because the agencies producing photography generally did so at established scales. Counties were the basic geographic unit that was covered by early USDA flights. The second part is a list of flight projects that cover more than one county with project name, counties covered, number of index sheets, and scale of photographs. This guide does not identify the specific photograph needed. It assists potential National Archives researchers in determining the years of coverage held at the Archives. Set indexes will still need to be consulted either by the individual or by Archives staff.

Guide to Cartographic Records in the National Archives

Looking under "Aerial Photography" in *Guide to Cartographic Records* leads to a list of 57 record groups representing aerial photographs taken between 1918 and 1947. The photographs cover locations throughout the world. At times there is not strict correspondence between the index entry and the text describing the record group. For instance, Record Group 208, which the index describes as an aerial photograph of Camp Bragg, North Carolina, in 1920–1921, also seems to include, according to the entry describing the record group, some photomaps of Coblenz, Germany, the Rhine River, and Washington, D.C. Because the *Guide* is somewhat dated, the list of record groups including aerial photography will be out of date. *Guide to Federal Records in the National Archives of the United States* can be used to find materials added since 1971. The print version is three volumes; there is a Web-based version (http://www.archives.gov/research_room/federal_records_guide/) that continues to be updated as new materials are received and processed. The NARA Archival Research Catalog (ARC) (http://www.archives.gov/research_room/arc/) describes approximately 13% of NARA's nationwide holdings. Some of the descriptions go beyond text to scanned images, including aerial photographs. ARC is a fairly new endeavor; very few aerial photographs are currently in the database but more will appear as the database is expanded.

When requesting assistance in locating photography, the Archives requests that both a map with the site clearly marked and a verbal description of the site and its relative location to other areas be sent. The staff will use this information to determine which photographs in the collection best cover the area. Reproductions cannot be purchased directly through the Cartographic Archives; all copies are sold through private vendors. Information about the vendors is available through the National Archives Web site. To order copies, information about the specific record series and item number must be sent directly to the vendor. The vendors will arrange to have ordered materials pulled, will make the copies, and will mail the copies to the orderer. All bills will be issued by and paid to the vendor. The Archives charges a fee to pull items for copying; this cost will be passed on by the copy vendors. Regional archives facilities also might hold aerial photography; each regional facility will need to be contacted individually.

EROS Data Center

The United States Geological Survey makes aerial photography available for purchase through the Earth Resources Observation Systems (EROS) Data Center in Sioux Falls, South Dakota. The EROS Data Center was originally opened in the 1970s to house and distribute data from NASA's Landsat satellites. The center's mission has expanded to include remotely sensed data from other sources, aerial photography, and cartographic data. According to the center's Web site (http://edcwww.cr.usgs.gov), "EDC's archives also hold the world's largest collection of civilian remotely sensed data covering the Earth's land masses, housing millions of satellite images and aerial photographs." From the EROS Data Center's Web site, users can find out about the kinds of data housed at EROS, data collection programs under way, and how to search for and order data. There are a number of search and order mechanisms available through the Web site; two include aerial photography. The order delivery time for aerial photography is four to six weeks and for data is one to three weeks. Data can also be ordered for "FTP pickup" and has a turnaround time of two days.

PhotoFinder (http://edcsns17.usgs.gov/finder/finder_main.pl?dataset_name=NAPP)

PhotoFinder is straightforward and simple to search by first entering the name of a populated place or a zip code, or by clicking on a map. Entering a place name or zip code will speed getting to a map of the appropriate area. Once the desired area is displayed, center points of photographs can be selected to see the photograph footprints. The photographs available through PhotoFinder are only from the NAPP coverage. Orders can be placed through the PhotoFinder Web site directly to the EROS Data Center.

EarthExplorer (http://edcsns17.cr.usgs.gov/EarthExplorer/)

EarthExplorer, the replacement for the USGS Global Land Information System (GLIS), has a broader focus than PhotoFinder. A Java-script application, it includes maps, map and satellite data, and aerial photography, specifically NHAP, NAPP, and DOQs. Users have the option to log into the system as a guest or as a registered user; the only difference between the two is that registered users can save their searches, search results, and order information. Specific types of data, including the three groups of aerial photographs, can be selected to search against. Search areas are defined spatially by bounding rectangle, place name or zip code, or coordinates. A "Results Summary" page will display while the search is running and will update every 10 seconds. Once the search has been completed, the results can be viewed. DOQ results allow the display of a browse or preview image. NHAP and NAPP photographs do not display, but their footprint can be displayed on a map of the area of interest. Orders for

TABLE 10.2

LANDSAT 1–3 MSS BANDS.

Band number	Wavelength (μm)	Spectrial Location	Useful for
4	0.5-0.6	Green	Water features
5	0.6-0.7)	Red	Vegetation (chlorophyll absorption)
6	0.7-0.8	Near Infrared	Surface features, moisture content
7	0.8-1.1	Near Infrared	Surface features, moisture content

data files and photographs are placed on-line through the Web site using "shopping cart technology." There are a number of links from within the site's pages that lead to appropriate help sections. Because this search and order system has multiple screens and a number of them contain a large amount of information, EarthExplorer can be confusing to work with initially. Users need to know what the products appropriate for their needs are before tackling searching and ordering through EarthExplorer.

Aerial Photography Summary Record System (APSRS)

The USGS has available for sale a CD-ROM "union list" of aerial photography projects called the Aerial Photography Summary Record System (APSRS). The APSRS database contains over 2.8 million records describing groups of photography, not individual photographs, produced by more than 600 federal, state, and local governments and private companies. The 2.8 million records correspond to over 600,000 projects. Each record uses the 7.5-minute topographic grid to group photographs from the same project together. A record may represent more than one photograph but will not include information about which photographs specifically.

APSRS consists of two databases, a database of project/group records and a database of contributors containing the name, address, and telephone number of each contributor. This product is becoming somewhat dated; its last version was released in May 1996. The database has been under consideration by the survey for transfer into the Internet realm but that has not happened yet. APSRS does not provide any kind of ordering information, nor does it explicitly identify specific photographs. The user must contact the producers or their agents to find out about availability and price.

State and Regional Sources

APSRS is a good place to begin searching for photographs produced at the state, regional, or local level but it does not fully reflect all aerial photograph producers. APSRS-listed producers are voluntary participants. Other, locally based commercial aerial photographers, can be found through the telephone book under entries such as "Photographers—Aerial." Many of the local producers are small firms that specialize in oblique photography. APSRS also does not include library or library-like collections of aerial photography. Many college and university libraries, as well as state and regional agencies, have collections of photography produced by different agencies covering different time periods. State and regional agencies that typically would have photography include departments of geology, environment resources or management, transportation, and planning. These agencies might also be good local resources for obtaining NHAP and NAPP photography. While some agencies might allow nonagency or nongovernmental use, others may restrict access to their collections. Some agencies, and increasingly libraries, will have descriptions of their collections and access policies posted on the Web.

REMOTE SENSING

Landsat Program

The Landsat program is a staple of U.S. civilian remote sensing analysis. Landsat 1–3 carried multispectral scanner (MSS) sensors (Table 10.2). Landsat 4 and 5 carry the more advanced Thematic Mapper (TM) sensor along with MSS (Table 10.3), and Landsat 7, launched in 1999, has an Enhanced Thematic Mapper (ETM) sensor that includes all of the TM bands plus a panchromatic band. The ground reso-

TABLE 10.3

Landsat 4–5 TM Bands.

Band number	Wavelength (μm)	Spectrial Location	Useful for
1	0.45-0.52	Blue-green	Underwater features; soil/rock vs. vegetation; cultural features
2	0.52-0.6	Green	Water turbidity differences; vegetation classification
3	0.63-0.69	Red	Vegetation vs. soil; snow cover; urban vs. rural
4	0.76-0.90	Near Infrared	Vegetation differences; soil moisture; water body location
5	1.55-1.75	Mid Infrared	Plant and soil moisture content;iron content in rocks; snow cover vs. clouds
6	10.40-12.50	Thermal Infrared	Heat mapping – estimates of soil moisture; rock identification; thermal water pollution
7	2.08-2.35	Mid Infrared	Vegetation and soil moisture

lution for the Landsat 7 bands is 30 meters, except for band 6 at 60 meters and the panchromatic band at 15 meters. Landsat 6, which had an ETM sensor, did not reach orbit when it was launched in 1993. The Landsat 7 Project Science Office maintains a Web site (http://landsat.gsfc.nasa.gov/index.html) that includes links to data resources, images, program documentation and news, and information about the agencies involved with the project.

Individually, the bands collected by Landsat display in black-and-white. Three bands can be combined to create false-color composites that can assist in identifying land cover circumstances. Colors in false-color composites can generally be interpreted thusly: black, clear water, lava, or asphalt; blues, silty water; reds, healthy vegetation; silver or gray, leafless or dead trees; blue gray, towns; white, snow or clouds, sand.

Other U.S. Programs

The National Oceanic and Atmospheric Administration (NOAA) has been launching meteorological data collecting satellites since 1970. NOAA has two different kinds of satellites monitoring weather conditions: Geostationary Operational Environmental Satellites (GOES), which maintain a position over a specific place on Earth in a geosynchronous orbit, and Polar Orbiting Environmental Satellites (POES), which orbit Earth by passing over both of the poles. These are the satellites that provide much of the imagery for television and Web weather broadcasts and forecasts. Of course, the sensors that these satellites carry are instrumental in tracking weather systems through data about temperatures, humidity, and cloud coverage, but other events that affect the atmosphere, such as major forest fires and volcanic eruptions, can also be monitored. Information about GOES and POES is available from NOAA's Office of Satellite Operations (http://www.oso.noaa.gov).

Beyond Landsat, NASA launched a number of its own weather satellites, including 14 TIROS (Television Infrared Observation Satellite) or TIROS-N/NOAA satellites (http://www.earth.nasa.gov/history/tiros/) in service from 1960 to the present; 9 ESSA (Earth Sciences Service Administration) satellites in service from 1966 to 1972; and 7 Nimbus satellites (http://www.earth.nasa.gov/history/nimbus/) in service from 1964 to 1994. A retrospective view of NASA's remote sensing and satellite activities is available at the Web site that celebrates 40 years of agency earth science activities (http://earth.nasa.gov/history/).

The United States Geological Surveys Earth Science Information Center's (ESIC) Web page on satellite imagery (http://ask.usgs.gov/satimage.html) includes links to information about satellite technology, remote sensing, and federal remote sensing programs. Information about purchasing data, including prices, can also be accessed from this site.

SPOT

The French SPOT (Système Pour l'Observation de la Terre) program is somewhat analogous to Landsat in that it provides full Earth coverage. Although it has roots in French governmental agencies, SPOT Image (http://www.spot.com) is a fully commercial enterprise. Five SPOT satellites have been launched since 1986. The SPOT satellites can collect data in both a black-and-white panchromatic mode (green-red spectral range) with a 10-meter ground resolution or a multispectral mode (three or four bands in green, red, and near infrared spectral ranges) with a ground resolution of 20 meters. SPOT attained international prominence with its coverage of the 1986 Chernobyl accident, Desert Storm preparations, and post-Gulf War United Nations inspections (*Commercial Observation Satellites,* 195).

Data and Printed Image Sources

Data and printed images are available from both the U.S. government and from commercial vendors. The biggest data vendor in the United States is the United States Geological Survey (USGS). Data from Landsat and other civilian projects can be searched for through the same EarthExplorer interface that is used to locate aerial photography.

Data also can be purchased from commercial suppliers, such as SPOT and Space Imaging (http://www.spaceimaging.com). Some older, "heritage" data is available for free from the NASA Landsat Web site, but it will require considerable preprocessing. Because digital satellite data can be very expensive both in terms of money and time, most individuals will probably not elect to purchase data, instead preferring to purchase photograph-like prints or posters.

Satellite imagery is often sold as decorative poster prints. Spaceshots (http://www.spaceshots.com) sells "natural color" satellite posters of areas such as countries, peninsulas, major metropolitan areas, and continents. Spaceshots posters are usually vividly colored,

with an emphasis on bright blues and greens. The scale of the images tends to be too small to do any intense analysis, but a viewer can get a general impression of terrain and urban pattern from the images.

Southwest Satellite Imaging has been specializing in poster images of areas in the arid southwest including the Grand Canyon, Big Bend National Park, and Death Valley. These images are usually at scales of 1:100,000 or 1:125,000, considerably larger than the Spaceshots images, because they focus on much smaller areas, and are not natural color, focusing on geologic formations, not vegetative land cover. Southwest Satellite Imaging products are available from Map Link (http://www.maplink.com).

The United States Geological Survey also produces poster-like printed satellite images. Sometimes there are topographic maps at the same scale on the verso. A list of satellite images is posted on the USGS Web site (http://mac.usgs.gov/mac/isb/pubs/forms/satimg.html) . Most of the USGS images are of the United States; there are also a number of images of Antarctica.

RESOURCES ABOUT REMOTE SENSING

Interpretation of Airphotos and Remotely Sensed Imagery
  Interpretation of Airphotos and Remotely Sensed Imagery is a lab manual with introductory text and exercises based on figures and illustrations included throughout the volume. The early chapters present essential information for successful aerial photography usage and for the use of imagery in general. The first three chapters cover basics of scale, measurement, and "image signatures," including information about the electromagnetic spectrum and image aspects (pattern, shape, orientation, size, etc.) that need to be considered in photograph interpretation. Chapters 4 through 8 focus on aerial photography and the remaining six chapters focus on satellite-based data collection and imagery. The text contained in *Interpretation of Airphotos and Remotely Sensed Imagery* is less technical, and somewhat more to-the-point, than that found in traditional textbooks. Not all of the questions posed by the exercises are about interpreting imagery; some work toward putting image interpretation and use into the context of research and problem solving. A selected bibliography and glossary of remote sensing terms are included. *Interpretation of Airphotos and Remotely Sensed Imagery* could serve as a quick introduction to data collection and image creation and interpretation.

Introductory Remote Sensing: Principles and Concepts

Introductory Remote Sensing: Digital Image Processing and Applications

Introductory Remote Sensing: Principles and Concepts and *Introductory Remote Sensing: Digital Image Processing and Applications* are companion texts. *Principles and Concepts* introduces remote sensing theory and applications by addressing in four chapters four fundamental questions: What is remote sensing?; What principles govern remote sensing?; How are remote sensing data obtained?; and What are the applications of remote sensing? (*Principles and Concepts*, xv). Although imagery is stressed, aerial photography is also discussed. Each chapter begins with a chapter outline and concludes with a self-assessment test and brief bibliography of suggested further readings. All of the chapters are extensively illustrated and include boxed examples (often mathematical problems with worked answers) and shaded boxes with complex descriptions and definitions. There also is a center section of color photographs and images. Answers to the self-assessment tests, along with a list of acronyms, a glossary, bibliographies, information about data sources, and a preview of *Introductory Remote Sensing: Digital Image Processing and Applications,* are included as appendices. *Introductory Remote Sensing: Principles and Concepts* is accompanied by a free Web site (http://www.remote-ensing.routledge.com/remote-sensing/default.html) that will expand the learning experience through image examples and exercises.

Introductory Remote Sensing: Digital Image Processing and Applications follows the same structure as *Principles and Concepts*. Digital remotely sensed data cannot be used without some kind of processing having been done. After an introductory chapter that reviews central remote sensing concepts, three chapters explains preprocessing data (the activities needed before images can be viewed), enhancing imagery to emphasize specific kinds of features or classify displayed data to discover patterns, and techniques used in environmental monitoring. The final chapter introduces case studies that explore how the previously discussed techniques are applied. As with its sister volume, *Digital image Processing and Applications* includes a center section of color illustrations and black-and-white illustrations throughout. The same appendices conclude the volume as in *Principles and Concepts. Digital Image Processing and Applications*

is accompanied by a CD-ROM with an image-processing software package and 77 data sets to provide a hands-on learning opportunity.

Introductory Remote Sensing, especially *Principles and Concepts,* may be a good first choice for reading about satellite-based imagery. The chapters are not overly mathematical; readers will not be bogged down either by equations or by lengthy passages of technical prose. Because the volumes are not large, they feel more approachable, not daunting like some of the other textbooks that are available.

Fundamentals of Remote Sensing and Airphoto Interpretation. 5th ed.

Fundamentals provides introductory college-level text information on both aerial photography and remote sensing. Basic understanding of map reading and math proficiency will be helpful in reading the text. Four chapters are devoted to aerial photography production and acquisitions, and three focus on non-photographic methods. The remaining seven chapters show how aerial photography and remotely sensed data are applied in different applications. Each chapter concludes with a short question set and a bibliography of further readings. This book is not for the casual reader. The information presented is densely written and may be technically challenging for the beginning interpreter. Nevertheless, the technical information is necessary for both understanding how aerial photography is created and for communicating with aerial photography producers. The chapters that examine photograph and image use in different disciplines are especially valuable because of the solid, real-world examples with illustrations and explanations that highlight the wide variety of applications for remotely gathered information. To take full advantage of the illustrations, a stereoscope will be needed.

Introduction to Remote Sensing. 3rd ed.

Most of *Introduction to Remote Sensing* focuses on satellite-based data collection and imagery. Twenty chapters are divided into four parts: "Foundations" which includes a historical overview and a review of electromagnetic radiation concepts, "Image Acquisition," "Analysis," and "Applications." Chapters include black-and-white illustrations (a section of color illustrations is in the center of the volume), review questions, and a bibliography. In many chapters, the text includes a number of Web site URLs as well as surface mail and telephone contact information for aerial photography, data, and imagery producers and vendors. The "Image Acquisition" chapters are syntheses of history, core concepts, and technological advances describing standard methods and programs for collecting remotely sensed data. The "Analysis" chapters occasionally require an advanced understanding of mathematical concepts to fully benefit from the information, hardly surprising because data collection and image interpretation is technologically and computationally complex. The chapters about applying imagery to specific kinds of research needs include plant sciences, geology, hydrology, and land use/land cover. The "Applications" part also includes an overview of geographic information systems (GIS) and incorporating imagery into GIS applications and a final chapter about expanding the use of remotely sensed imagery to investigate global patterns. Though the "Applications" chapters could be read without first reading the previous three chapters, if the reader does not have a prior grounding in imaging concepts, some of the information may be difficult to understand. All of the "Applications" chapters include contact information to assist in locating other kinds of appropriate data.

For the casual or first-time reader, *Introduction to Remote Sensing* will be daunting. Nevertheless, this is a foundation text. It thoughtfully and thoroughly conveys essential information about a complex topic through both theory and applications.

Commercial Observation Satellites

Instead of focusing on techniques of image interpretation or applications of remote sensing, *Commercial Observation Satellites* discusses the movement of satellite-based technology from governmental control into the hands of commercial corporations. Twenty-six chapters, divided into four sections, explore, summarize, and forecast current and emerging national and international policies; markets; national remote sensing programs; and environmental, political, and social applications of remotely sensed data. *Commercial Observation Satellites* will not aid in learning technical skills but it will help in situating technological advances; in making connections between governments, policies, and data availability; and in understanding how national policies and actions can have global data implications. In particular, the chapters in the "National Remote Sensing Programs & Policies" section are good digests of programs that either collect or use data. All of the chapters conclude with bibliographies, some including Web site references. Previous exposure to remote sensing concepts, agencies, and common acronyms would be helpful in reading *Commercial Observation Satellites,* but it is not

necessary. Because the text is packed so full with details, this volume is not light reading. *Commercial Observation Satellites* will ground readers in the organizational environments both commercial and governmental, in which remote sensing, including data collection, dissemination, and use, occurs.

The Remote Sensing Data Book

The Remote Sensing Data Book does not point to data resources. It is a dictionary of more than 700 common remote sensing terms and concepts. Programs, technologies, techniques, and characteristics of Earth's atmosphere and surface qualities are defined, often with cross-references to other definitions. Most of the illustrations are graphs, and many definitions include mathematical formulas. Some of the definitions also include Web site URLs. The entries vary in length from one or two lines to two pages. A brief bibliography concludes the volume. *The Remote Sensing Data Book* will be a useful complement to textbooks. It may also be of interest to remote sensing researchers to have on their office bookshelves.

The Remote Sensing Core Curriculum
(http://www.research.umbc.edu/~tbenja1/umbc7/)

The Remote Sensing Core Curriculum is an ongoing interorganizational project to develop five contributed volumes: Introduction to Photo Interpretation and Photogrammetry; Overview of Remote Sensing of the Environment; Introductory Digital Image Processing; Applications in Remote Sensing; and K-12 Education. The project has as its goal the provision of "resources to support a state-of-the-practice educational experience at our national and international collegiate institutions." The volumes vary in their states of completeness and level of detail. Many of the "chapters" are both text- and illustration-intensive and some will require substantial mathematical understanding. Much of the foundation material presented can be found in traditional ink-on-paper textbooks. The advantage to this presentation method is that the illustrations are in color and newer applications can be explored in shorter forms than they would have appeared as in professional or academic journals. An additional bonus is the list of links to satellite images available through the Web. Paper textbooks and lab manuals may better serve interested novices; this group of Web sites will work to whet appetites or quickly refresh memories.

Aerial photographs and images created from remotely sensed data give a different view of Earth from highly generalized and interpreted maps. Photographs and images give the user more control or input into the interpretation of land cover and land use along with a different understanding of how processes create landscapes.

BIBLIOGRAPHY

Aerial Photographs in the National Archives. Special List no. 25. Charles E. Taylor and Richard E. Spurr. Washington, D.C.: National Archives and Records Service, 1973.

Aerial Photography Summary Record System: APSRS CD-ROM. May, 1996. Reston, Va.: U.S. Geological Survey, Earth Science Information Center, 1996.

The Aerial Photo Sourcebook. Mary Rose Collins. Lanham, Md.: Scarecrow Press, 1998. ISBN: 0-8108-3519-3.

Basic Photo Interpretation: A Comprehensive Approach to Interpretation of Vertical Aerial Photography for Natural Resource Applications. Michael E. Rasher and Wayne Weaver. Fort Worth, Tex.: USDA Soil Conservation Service, National Cartographic Center, 1990.

Commercial Observation Satellites: At the Leading Edge of Global Transparency. John C. Baker, Kevin M. O'Connell, and Ray A. Williamson, eds. Santa Monica, Calif: RAND; Bethesda, Md.: American Society for Photogrammetry and Remote Sensing, 2000. ISBN: 0-8330-2872-3.

Fundamentals of Remote Sensing and Airphoto Interpretation. 5th ed. Thomas Eugene Avery and Graydon Lennis Berlin. New York: Macmillan, 1992. ISBN: 0-13-861006-1.

Guide to Cartographic Records in the National Archives. National Archives and Records Administration, Washington, D.C.: National Archives and Records Service, 1971. ISBN: 0-911333-19-3.

Guide to Federal Records in the National Archives of the United States. Robert B. Matchette and Anne B. Eales, comps. Washington, D.C.: National Archives and Records Administration, 1995. ISBN: 0-16-048312-3.

Interpretation of Airphotos and Remotely Sensed Imagery. Robert H. Arnold. Upper Saddle River, N.J.: Prentice Hall, 1997. ISBN: 0-02-303924-8.

Introduction to Remote Sensing. 3rd ed. James B. Campbell. New York: Guilford Press, 2002. ISBN: 1-57230-640-8.

Introductory Remote Sensing: Digital Image Processing and Applications. Paul J. Gibson. London: Routledge, 2000. ISBN: 0-415-18962-4.

Introductory Remote Sensing: Principles and Concepts. Paul J. Gibson. London: Routledge, 2000. ISBN: 0-415-19646-9.

The Remote Sensing Data Book. Gareth Rees. Cambridge: Cambridge University Press, 1999. ISBN: 0-521-48080-X.

On-line References

"Aerial Photographs." U.S. Geological Survey, 28 May 2003. <http://ask.usgs.gov/photos.html> (17 October 2003).

"Aerial Photography Summary Record System." Fact sheet 220–96, August 1998. U.S. Geological Survey, 31 December 2002. <http://mac.usgs.gov/mac/isb/pubs/fact sheets/fs22096.html> (17 October 2003).

"Aerial Products." U.S. Geological Survey, Earth Resources Observation Systems (EROS) Data Center, 2003. <http://edc.usgs.gov/products/aerial.html> (17 October 2003).

ARC: Archival Research Catalog. National Archives and Records Administration, 2003. <http://www.archives.gov/research_room/arc/> (17 October 2003).

Digital Orthophoto Quadrangle. U.S. Geological Survey, Western Mapping Center, 2003. <http://www-wmc.wr.usgs.gov/doq/> (17 October 2003).

"Digital Orthophoto Quadrangles (DOQ)." U.S. Geological Survey, Earth Resources Observation Systems (EROS) Data Center, 14 March 2003. <http://edc.usgs.gov/products/aerial/doq.html> (17 October 2003).

EarthExplorer. U.S. Geological Survey, Earth Resources Observation Systems (EROS) 1 May 2003. <http://edcsns17.cr.usgs.gov/EarthExplorer/> (17 October 2003).

Earth Resources Observation Systems (EROS) Data Center. Home page. U.S. Geological Survey, Earth Resources Observation Systems (EROS) Data Center, 2002. <http://edcwww.cr.usgs.gov> (17 October 2003).

Guide to Federal Records in the National Archives of the United States. Web version, updated from *Guide to Federal Records in the National Archives of the United States,* comp. Robert B. Matchette and Anne B. Eales. National Archives and Records Administration, 2003. <http://www.archives.gov/research_room/federal_records_guide/> (17 October 2003).

Introductory Remote Sensing (Principles and Concepts). Paul Gibson. Routledge, 30 March 2001. <http://www.remote-sensing.routledge.com/remote-sensing/default.html> (17 October 2003).

Landsat 7. National Atmospheric and Space Administration, Landsat 7 Project Science Office, 7 October 2003. <http://landsat.gsfc.nasa.gov/index.html> (17 October 2003).

Looking at Earth from Space: 40 Years of NASA Earth Science. NASA, SAIC Information Services, 15 July 2003. <http://earth.nasa.gov/history/> (17 October 2003).

Map Link. Home page. Map Link, 2003. <http://www.maplink.com> (17 October 2003).

The Nimbus Program. NASA, SAIC Information Services, 13 November 2001. <http://www.earth.nasa.gov/history/nimbus/> (17 October 2003).

Office of Satellite Operations. Home page. NOAA, National Environmental Satellite, Data, and Information

GEOGRAPHIC INFORMATION

176

Service, 23 September 2003. <http://www.oso.noaa.gov> (17 October 2003)

Photo Finder. U.S. Geological Survey, EROS Data Center, 25 March 2002. <http://edcsns17.cr.usgs.gov/finder/finder_main.pl?dataset_name=NAPP> (17 October 2003).

Remote Sensing Core Curriculum. Home page. Various contributors. Hosted by University of Maryland, Baltimore County, 25 August 1999. <http://www.research.umbc.edu/~tbenja1/umbc7/> (17 October 2003).

"Research Room: Cartographic and Architectural Records." National Archives and Records Administration, 2003. <http://www.archives.gov/research_room/media_formats/cartographic_and_architectural_records.html> (17 October 2003).

"Satellite Image Maps List." Product List 67-0035, February 2000. U.S. Geological Survey, 31 December 2002. <http://mac.usgs.gov/mac/isb/pubs/forms/satimg.html> (17 October 2003).

"Satellite Imagery." U.S. Geological Survey, 6 June 2003. <http://ask.usgs.gov/satimage.html> (17 October 2003)

Space Imaging. Home page. Space Imaging, 2003. <http://www.spaceimaging.com> (17 October 2003).

Spaceshots: Images and Imagination. Home page. Spaceshots, 2003. <http://www.spaceshots.com> (17 October 2003).

SPOT Image Corporation. Home page. SPOT, 28 September 2003. <http://www.spot.com> (17 October 2003).

Terraserver, Home page. Microsoft, 2003. <http://terraserver-usa.com> (17 October 2003).

The TIROS Program: Television Infrared Observation Satellite. NASA, SAIC Information Services, 15 July 2003. <http://www.earth.nasa.gov/history/tiros/> (17 October 2003).

USDA Aerial Photography Field Office, Home page. U.S. Department of Agriculture, Aerial Photography Field Office, 2003. <http://www.apfo.usda.gov/> (17 October 2003).

CHAPTER 11
Geographic Information Systems

TOPICS COVERED

Uses of GIS
GIS Components
    Hardware
    Software
    Data and Metadata
        Raster vs. Vector Data
        Attribute Data
        Data Conversion from Paper to Digital
        Data Collection
        Metadata
        Spatial Data Transfer Standard
        Data Sources
    People
    Queries or Problems
Finding Out More about GIS
    Books
    Periodicals
    Web Sites
    Organizations

MAJOR SOURCES DISCUSSED

"2001 Recommended Specifications for Public Access Workstations in Federal Depository Libraries"
ESRI ArcExplorer
MapInfo ProViewer
GRASS

GIS Data Sources
Spatial Data Transfer Standard
National Geospatial Data Clearinghouse
Starting the Hunt
The Geography Network
The Manual of Federal Geographic Data Products
Digital Maps & Data
Geographical Information Systems
Geographic Information Systems and Science
The GIS Book
Fundamentals of Geographic Information Systems
Getting Started with Geographic Information Systems
Principles of Geographical Information Systems
ESRI Press Dictionary of GIS Terminology
GeoWorld
ARCNews and *ARCUser*
Map Info Magazine
International Journal of Geographical Information Science
Cartography and Geographic Information Science
Geographic Information Systems
GIS.com
About GIS.com
The GIS Portal
Association of American Geographers Geographic Information Specialty Group
Geospatial Information and Technology Association (GITA)
Urban and Regional Information Systems Association (URISA)

Geographic information systems (GIS) are computer hardware, software, data, and people combined to answer spatially based questions and to provide new ways of looking at geographic information to find solutions or make decisions. GIS brings together expertise from many different disciplines and is used in areas as diverse as archaeology and precision agriculture. GIS has roots in geography, cartography, surveying, computer and information science, and photogrammetry and remote sensing.

Using a GIS goes far beyond making a map; GIS allows for data from disparate sources to be viewed and analyzed in new combinations and contexts. A map is only one of a number of possible results when querying a GIS. But because the end result of using a GIS is so often a map, many think that GIS is no more than using a computer to create maps. GIS is much more than computer assisted cartography (CAC) or computer aided design and drafting (CADD). Neither CAC nor CADD has the capabilities of a GIS for analyzing spatial data, comparing, contrasting, measuring, finding relationships, or building predictions.

There is not a single agreed-upon definition for GIS although they are all similar to each other in many regards. The United States Geological Survey's GIS Web site (http://erg.usgs.gov/isb/pubs/gis_poster) reads, "A GIS is a computer system capable of capturing, storing, analyzing, and displaying geographically referenced information; that is, data identified according to their locations. Practitioners also define a total GIS as including the procedures, operating personnel, and spatial data that go into the system." An earlier definition published in 1989 by Dueker and Kjerne specifically indicates that a GIS focuses on the Earth: A system of hardware, software, data, people, organizations and institutional arrangements for collecting, storing, analyzing, and disseminating information about areas of the Earth (*Multipurpose Cadastre*, 7–8). GIS can refer to a software package, the integration of many components as indicated in these two definitions, or the process of analysis required to transform data into usable information for decision making, problem solving, and discovery.

Assembling, storing, manipulating, and displaying data should be thought of as the four essential subsystems of a GIS. If just one is lacking, a GIS is not fully functional. Assembling data, or data input, is necessary because this is how data are fed into the system. Without data there is no information for the system to work on. Data can come from a number of different sources and can be in a variety of formats. It could be scanned or digitized maps and photographs, remotely sensed data, or data that describes attributes of places and features. The data must be managed (stored) in such a way that appropriate data can be located in consistent ways and queried. Storing and then retrieving data by selecting data that meet specified parameters is as essential as being able to input data in the first place.

The ability to manipulate or analyze data, going beyond merely finding data that meet a certain set of requirements (retrieval) to being able to compare, aggregate, reclassify, and create projections of future situations, is the heart of a full GIS. Analysis includes combining different kinds of data, such as the number of people in a county and the square mileage of a county, to create new data, population density. The ability to have a GIS analyze large data sets is core to being able to answer basic geographical questions, such as "Why is this here?" and "How does this place impact other places?" With analysis capabilities, new data and information can be generated to find solutions to problems. Without analysis, a GIS is little more than an input-output system. Analysis capabilities are what is most likely to be removed or reduced in less-than-full GIS systems.

Displaying data, the final subsystem, can be done in a number of different ways through a GIS. A single number could be displayed; for instance, a query could be constructed to return the total number of bears found in a six-county region. To generate a table, the bear-related query might request the number of female and the number of male bears tagged in each of the six counties, giving a three-column table (county name, number of female bears, number of male bears). A graph could be created showing the number of miles covered per day by a specific bear as indicated by the data sent by a transmission collar, and a bear map might show where each of the tagged bears was captured and released or could show territories of individual bears.

Overlays, or layers, are how a GIS works with data; data about a single aspect, for example roads, are entered into the system in such a way that the data layer can be displayed, or not displayed, as a single element. A GIS user can decide to display many layers or just a selected few. Within a layer, the objects and locations represented can have different attributes. A roads layer might show interstates and federal highways, state highways, county roads, and unmaintained gravel roads. A soils layer could either show where specific kinds of soils are located or could show different rates of drainage. A surface water layer could display where rivers are located with the appropriate names plus flow rates coded into the database. Using the appropriate layers, specific sites can be located and connections between sites can be determined. Densities of populations and occurrences of events can be tracked.

Spatial relationships between activities and sites can be discovered or predicted.

USES OF GIS

Possible uses of GIS range from tracking land use permits in a city to forecasting impacts of changes in the jet stream on types of forest distribution. From local to global, from societal to environmental, if an activity or action has a geographic aspect, it can be investigated using GIS. Many applications can be read about in academic journals and trade magazines. Displaying results of GIS-based investigations and making GIS data available for manipulation through the Web is becoming increasingly common. The previously mentioned USGS Web site on geographic information systems includes very brief descriptions of basic GIS capabilities along with examples of using GIS to make maps, select sites, plan for emergency response, and simulate environmental conditions in varying scenarios.

Web services maintained by local governments can assist users in determining which service districts a specific site is in, and what the topography is like, and, if zoomed in far enough, might display recent aerial photography. Sample local government Web sites can be located by searching for "interactive gis" with terms such as county, city, village, or town.

National atlases on the Web such as the *National Atlas of the United States* (http://www.national atlas.gov), the *National Atlas of Canada* (http://atlas. gc.ca/site/index.html), and the *Australian Natural Resources Atlas* (http://audit.ea.gov.au/anra/atlas_home. cfm) are basic GIS applications. Each allows different layers to be displayed to facilitate discovering connections and causalities between places and events. These sites only allow for displaying data in ways predetermined by the Web site designers and developers. Layers can be turned on and off, maps can be zoomed and panned, but the layers cannot be displayed or visually stacked in any order other than determined by the designer. Display colors cannot be changed, and there is no way to query the database to determine how many acres with a specific state or in a user-determined area were planted in alfalfa, received more than 100 inches of rain during the previous year, or are devoted to strip-mining or clear-cutting.

The road map and routing utilities available through the Web, such as MapBlast (http://www.mapblast. com) and MapQuest (http://www.mapquest.com), use basic GIS capabilities: displaying maps, address matching to find starting and ending points, and creating routes based on specific parameters and constraints. Selecting options and inputting addresses into one of these services to prepare a map with textual directions for driving from a specific address in Minneapolis, Minnesota, to Atlanta, Georgia, avoiding tollways and taking the most scenic route, is just like building a query in a GIS. These free driving directions services are available through the Web for the United States because the United States government provides access to basic, federally collected geographic data at low or no cost with few copyright or licensing restrictions placed on its use. All of the Web driving directions utilities are based on the same set of U.S. data, cleaned up and corrected to varying degrees. Although the display will vary, the results from these services will be similar. Most of the trip will be routed on federal interstate highways, ignoring other U.S. or state highways that might be more direct.

These Web-based GIS applications are all end products of completely functioning GIS installations that were used to massage, aggregate, and package raw data so that it could be easily displayed through a Web viewer. Viewers do not allow much flexibility in data display and usually do not allow for importing additional data from outside sources. In these ways, Web site developers maintain control over the data being displayed through their sites.

Results from GIS activities that solve specific problems or are applied to narrow applications, beyond the general display and dissemination of data, can be found in academic journals, trade magazines, and on the Web. Many of the U.S. federal agencies describe on their how they are using GIS. At the National Park Service site (http://www.nps.gov/gis/), the programmatic goal for using GIS is "to provide usable geographic data and information...for scientifically based management of park resources and for park planning." GIS has been specifically used to help restore bighorn sheep to western parks, to share data between numerous agencies about land development in the Blue Ridge Parkway Region, and to map shoreline attributes in Glacier Bay National Park and Preserve. The National Park Service also is working with the United States Geological Survey to map vegetation communities in more than 250 national parks using both existing data and newly collected data.

GIS COMPONENTS

A fully functioning GIS requires a number of different pieces: hardware, software, data, and people and organizations. If one part is missing, GIS has not been implemented.

Hardware

Since GIS is inherently computer-based, some consideration needs to be given to acquiring appropriate computer hardware and peripherals. The Federal Depository Library Program of the Government Printing Office has published a group of recommended standards in *Administrative Notes;* the standards also have been added to the Federal Depository Library Program's Web site (http://www.access.gpo.gov/su_docs/fdlp/computers/rs.html). The recommendations, "2003 Recommended Specifications for Public Access Workstations in Federal Depository Libraries," are intended to cover both workstations that access text and statistical data and workstations used for GIS applications. Throughout the document, there are additions labeled "For Cartographic Data Use"; these additions need to be taken seriously if planning for GIS because they substantially increase the computing capabilities of the workstations. They also may substantially increase the price of a workstation. The Federal Depository Library Program's recommendations cover the processor, memory, ports, I/O bus, video and audio, drive bays, hard disk space, external or removable storage, DVD and CD-R/W drives, monitor, printer, keyboard and mouse, and external connectivity. Software, including operating system, is also discussed with the specific recommendations for cartographic use including ArcView 3.0 or higher, Landview, MapInfo 4.5 or higher, or similar packages. While the Federal Depository Library Program's recommendations are a good starting point, the software package selected and its intended uses and output needs need to also be considered.

Software

GIS capabilities can be found at three different levels: viewer, desktop, and workstation or professional. Viewer software, allowing visual "inspection" of data, is often free, tends to require both less-intensive computer system capabilities and less-extensive training to use. Some desktop packages are free while others can cost more than $3000. The desktop packages are similar in some ways to common word processing and spreadsheet software packages. They may require some hands-on training, at minimum working with a manual and through examples. Desktop packages will be appropriate for single-person or smaller implementations of GIS. Workstation-based GIS, although often similar in look and feel to desktop GIS, is most appropriate for large implementations and will require a system administrator. These also are the most expensive to purchase.

GIS software must have a wide range of capabilities. GIS software assists in converting data to information. At the most fundamental level, the software stores and analyzes data and displays the, hopefully meaningful, results or information. The software must have appropriate capabilities for entering data, for storing data using a database management system, for querying and analyzing the data, and for presenting the results of the queries. The query and analysis tools included in a GIS software package will determine the package's flexibility in being able to meet a variety of different applications and to use a wide range of data types. GIS software currently is tending more toward graphical user interfaces instead of command language interfaces. Early GIS software often was only able to work with either raster or vector data, not both; now nearly all packages, including free software that does little more than display data, work with both in many different file formats.

For Free (or nearly free). There are many GIS software options available; some are free and can be downloaded from the Web giving an opportunity to "taste" GIS before making a financial or time commitment. Many of these free software packages are earlier versions of commercial software, have many capabilities removed, or only allow data viewing. The choice of viewer will depend on the format that most of the data needing to be examined is in and the "full" GIS system that might have already been made by an affiliated parent organization or some other related group.

ESRI ArcExplorer (http://www.esri.com/arcexplorer)

ESRI's ArcExplorer can be downloaded without charge from the ESRI Web site or purchased on CD-ROM for a minimal fee. While it supports a number of different data formats, including a number of image formats, no data editing can be done, only querying and viewing. Maps can be made using already existing and appropriately formatted data. Multiple layers can be displayed, maps can be zoomed, panned, and printed. Some basic analysis, including address matching, can be performed. ArcExplorer can also assist in downloading data from the Web. Plus, ArcExplorer can be licensed so that it can be included on CD-ROM-based publications.

MapInfo ProViewer (http://www.mapinfo.com/
   products/Download.cfm?ProductID=1062)

MapInfo's ProViewer allows the viewing of data created using MapInfo Professional. It performs basic functions such as zooming and panning, selecting objects and displaying statistics for those objects, and printing. ProViewer can also facilitate inserting maps in Word documents. Download of ProViewer from MapInfo's Web site is free, although registration is required. The ProViewer download includes a set of basic world data to help learn how to use the software.

GRASS (http://grass.itc.it/index.html)

Although it is free, GRASS is far more than the ArcExplorer and ProViewer GIS data viewers. GRASS, Geographic Resources Analysis Support System, is a fully functional GIS software package originally developed by the U.S. Army Construction Engineering Research Laboratories (USA-CERL) for use in military land management and environmental planning activities. The authors of the GRASS Web site refer to GRASS as "the world's largest open source GIS." GRASS is primarily a server- or main-frame-mounted package. In 2001, the developers were working on porting the software to a Microsoft Windows (NT and 2000) environment. GRASS was originally command line driven, but it now operates using a graphical user interface.

For Fee. Full GIS software packages are available for purchase from a number of different companies, all of which have Web sites and advertise in the GIS trade magazines. Reviews can be found in popular GIS magazines and at GIS Web sites. While the ways in which these different software packages operate internally differ, they will all perform the same basic functions on data: input, storage, management, query or search, analysis, and output of results. Responding to desktop and Internet usage, GIS software packages have become increasingly customizable using standard development tools such as Visual Basic and Java.

GIS operations no longer occur just in a mainframe office environment. In response to the need to move GIS onto desktops, handhelds, and through the Internet, the largest of the GIS software vendors have developed interoperable product "families" containing members that use the same data structure but have slightly different processing mechanisms or capabilities. ESRI's (http://www.esri.com) suite of GIS software includes ArcExplorer, ArcIMS, ArcPad, ArcView, and ArcInfo. Recently, ESRI began labeling its suite of software products as the "ArcGIS Scalable System" to help its clients understand that the different software packages were related. Autodesk (http://www.autodesk.com), which originally sold CAD (computer assisted drafting) software, has created AutoCAD LT, MapGuide, On-Site, World, and AutoCAD/World. Unlike ESRI's ArcInfo, which was originally a command line driven package, MapInfo's (http://www.mapinfo.com) products, ProViewer, MapXtreme, MapXtend, and MapInfo Professional, have always been Windows-based. There are many more companies from which to choose beyond these three.

Data and Metadata

Without data, a geographic information system would have nothing to process and thus would produce no analyses or any other kind of result. But data are expensive. As much as 75 percent of a GIS implementation budget could be devoted to data collection or acquisition. Unfortunately, not all data "are created equal." Data can be collected, or aggregated after collection, at large (fine-level of detail) scale or small, and data do not necessarily all have the same level of accuracy or reliability.

Data for GIS applications are produced by many different organizations and originate from a number of different data collection activities. The spatial nature of data is essential for use in a GIS because data are overlaid and analyzed, in part, because of their co-location in geographic space. Data can be collected in the field by using a global positioning system (GPS) or by collecting field samples. Datasets, such as census counts in tabular format, can be imported into a GIS. Often, scanned or digitized maps along with remote sensing images and scanned aerial photographs are harvested for their data content or are used as base layers.

GIS Data Sources

GIS Data Sources provides an overview of geospatial data basics with a focus on locating data. The 10 chapters build sequentially on each other from defining data needs to understanding problems of using data and knowing trends to watch. Five appendices list and describe data sources grouped by government or source type, and a glossary of terms is also included.

Near the beginning of each chapter is a "GIS Data Law" that functions as a focal or summary statement for the chapter. The text is straightforward, concise, and jargon-free. Some of the chapter sections include bulleted lists of points to remember or consider when making data acquisition and manipulation decisions. Readers will become acquainted with data formats, data clearinghouses, metadata, storage and transfer mechanisms, pros and cons of creating data as well as basic steps in creating digital geospatial data, and a wide variety of common data-use problems with potential solutions and things to think about to avoid those problems.

The five appendices of data sources focus on Internet-based resources. Each entry in the U.S. federal, state, or regional and local appendices includes the name of the data source, a Web site URL, e-mail and telephone contact information, and a brief description of the kinds of data available. The federal and state sites are primarily government agencies or universities. The regional and local sites are groups that focus on the needs of county or local governments; these sites might not have data available directly but will facilitate contacting appropriate offices and officials. The private sources appendix lists geospatial data "aggregators," mainly focusing on U.S. federal products. The foreign sources appendix lists 22 international, federal-level, and some state-level Web sites; most focus on western Europe, North America, or Australia. The final appendix, "other," includes on-line directories to GIS resources and Web sites for organizations with an interest in GIS.

GIS Data Sources will provide a solid introduction and fundamental grounding in looking for and acquiring geospatial data. It should help the reader pose questions about determining the appropriateness of a data set for a specific project.

Raster vs. Vector Data

GIS software and automated mapping packages require geographic data to be in specific, sometimes proprietary, file formats in the same way that Microsoft text documents are labeled ".doc" and Word Perfect documents are ".wpd." Underlying the formats are two kinds of data structures, raster and vector.

Raster data could be thought of as being arranged in a grid, rows and columns of cells uniform in size and shape; in some circumstances these cells might be referred to as pixels. The cells might not be square; triangular, rectangular, and hexagonal cells could also

be used. Each cell has an assigned value—even "zero," "null," "not present," or "no data available" will be coded. Every place on the landscape has a value because the raster format treats the landscape as a continuous surface. Because of the regular shape of the cells, a raster file can only approximate the shape of objects or landscape features. The ground area represented by a pixel, the resolution, will differ between data sets depending upon the original data collection and how the data have been aggregated. An approximation that more closely represents a feature's shape can be created by collecting and storing data using a finer grid with smaller cells or pixels, but finer grids with higher resolutions create larger files. Depending on the collection scale and resolution, some of the values assigned to pixels will represent exactly what is on the ground at the corresponding location. Other values can be generated as needed by the GIS by applying techniques like weighted averages, which determines how much a location is like other locations dependent on the distance away from other places. Pixels in remotely sensed images will be the average of all the ground cover types sensed for the area covered by the pixel. TIFF, GIF, JPG, and BMP are all raster data formats. Types of data often stored as raster data include satellite imagery, scanned maps and aerial photographs, elevation models, forest types, and soils. Scanned USGS topographic maps are a very common government raster product.

Vector data are the x and y location coordinates for points, lines, and polygons. Features represented as points, such as traffic signals, street lights, individual trees, or water towers, are designated in the database using a single coordinate pair. Line features, like railroads, highways, streams, or high-tension power lines, are represented by strings of coordinate pairs that include a starting point, an ending point, and points in between where the linelike feature changes direction. Polygons, features with areas like ponds, farm fields, national forests, and cities, are indicated in the database by a closed loop of coordinate pairs; the sequence will begin and end at exactly the same point with intervening points giving the polygon's specific shape. For objects represented as lines or polygons, using more coordinate pairs to define the object's shape will result in a shape that more closely fits the object's actual shape. Vector format files generally are not used to represent continuous surface data; vector data are usually used to represent discrete landscape elements. Boundaries of census areas and counties are commonly vector format files as are files depicting railroads, watersheds, wetlands, and earthquake epi-centers. All of the major commercially produced GIS software packages have their own vector file format; most of the packages are able to read or convert files from other producers. TIGER files from the United States Bureau of the Census and digital line graphs (DLGs) from the United States Geological Survey are two common vector products created by the federal government.

Attribute Data

Vector and raster data are spatial or geographic in nature. They show where a certain kind of object is located such as oak or pine forests or four-lane interstate highways. Detailed information, called attribute data, about objects, such as forest age and density or a time series of traffic volume, is often stored in a separate database that might appear very similar to a spread-sheet. Vector and raster data describe where, and attri-bute data describe what about where, including dates, measurements, names, and values. In a GIS applica-tion focusing on railroads, vector data might be used to locate rail lines while attribute data would record information about track maintenance, weekly traffic amounts, which companies were renting the rail line, and schedules. *The National Atlas of the United States* Web site includes a number of data table files (.dbf) for attributes, such as information collected during the 1980 and 1990 censuses, distributions of butterflies and invasive plant species, West Nile Virus, and wildlife mortality.

Data Conversion from Paper to Digital

The data presented graphically by maps can be con-verted to electronic formats by two different processes, scanning and digitizing. Data conversion can be expen-sive in terms of time and labor. The need to convert data from paper to digital form must be carefully considered, as does the method of conversion, before beginning.

Scanning captures a raster image of the entire printed item, everything on the item including printed symbols, handwritten notes, folds, dirt stains, and cof-fee cup rings. Generally, higher resolution scanning is necessary for converting graphics for GIS use. If the selected pixel size or number of dots per inch is set too low, small features might not appear in the resulting file because they were too small to be captured and stored. Similarly, if the scanning resolution is too low, objects next to each other could be merged together because the space between them was too small to be

detected and recorded by the scanner. Higher scanning resolutions, as well as larger original objects, create larger files. Small, office-sized flat document scanners can produce high quality scans fairly inexpensively. Unfortunately, office scanners often cannot handle an image larger than 8.5-by-14 inches, but seaming soft-ware can be used to merge sections of a large item to-gether. There are also large format scanners including drum scanners, flatbed scanners, and roll scanners. These all require considerable expertise as well as capital outlay. For casual or occasional use, a smaller document scanner might be more than adequate to meet scanning needs.

Digitizing maps, and creating vector format files, mimics the process of drawing a map. Digitizing is not an automated process like scanning; it requires a human operator to trace geographic features. After at-taching a map to a digitizing tablet, which has a grid of wires inside to sense the location of the digitizing puck, which looks very much like a computer mouse, the operator manually traces the required features, pressing a button on the puck in any place that the dig-itizing system needs to record a location. Digitizing systems can also be configured to collect data point locations automatically at a predetermined interval, either time or distance, as the operator moves the puck from the starting to the ending point. The more often the button is pressed or the location is automatically recorded, the more detailed and larger the resulting file. Digitizing will be more labor and time consuming for more complex or detailed maps. Because digitiz-ing relies so heavily on the training and abilities of a human operator, the quality of data capture, in partic-ular the accuracy of location, can vary widely. Digitiz-ing works well for simple graphics. For more involved maps, the image could be collected by scanning, cre-ating a raster format file that could later be converted to a vector format file if necessary.

Data Collection

Data for GIS applications can be collected in a number of different ways. Data can be harvested from paper maps and photographs by scanning or digitiz-ing. Attribute data can be collected via surveys such as the decennial census, telephone polls, or voting exit polls. Historic data can be gleaned from old records or first-person accounts. Data also can be collected by satellite.

Current conditions can be inventoried by hand in the field with location information recorded using global positioning system (GPS). GPS uses multiple satellites that send and receive synchronized radio signals to assist in measuring the distances between a location on the ground and three or four satellites simultaneously. Each of the individual satellite-to-ground lengths creates an arc of points equidistant from the satellite. The location of the GPS receiver on the ground is determined by trilateration (similar to triangulation); it is at the location where the arcs intersect. The GPS satellite network and technology was originally developed by the United States Department of Defense for launching missiles from submarines. Until May 2000, GPS signals were intentionally degraded so that non-U.S. or nonmilitary GPS users would not be able to pinpoint locations with the same accuracy as U.S. military users. GPS users had to be able to correct for deliberately programmed location errors. But because GPS had become a global navigational and scientific resource, the intentional degradation, officially called Selective Availability, was turned off on May 1, 2000, with no intention of turning it back on. Information about discontinuing Selective Availability, including President William Clinton's remarks and a list of how increased GPS accuracy benefits civilians, is available through the Web (http://www.igeb.gov/sa).

Beyond serious location work, GPS is being used by the "Degree Confluence Project" to locate, visit, and photograph each place where integer latitude and longitude designations intersect (http://www.confluence.org/index.php). The sport of geocaching is a treasure hunt, using a GPS unit and some basic maps, to locate "treasure troves" identified only by their latitude/longitude coordinates (http://www.geocaching.com).

Understanding the GPS includes introductory information about GPS and GPS use. Each topic, or subtopic, contained is covered in two pages, the first a graphic similar in appearance to an overhead transparency or slide from a lecture presentation and the second page containing brief text. The volume also includes a glossary and a short bibliography. Although short on specifics and details, *Understanding the GPS* will give a quick overview as well as a grounding in fundamental GPS concepts. Trimble Navigation, one of the leading manufacturers of GPS equipment, has developed a nontechnical Web-based tutorial on GPS, "All About GPS" (http://www.trimble.com/gps/index.html). The illustrated discussion about GPS found at Geographer's Craft (http://www.colorado.edu/geography/gcraft/notes/gps/gps_f.html) is more technical than Trimble's.

Metadata

Federal agencies responsible for collecting or creating digital geospatial data sets are mandated to document the collection, creation, and manipulation processes that ultimately result in a data set. The description of these processes, as well as descriptions of a data set's subject and geographic scope, quality, and the people or agency responsible for creating the data, is called *metadata,* data about data. Metadata is very similar to descriptions of books in library catalogs, but it is much more detailed because digital geospatial data cannot be visually previewed without assisting technologies. Also, digital geospatial data do not have conventional parts such as title pages or title panels in books or maps. The metadata is necessary to identify the data set.

The federal metadata standard, developed by the Federal Geographic Data Committee (FGDC), consists of seven basic kinds of information: identification, data quality, spatial data organization, spatial reference, entity and attribute, distribution, and metadata reference. Identification information is very similar to a book's title page information: data set title, geographic area covered, age of data, and information about acquiring or accessing the data set. Data quality information includes information that will help in assessing the data set's accuracy, precision, and completeness plus a description of how the data were prepared. Spatial data organization describes whether the data are vector, raster, or a table of attributes. Spatial reference information will indicate the kind of coordinate system and the set's projection. Entity and attribute information names and defines the different kinds of objects represented in the data set. Distribution information will include specific contact information as well as use restrictions, data formats and physical media available, and purchase or use fees. Metadata reference information helps track how and when the metadata was prepared.

Because the federal government is the largest producer of digital geospatial data in the United States and because standardized metadata assists in sharing data through geospatial data clearinghouses, many state and local agencies as well as private corporations are using the FGDC metadata standard to prepare metadata. Ideally, metadata is created by the data producer at the same time that the data set is being prepared. When downloading free data from the Web, or using data from other sources, the metadata will be important for being able to judge the compatibility of one data set with others. For instance, data about land use collected at a very gross scale, perhaps only five or six sample locations within a square mile, is too generalized to be appropriate for overlaying with data collected by the Bureau of the Census that have been aggregated to areas the size of city blocks. If there is a great scale, and ensuing generalization, difference between a data set that represents Great Lakes shorelines and a second data set that represents lakeside forests, forests could appear to be growing in Lake Superior. The information supplied by the metadata will also indicate what kinds of transformations might be needed to coordinate systems or projections so that data sets will overlay correctly.

A fact sheet about metadata is available through the Federal Geographic Data Committee's Web site on metadata (http://www.fgdc.gov/metadata/metadata.html). This Web site also includes the metadata content standard, training materials for learning how to create metadata, tools that might help create metadata, and other general informational pieces.

Spatial Data Transfer Standard

The federal government has put into place a Spatial Data Transfer Standard (SDTS) to facilitate exchange of geospatial data between governmental agencies. As with the metadata standard, federal agencies are required to use SDTS, and the standard has been made available to and is being used by state and local governments as well as academic and commercial data producers. SDTS does not directly transform geospatial data from one proprietary format to another; it functions as an intermediate step, identifying and encoding data from the original format into a commonly understood format that other proprietary software platforms can manipulate and translate into the required format. Because federal agencies are required to distribute their data according to the SDTS standard, any GIS application will be able to ingest and manipulate the data. Saving data following SDTS is somewhat analogous to saving a word processing document as a .txt file or a database as a comma-delimited ASCII text file. Both of these file types can be read by a number of, often competing, software packages.

Information about SDTS is available through the United States Geological Survey (http://mcmweb.er.usgs.gov/sdts). The standard itself is quite lengthy but some general overviews are available at the users guides and training materials portion of the Web site, including one for "senior managers" that is concise

and less technical and another for "technical managers" that is intended as an introduction for individuals responsible for implementing SDTS or using SDTS-based files. Many of the United States Geological Survey's data sets are in SDTS; older geospatial data might still be in USGS custom ASCII formats but the survey encourages use of SDTS.

Data Sources

Coupling FGDC metadata standard use with SDTS compliance has facilitated the development of geospatial data clearinghouses. These Web-based services are often decentralized systems of servers that host searchable descriptions, a.k.a. metadata, for geospatial data sets. The ANSI Z39.50 standard is used for query development, database search, and results presentation. Metadata descriptions will always be the result of a query and search, but some of the metadata might include links that will enable data downloads or direct the reader to information about data licensing or purchase options.

National Geospatial Data Clearinghouse

The Federal Geographic Data Committee maintains a Web site about its clearinghouse work (http://www.fgdc.gov/clearinghouse/clearinghouse.html) that includes an entry point into the National Geospatial Data Clearinghouse, "Search for Geospatial Data." The National Geospatial Data Clearinghouse includes databases from U.S. federal agencies; regional, state, and local agencies and organizations; and non-U.S. national- and state-level agencies as well as international organizations.

First, the user must select the closest clearinghouse gateway from a group of six; the servers searched through the six gateways is exactly the same for each. The clearinghouse can be searched in three different ways: by completing a Web form with bounding coordinates or desired text, by using a Web form that searches desired text but includes an interactive map instead of bounding coordinate input boxes, or by working through a sequence of wizard pages that assist in building a query. The first two search options require the user to specifically select data servers to be searched. The wizard function guides the user in selecting servers without naming the servers specifically but by asking the user to select topics of interest. Twenty-one interest groups, reflecting different aspects of both human and physical geography, can be searched.

For all three search methods, users must be aware of the differences between searching with "and" and searching with "or." Selecting specific databases for searching without using the wizard gives the searcher greater control and possibly better focused results. The wizard makes some strange suggestions for databases; when searching for transportation information for Illinois, the wizard suggested the Chile Instituto Geographic Militar, a Guatemalan clearinghouse; the Honduran Centro de Informacion Geograica; and the Southwest Region Road Map of National Resource Data and Information—none at all geographically related to Illinois and none with any matching results. It will speed searching if the user removes databases that seem to be unlikely to produce appropriate results from the list of suggestions before beginning the search.

The United States federal government is the largest producer and distributor of geographic data in the United States. Some of the data identified through searching the National Geospatial Data Clearinghouse can be accessed directly through the appropriate agency's Web site. TIGER/Line files and other geographic products can be downloaded from the continuously updated Bureau of the Census site (http://www.census.gov/geo/www). National Wetlands Inventory data can be downloaded from the Fish and Wildlife Service (http://www.nwi.fws.gov); and digital line graphs (DLGs) and digital elevation models (DEMs) are available through the United States Geological Survey (http://edc.usgs.gov/geodata/). The National Geospatial Data Clearinghouse is most useful for quickly searching across the entire universe of data possibilities or when a likely producer agency is not known; using the clearinghouse to access data is not required.

Many regional, state, and local agencies have their own clearinghouses or geospatial information available through the Web that might not appear in the national clearinghouse. These information resources often can be found by using Web browsers and searching for "[state name] clearinghouse GIS." The GIS is important for this search because some states have clearinghouses for other kinds of information such as pollution reduction, educational management, or science and technology developments. "[State or city name] GIS data" or just "[state or city name] GIS" may also be helpful in locating state or local data. The University of Oregon Map Library is maintaining a page of "State GIS Data Resources" (http://libweb.uoregon.edu/map/map_section/map_Statedatasets.html).

Starting the Hunt: Guide to Mostly On-Line and Mostly Free U.S. Geospatial and Attribute Data (http://www.cast.uark.edu/local/hunt/index.html)

Starting the Hunt, compiled at the University of Arkansas-Fayetteville's Center for Advanced Spatial Technologies, is a vast set of links to geospatial data resources including state agencies and clearinghouses. The list is arranged in five broad sections: a subject-oriented list; general; international sites that include U.S. data; United States organizations with national-level data; and state GIS and base map data. The subjects in the subject-oriented list cover both the natural and the manmade environment. "General Level" contains a handful of links to other sites that deal with GIS in general or that serve as link aggregators. While Starting the Hunt might not be exhaustive, it does include links to fundamental state and national GIS data sources.

The Geography Network (http://www.geographynetwork.com)

Sponsored by ESRI, The Geography Network is intended to enable worldwide data sharing through the Web with a growing set of links to data and to Internet-based interactive mapping sites and services. The data available for download directly through The Geography Network site or through links from the site are primarily global or North American. Much of the data are formatted for use with ESRI products. Some of the data sources allow geographic customization so that specific areas of interest can be "carved" from the data instead of downloading the entire set. The Geography Network also includes links to GIS data clearinghouses and Web sites, some for very specific locations like an individual national forest or city, that allow data downloads.

The Manual of Federal Geographic Data Products

The Federal Geographic Data Committee published *The Manual of Federal Geographic Data Products* in 1992 to promote "coordinated development, use, sharing, and dissemination of surveying, mapping and related spatial data." The products described are national in scope, are generally available for public use, and include both paper-based and electronic titles. The *Manual* is organized alphabetically by department; individual agencies are filed in the appropriate department. The first page of each agency's product descriptions is a data product-keyword matrix that lists each of the products indexed with appropriate descriptive content terms. The product descriptions follow a standard format and include the list of keywords from the matrix, a summary description that includes information about appropriate or possible uses and (occasionally) production information, geographic extent (usually national or global), available product coverage giving more specifics about areas reported on, information content describing data collection and types of features included, product delivery format, and ordering and availability information. Most of the product descriptions are one or two pages; some include illustrations. Unfortunately, the paper-based product has not been kept up-to-date and a digital version is no longer available through the Web, although information about obtaining a paper or microfiche copy is (http://www.fgdc.gov/FGDP/title.html). Although *The Manual of Federal Geographic Data Products* is somewhat dated, it contains basic descriptions of fundamental federal geographic products. Some products might no longer be produced or have been renamed and a number of the digital products might be available through the Web or on CD-ROM instead of on magnetic tape, but the core information and descriptions found in the *Manual* still reflect government geographic data products and will be helpful in determining appropriate agencies to contact or in formulating viable Web searches for data.

The USGS has a Web page devoted to "Digital Maps & Data" (http://ask.usgs.gov/digidata.html) with links to descriptions of data and to sites that allow downloading. The kinds of data included at this site are: digital raster graphics (DRG); digital elevation models (DEM); digital line graphs (DLG); digital orthophotograph quadrangles (DOQ); data from *The National Atlas of the United States;* the National Hydrography Dataset (NHD); the National Elevation Dataset (NED); National Wetlands Inventory (NWI) maps; land use and land cover data; and other biological, mineral, and hydrographic resources. The wide variety of data available, much of it focusing at the 1:24,000-scale, is being conceptually grouped together by the USGS as "The National Map" (http://nationalmap.usgs.gov).

One of the resources that the USGS digital data page points to is EarthExplorer (http://edcsns17.cr.usgs.gov/EarthExplorer/). EarthExplorer searches USGS data sets for data covering coordinates as determined by the user with the assistance of a wizard. EarthExplorer displays data that meet the user's location and data type requirements and will facilitate placing an on-line order. Not all of the data included in the EarthExplorer search are digital. EarthExplorer searches for aerial photography, DLGs, DEMs, DRGs, maps, and remotely sensed images.

People

One of the most important things to remember about GIS is that GIS applications do not function in an organizational vacuum. The nature and mission of the "home" of a GIS system will be instrumental in driving the GIS's development and applications.

Training in using GIS software is available in a number of different places. Increasingly, community colleges are offering sequences of courses that could lead to working as a GIS technician. College and university programs, often found in departments of geography, urban planning, or civil engineering, focus less on learning how to use specific software packages, although GIS packages are used in laboratory situations to support lecture material, and more on fundamental principles of GIS application, data development, and the impacts of GIS usage. Many courses make their syllabus available for viewing through the Web; for individuals interested in pursuing self-study, these materials might be helpful in selecting books and articles to read.

GIS training is also becoming available through the Web. ESRI has an extensive list of courses, some free, available through its Virtual Campus (http://campus.esri.com). Most of the ESRI courses focus on using ESRI software, but some, mainly found in the "GIScience" section, cover foundation material that can be applied to other GIS packages and a multitude of GIS situations. The National Center for Geographic Information Analysis (NCGIA) has created a *Core Curriculum in GIScience* as well as a *GIS Core Curriculum for Technical Programs*. Both can be found under the education portion of the NCGIA Web site (http://www.ncgia.ucsb.edu). NCGIA also makes available through its site a number of publications and technical reports, including sets of laboratory exercises.

Queries or Problems

Without a question to answer, a problem to solve, or a decision to make, there would be no reason to implement a GIS. Every GIS has an application or set of intended applications. Additional applications might be discovered after using a GIS. Applications generally revolve around questions that require the system to describe the current situation or predict possible connections or future impacts and outcomes of different actions.

FINDING OUT MORE ABOUT GIS

Books

An overwhelming number of publications appear each year about GIS. Many have specific topics such as error analysis, database management, using remotely sensed data, and depicting time as one of a place's attributes. Others delve into the philosophy and ethics of GIS or attempt to synthesize a history of the development of GIS both as a tool and as a discipline of study. There are also numerous publications on applying GIS to specific fields or problems; archaeology, coastal erosion management, gypsy moth population spread, social services for an aging population, or developing emergency services are all typical publication topics. Finally, there is a large market, and correspondingly a large publication output, for after-market guides to common software packages.

Many of these publications can be found in library or booksellers' catalogs by searching "geographic information systems" or the name of the desired software package as a subject. The Web sites for producers of GIS software often include bookstores or advertisements, and the trade magazines such as *GeoWorld* include many advertisements. Book reviews, similar to those at Amazon.com, are submitted by readers to the Web site for the ESRI Virtual Campus' Library (http://campus.esri.com/library). After going to the Library Web page, select one of the material types under the "Browse" section. Books are divided into a number of subject groupings. Clicking on a subject will display a list of titles; if a book has an on-line review, its title will be followed by a number of red stars. The titles all link to descriptions, images of book covers, and if available brief reviews.

Geographical Information Systems. 2nd ed. Vol. 1. *Principles and Technical Issues.* Vol. 2. *Management Issues and Applications.*

The two-volume, boxed set *Geographical Information Systems* was rightly called the "Big Book of GIS" in its previous edition. *Geographical Information Systems* is an encyclopedic omnibus of 72 contributed chapters or essays, intended by the authors and editors to be "benchmark reviews," on all aspects of GIS from fundamental principles of dealing with changes in space through time to descriptions of applications of GIS to real-world problems. Both of the volumes are divided into two parts, volume one into "Principles" and "Technical Issues" and volume two into "Management Issues" and "Applications." The parts are divided into lettered sections such as "Data Quality" (principles), "Technical Aspects of GIS Data Collection" (technical issues), "The Impact of Broad Societal Issues on GIS" (management issues), and "Operational Applications" (applications). The sections begin with an introductory essay by the authors that is followed by three or more chapters contributed by subject specialists. Each of the chapters includes a list of references, and a consolidated bibliography appears at the end of the second volume. Chapters are illustrated with black-and-white maps, charts, and tables, and both volumes include a center section of color illustrations. Both of the volumes have an appendix of glossary resources and acronyms along with an author and a subject index.

As a global view of GIS, *Geographical Information Systems* touches on all aspects of a broadly applied technology and discipline with disparate views. The chapters are straightforward, presenting core concepts with applicable illustrations and references to other source materials. *Geographical Information Systems* may not be a publication to read from the introduction through the epilogue. Instead, readers will be better served by focusing on only the chapters that touch on their immediate interests, using *Geographical Information Systems* as a reference work instead of as a text.

All of the chapters are completely new to the second edition of *Geographical Information Systems,* so it might be worthwhile to take a look at the first edition also. Although trends and technical issues may have changed in the eight years between editions, the essays in the first edition reflect the state of the discipline in the late 1980s and could prove valuable for tracing developments historically.

As the first edition was, the second edition of *Geographical Information Systems* will become a touchstone for those with a serious interest in GIS. While its price may exclude it from personal collections, *Geographical Information Systems* should be considered an essential and required library purchase, especially for libraries supporting any kind of work with GIS.

Geographic Information Systems and Science

Written by the same team that created *Geographical Information Systems, Geographic Information Systems and Science* is an intermediate level textbook full of examples from business and government. Twenty chapters are grouped into three major sections: Principles, Techniques, and Practice.

Each chapter begins with a page that briefly outlines the chapter's content as well as lists a short set of learning objectives. Chapters are heavily illustrated with screen shots, photographs, maps, and graphs. Summary statements and fundamental principles, printed in blue, appear throughout the densely written chapters. There is an extensive amount of boxed text that expands on topics touched upon by the main text; illustrates a specific principle, concept, or application; or introduces the reader to key people in the development and current implementation of GIS. The chapters typically conclude with study questions, a list of on-line resources, "Reference Links" to chapters in both the first and second editions of *Geographical Information Systems,* and a list of references.

The authors of *Geographic Information Systems and Science* are particularly aware of the need to apply the principles and foundations laid by geographic information science to the work being done with geographic information systems. For all of its wonderful illustrations, case studies, and supporting materials, *Geographic Information Systems and Science* is not for the technologically faint-at-heart or the beginning GIS reader. This text truly is for an intermediate-level student who already has a firm foundation of GIS fundamentals.

The GIS Book. 5th ed.

The GIS Book is a non-technical introduction to GIS fundamentals, in particular "the selection, implementation, uses, benefits, and management of geographic information systems" (*GIS Book,* ix). It is intended to reach a broad audience going far beyond geographers and engineers to environmental science, politics, and business.

The text is divided into three parts: Understanding GIS, Selecting and Implementing a GIS, and Considerations for Making GIS Decisions. Each part has 9 or 10 chapters. All three parts begin with a two-page summary of the part that includes one or two sentences explaining the part and a list of the chapters each with a brief qualifying statement. Similarly, all of the chapters begin with a single-paragraph "In This Chapter..." The chapters feature brief sections with bold titles, often containing bulleted lists. Many of the chapters feature descriptions of real applications of GIS; the final three chapters are devoted completely to case studies. *The GIS Book* takes a practical approach to many of the issues associated with implementing

GIS. There are chapters on both how to succeed with GIS and what possible pitfalls might be along with chapters on selecting a GIS, descriptions of four major GIS software vendors, and justifying a GIS financially. Although *The GIS Book* takes a nontechnical approach, this does not preclude the inclusion of chapters on data quality, data formats, and the different kinds of analysis that can be done using GIS. *The GIS Book* is not as heavily illustrated as some other works on GIS; this may be due, in part, to the straightforward presentation of core concepts. Illustrations are not as necessary to be sure that the author's intent is clear. Some of the chapters, but not many, conclude with a list of references.

There is a bibliography of core books in one of the appendices. The appendix titles are "GIS Exercises Using Free GIS Software and Data," "Resources for GIS Information and Training," and "GIS Data Sources." The resources appendix focuses on organizational and information sources, including GIS education options, professional associations and events, the aforementioned bibliography, a list of periodicals with contact information including Web sites, and a list of some colleges and universities that offer GIS course work. The data sources appendix is a table of federal and commercial data producers that logs the types of data available. The volume concludes with a glossary and index.

Reading *The GIS Book* will not produce instant expertise in GIS, but it will help ease a potential GIS user (or budget approver) painlessly into being able to begin understanding this complex and multifaceted technology. The practical and everyday tone of *The GIS Book* will complement more technical and theoretical texts.

Fundamentals of Geographic Information Systems.
    2nd ed.

Fundamentals of Geographic Information Systems invites the reader to take a "trip into the modern world of geographic exploration" (*Fundamentals,* 4). The 15 chapters are organized into 6 units: Introduction; Geographic Data, Maps, and Automation; Input, Storage, and Editing; Analysis: The Heart of GIS; GIS Output; and GIS Design. Half of the chapters fall into "Analysis: The Heart of GIS," an indication of how important the analysis subsystem is to full GIS capabilities. As *Fundamentals of Geographic Information Systems* is intended to be used as a textbook, each chapter begins with a list of learning objectives and concludes with a list of terms, review questions, and references. The author does not assume that his readers are cartographers, although there is an implicit assumption that the readers have some comprehension of how to read maps and some of the steps that go into map creation. The chapters are full of fundamental concepts about GIS and using GIS. The book also includes a great deal of commonsense, everyday advice for working with both people and GIS. For instance, in the section about map scale, the reader is reminded that people do not necessarily communicate about scale precisely or accurately, that verbal shorthands are often used when discussing the scale of photography, maps, or data collection. Often more than one way of thinking through and solving a problem is presented. Advantages and pitfalls to specific approaches are also included in their descriptions.

Fundamentals of Geographic Information Systems includes a number of illustrations but very few of them are actual output from a GIS. Most are schematic diagrams showing database structures or hypothetical results from statistical operations, data editing, and error analysis. *Fundamentals of Geographic Information Systems* concludes with a list of "Software and Data Sources," information about using the author's and publisher's Web sites to find data and examples, and a glossary.

Fundamentals of Geographic Information Systems is densely written, presenting foundation concepts in a straightforward manner with explanations couched in such a way that readers will be introduced to, but not overwhelmed by, technical terms. This is not the title to pick up if looking for examples of GIS applications and output. That need would be better served by the *ESRI Map Book* or by any of the GIS trade magazines.

Getting Started with Geographic Information Systems. 3rd ed.

Getting Started with Geographic Information Systems is a popular choice as a textbook for college and university GIS courses. This work covers GIS basics in 10 chapters that could be roughly grouped into 3 areas: GIS foundations, the scope of GIS issues and applications, and critical thinking about GIS capabilities. After two chapters that define GIS and cover basic cartographic definitions, there are four chapters about data, describing how geographically distributed phenomena can be represented numerically, how data are entered into a GIS, how a GIS manages data and searches databases, and how data can be analysed. The following two chapters cover map production with GIS and selecting a GIS software package. The last chapters include case studies and a view of GIS's potential future.

The text is straightforward to read, and all of the chapters include black-and-white illustrations. Each chapter concludes with a study guide section that includes a bulleted list of important points, study questions, laboratory assignments, a list of references, and a chapter glossary. There also is a glossary at the end of the volume. Five of the chapters include interviews with key individuals who use or study GIS. The publisher is maintaining a Web site (http://cwx.prenhall. com/bookbind/pubbooks/clarke/) that includes Power-Point instructor lectures, laboratory exercises that use ArcView, quizzes, glossaries, and links to GIS Web sites.

Because *Getting Started with Geographic Information Systems* is intended as a textbook for introducing basic concepts about GIS, it will be an ideal starting point for learning about GIS capabilities and applications.

Principles of Geographical Information Systems

Principles of Geographical Information Systems could be considered one of the classics of GIS literature. It introduces broad theoretical and technical foundations for GIS work in a scholarly yet straightforward style. Basics such as data acquisition, how sampling is used to collect data, and core data analysis techniques are covered as well as statistical analysis and using digital elevation models. But there also is information about more advanced topics such as fuzzy objects and error analysis. The volume begins with a chapter on the history of GIS and concludes with a short chapter on current issues and trends. Each chapter includes a set of study questions and a short list of additional reading. The chapters are amply illustrated with maps, graphs, and tables. The maps in the chapters are black-and-white; there is a center section of color illustrations. Most of the sample GIS outputs appear to be from a raster system and show examples from European applications. There is a glossary, a list of Web sites for geography and GIS, information about the data used for some of the examples, a bibliography, and an index.

Principles of Geographical Information Systems is often used as a textbook for college and university courses on GIS. *Principles of Geographical Information Systems* will appeal to a somewhat technically oriented reader; it might be a difficult read if it is the first publication encountered about GIS. The text is composed generically so that it is virtually free of references to proprietary GIS software. *Principles of Geographical Information Systems* does well at introducing core concepts and application of GIS without resorting to examples driven by specific software, making the publication a textbook, not a software training manual.

Publications produced by ESRI are unabashedly vehicles for promoting ESRI's products, in particular ArcView. All of the ESRI Press publications are about GIS and GIS applications, with a wide variety of applications covered. Some of the titles are more general in nature such as basic guides to GIS and the annual *ESRI Map Book*. There also is a case studies series, a group of publications of which each focuses on a specific type of GIS application; areas such as natural resources management, landscape architecture, health care provision, and public safety have been covered. Of course, the ESRI Press also publishes aftermarket workbooks and documentation to assist users of ESRI software. Most of the ESRI Press books are extensively illustrated, often using screen captures, and nearly always including lots of color.

ESRI Press Dictionary of GIS Terminology

Containing more than 1000 terms and cross references, the *ESRI Press Dictionary of GIS Terminology* is a disciplinary- or technology-based dictionary that might be useful to beginning GIS users. The definitions are generally brief, more like those typically found in a glossary, with some accompanying illustrations. Some of the definitions include a reference to the discipline or technology from which the term originated, for example "ellipsoid" is qualified by "geometry" and "metes and bounds" by "surveying." There also is a list of acronyms, but beyond acronym and full name or phrase there is no definition or explanation. Another GIS dictionary to look for, although smaller and older than the *ESRI Press Dictionary,* is the *International GIS Dictionary*.

Periodicals

GeoWorld

GeoWorld is a monthly glossy trade magazine. Its subtitle claims that it is "The World's Leading Integrated Spatial Technologies Publication." The contents of *GeoWorld* touch on a wide variety of GIS-related arenas. Each month, four or five feature articles highlight current GIS applications or individuals and organizations involved with GIS. There are also a number of regular columns; most discuss practical problems and solutions or explain important GIS concepts. Space near the front of each issue, titled "NewsLink," is reserved for shorter articles; often in-

formation about changes in corporate ownership, industry-education cooperative programs, and grant awards can be found. "NetLink" focuses attention on changes to corporate Web sites and always includes a "Internet Resource of the Month," which usually is an unique GIS application, a data resource, or a basic government site. "PeopleLink" will include obituaries and information about people, often corporate employees, active in GIS. The final two news sections, "Federal Connection" and "Conference Connection," focus on GIS developments in the U.S. federal government and conference events, respectively. A "Product News" and a "Business News" section follow the feature articles along with a short review section that usually evaluates a software package, classified advertisements, and a worldwide GIS events calendar. Color advertisements are found throughout the magazine. The companies advertising in *GeoWorld* go beyond software producers to include companies selling GPS systems, data vendors, computer hardware and peripherals, and aerial photography companies.

Information about *GeoWorld* can be found on the Web at the GeoPlace site (http://www.geoplace.com). Features and columns can be read on-line, and an archives of previous issues can be searched and viewed. Also at the Web site is a subscription form; *GeoWorld* is distributed free in the United States and Canada to those who qualify. The GeoPlace Web site also includes product reviews, directories, calendars, and a news center.

GeoWorld is an easy way to stay aware of how GIS is being applied to real problems. The articles are not overly technical and are always illustrated with screen shots, photographs of the physical environment being discussed, or graphs. The articles usually do not include a bibliography or references but often are accompanied by contact information for the author or a URL for further information.

ARCNews and ARCUser

ARCNews and *ARCUser* are quarterly publications from ESRI. They primarily celebrate the usage, and the users, of ESRI's suite of GIS products. *ARCNews* is in a tabloid newspaper format and usually includes four to seven cover stories, all of which begin on the front page and are completed in the following four to six pages. The cover stories are often about environmental or social applications of ESRI products that impact large groups of people or large tracts of land. Other cover stories are about the company, including software developments, cooperative work on standards, and new ways that ESRI executives and employees are thinking about geospatial data. A number of regular sections follow the cover stories, including: Software News; GIS in Action; GIS Trends in [various topics]; Community News; and Focus on GIS in [various specialties]. All of the cover stories and many of the regular sections include either URLs or contact information (e-mail addresses) for individuals responsible for the project described. There also is a section of descriptions of open positions at ESRI and a directory of contact information for ESRI offices worldwide. All of the advertisements are either for ESRI products or for ESRI business partners. Partial contents of *ARCNews,* both current and previous issues, is available through ESRI's Web site (http://www.esri.com/news/arcnews/arcnews.html). This also is where corrections to printed articles might be posted. The URLs that appear in the printed version are all linked in the on-line version.

ARCUser is in a glossy magazine format. Each issue has a special focus; thus far these have included topics such as transportation, GIS in education, utilities, and "G-government" (government use of GIS to deliver services and make decisions). Beyond the articles in the focus section, there are usually three to five other feature articles, reviews of GIS-related publications, short tutorials, and contact lists for ESRI-authorized instructors and learning centers. Unlike *ARCNews,* which is mostly authored by ESRI employees, many of the articles in *ARCUser* are written by ESRI software users. Some of the articles are accompanied by brief lists of references, and nearly all of the articles and columns include contact information, either a specific person or a Web site, for further information. In general, the articles and columns in *ArcUser* are devoted to real-world problems and GIS-based solutions. *ARCUser* is also available on-line through ESRI's Web site (http://www.esri.com/news/arcuser/index.html). Some of the articles are text files that have been imported into the Web site, while others, primarily those that include technical instructions or those that are tutorial in nature, are in PDF format.

Access to both *ARCNews* and *ARCUser* through the Web is free of charge, as are the print publications, and does not require any kind of password or permission to view.

MapInfo Magazine

Like the ESRI products, *MapInfo Magazine* is available free of charge as PDF files from the MapInfo literature Web site (http://www.mapinfo.com/company/literature/index.cfm). Readers will need to register to be able to view the PDF files. Issues from 1999 to the present are available through the Web site; prior to 2001 the magazine was titled *MapWorld Magazine.* Each issue has a theme; recent issues have focused on retail applications, wireless technology, and the public sector (in particular e-government). A number of the issues have incorporated a continuing theme of MapInfo products' application to solving problems of customer relationship management (CRM). The magazine also contains a number of columns or departments as well as advertising specifically related to MapInfo products and development partners.

International Journal of Geographical Information Science

International Journal of Geographical Information Science (IJGIS), which appears 10 times yearly, is much more scholarly and academic than *GeoWorld* or the ESRI quarterly publications. An interdisciplinary, refereed journal, IJGIS is a publication outlet for practitioners, researchers, and academics who think about GIS and GIS applications at either a very theoretical or highly advanced level. IJGIS is not light reading! Typical issues will include five or six research articles and perhaps some book reviews. Occasionally an issue will have a specific theme. The articles range in content from applying GIS algorithms for improving soil mapping to new ways of examining human-computer interactions in a GIS setting. IJGIS is published in Great Britain and has an international, and internationally renowned, editorial board. IJGIS is a core journal for academic and research GIS users and researchers. Its content goes well beyond demonstrating how GIS, with the *S* standing for *System,* can be used for specific needs to illuminating how GIS, with *S* standing for *Science,* is shaping how geographic data explored and expanded into information.

Cartography and Geographic Information Science

Cartography and Geographic Information Science (CAGIS) is published quarterly by the American Congress on Surveying and Mapping (ACSM) with co-sponsorship by the Cartography and Geographic Information Society, part of the congress. Officially, CAGIS is "devoted to the advancement of cartography in all its aspects." Typically, most of a CAGIS issue will be devoted to research articles, many of which touch on GIS by discussing aspects of producing maps using computers. Occasionally a technical paper will appear, as will book reviews and listings of recent cartographic and GIS publications. Winning maps from the annual ACSM Map Design Competition are published in CAGIS. One issue each year is a theme issue, and every four years CAGIS publishes the United States Report to the International Cartographic Association.

Web Sites

Geographic Information Systems (http://www.icls. harvard.edu/gis/contents.html)

The Institute for Cultural Landscape Studies, part of The Arnold Arboretum of Harvard University, has created a set of Web pages full of GIS basics. There is a "summary of key issues," 10 chapterlike pages, two case studies, and three groups of links to other resources including information about GIS applications and GIS in general and citations to printed publications. Except for the chapter of maps created using GIS, this site is primarily text or text in boxes. It is succinct and highly readable. This site might be a good first choice for an introduction to GIS, but it could serve better as a quick reminder or checklist of issues to keep in mind when selecting or working with GIS. It attempts to provide balanced coverage, pointing out both pros and cons of implementing GIS.

GIS.com (http://www.gis.com)

GIS.com is a good place to start on the Web when looking for basic information about GIS; this portal, developed by ESRI, has a definite ESRI slant. ESRI is the only company with a direct link from the Web site. All other companies are accessed via third-party link aggregators. Aside from this obvious bias, GIS.com presents basic information about what GIS is all about. Each aspect of a GIS, except for hardware, is explored quickly with links to other Web sites. The group of pages on data is especially helpful with information on data types and a list of 14 questions that should be considered when looking for appropriate data. Six different kinds of GIS use are briefly described: Mapping Where Things Are; Mapping Quantities; Mapping Densities; Finding What's Inside; Finding What's Nearby; and Mapping Change. The site also includes a brief step-by-step guide of how to use a GIS to analyze data. Applications of GIS to specific subject specialties are illustrated. There are links to GIS/Web-based interactive mapping sites and links to additional resources, such as information about GIS training and education, glossaries, and careers revolving around GIS.

GIS.com's content is very much at the brief introductory level. The text contained in the site reads quickly; perhaps the site could be used as an introduction to GIS for a busy administrator. Concepts are introduced in a basic and bare-bones fashion, enough for rudimentary grounding but not exceeding or meeting the level of detail available through printed texts. GIS.com is a wonderful public relations tool for GIS in general and ESRI specifically.

GIS—Geographic Information Systems (http://gis. about.com/gis/index.htm)

Like the other About.com sites, About GIS.com has a rich assortment of links to information about Web-based GIS resources. Some of the site's content is text written by About.com, such as text titled "What is GIS?" and short descriptions of commercial software companies. But by far, most of this site is made up of links to other Web sites and descriptions of the linked resources. There are over 20 categories of information in the subjects list. The site includes fundamental definitions of GIS, information about core GIS and data processing activities, a glossary of GIS-related terms, links to GIS education including university programs and on-line tutorials, plus information about discussion and mailing lists and user groups.

The GIS Portal (http://www.gisportal.com

Also known as "Great GIS Net Sites," the GIS Portal is hosted by HDM, Harvard Design and Mapping Company, Inc. Links to more than 1,000 sites are maintained, grouped into 17 categories including jobs, data, on-line GIS, WWW resources, software companies, books, higher education, companies, and governmental agencies at a variety of levels. This site does not provide any kind of summary of linked sites' contents nor does it include any evaluative comments—just site name links.

Clicking on the link to HDM's Web site (http://www.hdm.com), at the bottom of the page, will lead to information about the company. The list contained in the left-hand frame of the "About Us" page includes "6 Steps to a Successful GIS," HDM's approach to managing GIS installation and use. The six steps group fundamental questions or concerns that should be answered when considering working with a GIS: requirements analysis, system configuration, data development, application development, training and support, and system and data maintenance—all important to using GIS effectively in any kind of setting.

Organizations

Association of American Geographers Geographic Information Systems Specialty Group (AAG-GIS)

The Association of American Geographers has a GIS specialty group with the mission "to promote the development and practice in computer-based hardware, software and graphic capabilities that encode, analyze and display natural, cultural and economic information." Members of the group are either involved in using GIS as a research tool or doing research about GIS. The specialty group sponsors paper and poster sessions at the annual AAG meeting. AAG-GIS also has a Web site (http://www.cla.sc.edu/gis/aaggis/index.html) and a listserv. The Web site includes information about the specialty group's officers, job postings and calls for conference papers, a membership list that includes e-mail addresses, and other GIS links. The AAG-GIS Web site might be most useful as a way to find contact information for people involved with GIS.

Geospatial Information and Technology Association (http://www.gita.org)

The Geospatial Information and Technology Association (GITA), formerly named AM/FM International, focuses "on the use and benefits of geospatial information and technology in telecommunications, infrastructure, and utility applications worldwide." The organization serves specific utilities: electric, gas, telecommunications, water/wastewater, public works/local government, and oil and gas pipelines. The organization holds an annual meeting, and local, regionally based chapters in North America also hold regular events. GITA is a distributor for a videotape about GIS, *The World in a Box,* that includes a number of real-life case studies or illustrations of GIS applications including natural resource management, law enforcement, and African famine prevention.

Urban and Regional Information Systems Association (http://www.urisa.org)

Urban and Regional Information Systems Association (URISA) members focus on using GIS and other information at state, regional, and local levels. Members have specific interest in planning, emergency preparedness, and infrastructures such as transportation and utilities. Many of this organization's members are involved in state or local government. An annual meeting is held and many of the state or regional chapters are also active. URISA members receive a newsletter and a quarterly journal.

A full GIS can be expensive to implement, expand, update, and maintain in terms of both money and time. One of the most important things to remember about GIS is that GIS applications do not function in an orga-

nizational vacuum. The nature and mission of the home of a GIS system will be instrumental in driving the GIS's development and applications. Nevertheless, individuals interested in current as well as some historic geographically referenced data might find their information needs met by Web-based GIS applications that have been prepared by governmental agencies and organizations with specific scientific or cultural missions.

BIBLIOGRAPHY

"2003 Recommended Specifications for Public Access Workstations in Federal Depository Libraries." *Administrative Notes,* vol. 24, no. 7 (15 June 2003): 7–12.

ARCNews. Redlands, Calif.: Environmental Systems Research Institute (ESRI), 1987– . Quarterly. ISSN: 1064-6108.

ARCUser. Redlands, Calif: ESRI, 1998– . Quarterly. ISSN: 1064-6108.

Cartography and Geographic Information Science (CAGIS). Bethesda, Md.: American Congress on Surveying and Mapping, 1974– . Quarterly. Former titles: *American Cartographer; Cartography and Geographic Information Systems.* ISSN: 1523-0406.

ESRI Map Book. Redlands, Calif.: ESRI Press, 1984– . Annual. ISBN: 1-58948-015-5.

ESRI Press Dictionary of GIS Terminology. Heather Kennedy, ed. Redlands, Calif.: ESRI Press, 2001. ISBN: 1-879102-78-1.

Fundamentals of Geographic Information Systems. 2nd ed. Michael N. DeMers. New York: J. Wiley & Sons, 2000. ISBN: 0-471-31423-4.

Geographical Information Systems. David J. Maguire, Michael F. Goodchild, and David W. Rhind, eds. Vol. 1: Principles; Vol. 2: Applications. New York: Wiley, 1991. ISBN: 0470217898 (set).

Geographical Information Systems. 2nd ed. Paul A. Longley, et al., eds. Vol. 1: *Principles and Technical Issues;* Vol. 2: *Management Issues and Applications.* New York: J. Wiley & Sons, 1999. ISBN: 0-471-32182-6.

Geographic Information Systems and Science. Paul A Longley, et al. New York: J. Wiley & Sons, 2001. ISBN: 0-471-89275-0.

GeoWorld. Arlington Heights, Ill.: Adams Business Media. 1989– . Monthly. Former title: *GIS World.* ISSN: 0897-5507.

Getting Started with Geographic Information Systems. 3rd ed. Keith C. Clarke. Upper Saddle River, N.J.: Prentice Hall, 2001. ISBN: 0-13-016829-7.

The GIS Book. 5th ed. George B. Korte. Albany, N.Y.: OnWord Press, 2001. ISBN: 0-7668-2820-4.

GIS Data Sources. Drew Decker. New York: J. Wiley & Sons, 2001. ISBN: 0-471-43773-5.

International GIS Dictionary. Rachel McDonnell. Cambridge, England: GeoInformation International; New York: J. Wiley & Sons, 1995. ISBN: 0470236078.

International Journal of Geographical Information Science
(IJGIS). London: Taylor & Francis, 1987– . 8 per year.
Former title: *International Journal of Geographical Information Systems.* ISSN: 1365-8816.

The Manual of Federal Geographic Data Products. Reston,
Va.: Federal Geographic Data Committee, 1992.

Multipurpose Cadastre: Terms and Definitions. Kenneth J.
Dueker and Daniel Kjerne. Falls Church, Va.: American
Society for Photogrammetry and Remote Sensing and
American Congress on Surveying and Mapping, 1989.
ISBN: 0-614-06098-2.

Principles of Geographical Information Systems. Peter A.
Burrough and Rachael A. McDonnell. New York: Oxford University Press, 1998. ISBN: 0-19-823365-5.

Understanding the GPS: An Introduction to the Global Positioning System: What It Is and How It Works. Gregory
T. French. Bethesda, Md.: GeoResearch, 1996. ISBN: 0-9655723-0-7.

The World in a Box. (VHS video) Victoria Eubanks and Cal
Lewin. Opticus, 2001.

On-line References

"2003 Recommended Specifications for Public Access Workstations in Federal Depository Libraries." Federal Depository Library Program, 2 June 2003. <http://www.access.gpo.gov/su_docs/fdlp/computers/rs.html> (20 October 2003).

"All about GPS." Trimble Navigation Ltd., 2003. <http://www.trimble.com/gps/index.html> (20 October 2003).

"ArcExplorer." Free GIS data viewer. ESRI, 2003. <http://www.esri.com/arcexplorer> (20 October 2003).

ArcNews Online. Selected articles form *ArcNews.* ESRI, 2003. <http://www.esri.com/news/arcnews/arcnews.html> (20 October 2003).

ArcUser Online. ESRI, 2003. <http://www.esri.com/news/arcuser/index.html> (20 October 2003).

Association of American Geographers Geographic Information Systems (AAG-GIS) Specialty Group. Home page. University of South Carolina, Department of Geography, 26 June 2003. <http://www.cla.sc.edu/gis/aaggis/index.html> (20 October 2003).

Australian Natural Resources Atlas. National Heritage Trust, National Land & Water Resources Audit (Australia), 2003. <http://audit.ea.gov.au/anra/atlas_home.cfm> (20 October 2003).

Autodesk. Home page. Autodesk, Inc., 2003. <http://www.autodesk.com/siteselect.htm> (20 October 2003).

"Census Bureau Geography." U.S. Census Bureau, 1 October 2002. <http://www.census.gov/geo/www/> (20 October 2003).

"Clearinghouse." Federal Geographic Data Committee, 27 March 2003. <http://www.fgdc.gov/clearinghouse/clearinghouse.html> (20 October 2003).

Degree Confluence Project. Home page. Alex Jarrett, 2003. <http://www.confluence.org/index.php> (20 October 2003).

"Digital Maps & Data." U.S. Geological Survey, 10 July 2003. <http://ask.usgs.gov/digidata.html> (20 October 2003).

EarthExplorer. U.S. Geological Survey, Earth Resources Observation Systems (EROS) Data Center, 1 May 2002. <http://edcsns17.cr.usgs.gov/EarthExplorer/> (20 October 2003).

ESRI. Home page. ESRI, 2003. <http://www.esri.com> (20 October 2003).

ESRI Virtual Campus. ESRI, 2003. <http://campus.esri.com> (20 October 2003).

"ESRI Virtual Campus Library." ESRI, 2003. <http://campus.esri.com/library> (20 October 2003).

Geocaching. Groundspeak, 2003. <http://www.geocaching.com> (20 October 2003).

"Geographic Information Systems." Harvard University, Institute for Cultural Landscape Studies, 4 January 2001. <http://www.icls.harvard.edu/gis/contents.htm> (20 October 2003).

"Geographic Information Systems." U.S. Geological Survey, Eastern Region Geography, March 2003. <http://erg.usgs.gov/isb/pubs/gis_poster> (20 October 2003).

"Geographic Information Systems: State Datasets." University of Oregon, Map and Aerial Photography (MAP) Library. <http://libweb.uoregon.edu/map/map_section/map_Statedatasets.html> (20 October 2003).

Geography Network. ESRI, 2003. <http://www.geographynetwork.com> (20 October 2003).

GeoPlace. Adams Business Media, 2003. <http://www.geoplace.com> (20 October 2003).

"Geography and Mapping Technologies: Geographic Information Systems." National Park Service (U.S.), 15 August 2003. <http://www.nps.gov/gis> (20 October 2003).

Geospatial Information and Technology Association (GITA). Home page. GITA, 3 October 2003. <http://www.gita.org> (20 October 2003).

Getting Started with Geographic Information Systems. Companion Web site. Keith C. Clarke. Prentice-Hall, 2 August 2002. <http://cwx.prenhall.com/bookbind/pubbooks/clarke/> (20 October 2003)

GIS.com. ESRI, 2003. <http://www.gis.com> (20 October 2003).

"GIS-Geographic Information Systems." Geography home page. About.com, 2003. <http://gis.about.com/cs/gis/index.htm> (20 October 2003).

"GIS, GPS, and Technology in Geography." Geography home page. About.com, 2003. <http://gis.about.com/cs/gisgpstech/> (20 October 2003).

The GIS Portal: Great GIS Net Sites. Harvard Design and Mapping, Inc., 2003. <http://www.gisportal.com> (20 October 2003).

"Global Positioning System Overview." Peter H. Dana. Department of Geography, The Geographer's Craft Project, The University of Colorado at Boulder, 1994. Revised May 2000. <http://www.colorado.edu/geography/gcraft/notes/gps/gps_f.html> (20 October 2003).

"GRASS GIS." Home page. GRASS Development Team. <http://grass.its.it/index.html> (20 October 2003).

"Literature." MapInfo Corp., 2003. <http://www.mapinfo.com/company/literature/index.cfm> (20 October 2003).

"Manual of Federal Geographic Data Products." Federal Geographic Data Committee, 2003. <http://www.fgdc.gov/FGDP/title.html> (20 October 2003).

MapBlast. Microsoft, 2003. <http://www.mapblast.com> (20 October 2003).

MapInfo. Home page. MapInfo Corp., 2003. <http://www.mapinfo.com> (20 October 2003).

"MapInfo ProViewer—Demo Download." Free download. MapInfo Corp., 2003. <http://www.mapinfo.com/products/Dowload.cfm?ProductID=1062> (20 October 2003).

MapQuest. MapQuest.com, Inc., 2003. <http://www.mapquest.com> (20 October 2003).

"Metadata." Federal Geographic Data Committee, 19 April 2003. <http://www.fgdc.gov/metadata/metadata.html> (20 October 2003).

National Atlas of Canada. Geographical Services Division (Canada), 2003. <http://atlas.gc.ca/site/index.html> (20 October 2003).

National Atlas of the United States. U.S. Geological Survey, 28 February 2003. <http://www.nationalatlas.gov> (20 October 2003).

National Center for Geographic Information & Analysis (NCGIA). University of California, Santa Barbara, NGCIA, 21 May 2003. <http://www.ncgia.ucsb.edu> (20 October 2003).

"The National Map." U.S. Geological Survey, 29 August 2003. <http://nationalmap.usgs.gov/> (20 October 2003).

"National Wetlands Inventory." Home page. U.S. Fish & Wildlife Service, NWI, 8 July 2003. <http://www.nwi.fws.gov> (20 October 2003).

"President Ends Selective Availability." Interagency GPS Executive Board (U.S.), 2003. <http://www.igeb.gov/sa> (20 October 2003).

Spatial Data Transfer Standard (SDTS) Information Site. U.S. Geological Survey, 8 March 2002. <http://mcmcweb.er.usgs.gov/sdts> (20 October 2003).

"Starting the Hunt: Guide to Mostly On-Line and Mostly Free U.S. Geospatial and Attribute Data." Stephen Pollard. University of Arkansas, Fayetteville, Center for Advanced Spatial Technologies, 13 February 2003. <http://www.cast.uark.edu/local/hunt/index.html> (20 October 2003).

Urban and Regional Information Systems Association (URISA). Home page. URISA, 17 October 2003. <http://www.urisa.org> (20 October 2003).

"USGS Geographic Data Download." U.S. Geological Survey, 2 July 2003. <http://edc.usgs.gov/geodata/> (20 October 2003).

CHAPTER 12
Geography Standards and the Curricula

TOPICS COVERED

Standards
Organizations
Instructional Resources
Commercial Publications
Careers in Geography

MAJOR SOURCES DISCUSSED

Guidelines for Geographic Education: Elementary and Secondary Schools
Goals 2000: Educate America Act
Geography for Life: National Geography Standards
Content Knowledge: A Compilation of Content Standards for K–12 Curriculum
State Geography Standards: An Appraisal of Geography Standards in 38 States and the District of Columbia
National Council for Geographic Education
Geographic Education National Implementation Program
Geographic Alliances
Geography Awareness Week
National Council for the Social Studies
Geography for Educators: Standards, Themes, and Concepts
Spaces and Places: A Geography Manual for Teachers
Using Internet Primary Sources to Teach Critical Thinking Skills in Geography
ARGUS: Activities and Readings in the Geography of the United States
ARGWorld: Activities and Resources for the Geography of the World
Lesson Plans at Geographic Alliance Web sites
Lesson Plans—Discovery School
Economics and Geography Lessons for 32 Children's Books
Education World—Geography
USGS Educational Resources Learning Web
AskERIC Lesson Plans
Early Childhood: Where Learning Begins—Geography
Helping Your Child Learn Geography
Advanced Placement (AP) Human Geography
AP Central
Geography About.com
Rand McNally
Prentice-Hall
Houghton Mifflin Education Place

Geography as a stand-alone subject disappeared from elementary and secondary schools with the educational reforms that took place in the United States after the First World War. Individual subjects were replaced with broadly defined curricular fields including social studies, initially a combination of geography, history, and civics, but later expanded to include economics, sociology, anthropology, and political science. Greater emphasis was placed on the child's social adjustment and individuals' self-expressed and presumed learning needs. These reforms reduced the need for subject specialists in elementary and secondary schools. The interrelationships between the fields contained in social studies led both to generalization and compression of fundamental concepts and knowledge. Social studies became increasingly diffused as it "embraced nearly all of man's social relations, almost any subject or topic could be included as legitimate content for social studies education" ("Social Studies Education," 282).

During the 1960s and 1970s, a "new" social studies was developed following the lead of the "new" math and science from the 1950s. A university-based curriculum materials project in the sciences had been given a boost by the 1957 success of Sputnik with increased allocation of funds for curricular reform. Reform of the social studies curricula, with emphasis on developing student thinking abilities through both conceptual and inquiry-based learning approaches, took place later and was much slower because there was not the same kind of focused funding infusion. As with the sciences, but in the 1970s instead of in the 1960s, social studies began to reconnect with academic social sciences disciplines. Unfortunately, there were still many social studies teachers who had little geography background, and geography retained its reputation as being no more than memorizing lists of places, products, and levels of gross national production.

In the 1980s, a number of events occurred that increased awareness of geography and highlighted geography's potential importance in curricula. From data collected by the National Commission on Excellence in Education for *A Nation at Risk: The Imperative for Educational Reform,* it became apparent that fewer students were enrolling in geography courses. Following on this report, a number of tests and studies were done to ascertain student geographic knowledge; overall, the results were weak. The National Geographic Society increased its work with educators by founding the Geographic Alliance program and by creating the National Geographic Society Education Foundation. Finally, fundamental geographic themes were articulated in *Guidelines for Geographic Education: Elementary and Secondary Schools* and illustrated through *K-6 Geography: Themes, Key Ideas and Learning Opportunities* and *Geography in Grades 7–12: Themes, Key Ideas and Learning Opportunities.*

STANDARDS

Current geographic education standards were built on top of previous guidelines and standards.

Guidelines for Geographic Education: Elementary and Secondary Schools

A joint committee of the National Council for Geographic Education and the Association of American Geographers prepared *Guidelines for Geographic Education* in the early 1980s. This work is a foundation for *Geography for Life,* which was published 10 years later. Of particular interest are the five "Fundamental Themes in Geography": location, position on the Earth's surface; place, physical and human characteristics; relationships within places, humans and environments; movement, humans interacting on the Earth; and regions, how they form and change. Al-

though these themes are not explicitly stated in *Geography for Life,* they are woven through the later set of essential elements and learning standards. *Guidelines for Geographic Education* also introduces readers to how geography adds value to the curricula and its relationship to other subjects, and it suggests a potential sequence of graded concepts and learning outcomes for elementary grades and possible courses and appropriate geographic skills for secondary grades.

Goals 2000: Educate America Act (1991) (PL 103-227)

Signed into law by President William J. Clinton, "Goals 2000: Educate America Act" specifically includes geography as a core subject for elementary and secondary schools. The third point of Section 102, "National Education Goals," states that:

By the year 2000, all students will leave grades 4, 8, and 12 having demonstrated competency over challenging subject matter including English, mathematics, science, foreign languages, civics and government, economics, arts, history, and geography.

Two of the objectives under the goal can be linked specifically to geography: ii. the percentage of all students who demonstrate the ability to reason, solve problems, apply knowledge, and write and communicate effectively will increase substantially; and vi. all students will be knowledgeable about the diverse cultural heritage of this Nation and about the world community. National and state standards have been developed to meet this goal and objectives.

Geography for Life: National Geography Standards

Geography for Life was developed by the Geography Education Standards Project, a team of people drawn from higher education, the National Geographic Society, and the National Council for Geographic Education, on behalf of four major geography organizations (American Geographical Society, Association of American Geographers, National Council for Geographic Education, and National Geographic Society). It responds to the portion of Goals 2000: Educate America Act that treats geography as a core subject.

The first chapter, "The Geographic View of Our World," answers the questions "What is geography?," "Why geography?," and "Why geography standards?" using maps, each with questions (and answers) that can be posed using maps, real-life brief examples, and photographs. The second chapter discusses "The Components of Geography Education" by describing how subject matter, skills, and perspectives are interwoven, briefly relating the importance of both space and place, defining geography, listing the "six essential elements" into which the standards can be grouped, and introducing the 18 standards. Essentially, this chapter lays the groundwork for the heart of *Geography for Life* contained in the subsequent six chapters.

Chapter 3 delves into "Geographic Skills and Perspectives." Five different skill sets are specifically articulated: asking geographic questions, acquiring geographic information, organizing geographic information, analyzing geographic information, and answering geographic questions. After discussing the principles behind these five skill sets, the chapter illustrates appropriate activities and capabilities for three benchmark years: 4th grade, 8th grade, and 12th grade. The remainder of the chapter quickly covers two geographic perspectives from which to study the world, spatial and ecological, and two complementary perspectives, historical and economic. Chapter 4, "The Subject Matter of Geography," explains, expands, and illustrates the 18 geography standards. Chapters 5, 6, and 7 explicitly list what students should know and understand and be able to do at the end of the 4th, 8th, and 12th grades. Chapter 8, "Student Achievement in Geography," summarizes the assessment of students aspiring to standard, at standard, and beyond standard for the three benchmark grades. "Thinking Geographically," the conclusion chapter, is largely for parents, highlighting the importance of parents in a child's education and including three lists of geographical skill and activity questions titled "What does your [4th, 8th, or 12th] grader know?"

Geography for Life concludes with a set of appendices on the development of the National Geography Standards, use of the standards in the classroom, and geographic information systems. There also is a glossary and an index.

A Web-based tutorial for *Geography for Life* is available through the National Council for Geographic Education Web site(http://www.ncge.org/publications/tutorial/index.html). The tutorial has four sections, a brief section on the history of the geography standards, a countdown to geographic awareness, discussion of the 18 standards, and information on how to ask questions about the geography standards. Access to the tutorial is free of charge.

Additionally, the standards appear as part of the National Geographic Society's Xpeditions Web site (http://www.nationalgeographic.com/xpeditions/standards/) along with suggestions of lesson plans for all of the standards developed for grade levels kindergarten through 2nd, 3rd through 5th, 6th through 8th, and 9th through 12th.

Content Knowledge: A Compilation of Content Standards for K–12 Curriculum.. 3rd ed. (http://www.mcrel.org/standards-benchmarks/index.asp)

Mid-continent Research for Education and Learning (McREL) focuses on improving education, promoting best practices in instruction through applied research and development. One of its most widely used products is *Content Knowledge: A Compilation of Content Standards for K–12 Curriculum.* This Web-based publication creates an internally consistent model of standards and benchmarks and applies it to the wide variety of standards across disciplines. After identifying significant reports and selecting the central reference document for each discipline, information from other standards and benchmark documents were integrated into the central reference document following the project-established format.

For geography, the result is 18 standards grouped into 6 sections; these standards subtly restate the standards found in *Geography for Life.* The fifth standard in *Geography for Life* is "That people create regions to interpret Earth's complexity" and the corresponding *Content Knowledge* standard reads "Understands the concepts of regions." Similarly, the eighth *Geography for Life* standard, "The characteristics and spatial distribution of ecosystems on Earth's surface," became "Understands the characteristics of ecosystems on Earth's surface." Underneath each *Content Knowledge* standard are more specific learning benchmarks graded into four different levels, kindergarten through 2nd, 3rd through 5th, 6th through 8th, and 9th through 12th, to more closely correspond to primary elementary, upper elementary, middle school, and high school. In a details section, each of the learning standards and benchmarks is keyed to the standard or document from which it was gleaned; some of the standards and benchmarks appeared in multiple documents. Additionally, some activities keyed specifically to *Content Knowledge* standards are available as are links to other Web-based resources.

Articles drawn from *Ubique,* the American Geographical Society's newsletter, on implementing *Geography for Life* are available through the "Geography for Life" portion of the Geographic Education National Implementation Project (GENIP) Web site (http://genip.tamu.edu). The articles, written between 1994 and 1999, are short and tend to be broad-brush descriptions of the learning standards and their potential and general accounts of applying the ideas found in *Geography for Life.*

The standards advocated in *Geography for Life* are voluntary but many states have incorporated them, along with the five themes articulated in *Guidelines for Geographic Education: Elementary and Secondary Schools* and standards established by the National Council for the Social Studies, into their statewide learning standards. There does not seem to be a Web site available that lists links to all of the on-line state learning standards but searching for "learning standards geography" or "state standards geography" should result in links to many of those that are available electronically.

State Geography Standards: An Appraisal of Geography Standards in 38 States and the District of Columbia (http://www.edexcellence.net/standards/geography/geograph.htm)

The Thomas B. Fordham Foundation commissioned a study titled "State Geography Standards: An Appraisal of Geography Standards in 38 States and the District of Columbia" as part of a set of five studies in the core subjects (geography, science, English, history and math) that were designated by state governors and President George H.W. Bush at the 1989 Education Summit (prior to the Goals 2000: Educate America Act) held in Charlottesville, Virginia. According to the study, "Among them, geography is a unique case: the core subject that most U.S. schools have most egregiously neglected, the field that has had to start practically from scratch to win its proper place in the academic curriculum." In the eyes of the study authors, most sets of state learning standards in geography are weak because they are not clear, specific, or balanced; do not give guidance to instructors; they do not use active verbs against which progress can be measured; and they do not include benchmarks. State standards also often were judged to be less comprehensive than needed and in general not assisting in equipping students with the ability to ask "why" and then work toward answering their own questions. The report includes summary information about how the study was conducted and specific comments about each state's set of learning standards. Because the comments about each set of geography learning standards are in a standard format, it is fairly easy to quickly do a surficial comparison between states.

ORGANIZATIONS

The work of organizations interested in geographic education is often done cooperatively or interweaves with the work done by others.

National Council for Geographic Education

The National Council for Geographic Education (NCGE) "works to enhance the status and quality of geography teaching and learning" through communication, research, publication, and cooperation with other organizations. Its members include K–12 teachers and college/university instructors. An annual meeting is held, usually four days in October, with paper sessions, workshops, field trips, and exhibits. Each spring, NCGE organizes a nationwide geography competition, the National Geography Olympiad, was renamed in 2003 the National Geography Challenge. The organization also sponsors a number of awards to promote excellence in geographic education, including scholarships, mini-grants, service awards, and publication awards.

NCGE publishes a bimonthly scholarly journal, *Journal of Geography,* and a bimonthly newsletter, *Perspective.* The journal is a "forum for educators and scholars to present results from teaching and research that advance our understanding and practice of geographic education from pre-Kindergarten through the post-graduate levels." Each issue includes three to five research- or instruction-based articles. Semi-regular columns include "Teacher's Notebook," with descriptions of innovative teaching strategies that demonstrate geographical concepts, and "Agenda for the 21st Century," which presents discussion papers about geographic education challenges and opportunities. Occasionally, the journal's primary contents are a collection of short, related articles ("Symposium") on a current geographic education issue. Book reviews and letters to the editor also appear. For non-geographer educators, *Journal of Geography's* contents are a practical eye-opener to many facets of geography and geography pedagogy. For geographers, the journal will be a reminder of how exciting a geographical viewpoint can be.

Perspective includes typical newsletter information: upcoming conference information; a president's column; news from other geography organizations; descriptions of and advertisements for NCGE publications; slates of NCGE election candidates; contact information for subject specialists; and calendars for workshops, summer institutes, and other training opportunities. Regular columns include "Resources in Non-Geographic Periodicals," a bibliography of articles in easily available periodicals of a less specific nature, along with suggestions of the kind of courses to which the articles could be applied, and "Geography in the News," a one-page digest of a recent event placed into geographic context with an accompanying map. Each issue also includes a focused "Learning Activity" lesson plan and a list of "Resources for Teachers."

NCGE also publishes the *Pathways in Geography* series. Each title in the series presents a specific theme or concept to support instruction. The most recently published is *Fieldwork in the Geography Curriculum: Filling the Rhetoric-Reality Gap.* Others have focused on political geography, global hydrology, wetlands, map reading, remote sensing and landscape analysis, and regional descriptions. Additionally, NCGE has slide sets available for purchase that could support instruction about places and geographical topics worldwide.

Information about NCGE activities and publications is readily available through the council's Web site (http://www.ncge.org). Beyond the previously mentioned *Geography for Life* tutorial, the Web site also includes information on high schools offering Advance Placement human geography, links to geography assessments and information about assessments, links to other geography education related Web sites, and the council's publications catalog, pamphlets on geography, and electronic reprints of classic articles from the *Journal of Geography*.

Geographic Education National Implementation Program (http://genip.tamu.edu)

Organized in 1985 in part because of positive reaction to *Guidelines for Geographic Education: Elementary and Secondary Schools,* the Geographic Education National Implementation Program (GENIP) is a consortium of the four major geography or geographic associations in the United States: American Geographical Society, Association of American Geographers, National Council for Geographic Education, and National Geographic Society. GENIP was the driving force behind *Geography for Life,* and since *Geography for Life*'s publication, the consortium has been working toward integrating standards-based geography education. GENIP has focused on six key areas or issues:

- the dissemination and implementation of the content, skills, and perspectives of the National Geography Standards in both formal and informal education settings;
- the use of geographic tools and technology (computer-based geographic information systems, remote sensing);
- spatial data (available on CD-ROMs and the Internet) in education;
- the development of effective materials and programs in pre-service and in-service education;

- the development of partnerships with other stakeholder organizations; and
- public advocacy for geography education.

Most recently, GENIP has spearheaded the development and dissemination of an Advanced Placement course in human geography. GENIP has also consulted with publishers of geography-based materials, has sponsored workshops at association meetings, and has published a number of titles about geography education and standards.

Geographic Alliances

The National Geographic Society, through its Geography Education Program, has established state geographic alliances in each state, the District of Columbia, Canada, and Puerto Rico; all have the goal of promoting and improving geographic education. Members in these alliances include K–12 teachers and college and university faculty members. The alliances receive funding from the society's Education Foundation and are expected to raise matching funds. The alliances support teacher professional development and the development of classroom materials and encourage including geography in state education learning standards or curricula. Information about state alliance activities appears regularly in the *AAG Newsletter* and the NCGE *Perspective.* Part of the National Geographic Society's Web site describes the Geographic Alliance Network and lists state alliance Web sites and contact points (http://www.national geographic.com/education/alliance.html).

Geography Awareness Week

The National Geographic Society has also played a leading role in creating and promoting Geography Awareness Week, which occurs annually during the third week of November as part of the society's "Geography Action!" conservation and awareness program (http://www.nationalgeographic.com/geography action/). One day of Geography Awareness Week is designated as GIS Day (http://www.gisday.com). Each year the program, which runs May through April, and the week have a different theme. The society is partnering with a wide variety of government agencies, interest groups, and corporate sponsors to provide Web-based resources, sponsor workshops, and disseminate curricula support materials to teachers. State geographic alliances will be good local contact points about "Geography Action!," Geography Awareness Week, and GIS Day.

The National Geographic Society also has an education Web page (http://www.nationalgeographic.

com/education/) with lesson plans, descriptions of successful activities, links to printable maps, content that ties into *World* magazine features, and information about the Geographic Alliance program and educational grants available through the National Geographic Society Education Foundation.

National Council for the Social Studies (http://www.ncss.org or http://www.socialstudies.org)

The mission of the National Council for the Social Studies (NCSS) is "to provide leadership, service, and support for all social studies educators." NCSS has members in all of the states and includes all of the social sciences that are touched on by social studies instruction, including geography. The council's Web site includes annual bibliographies of "Notable Social Studies Books for Young People" and teaching resources. It also includes the executive summary and first chapters of *Expectations for Excellence: Curriculum Standards for Social Studies* (http://www.social studies.org/standards/stitle.html). The full text of these standards was published as the council's *Bulletin* 89 and can be purchased from NCSS. Many of the 10 themes or strands have clear, although not always stated, geographical content: I. Culture; II. Time, Continuity, and Change; III. People, Places, and Environments; VII. Production, Distribution, and Consumption; and IX. Global Connections. *Expectations for Excellence* includes performance expectations for elementary, middle, and high school levels for each of the themes along with examples, "Standards into Practice," for all themes at all levels.

INSTRUCTIONAL RESOURCES

Most of the instructional resources that support geographic education have been created with nongeographers in mind.

Geography for Educators: Standards, Themes, and Concepts

Geography for Educators is a geography textbook for classroom teachers revolving around *Geography for Life.* Filled with geographical foundations intended to be applied at all levels, kindergarten through 12th grade, *Geography for Educators* is a basic introduction to both human and physical geography structured around the five fundamental themes found in *Guidelines for Geographic Education* and further expanded upon in *Geography for Life.* A color diagram on the inside cover, reproduced in grayscale in chapter 1, illustrates the connections between the 5 themes, 18

learning standards, and specific *Geography for Educators* book chapters. The first two chapters set the context for geography education by describing the field of geography and by comparing the development of geography education in a number of countries and regions worldwide. The next 10 chapters are strongly tied to the 5 fundamental themes. Chapter 3 focuses on the theme of location; chapters 4 through 9 on different aspects (physical, cultural, economic, urban) of the theme of place; chapter 10 on human-environment interaction; chapter 11 on movement; and chapter 12 on regions. Clearly from this distribution, understanding the concept of place, how places develop their unique characteristics and how they are related to each other, is the primary geography key. The final chapter presents four geographical case studies to show how the themes and learning standards can be tied together to create a interpretation of events, distributions, and resources.

Each chapter begins with a listing of the learning standards covered. The body of the chapters survey systemic human and physical geography. Chapters include many black-and-white or grayscale illustrations along with boxed text that examines specific aspects of the focus theme and a description of a "Geographer at Work." All of the chapters conclude with a list of key concepts and a further reading bibliographic essay. Five of the chapters also include brief descriptions of learning outcomes. *Geography for Educators* concludes with a glossary and index.

Geography for Educators does not include lesson plans, teaching tips, or methodological approaches for teaching geography or including geography as part of the curricula. Its intention is to provide a holistic and integrated introduction to the field of geography using the 5 fundamental themes and 18 learning standards as a structure. The nongeographer classroom teacher will find geographical grounding in *Geography for Educators* with suggestions for further study or exploration that could be used either by the teacher or by advanced students.

Spaces and Places: A Geography Manual for Teachers

Spaces and Places is a loose-leaf resource guide that touches on the entire context of classroom geographic education including definitions of geography; a discussion of the standards proposed in *Geography for Life*; lesson plans and teaching strategies; teaching fundamental skills such as asking and answering questions; using maps and technology in the classroom; and assessment of student achievement. Each of the

12 chapters is written by a geographer or geographic educator and begins with an abstract and list of key words. Chapter text tends to be broken into short sections, often with subsections or numbered or bulleted lists. All of the chapters conclude with a list of references and a biographical sketch about the chapter author. Depending on the chapter topic, some chapters include sample lesson plans, activities, or teaching suggestions. *Spaces and Places* is not a geography survey textbook in the way that *Geography for Educators* is; it is an entry-level guide to incorporating geography and geographical ideas in the classroom.

Using Internet Primary Sources to Teach Critical Thinking Skills in Geography

Although intended for school teachers and librarians, *Using Internet Primary Sources to Teach Critical Thinking Skills in Geography* could be used by anyone interested in finding core Internet sites that focus on presenting information that would be useful in geographically based inquiries. The initial four chapters will ground the reader in the basics of critical thinking, geography, and types of geographic information resources. Six sections reflecting the *Geography for Life* "six essential elements" framework containing information about 75 Internet sites follow the four chapters: The World in Spatial Terms; Places and Regions; Physical Systems; Human Systems; Environment and Society; and Uses of Geography. Each of the numbered entries includes the Web site's URL, one- or two-word indications of the type of data, and a list of key terms. A paragraph is devoted to explaining each Web site's "Geographical Context" and four brief activities and exploration questions are included in "Thinking Critically." The activities and exploration questions are geared to the secondary school or college-level investigator. Some of the entries include URLs to additional or related sites. The volume concludes with a list of additional resources and an index.

For nongeographers, the first four chapters of *Using Internet Primary Sources to Teach Critical Thinking Skills in Geography* will be valuable because they succinctly describe geography as a discipline, the kinds of questions asked by geographers, and the primary resources often used by geographers. Throughout the chapters, Web sites beyond the 75 treated in depth are quickly described, discussed, and placed into the contexts of geographical inquiry and other available resources. Unfortunately, there is no bibliography or listing in the book of all of the Web sites discussed or just mentioned as other resources.

ARGUS: Activities and Readings in the Geography of the United States
ARGWorld: Activities and Resources for the Geography of the World

The Association of American Geographers is sponsoring the development of active learning materials to support instruction on United States and world geography. These sets of materials will lend themselves to either topically or regionally organized instruction. The print materials for *ARGUS: Activities and Readings in the Geography of the United States* are organized into five broad categories: Geographical Themes; Population Geography; Economic Geography; Political Geography; and Environmental Issues. An overview text, teacher's guide, and 35 student activities have been produced. In 1999 a CD-ROM containing 190 units, 3,500 photographs, and 600 maps was created for use with the ARGUS student activities but also to support instruction with other texts or to be used as a stand-alone resource. Most recently, the association has been working on *ARGWorld: Activities and Resources for the Geography of the World,* which will be a CD-ROM and a set of issues-oriented student activities geared toward secondary school students. The CD-ROM will contain many scanned photographs, maps, and remotely sensed images as well as other geographic information resources and links to appropriate Web resources. Other Association of American Geographers projects for secondary and higher education described at the association's Web page (http://www.aag.org) under "Geography Education," include "Hands-On! Human Dimensions of Global Change" and "My Community, Our Earth: Geographic Learning for Sustainable Learning."

Lesson Plans at Geographic Alliances Web Sites

Many sample lesson plans can be found on the Web by searching "geography lesson plans" or by adding a geographical designation such as state, country, or region name to the search. Some are sponsored by state geographic alliances, others by commercial publishers or federal agencies and affiliates. Although the lesson plans might not be exactly replicable in specific situations, they do provide ideas and contact points for help in applying the framework found in *Geography for Life.*

The lesson plans found at the New Mexico (http://www.unm.edu/~nmga/programs/lessonplns.html), Florida (http://fga.freac.fsu.edu/lessonplans.html), and Oregon (http://geog.pdx.edu/oga/index.html) geographic alliance Web sites are a mixture of lesson plans that focus on specific local features and events and lesson plans that illustrate broader concepts and phenomena. New Mexico includes lesson plans that center on New Spain, the Santa Fe Trail, and immigration to New Mexico, and the Oregon site includes a unit on change in Portland and effects of damming the Deschutes River. Lesson plans at the Florida and Oregon sites also cover a broader geographic scope, still with a specific location. Examples from Oregon include The African Puzzle, The Aral Sea: A Time For Change, and The Russian View of Territorial Encroachment. Examples from Florida include Africa-European Imperialism, East India Trading Company, Seven Wonders of the Ancient World. Other lessons tackle broad concepts such as crustal drift, mental maps, vegetation zones, biomes, map scale and other aspects of map reading and interpretation, migratory patterns (human and otherwise), and urban growth. Some of the seemingly geographically narrow lesson plans could be rescoped to examine a different area. The Oregon Geographic Alliance site includes a lesson plan that examines the geographic coverage of stories published in the *Oregonian,* the Portland newspaper. Depending on location, this lesson could be done with newspapers such as the *Detroit Free Press,* the *Atlanta Journal-Constitution,* or the *Houston Chronicle.* The lesson plan that explores how Oregon's physical geography changes from east to west along a single line of latitude could be rewritten to explore a similar east-west path in Montana or Pennsylvania or a north-south path in Illinois or California. Of course, recasting the geography of a lesson plan will need to be done carefully because the phenomena that clearly illustrate a concept in one location might not be present in another.

Lesson Plans—Discovery School (http://school. discovery.com/lessonplans)

The Discovery School Web site includes lesson plans for a number of topics including geography, earth science, and weather. The lesson plans are grouped into three grade levels, kindergarten through 5th, 6th through 8th, and 9th through 12th. Regardless of topic or level, the lesson plans follow the same basic format of listing objectives, materials needed, procedures, ways of adapting the procedures, discussion questions, evaluation, lesson extensions and reading suggestions, vocabulary (including audio pronunciations), and applicable learning standards. The standards connections are not to *Geography for Life* but instead to *Content Knowledge: A Compilation of Content Standards for K–12 Curriculum,* National

Science Education Standards, or standards developed by the National Council for the Social Studies. Most of the lesson plans, by far, are intended for grades five through eight. The content of the lessons ranges from very specific, "Ivory Wars" about killing African elephants for tusk ivory, to quite broad, "Landmarks of Civilization," an opportunity to explore the importance of the built environment, especially monumental structures. Some of the lessons have somewhat misleading titles. "Rainforests," which is grouped under geography, plants, and human body, is about sources of pharmaceutical drugs.

Many of the lessons, although they have been grouped under geography or a geography-like topic, are not clearly focused on geographical concepts. The lesson titled "Dictator for a Day" has two objectives:

1. experience and analyze the pros and cons of a dictatorship; and
2. apply these ideas to their understanding of life in ancient Rome.

Neither of these can be tied to the stated geographic standard, "Understands how geography is used to interpret the past," but the expansion plan for the lesson could be used to incorporate the standard. Geographically appropriate lesson ideas can be found throughout the Discovery School Lesson Plans Web site because geography integrates materials from many different disciplines. Potential users will need to consider carefully how particular lessons might meet stated standards or possibly other standards before adapting the lessons for use in the classroom.

Economics and Geography Lessons for 32 Children's Books (http://www.mcps.k12.md.us/ curriculum/socialstd/Econ_Geog.html)

The Montgomery County Public Schools in Maryland have taken a slightly different approach to incorporating geography into the curricula. The Economics and Geography Lessons for 32 Children's Books Web site illustrates how specific books included in the county curricula can be used to discuss geographical concepts. *Make Way for Ducklings* is used as a background for exploring cardinal directions, discovering how communities grow, and examining the environment's impacts on life choices. *Sarah, Plain and Tall* gives the teacher an opportunity to talk about environmental and lifestyle differences between regions as well as connections among regions. The lesson plan for *Everybody Cooks Rice* includes an exercise about diffusion plus cultural differences that exist for the same natural resource. These lesson plans might point the way to looking at familiar books and language arts resources to facilitate strengthening the incorporation of geographical concepts.

Education World—Geography (http://www.education-world.com/a_special/geography_aware_98.shtml)

Education World, a free on-line resource for educators and parents, includes lesson plans and idea articles as part of its content. A recently developed page assembled to assist with Geography Awareness Week planning provides links to a number of geography-related articles and resources available at the Education World site. Included are an article that focuses on the five themes of geography with five activity ideas for each theme; ideas for using playground maps to teach basic map-reading skills or to accompany other activities at a playground scale instead of at a desk scale; virtual field trips; and geographic scavenger hunts.

USGS Educational Resources Learning Web
(http://ask.usgs.gov/education.html)
AskERIC Lesson Plans (http://askeric.org/cgi-bin/lessons.cgi/Social_Studies/Geography)

Many United States federal government agencies include educational materials, some of which are geographical in nature, on their Web sites. The United States Geological Survey Earth Science Information Center has a Learning Web site (http://ask.usgs.gov/education.html). For kindergarten through 12th-grade students, there is an extensive table of project ideas, including instructions on how to make paper, modeling clay, and papier-mâché volcanoes; create weather forecasts; and model a wetland. In the homework help section, there are links to many survey publications on geology, natural disasters, glaciers, weather, and dinosaurs. The teachers' section has lesson plans on life sciences, geology, map skills, and the environment. Some of the lesson plans rely on packets, often larger format materials such as maps and posters or more substantial book-like publications, that are available inexpensively through the Information Center. "Explorers" will find links to a number of discipline-specific glossaries. The survey's Rocky Mountain Mapping Center also hosts a Web site (http://rocky-web.cr.usgs.gov/public/outreach/) that highlights USGS educational and outreach resources and provides some lesson plans and ideas not available at the central Ask USGS site. Included at the Rocky Mountain site are "Teaching with Topographic Maps—25 Ideas for Educational Lessons" (http://rockyweb.cr.

usgs.gov/public/outreach/topoteach.html) and "Map Mysteries: 74,796 Ready-To-Go Lesson Plans, Exploring Human and Physical Geography with USGS Topographic and Thematic Maps" (http://rockyweb.cr.usgs.gov/public/outreach/mapmys.html).

Nearly 60 lesson plans are listed under "Geography" at the Ask ERIC Lesson Plans Web site (http://askeric.org/cgi-bin/lessons.cgi/Social_Studies/Geography). A large number of the lessons were the result of a Columbia Education Center's Summer Workshop. Many are related to map reading and construction, but other topics covered include physical geography, climate, geography-related careers, regional geography, and, historical and political geography. Although goals and objectives along with grade levels are included in the lesson plans, there is no indication of which learning standard the lesson plans are intended to meet.

Early Childhood: Where Learning Begins—
  Geography (http://www.ed.gov/pubs/Geography/)
Helping Your Child Learn Geography
  (http://www.ed.gov/pubs/parents/Geography/index.html)

The United States Department of Education has published two booklets full of activity ideas, geared primarily to parents, to promote geographical education and awareness. Both *Early Childhood: Where Learning Begins—Geography* and *Helping Your Child Learn Geography* are organized following the five fundamental themes of geography. *Early Childhood* is intended for children between the ages of 2 and 5, while *Helping Your Child Learn Geography* is for children between 5 and 10. The chapters are arranged in similar fashions. They begin with background information about the focus theme and examples of questions typically asked about the theme. In *Early Childhood,* related developmental skills are explained and two sets of activities are included, one for ages two to three and the other for ages four to five. The activities included in both publications are grouped topically. In the *Helping Your Child Learn Geography* chapter on patterns of movement, there are activities about modes of travel, tracking the movement of people and objects, and tracking the movement of information, and the chapter on human interaction with the environment is divided into understanding controlling one's surroundings and adapting to one's surroundings. The *Early Childhood* chapter on place includes activities that highlight "What is my home like?" and "What is the weather today?" Both of the booklets include a list of references and a glossary. *Early Childhood* also includes a list of resources and a bibliography of picture and early reading books. *Helping Your Child Learn Geography* concludes with suggested reading lists for younger and older readers and bibliographic information about atlases and computer software as well as information about Internet resources and obtaining free or inexpensive materials. *Helping Your Child Learn Geography* also reprints "What does your fourth-grader know?" from *Geography for Life*.

Most of the activities in *Early Childhood* for the two to three age group revolve around conversations that might already be occurring between child and parent. The activities for the four to five age group expand the conversations to include the world beyond what the child experiences directly. Many of the activity ideas in *Helping Your Child Learn Geography* use common objects such as maps, coins, board games, newspaper articles, and photographs to facilitate thinking and communication about the world. *Early Childhood* and *Helping Your Child Learn Geography* dovetail with each other to help parents, and potentially teachers, find simple ways to begin geographical exploration. Both of these publications are available as printed publications or for free download from the United States Department of Education Web site.

APCentral (http://apcentral.collegeboard.com)
"Advanced Placement (AP) Human Geography"
   (http://geography.about.com/cs/advanced
   placement/index.htm)
College Board offered an Advanced Placement exam in human geography for the first time in May 2001; the course is equivalent to a half-year college course. The course's purpose "is to introduce students to the systematic study of patterns and processes that have shaped human understanding, use, and alteration of Earth's surface." At the completion of the course, the students are expected to: use and think about maps and spatial data sets; understand and interpret the implications of associations among phenomena in places; recognize and interpret at different scales the relationships among patterns and processes; define regions and evaluate the regionalization process; and characterize and analyze changing interconnections among places. These learning goals are loosely structured on the standards found in *Geography for Life*. The course outline has seven sections: Geography, Its Nature and Perspectives; Population; Cultural Patterns and Processes; Political Organization of Space; Agriculture and Rural Land Use; Industrialization and Economic Development; and Cities and Urban Land Use.

The official College Board Advanced Placement Web site (http://apcentral.collegeboard.com) offers a brief overview of the human geography course and a course description in PDF format. The Geography About.com site (http://geography.about.com/cs/ advancedplacement/index.htm) includes links to the College Board site, geography unit outlines and projects, a list compiled by the National Council for Geographic Education (NCGE) of high schools offering Advanced Placement Human Geography, and a book list compiled by the 1997 AP Geography Summer Institute held at Macalester College in St. Paul, Minnesota.

Links to additional resources for geographical education appear at the Geography About.com site (http://geography.about.com/cs/geoeducation/). Students, parents, and teachers will find information, resources, and contacts conveniently assembled.

COMMERICAL PUBLICATIONS

Commercially produced geographic education publications are available from many of the large and mainstream textbook publishers.

Rand McNally (http://www.k12online.com/
   default2.asp)
Rand McNally may be one of the United States' best known commercial publishers of geographic materials because of its annual road atlas for the United States, Canada, and Mexico. Rand McNally also supports geographical and social science education through its publishing program and K12online.com Web site (http://www.k12online.com/default2.asp). Teachers and nonteachers can log into the "Teachers' Corner" to find out how Rand McNally educational materials correlate to state and national standards and to request assistance in purchasing material or determining if maps and globes need to be updated. The Web site includes PDF files for color maps of states and thematic maps of the United States, continents, and the world. There also are black-and-white PDF outline maps of states, nations, and continents. The site also includes textual materials, one- and two-page "research articles," somewhat like long dictionary or short encyclopedia entries, about places, cultures, and historical events. Through the Web site, wall maps and other maps ranging in size from page-size outline maps to floor maps, atlases, globes, and software can

be purchased. Rand McNally makes freely available its annual catalog of "Classroom Resources."

Prentice-Hall (http://www.phschool.com/atschool/ world_geo/index.html)

The Prentice-Hall school Web site is intended to extend the use of Prentice-Hall publications. The "Resource Library" at the geography portion of the Prentice-Hall Web site includes Internet-based learning activities; links to biographies of geographers, cartographers, and explorers at Infoplease.com; and descriptions of careers in geography. The careers information is divided into education, human, physical, and technical geography and includes links to the Bureau of Labor Statistics's *Occupational Outlook Handbook* as well as to information at other federal agency sites.

Houghton Mifflin Education Place: K–8 Resources, Social Studies Center
(http://www.eduplace.com/ss/)

The Social Studies Center found at Houghton Mifflin's Education Place includes "GeoNet," a game based on the National Geography Standards for grades four and above. PDF-format outline maps of the world, continents, regions, and countries can be printed from the site, and there are projects and activities along with worksheets for classroom use. Like the Prentice-Hall site, this Web site is geared toward supporting and enhancing the use of Houghton Mifflin materials.

CAREERS IN GEOGRAPHY

Because geography is such a diverse field of study, students and parents often wonder what can be done with course work or a degree in geography. Geography organizations and college and university geography departments can help answer career path questions.

The Association of American Geographers has an extensive amount of information about careers for which geographers are well suited at the "Careers in Geography" portion of the association's Web site (http://www.aag.org). The Web site includes 10 quickly answered questions that might help respond to "How do you know if you want to be a geographer?" such as: Do you prefer the window seat on airplanes?; Are you good at seeing connections among seemingly unrelated processes?; and Are you interested in connections between humans and the environment? Also included are lists of careers; descriptions of geography and the kind of geographical training needed for certain kinds of careers; suggestions for the job

search; and contact points for further information. The association has recently published a new and colorful "Careers in Geography" brochure. The brochure highlights aptitudes that might lead toward geography as an area of study, technology used in geographical work, and areas of employment as well as how to get further information.

The University of North Carolina at Wilmington maintains an extensive Web site (http://www. uncwil.edu/stuaff/career/Majors/geography.htm) about geographical careers and links to other Web sites about geography vocations. The University of Wisconsin-Oshkosh "Careers in Geography" Web site (http://www.uwosh.edu/departments/geography/ careers.html) lists job titles with potential geographical ties and workplaces in private firms and at different levels of government where geographical positions can be found. Other Web-based resources can be easily found by searching "geography careers."

Geographic education is not about memorizing place names or facts about products, economies, or climate. While a fundamental understanding about characteristics of locations is important, geography at the beginning of the twenty-first century is about making connections between places, seeing how one place influences or impacts another, and being able to pull together seemingly unrelated information to describe places and connections and to forecast probable outcomes. Geography ties together an understanding of the Earth with knowledge of how humans impact their environments, natural and built, and how different environments impact human endeavor.

BIBLIOGRAPHY

ARGUS: Activities and Readings in the Geography of the United States Washington, D.C.: Association of American Geographers, 1995 (print), 1999 (CD-ROM). ISBN 0892912197 (backbone text); 0892912219 (teacher's guide); 0892912200 (activity masters); 0892912227 (transparency masters).

ARGWorld: Activities and Resources for the Geography of the World CD-ROM. Test version 5.2. Washington, D.C.: Association of American Geographers, 2001.

"Careers in Geography." Washington, D.C.: Association of American Geographers, 2002.

Early Childhood: Where Learning Begins—Geography: With Activities for Children Ages 2 to 5 Years of Age. Carol Sue Fromboluti and Carol Seefeldt. Washington, D.C.: U.S. Dept. of Education, Office of Educational Research and Improvement, 1999. ISBN: 0-16-049840-6.

Expectations of Excellence: Curriculum Standards for Social Studies. National Council for the Social Studies

Bulletin No. 89. Washington, D.C.: National Council for the Social Studies, 1994. ISBN: 0879860650.

Geography for Educators: Standards, Themes, and Concepts. 2nd ed. Susan W Hardwick and Donald G Holtgrieve. Upper Saddle River, N.J.: Prentice Hall, 1995. ISBN: 0-13-442377-1.

Geography for Life: National Geography Standards. Sarah Witham Bednarz, et al. Washington, D.C.: National Council for Geographic Education, 1994. ISBN: 0-7922-2775-1.

Geography in Grades 7–12: Themes, Key Ideas and Learning Opportunities. Washington, D.C.: National Council for Geographic Education, 1989.

Goals 2000: Educate America Act: To Improve Learning and Teaching by Providing a National Framework for Education Reform; to Promote the Research, Consensus Building, and Systemic Changes Needed to Ensure Equitable Educational Opportunities and High Levels of Educational Achievement for All Students; to Provide a Framework for Reauthorization of All Federal Education Programs; to Promote the Development and Adoption of a Voluntary National System of Skill Standards and Certifications; and for Other Purposes. Public Law 103-227. Washington, D.C.: U.S. Government Printing Office, 1994. ISBN: 0160414822.

Guidelines for Geographic Education: Elementary and Secondary Schools. Washington, D.C.: Association of American Geographers, 1984. ISBN: 0892911859.

Helping Your Child Learn Geography: With Activities for Children from 5 to 10 Years of Age. Prepared by Kathryn Perkinson. Washington, D.C.: U.S. Dept. of Education with U.S. Geological Survey and National Geographic Society, 1996. ISBN: 1-57979-183-2.

Journal of Geography. Indiana, Pa.: National Council for Geographic Education, 1902– . 6 per year. ISSN: 0022-1341.

K–6 Geography: Themes, Key Ideas and Learning Opportunities. Washington, D.C.: National Council for Geographic Education, 1987.

National Geographic World. Washington, D.C.: National Geographic Society, 1975– . 10 per year. ISSN: 0361-5499.

A Nation at Risk: The Imperative for Educational Reform. Washington, D.C.: National Commission on Excellence in Education, 1983.

Pathways in Geography. Series. Indiana, Pa.: National Council for Geographic Education, 1991– . Recent titles include: *Asian Women and Their Work: A Geography of Gender and Development* (No. 17, Carolyn V. Prorok and Kiran Banga Chhokar, 1998, ISBN: 1884136125); *Teaching American Ethnic Geography* (No. 18, Lawrence E. Estaville and Carol J. Rosen, 1997, ISBN: 1884136133); *Teaching Political Geography* (No. 19, Fiona M. Davidson, 1998, ISBN: 188413615X); *Renaissance in the Heartland: The Indiana Experience* (No. 20, John E. Oliver, ed., 1998, ISBN: 1884136141);

Boston and New England: Advancing the Revolution in Geographic Education in a Region of Change (No. 21, Theodore S. Pikora and Stephen S. Young, 1999, ISBN: 1884136168); *Fieldwork in the Geography Curriculum: Filling the Rhetoric-Reality Gap* (No. 22, Gwenda A. Rice and Teresa L. Bulman, 2001, ISBN 1884136192).

Perspective. Chicago: National Council for Geographic Education, 1969– . 6 per year. ISSN: 0555-974X.

"Social Studies Education: Trends." John Jarolimek. In *Encyclopedia of Education,* ed. Lee C. Deighton. Vol. 8. New York: Macmillan, 1971, pp. 281–86.

Spaces and Places: A Geography Manual for Teachers. Washington, D.C.: Geographic Education National Implementation Project (GENIP), 1995. ISBN: 0528178999.

Ubique: Notes from the American Geographical Society. New York: American Geographical Society, 1968– , excluding 1975–78. Previously titled *Newsletter.* 3 per year.

Using Internet Primary Sources to Teach Critical Thinking Skills in Geography. Martha B. Sharma and Gary S. Elbow. Westport, Conn.: Greenwood, 2000. ISBN: 0-313-30899-3.

On-line References

"Advanced Placement (AP) Human Geography." Course and exam information. About.com, 2003. <http://geography.about.com/cs/advancedplacement/index.htm> (20 October 2003).

"APCentral." College Board, 2003. <http://apcentral.collegeboard.com> (20 October 2003).

Association of American Geographers. Home page. AAG, 2003. <http://www.aag.org> (20 October 2003)

"Careers in Geography." About.com, 2003. <http://geography.about.com/cs/careersingeograp/> (20 October 2003).

"Careers in Geography." University of Wisconsin-Oshkosh, 12 July 2003. <http://www.uwosh.edu/departments/geography/careers.html> (20 October 2003).

"Career Services: Geography." University of North Carolina at Wilmington, 10 September 2003. <http://www.uncwil.edu/stuaff/career/Majors/geography.htm> (20 October 2003).

"Celebrate Geography Awareness Week." Education World, 2 November 2001. <http://www.education-world.com/a_special/geography_aware_98.shtml> (20 October 2003).

Content Knowledge: A Compilation of Content Standards for K–12 Curriculum. 3rd ed. McREL, 2003. <http://www.mcrel.org/standards-benchmarks/index.asp> (20 October 2003).

Early Childhood: Where Learning Begins—Geography. Carol Sue Fromboluti and Carol Seefeldt, January 1999. U.S. Department of Education, 23 August 2003. <http://www.ed.gov/pubs/Geography/index.html> (20 October 2003).

"Economics and Geography Lessons for 32 Children's Books." Patricia King Robeson and Barbara Yingling. Montgomery County (MD) Public Schools, 25 March 1998. <http://www.mcps.k12.md.us/curriculum/social-std/Econ_Geog.html> (20 October 2003).

"Education." U.S. Geological Survey Rocky Mountain Mapping Center, 2 September 2003. <http://rockyweb.cr.usgs.gov/public/outreach> (20 October 2003).

Expectations for Excellence: Curriculum Standards for Social Studies. Executive Summary and Chapters 1 & 2. National Council for the Social Studies, 2003. <http://www.socialstudies.org/standards/stitle.html> (20 October 2003).

"FGA Lesson Plans." Florida Geographic Alliance, 2003. <http://fga.freac.fsu.edu/lessonplans.html> (20 October 2003).

"Five Times Five: Five Activities for Teaching Geography's Five Themes." Gary Hopkins. Education World, 2 July 2001. <http://www.education-world.com/a_lesson/lesson071.shtml> (20 October 2003).

"Geographic Alliance Network." National Geographic Society, 23 April 2003. <http://www.nationalgeographic.com/education/alliance.html> (20 October 2003).

Geographic Education National Implementation Program (GENIP). Home page. GENIP, 19 April 2003. <http://genip.tamu.edu/> (20 October 2003).

Geography Action! Home page. National Geographic Society, 2003. <http://www.nationalgeographic.com/geographyaction/> (20 October 2003).

"Geography Education and Teaching Geography." About.com, 2003. <http://geography.about.com/cs/geoeducation/> (20 October 2003).

"Geography Lesson Plans." AskERIC, Educational Resources Information Center (ERIC) Clearinghouse, 2003. <http://askeric.org/cgi-bin/lessons.cgi/Social_Studies/Geography> (20 October 2003).

"Geography Lesson Plans for New Mexico Teachers." New Mexico Geographic Alliance, 11 February 2001. <http://www.unm.edu/~nmga/programs/lessonplans.html> (20 October 2003).

"Geography Standards." Geography for Life national standards. National Geographic Society, 8 September 2003. <http://www.nationalgeographic.com/xpeditions/standards/> (20 October 2003).

GIS Day. Home page. ESRI, 2003. <http://www.gisday.com> (20 October 2003).

Helping Your Child Learn Geography. Kathryn Perkinson, October 1996. U.S. Department of Education, 23 August 2003. <http://www.ed.gov/pubs/parents/Geography/index.html> (20 October 2003).

"Human Geography Overview." Course information. AP Central, Collegeboard.com, 2003. <http://apcentral.collegeboard.com/repository/ap03_cd_humangeo_0405_4322.pdf> (20 October 2003).

"Implementing Geography for Life." Articles from *Ubique* (American Geographical Society). Geographic Education National Implementation Project (GENIP), 19 April 2003. <http://genip.tamu.edu/collect.html> (20 October 2003).

K12Online.com. Rand McNally, 2003. <http://www.k12online.com/default2.asp> (20 October 2003).

"Lesson Plans Library: Geography." Discovery.com, 2003. <http://school.discovery.com/lessonplans/geog.html> (20 October 2003).

"Map Mysteries Activites." U.S. Geological Survey, Rocky Mountain Mapping Center, 26 March 2003. <http://rockyweb.cr.usgs.gov/public/outreach/mapmys.html> (20 October 2003).

"Model Lessons." Oregon Geographic Alliance, 16 June 2003. <http://geog.pdx.edu/oga/lessons_new.html> (20 October 2003).

"A Nation at Risk: The Imperative for Educational Reform, April 1983." U.S. Department of Education, 7 October 1999. <http://www.ed.gov/pubs/NatAtRisk/index.html> (20 October 2003)

National Council for Geographic Education. Home page. NCGE, 2003. <http://www.ncge.org> (20 October 2003).

National Geographic Education Guide. National Geographic Society, 2003. <http://www.nationalgeographic.com/education/> (20 October 2003).

"NCGE *Geography for Life* Tutorial." National Council for Geographic Education, 6 June 2003.<http://www.ncge.org/publications/tutorial/index.html> (20 October 2003).

"Social Studies Center." K-8 Education Place. Houghton Mifflin, 2003. <http://www.eduplace.com/ss/> (20 October 2003).

Socialstudies.org. National Council for the Social Studies, 2003. <http://www.ncss.org> or <http://www.socialstudies.org> (20 October 2003).

"State Geography Standards: An Appraisal of Geography Standards in 38 States and the District of Columbia." *Fordham Report,* vol. 2, no. 2: February 1998. Susan Munroe and Terry Smith. Thomas B. Fordham Foundation, 22 November 2002. <http://www.edexcellence.net/standards/geography/geograph.htm> (20 October 2003).

"Teaching with Topographic Maps." U.S. Geological Survey, Rocky Mountain Mapping Center, 26 August 2002. <http://rockyweb.cr.usgs.gov/public/outreach/topoteach.html> (20 October 2003).

Ubique. American Geographical Society, 19 May 2003. <http//:www.amergeog.org/ubique.html> (20 October 2003).

USGS Educational Resources Learning Web. U.S. Geological Survey, 22 November 2002. <http://ask.usgs.gov/education.html> (20 October 2003).

"World Geography." PHF@school. Prentice-Hall, 2003. <http://www.phschool.com/atschool/world_geo/index.html> (20 October 2003).

Index

ABOUT THE AUTHOR

JENNY MARIE JOHNSON is Map and Geography Librarian and Associate Professor of Library Administration at the University of Illinois at Urbana-Champaign. She is a member of the Association of American Geographers, the Map and Geography Round Table of the American Library Association, and the North American Cartographic Information Society.